Due to the impact of the epidemic in recent two years, the world economy has suffered great fluctuations. "Digital Finance", "Internet Finance" and "Science and Technology Finance" have gradually become hot spots in the industry, while enterprise development is also facing more challenges and difficulties. How should enterprises face the new situation and transformation? **Economic and Business Management 2022 discusses the topics below:**

- **Economics:** Marketing; Finance and Securities; Regional Economic; Tourism Economy; Economic Theory; Ecological Economy; Resources Economy; E-Commerce/Ebusiness; Finance and Tax.
- **Business Management:** Human resources; Market management; Sales management; Business management; Quality Management; Production management; Cultural system and mechanism; Fund management.

The book is of interest to academics and professionals involved or interested in the fields mentioned above.

PROCEEDINGS OF THE SEVENTH INTERNATIONAL CONFERENCE ON ECONOMIC AND BUSINESS MANAGEMENT (FEBM2022), ONLINE CONFERENCE, 24–25 OCTOBER 2022

Economic and Business Management 2022

Edited by

Bogdan Lent
Bern University of Applied Sciences, Switzerland & University of Science and Technology, Poland

Changzheng Zhang
Xi'an University of Technology, China

 CRC Press
Taylor & Francis Group
Boca Raton London New York Leiden

CRC Press is an imprint of the
Taylor & Francis Group, an **informa** business

A BALKEMA BOOK

First published 2023
by CRC Press/Balkema
4 Park Square, Milton Park, Abingdon, Oxon, OX14 4RN
e-mail: enquiries@taylorandfrancis.com
www.routledge.com – www.taylorandfrancis.com

CRC Press/Balkema is an imprint of the Taylor & Francis Group, an informa business

Library of Congress Cataloging-in-Publication Data
A catalog record has been requested for this book

ISBN: 978-1-032-24482-2 (hbk)
ISBN: 978-1-032-24486-0 (pbk)
ISBN: 978-1-003-27878-8 (ebk)

DOI: 10.1201/9781003278788

TypesetinTimesNewRoman
by MPS Limited, Chennai, India

Table of contents

Economic and Business Management – Lent & Zhang (Eds)
© 2023 the Editor(s), ISBN 978-1-032-24482-2

Preface

The Seventh International Conference on Economic and Business Management (FEBM2022) was successfully held online on October 24–25, 2022. The conference was an annual forum for researchers and application developers in the area of Economic and Business Management.

This conference proceeding includes 38 accepted articles selected from 80 submissions.

We would like to express our gratitude to the reviewers of these manuscripts, who provided constructive criticism and stimulated comments and suggestions to the authors. We are extremely grateful as organizers, technical program committee and editors and extend our most sincere thanks to all the authors for their excellent contribution and work. Our sincere gratitude also goes to the CRC Press/ Balkema (Taylor & Francis Group) editors and managers for their helpful cooperation during the preparation of the proceeding.

On behalf of the Organizing Committees of FEBM2022.

Bogdan Lent
Editor, Bern University of Applied Sciences, Switzerland;
University of Science and Technology, Poland

Changzheng Zhang
Co-Editor, Xi'an University of Technology, China

Committee Members

Conference Chair
Bogdan Lent, *Bern University of Applied Sciences, Bern, Switzerland; University of Science and Technology, Bydgoszcz, Poland.*

Conference Co-Chair
Changzheng Zhang, *Xi'an University of Technology, China*

Technical Program Committee Chair
Haoxun Chen, *University of Technology of Troyes, France*

Technical Program Committee
Fernando Merino de Lucas, *Facultad de Economía y Empresa, Universidad de Murcia, Spain*
Josu Takala, *Industrial Management at University of Vaasa, Finland*
Mykola Mykolaichuk, *Public Administration and Regional Studies department, Odesa; Regional Institute for Public Administration of National Academy for Public Administration, the President of Ukraine*
Libiao Bai, *Chang'an University, China*
Peng Zhu, *Nanjing University of Science and Technology, China*
Lin Wang, *Chinese Academy of Science and Education Evaluation; Hangzhou Dianzi University, China*
Jose Weng-Chou Wong, *Macau University of Science and Technology, China*
Carlos Pinho, *University of Aveiro, Portugal*
Dhouha Jaziri Bouagina, *University of Sousse, Tunisia*
NGUYEN QUYET THANG, *Vietnam Tourism Education Association (VITEA); Tourism & Hospitality Management – Ho Chi Minh City University of technology (HUTECH), Vietnam*
Maria Cristina Longo, *University of Catania, Italy*
Md Reza Sultanuzzaman, *Nanchang University of Technology (NTU), China*
Julien Chevallier, *University Paris VIII, France; IPAG Business School (IPAG Lab)*
Alicia Orea Giner, *Universidad Rey Juan Carlos (Madrid, Spain)*
Monika Hadaś-Dyduch, *University of Economics in Katowice, Poland*

Economic and Business Management – Lent & Zhang (Eds)
© 2023 the Author(s), ISBN 978-1-032-24482-2

Research on green investment strategies of Chinese enterprises in the context of the green BRI

Mengwen Xie & Yongjian Zong
School of Management & Economics, Nanjing University of Science & Technology, Nanjing, China

ABSTRACT: The "Belt and Road" Initiative (BRI) provides a greater opportunity and a broader space for China to carry out green investment. As one of the participating enterprises, how to carry out green investment in the BRI is a topic worth studying nowadays. This paper explains the current situation and significance of green investment in the BRI, analyzes the opportunities and challenges faced by Chinese enterprises in green investment in the BRI, and puts forward the strategic suggestions for green investment by Chinese enterprises.

1 INTRODUCTION

On March 28, the National Development and Reform Commission and other departments jointly launched the "Opinions on Promoting the Green Development of the 'Belt and Road' Initiative". It points out that by 2025, the joint construction of the green BRI will achieve obvious goals, and by 2030, the green development pattern of the joint construction of the BRI will basically take shape. This shows that the green development of the BRI is becoming mature.

Promote green BRI need to vigorously promote the BRI green investment. Green investment, also known as socially responsible investment, focuses on the evaluation of social and environmental factors in addition to economic factors, so that enterprises can improve their sense of social responsibility while pursuing economic interests. Relying on wind and solar energy, which are invested by capital-intensive economy, enterprises can protect the environment and reduce ecological damage caused by pollution while developing the economy.

As one of the main participants of the BRI, how to conduct green investments and promote the construction of green BRI has become a topic worth studying nowadays.

2 LITERATURE REVIEW

Studies on green investment in the BRI mainly focus on the financial policies related to China's participation in the green BRI. Green finance promotes the construction and development of the BRI, while green investment and financing is focused on the "going out" of green industries and green infrastructure construction (Wang 2017). China vigorously develops green finance, actively promotes the development and application of applicable green technologies, and cultivates and enhances the ability of enterprises to participate in the green BRI construction (Lan 2020; Liu 2021). However, Chinese enterprises' green development capacity in the BRI is insufficient (Lan 2020), and they are facing difficulties in financing implementation (Wang & Zhang 2020).

DOI: 10.1201/9781003278788-1

There is little research in the existing literature on how enterprises can participate in green investment in the BRI. Based on the current situation, opportunities and challenges of green investment in the BRI, this paper makes suggestions on the strategies for Chinese enterprises to implement green investment in the BRI.

3 THE CURRENT SITUATION AND SIGNIFICANCE OF THE BRI GREEN INVESTMENT

3.1 *The current situation of the BRI green investment*

3.1.1 *Green investment along the BRI is taking shape*

At the end of 2020, China's direct investment flow to countries along the BRI was US$22.54 billion, an increase of 20.6%. Among them, the scale of green investment including renewable energy investment and clean energy investment is expanding. According to the data tracked by China Investment Tracker, from 2013 to June 2021, the cumulative energy investment by Chinese investors along the BRI reached US$125 trillion. (See Figure 1) In recent years, Chinese investors' investment in renewable energy has been on an overall upward trend, and in 2021, Chinese investors' investment in renewable energy along the BRI accounts for 57% of the total investment volume.

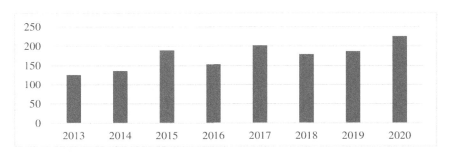

Figure 1.   China's investment in countries along the BRI from 2013 to 2020 (Unit: $ billion).
Source: Ministry of Commerce.

3.1.2 *Green investment targets mainly developing countries*

The BRI runs through the Eurasian continent, covering 71 countries, mostly developing economies. Developing countries along the route are rich in solar energy, wind energy, tidal energy and other resources, and have great potential for development, so they have also become the main body of green investment in China. In 2014, the successful start of the China-Central Asia Gas Pipeline D project and the China-Russia Eastern Gas Pipeline opened the door for China's green investment in countries along the BRI. In 2019, China Liaoning Lide Group and Bukhara Oblast of Uzbekistan jointly built Bukhara wind power plant. At the end of 2021, China Railway 12th Bureau and Kyrgyzstan signed the Issyk-Kul photovoltaic and hydroelectric power plant project in Kyrgyzstan. These investment projects have made great contributions to the infrastructure construction in the host countries along the BRI.

3.1.3 *Green investment efficiency is low*

China's green investment efficiency in the countries along the BRI is not high. The renewable energy and clean energy reserves of the countries along the BRI account for half of the global total, with huge investment space, while China's utilization rate of energy development in the countries along the BRI is low. The overseas industrial parks invested and built in the countries along the BRI are concentrated in traditional industrial enterprises, and the efficiency of green investment still needs to be improved.

3.2 *The significance of the BRI green investment*

In recent years, the world economic and political situation is grim. Many unfavorable factors have emerged in the process of global governance. The BRI is essentially global cooperation. Countries along the BRI have a low level of economic development in general, and their ecological environment is fragile. The implementation of green investment can help enhance their own sustainable development capacity.

On the other hand, for Chinese enterprises participating in the BRI, promoting green investment can give better play to the scale effect and improve production efficiency, while obtaining direct benefits. At the same time, it can also establish a good image of green investors and help to improve the international competitiveness of enterprises.

4 OPPORTUNITIES AND CHALLENGES FACED BY CHINESE ENTERPRISES TO PARTICIPATE IN THE BRI GREEN INVESTMENT

4.1 *Opportunities for Chinese enterprises to participate in the BRI green investment*

4.1.1 *Strong policy support*
At present, the World Bank, ADB, Silk Road Fund and other financial institutions are vigorously promoting green financing. The World Bank, a pioneer in global green financing, plans to increase the share of green financing to 35% of total financing between 2021 and 2025. The ADB has prioritized investment in sustainable infrastructure, and the Silk Road Fund has incorporated green development into its principles. Green bonds, green PPPs and other innovative green financial products of the BRI have emerged in large numbers. (Xu 2019).

In July 2021, China's Ministry of Commerce and Ministry of Ecology and Environment jointly issued the "Green Development Guidelines for Foreign Investment Cooperation" to provide guidance for Chinese enterprises to engage in green investment in the BRI countries. China's policy banks have become leaders in green finance, with data showing that by the end of 2019, China Exim Bank's BRI green credit balance had exceeded US $250 billion.

For Chinese enterprises, these policies can effectively reduce the cost of green certification for cross-border transactions and reduce the risk of overseas investments.

4.1.2 *Wide market space*
Under the promotion of domestic carbon neutrality target and green BRI, countries along the BRI are vigorously promoting energy transformation. China's overseas energy investment fields are gradually shifting from fossil energy to non-fossil renewable energy. In the future, with the deepening of low-carbon concept, more and more countries along the BRI will make carbon neutral commitments and put forward low-carbon policies. Therefore, there will be more and more opportunities for enterprises to invest in green energy. According to the Center for Finance and Development Studies of Tsinghua University, the demand for green investment in the four key sectors of power, transportation, construction and manufacturing in the BRI countries will be huge until 2030, averaging about 785 billion USD per year (Cheng & Chen 2021).

4.2 Challenges faced by Chinese enterprises to participate in the BRI green investment

4.2.1 Imperfect BRI green investment and financing system

The ADB and other financial institutions play an important role in building the green investment system, but there is no perfect solution to the huge demand for green funds. At the national level, most of the countries along the BRI are developing countries and emerging economies with low level of green technology and backward green investment and financing system, which makes it more costly for enterprises to implement green investment (Lan 2020).

At the enterprise level, many small and medium-sized enterprises are short of funds due to the COVID-19, which makes it difficult to guarantee continuous cash flow and increases the credit risk of banks. At the same time, green financial products are not abundant. Green bonds, green funds, and green capital management products are scarce, and the number of investors is limited, making it difficult for enterprises to raise funds.

4.2.2 Fierce green competition from developed countries

In recent years, as the problem of global warming and ecological environment deterioration has become more serious, developed countries also pay more attention to the global discourse in the field of green development, and continuously increase their investment in clean energy in the BRI countries. For example, the European Union has been increasing its investment in clean energy in India, South Africa and other countries, researching and promoting clean energy technologies, and developing green financial products in cooperation with the host country's financial industry; Japan is focusing on industrial and technological cooperation with Southeast Asian and South Asian countries in new energy, bioengineering, energy conservation and environmental protection. Many BRI developing countries were colonized by developed countries in the history, so developed countries have the first-mover advantage in market development and green investment in the BRI countries, which is bound to form fierce competition for green investment by Chinese enterprises.

4.2.3 Insufficient attention to green investment in the BRI

Experts point out that enterprises do not pay enough attention in the process of investment, and do not conduct enough consultation, investigation, communication and evaluation. The political, economic and cultural differences among countries along the BRI are huge. Many enterprises lack understanding of host country laws and regulations, and face the risk of default. Green investments are mostly infrastructure projects with long cycle time and large capital volume. Once defaulted, the loss will be huge. At the same time, the management concept of Chinese financial institutions is also immature, and there is no good disclosure on the implementation of green investment and financing guidelines.

5 STRATEGIES FOR CHINESE ENTERPRISES TO PARTICIPATE IN THE GREEN BRI

5.1 Optimize the location choice of green investment along the BRI

According to the different resource endowment and economic development characteristics of countries along the BRI, enterprises should take advantage of the situation to realize the optimal location selection of green investment. For example, Central Asia is rich in solar energy and biomass energy resources, enterprises should give full play to our technical and financial advantages in this field to improve the application and conversion efficiency of solar energy and biomass energy; Southeast Asia is rich in hydropower resources, enterprises should expand the scale of investment in hydropower in this region and promote the investment and construction of hydropower projects with international advanced technology standards; West Asia is rich in natural gas resources, but the investment risk is high, so enterprises should build a risk prevention and investment strategy for this region. Green investment in the region should build risk prevention, early warning, and emergency handling mechanisms, and actively build a natural gas cooperation platform between China and the region through direct investment and engineering services and other channels.

5.2 *Innovate methods of investment and financing*

From a micro level, enterprises need to innovate investment and financing methods to solve and overcome the obstacles of investment and financing. In 2016, China National Nuclear Corporation (CNNC) and Saudi Energy City signed a Memorandum of Understanding (MOU) on cooperation in the Saudi high-temperature gas-cooled reactor project, which opened a two-way cooperation in the field of nuclear energy. Based on the risky nature of new energy investments, this "compound investment" model can avoid the uncertainty that Chinese new energy companies face in one-way investments. The mutual investment with the resource countries to expand the cooperation of the whole industry chain makes the risk of cooperation more controllable.

At the same time, Chinese enterprises can learn from domestic model of wind power and photovoltaic poverty alleviation, and explore modes and mechanisms such as project co-construction and profit sharing. For example, innovative financing models such as power purchase agreements, financial leasing, crowdfunding and special purpose tools can be implemented on projects in countries along BRI according to local conditions (Li & Zheng 2020).

5.3 *Strengthen technology exchange and enhance independent innovation ability*

In response to the problem of low green level in countries along the BRI, Chinese enterprises can train the personnel of relevant enterprises in the host country before making investments, or invite them to visit and study the green demonstration industries in China. At the same time, they can actively learn from the overseas investment experience of enterprises in developed economies, deepen technical cooperation, absorb and utilize the advanced level of foreign countries so as to improve the utilization rate of green investment in host countries. It is worth noting that while learning from advanced technologies, enterprises should continuously improve their independent innovation capabilities, increase their scientific and technological research and development expenditures, and let the researchers of host country enterprises actively participate in scientific and technological innovation to make it more convenient for Chinese enterprises to carry out green investment activities in host countries.

5.4 *Fulfill social responsibility*

Chinese enterprises should actively communicate with local enterprises in the process of green investment. At the same time, they should strengthen the propaganda of green investment in the host country, which can bring certain economic and social benefits to the host country. By publicizing the vision of green BRI cooperation to the public, the local people's awareness of environmental protection will be enhanced and a consensus of green development will be formed, so that more local residents will accept China's green investment. At the same time, enterprises should pay attention to the construction of local people's livelihood, improve the recognition of residents while allowing more residents to participate in the construction of green investment, advocate green consumption in the daily life of residents, and create a good pattern of cooperation for green investment between China and the host country.

6 CONCLUSIONS

As one of the participants of BRI, Chinese enterprises play an important role in the green transformation process of BRI. This paper puts forward strategic suggestions in terms of location selection, financing, technological innovation and social responsibility of green investment, aiming at exploring ways for Chinese enterprises to participate in green investment in the BRI and promoting the construction of green BRI.

REFERNECES

Cheng Lin, Chen Yunhan. 2021. "Belt and Road" Green Investment in the Context of Carbon Neutrality. *China Finance* (22): 29–30.

Lan Qingxin, Liang Wei, Tang Wan. 2020. Current Situation, Problems and Countermeasures of Green "Belt and Road" Construction. *International Trade* (03): 90–96.

Li Lu, Zheng Xiaoling. 2020. Analysis of China's Green Investment Under the "Belt and Road" Initiative: A Case Study of Five Central Asian countries. *Journal of Baise College* (02): 74–78.

Liu Shiwei. 2021. Financial Institutions Help the Green Development of the "Belt and Road". *China Finance* (22): 25–26.

Wang Yuesheng, Zhang Yufei. 2020. Private Enterprises Boost the High-quality Development of the "Belt and Road": Advantages, Challenges and Countermeasures. *New Vision* (04): 24–31.

Wang Yao, Fan Gaoyan, Xia Hanwei. 2017. Research on the Path of Green Finance to Support the Construction and Development of the "Belt and Road". *Environmental Protection* 45(12): 56–59.

Xu Dongmei. 2019. Research on China's Green Investment Path to Countries Along the "Belt and Road". *China Collective Economy* (28): 33–34.

Preliminary analysis of the investment of *Cunninghamia Lanceolata* forest and *Camellia oleifera* forest in Anhui Province

Xuan Hu
Beijing-Dublin International College, Beijing University of Technology, Beijing, China

Fenglin Hu
College of Forestry and Gardening, Anhui Agricultural University, Hefei, China

ABSTRACT: In China, *Cunninghamia Lanceolata* forest is one of the main timber forests, and *Camellia oleifera* forest is one of the main economic forests. Twenty years of investment results of the two kinds of forests in Anhui Province showed that the annual average return on investment (ROI) of the two forests were 4.40% and 6.63%, respectively, which exceeded most of the investment return in the world. The ROI of investment in *C. oleifera* forest is 50.68% higher than that of investment in *C. Lanceolata* suggesting that the investment in *C. oleifera* forest is better. During the last 20 years, the labor wages of *C. oleifera* increased exponentially ($y = 5E\text{-}70e^{0.0806x}$), and its seeds price increased in a straight line ($y = 0.1227x - 245$); however, the timber price of *C. Lanceolata* increased very slow ($y = 35.894\ln(x) + 47.198$). This sharply increasing labor cost and slowly increasing price of timber suggest that *C. Lanceolata* is not the best tree for future investment in the Anhui Province.

1 INTRODUCTION

Forest is the main component of the earth's ecosystem which can regulate climate, purify the air, conserve water, and neutralize carbon dioxide emissions (Onker 2018; Xue 2010). To improve the ecological environment of our shared homeland, the Earth, there were several climate agreements signed by the world including Kyoto Protocol, the United Nations Framework Convention on Climate Change (UNFCC), and The Paris Agreement (The World Bank 2019; Zhang 2022). Xi Jinping, the President of the People's Republic of China declared to the world that China would strive to reach the peak of carbon dioxide emissions by 2030 and achieve carbon neutrality by 2060 (Zhang 2022; https://cnews.chinadaily.com.cn, 2020-09-23).

To achieve this goal, we need large-scale afforestation so that forests can soak up atmospheric carbon dioxide and form forest carbon sinks. Meanwhile, China is a country lacking in timber, 50% of which needs to be imported (Cheng 2021). Therefore, the government of China issued a number of preferential policies for afforestation such as granting saplings and management subsidies (Chen 2018; Yang 2021) which promoted timber forests investment.

Apart from timbers the forest products such as fruits, edible oils, herbal medicines and natural industrial raw materials are also valued by the Chinese. *C. oleifera* is one of the typical economic forest species which produces high-quality edible oil (Yang 2018). Economic forests can bring economic and ecological benefits at the same time (Guo 2020; Mao 2018).

Regarding forest investment there were several reports on the comparison of estimated income between different timber or economic forests which concluded that *C. Lanceolata* forest was one of the best trees for timber forest investment, whereas *C. oleifera* was one of the best trees for economic forest investment. However, there is a lack of detailed comparison of investment results between the two typical forests. Meanwhile, the timber price of *C. Lanceolata* was usually overrated and the labor cost is usually underestimated (Ding 2018; Liu 2017; Ma 2019; Wang 2020). This article will preliminarily suggest forest investment direction in Anhui Province on the basis of comparing the investment effects in the past 20 years between the two typical forests types in Anhui Province.

2 METHODS

Ten *C. Lanceolata* forests and 10 *C. oleifera* forests enterprises or forest farms were selected through visiting and field investigations. All the forests were invested from 2002.01 to 2021.12 and located at the foot of the mountain with gentle slopes and deep soil. The enterprises or farms should have detailed documents on forest production and financial management. Part of the information about product prices was searched by the Forestry Department of Anhui Province and the internet (http://www.wood168.net/price/ and https://lyj.ah.gov.cn/). The change trends were obtained by regression calculations.

3 RESULTS AND DISCUSSIONS

All of the average data of the forest enterprises and forest farms were listed in Table 1. Calculation results showed that the total investment including interest in *C. Lanceolata* forest in 20 years was 19200.7 USD/hm^2, and the corresponding total output was 36107.1 USD/hm^2. The total return rate was 88.05% and the annual average return rate was 4.40%. The total investment in *C. oleifera* forest in 20 years was 21457.2 USD/hm^2, and the corresponding total output was 49907.4 USD/hm^2. The total return rate was 132.60% and the annual average return rate was 6.63%. The ROI of investment in *C. oleifera* forest is 50.68% higher than that of investment in *C. Lanceolata*, which clearly shows that, the investment in *C. oleifera* forest was better. Despite the annual average return on investments of the two forests being just 4.4% and 6.6% which were not very high they exceeded most of the investment results in the world (Wei 2020).

Statistics of the 10 forest enterprises and forest farms showed that the average total labor in the production of *C. Lanceolata* forest was 676.7 day/hm^2, whereas for *C. oleifera* production, it was 1053.5 day/hm^2. The average wage of the labor was just 12.8 USD/day, and the total labor cost of the two investments account for 48.0% and 59.1% of the total investment. In the past 20 years, the average labor wage in Anhui increased exponentially (Figure 1). The average labor wage in the next 20 years investment will increase to 6.78 times and reach 86.9 USD/day according to the exponential equation $y = 5E-70e^{0.0806x}$ (Figure 1). When the labor cost rose, the price of *C. oleifera* products also increased (Figure 2). According to the price equation the average price will increase to 2.33 times in the next 20 years. Meanwhile, reports showed that the yield of the improved variety of *C. oleifera* can reach 4500 kg/hm^2 (Yang 2018) which is 2.73 times the average annual yield of the invested *C. oleifera* forest at the full fruit period. Investment using an improved variety of *C. oleifera* will have 6.36 times output in the next 20 years investment. The increased output can compensate for most of the increased labor cost. Therefore, *C. oleifera* forest still has investment value in the future in Anhui Province.

While the labor cost increases sharply, the timber price of *C. Lanceolata* increases very slowly (Figure 3). Timber forest has relatively higher carbon sequestration benefits, but the price is very low, that is, only 5.0 USD/t in the year 2016 and 7.1 USD/t in the year 2021 (He 2017; http://www.tanjiaoyi.com). This can't compensate for the increasing labor cost. It shows that, *C. Lanceolata* is not the best tree for investment in the future in Anhui. There are several quicker growing or higher value timber trees such as poplars, *Metasequoia*

Table 1. Expenditure and income of *C. Lanceolata* forest and *C. oleifera* forest.

Items	Time	Material (USD/hm^2)		Labor (USD/hm^2)		Average expenditure and income (USD/hm^2)	
		CL	CO	CL	CO	CL	CO
RL	2002					−2100.0	−2100.0
SP	2002	55.9±9.4	50.7±7.6	20.1±5.5	20.1±5.5	−76.0	−70.8
FC	2002	455.0±62.1	1288.6±137.4	107.1±13.6	159.6±16.8	−562.1	−1448.2
LR	2002	307.1±35.0	457.2±54.0	503.2±46.7	606.4±55.4	−810.3	−1063.6
P	2002	257.3±30.9	500.0±52.7	301.0±39.1	321.4±38.0	−558.3	−821.4
RPM	2002	69.0±14.4	78.6±19.0	297.0±34.2	451.4±49.3	−366.0	−530.0
AI of 2002						−4696.3	−6335.7
FM	2003	35.7±3.9	35.5±4.1	207.4±26.6	271.6±29.6	−243.1	−307.1
AI of 2003						−5175.2	−6959.9
FM	2004	35.5±3.7	35.9±3.8	208.1±25.4	271.2±27.7	−243.6	−307.1
AI of 2004						−5666.8	−7599.4
FMH	2005	38.6±4.0	37.1±3.9	212.1±26.3	284.0±35.2	−250.7	−45.8
AI of 2005 (including sales income of *C. oleifera* seeds 175.3±85.4 USD)						−6178.0	−8269.0
FMH	2006	39.7±4.1	40.0±4.5	218.0±23.5	339.7±38.1	−257.7	−104.9
AI of 2006 (including sales income of *C. oleifera* seeds 274.8±117.8 USD))						−6709.1	−8727.6
FMH	2007	9.3±1.9	47.4±5.3	131.4±17.9	348.0±38.9	−140.7	198.9
AI of 2007 (including sales income of *C. oleifera* seeds 594.3± 145.1 USD)						−7130.2	−8882.4
FMH	2008	12.7±2.3	52.0±5.0	124.3±17.2	336.2±37.3	−137.0	719.3
AI of 2008 (including sales income of *C. oleifera* seeds 1107.5±197.8 USD)						−7554.5	−8507.3
FMH	2009	10.1±2.3	54.7±6.5	113.9±16.2	323.7±35.5	−124.0	1171.6
AI of 2009, including sales income of *C. oleifera* seeds (1550.0±210.2 USD)						−7972.0	−7645.7
FMH	2010	13.4±1.8	55.6±6.7	101.9±15.7	352.6±39.4	−115.3	1548.4
AI of 2010, including sales income of *C. oleifera* seeds (1956.6±263.6 USD)						−8386.5	−6351.5
FMH	2011	13.6±1.7	57.3±7.1	128.4±17.0	382.7±39.1	−142.0	2231.4
AI of 2011, including sales income of *C. oleifera* seeds (2671.4±297.4 USD)						−8834.8	−4262.7
FMH	2012	84.7±8.9	59.7±7.0	583.0±52.7	425.0±43.6	1689.4	2558.2
AI of 2012, including sales incomes of *C. oleifera* seeds (3042.9±326.2 USD)or intermediate cuttings woods of *C. Lanceolata* (2357.1±694.6 USD)						−7438.9	−1740.9
FMH	2013	16.4±2.2	61.2±7.0	158.1±18.1	452.6±46.7	−174.5	3016.2
AI of 2013, including sales income of *C. oleifera* seeds (3530.0±348.5 USD)						−7844.0	1275.3
FMH	2014	16.1±1.9	63.4±7.0	125.2±16.5	515.0±52.2	−141.3	3537.3
AI of 2014, including sales income of *C. oleifera* seeds (4115.7±397.8 USD)						−8223.0	4812.6
FMH	2015	17.9±2.3	69.3±7.3	135.2±16.4	652.3±59.8	−153.1	3484.1
AI of 2015, including sales income of *C. oleifera* seeds (4205.7±415.9 USD)						−8621.4	8296.7
FMH	2016	17.6±2.2	70.3±6.9	190.1±23.8	677.4±63.0	−207.7	3096.3
AI of 2016, including sales income of *C. oleifera* seeds (3844.0±372.9 USD)						−9084.8	11393.0
FMH	2017	18.0±2.4	72.4±7.6	211.2±24.1	831.6±78.2	−229.2	3917.4
AI of 2017, including sales income of *C. oleifera* seeds (4821.4±464.5 USD)						−9581.1	15310.4
FMH	2018	20.3±2.6	76.1±7.7	197.0±21.7	935.6±89.3	−217.3	3438.9
AI of 2018, including sales income of *C. oleifera* seeds (4450.6±425.0 USD)						−10076.5	18749.3
FMH	2019	19.2±2.5	79.8±8.0	213.1±23.3	1133.0±98.9	−232.3	3471.5
AI of 2019, including sales income of *C. oleifera* seeds (4684.3±442.7 USD)						−10598.4	22220.8
FMH	2020	20.6±2.5	81.7±8.3	288.9±28.9	1252.4±119.3	−309.5	2917.3
AI of 2020, including sales income of *C. oleifera* seeds (4251.4±418.1 USD)						−11213.0	25138.1
FMH	2021	885.7±117.1	80.5±8.2	4439.8±421.8	1328.2±135.7	28424.5	3223.4
AI of 2021, including sales incomes of *C. oleifera* seeds (4632.1±452.5 USD)or clear cuttings woods of *C. Lanceolata* (33750.0±3574.2 USD)						16989.6	28361.5

Note: CL = *C. Lanceolata*; CO = *C. oleifera*; RL = Rent of land; SP = Survey and planning; FC = Facilities construction; LR = Land revitalization; P = Planting; RPM = Reinforcement planting and maintenance; AI = Accumulated income; FM = Forest management; FMH = Forest management and harvesting. Materials included saplings, fertilizers, pesticides, construction materials, fuel, tools and instruments (lease or purchase). The loan rate is 5%. The sale incomes were preferentially used to repay the loan. Some implicit costs and small incomes can be roughly offset each other and are not listed in the table.

9

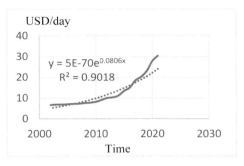

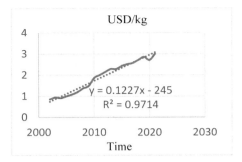

Figure 1. Average wage from the year 2002 to 2021. The solid line is average wage. The spotted line is fitting curve.

Figure 2. Average price of *C. oleifera* seeds from the year 2002 to 2021. The solid line is average price. The spotted line is fitting curve.

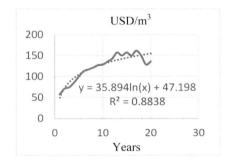

Figure 3. Average price of *C. Lanceolata* timber from the year 2002 to 2021. The solid line is average price. The spotted line is fitting curve.

glyptostroboides, *Cinnamomum camphora*, *Phoebe zhennan,* etc. (Cheng 2008) that could be invested in the future in Anhui Province. Meanwhile, mixed forests of *C. Lanceolata* and some broadleaf trees also have investment value in the future, as mixed forests usually have better growth rates, produce more timbers, and act as carbon sinks (Cui 2020; Li 2021; Ouyang 2017) which may compensate the increasing labor cost in the future.

4   CONCLUSIONS

From the above analysis we can conclude that the investments in *C. Lanceolata* and *C. oleifera* forests in Anhui Province over the past 20 years have been successful, as evidenced by the fact that the annual average returns (4.40% and 6.63%) exceed the returns of most investment around the world. The investment in *C. oleifera* forest was better than in *C. Lanceolata* forest in the past 20 years in Anhui Province. During the last 20 years the labor wages increased exponentially ($y = 5E\text{-}70e^{0.0806x}$), the seeds price of *C. oleifera* increased in a straight line ($y = 0.1227x - 245$), but the timber price of *C. Lanceolata* increased very slowly ($y = 35.894\ln(x) + 47.198$). In the future, the investment in *C. oleifera* forest will still be better than in *C. Lanceolata* because while the labor costs increase, the yield and price of *C. oleifera* seeds will increase. The sharply increasing labor cost and slowly increasing price of timber suggest that the ROI of investment on *C. Lanceolata* will be considerably lower in the future. Therefore, the investment in *C. Lanceolata* forest is not a good choice for the future in Anhui

Province. Some quicker-growing or higher value timber forests, or mixed forests of *C. Lanceolata* and some broadleaf trees may be a better choice than pure *C. Lanceolata* forest.

REFERENCES

Chen, W. Xiao, J. Liu X. & Huang, C. 2018. Study on the Influence of Ecological Compensation on Forestry Investment Assets Portfolio. *Issues of Forestry Economic* 38(2): 33–39.

Cheng, P. (ed.) 2008. *Selection and Cultivation Techniques of Afforestation Tree Species in Different Regions of Anhui Province.* Beijing. Chinese Forestry Publishing House.

Cheng, Y. Liu C. Yang, H. & Zhang, H. 2021. The Structure of Commercial Forests "Tending to Become Economic Forests": An Analysis of Causes Based on Labor Cost Effects and Relative-revenue Effects. *Scientia Silvae Sinicae* 57(7): 184–192.

Cui, S. Xiao, R. Wang, W. & Liu, B. 2020. Carbon Sink Structure of Coniferous and Broadleaved Mixed Forests in Lesser Khingan. *Forest Engineering* 36(6): 30–35.

Ding, Q. 2018. A Comparative Study on Investment and Return of Commercial Forest. *Modern Business* 5: 147–148.

Guo, M. Yang Y. Xu, Y. & Xi, R. 2020. Carbon Storage and Distribution Characteristics of *Camellia Gauchowensis* Plantation. *Journal of South China Agricultural University* 41(3): 86–92.

He, X. Wang, D & Zeng, S. 2017. Valuation for Forest Investment Projects with Carbon Sequestration Benefits—based on Real Option Pricing Theory. *Chinese Journal of Management Science* 25(3): 39–46.

Li, C. 2021. Comparison of Growth of Mixed Afforestation of *Cunninghamia lanceolata* and *Phoebe zhennan*. *Green Science and Technology* 23: 165–167.

Liu, Y. Fu, W. Zhao, J. & Liu, J. 2017. Study on the Forestry Investment and Ecological Services Value in China. *Ecological Economy* 33(1): 152–158.

Ma, A. 2019. Study on Risk and Countermeasure of Forestry Investment. *Agricultural Development & Equipments* 9: 80–82.

Mao, X. & Xu, Z. 2018. Forest Carbon Storage and Dynamic Change in the Mountain Region of Southern Anhui. *Journal of Forest and Environment* 38(2): 185–190.

Ouyang, JZ. 2017. Study on Ecological Effects of Chinese Fir Mixed Forest in South Fujian Mountainous Area. *Green Science and Technology* 12: 172–174.

Onker, J. Vander, H. Markewitz, D. Faaij, A. & Junginger, H. 2018. Carbon Balance and Economic Performance of Pine Plantations for Bioenergy Production in the Southeastern United States. *Biomass Bioenergy* 117: 44–55.

The World Bank. 2019. Review on Sustainable Forest Management and Financing in China. *Report* No: AUS0001069.

Wang, Q. & Chao, Y. 2020. Time Varying Characteristics of the Output Effect and Profit Effect of Forestry Investment in China. *Statistics and Decision* 544(4): 155–158.

Wei, W. & Zhang, B. 2020. International Comparison of China's Return on Investment and its Implications. *Enterprise.Economy* 39(10):111–120.

Xue, J. (ed.) 2010. *Forest Ecology.* Beijing. Chinese Forestry Publishing House.

Yang, X. Yin, S. Deng, J. Zhang, L. & Liu, C. 2021. Analysis on the Influence of Forestry Financial Subsidy Policy on Farmers' Forestry Investment and its Structure — Based on the Perspective of Crowd-in and Crowd-out Effect of Financial Subsidy. *Forestry Economics* 2: 5–20.

Yang, Y. Zhang, P. Xi, R. & Huang, R. 2018, Variation Characteristics of Oil Content and Fatty Acid Composition in *Camellia gauchowensis* Fruits at Different Producing Areas. *Nonwood Forest Research* 36 (4): 104–108.

Zhang, Y. Li, X. & Wen, Y. 2022. Forest Carbon Sequestration Potential in China Under the Background of Carbon Emission Peak and Carbon Neutralization. *Journal of Beijing Forestry Univesity* 44(1): 38–47.

Economic and Business Management – Lent & Zhang (Eds)
© 2023 the Author(s), ISBN 978-1-032-24482-2

Commuting of the self-employed – Experience from Slovakia

B. Mazúrová, J. Kollár & M. Martinkovičová
Faculty of Economics, Matej Bel University in Banska Bystrica, Banská Bystrica, Slovakia

ABSTRACT: This article explores the commuting to/from work in Slovak republic, with a focus on the differences in commuting of the self-employed compared to average of all workers. We analyze commuting in the context of time costs and monetary costs and the mode of transport. Using data from questionnaire survey on a sample of more than 1 000 workers, we compare the commuting behavior of all respondents and the self-employed. By processing the results, we can conclude that while time costs of commuting of self-employed do not differ compared to all respondents, there are significant differences in monetary costs. We also found out that the most common mode of transport using by all respondents is commuting by own car.

1 INTRODUCTION

Commuting to/from work is an undesirable personal employment tax. It is therefore very important to know the essential factors of commuting behavior of workers. Factors such as gender, education, marital status, the presence of children in the household, employed partners, industry and occupation, and the geographical location (e.g., living in urban area) may differentially affect workers in their commuting behavior. Previous research has shown that Slovaks are among the countries with lower time costs and that there is dependence between the length of commuting and the net monthly income of respondents (Kollár & Mazúrová 2019).

In Europe, the representation of self-employed workers ranges from 7% to 29% of the total working-age population. According to Giménez-Nadal et al. (2020) the average commuting time of female and male self-employed and employed workers depends on the degree of urbanization of their place of residence (urban areas, urban intermediate areas and rural areas). The results of their investigation showed that urban characteristics are important in such differences in commuting times, which appear to be smaller in urban areas than in rural areas, especially for female workers.

The importance of self-employed for the national economy is undeniable. In Slovakia, persons-entrepreneurs make up over 65% of the total number of entrepreneurs entities. They provide employment opportunities in the corporate economy of almost 75% of the active workforce and account for more than 50% of gross output and value added (Slovak Business Agency 2020).

The most self-employed persons in the Slovak Republic are small self-employed persons. Preferred spheres of activity are industry, construction and services (personal, business, educational, advisory, consulting, brokerage) and mostly the performance of work is situated locally or regionally. These conditions require no or minimal commuting to/from work by self-employed persons.

Nevertheless, entrepreneurship in Slovakia is still associated with spatial and temporal mobility, therefore we assume that in case of self-employed the time costs as well as monetary costs of commuting are higher compare to all respondents. At the same time, in the case

DOI: 10.1201/9781003278788-3

of both categories of workers can be assumed the preference of commuting by own car over alternative modes of transport. The aim of the article is to quantify average weekly time costs and monetary costs of commuting as well as mode of transport of self-employed and compare the results with a sample of all workers in Slovakia.

2 LITERATURE REVIEW

Commuting to and from work is part of everyday life, both professional and private. It can also be seen as a link between personal and working life, it enables access to the labor market and it can be a manifestation of gendered relations between women and men. Accordingly, commuting is a concern at both the individual and household levels as well as for policy and planning at various levels (Solá 2016).

According to Wheatley and Wu (2014), commuting time is a necessary work-related activity, but is distinct from work-time. Basmajian (2010, p. 77) presumes commuting as a "fluid experience equally blended into home life and work-place and points in between".

In the relationship between self-employment and commuting, prior research has found that the self-employed exhibit different behaviors in comparison to employees, with these differences being partially motivated by different job-search market structures (Giménez-Nadal et al. 2020). There is a presumption that the self-employed are better informed about the labor market compared to employees. The self-employed commute about 40-60 % less than employees (e.g. in the Netherlands according to Van Ommeren & Van der Straaten 2008). More recently, Gimenez-Nadal et al. (2018a) study differences in the time devoted to commuting by US employees and self-employed workers, finding a difference of about 17%. In addition, Albert et al. (2019) analyze the case of Spain, using information about commuting time from the Quality of Life at Work Survey, and find a difference between employees and the self-employed ranging from 13% to 19.5%. "Analyzing differences in commuting behavior between employees and self-employed workers is important in the case of Europe, since the latter represent a significant proportion - between 7% and 29% - of the working-age population" (Giménez-Nadal et al. 2020, p. 3).

As in the current paper, we aim to estimate individuals' marginal costs of commuting, we resume these costs include travel time costs and monetary costs, but they may also include other costs that affect the utility of travel (e.g. stress). Commuting costs play an important role in hundreds of studies that contribute to urban economics theory (e.g. Fujita 1989; Van Ommeren & Fosgerau 2009; Wheaton 1974).

3 DATA AND METHODOLOGY

The results that we present in this article were obtained by processing the data of a questionnaire survey. Trained interviewers distributed the questionnaire, consisting of eight interconnected parts, in the months of April–May 2018 to more than 700 Slovak households (with 1.819 members). The research team consisted of academic experts in economics, sociology, demography, statistics and psychology, who participated in the creation of the questionnaire (as the main tool for data collection). The research team was available to interviewers in case of questions or uncertainties during the data collection both on-line and in person. For the purposes of this article, we processed data related to the previous year 2017 from first and seventh module, which were focused at capturing commuting information. We used this method so that attendance information from respondents could be averaged over a more comprehensive period.

The research sample consisted of 1014 economically active respondents, aged 15-64 years (56% men, 44% women). The average age of respondents was 38 (a quarter of respondents were in the age category of 40–49 years old). The largest part consisted of secondary school-educated (more than 70%) and full-time employed (almost 80%) respondents working in the private sector of the economy (almost 80%). Most of them (93.1%) had only one paid job at the time of the survey, worked in the Slovakia (95%) and commuted daily (91%). Almost half of the respondents belonged to the income category from 401 to 800 €. Of the total economically active respondents, 143 were self-employed (14,1% of all respondents). This share of respondents roughly mirrored the actual share of self-employed persons in the Slovak Republic in the total number of work force. The information from the questionnaire was representative with respect to the structure of the Slovak population by gender, age and education of respondents. All data that we evaluated were adjusted from outliers and were processed using SPSS software.

4 RESULTS AND DISCUSSIONS

From the questionnaire survey, we processed the data and came to several findings. The average weekly commute time in hours (net time) of all respondents was 4.06 hours. This value does not include time that may be associated with commuting, such as waiting time for public transport, time spent by refueling, etc. The average weekly net commuting time for the self-employed is 4.30 hours. These results indicate that respondents who reported in the questionnaire survey that they are self-employed commute longer than the average for all employees. We also note that the values are comparable and we did not identify a significant deviation what is not consistent with the conclusions of analyses abroad (e.g. Albert et al. 2019; Gimenez-Nadal et al. 2018a; Van Ommeren & Van der Straaten 2008). A more detailed analysis of the data regarding average weekly commuting expenditures showed differences that are more pronounced. If the average weekly commuting expenses of all respondents were 13.19 €, for the self-employed there were 22 €. It can be stated that in the case of respondents involved in the survey who were self-employed, the average weekly expenditures are higher by more than 8 €, which is not insignificant in terms of monthly expenditures - it amounts to 32 €.

Based on results of the questionnaire survey, it is clear that the most frequently mode of transport by commuting for all respondents is by own car. An interesting finding is that while 46% of all respondents use this mode of transport, in the case of the self-employed it is as high as 65% of respondents. This fact may be one of the reasons explaining the higher average weekly monetary costs of commuting of the self-employed we identified earlier.

Other modes of transport by commuting such as using public transport, cycling, walking, car sharing and other transfer modes coming into consideration in Slovakia are used by all respondents as well as the self-employed to a much lesser extent. The results for mode of transport, time costs and monetary costs are detailed in Table 1.

Table 1. Mode of transport, monetary and time costs of commuting.

	Mode of transport	Average weekly monetary costs in €	Average weekly time costs in hours
all employees	own car	19.53	4.19
	public transport	8.85	4
	bicycle, walking	0.72	1.97
	shared car	10.83	4.77
	other	10	5.98
self-employed	own car	29.11	4.73
	public transport	8.96	5.46
	bicycle, walking	0.86	1.43
	shared car	15.76	4.71
	other	8	0.41

Source: Own processing based on questionnaire survey data.

14

The results we have reached are initial in the conditions of the Slovak Republic, but their interpretation is limited. For example, based on the primary data obtained, we cannot identify the average length (in km or miles) that commuters travel on average. At this stage of knowledge, we can only assume that the self-employed, taking into account monetary costs and the mode of transport, travel on average a greater distance compared to the employed.

The commuting time costs and monetary costs as well as the mode of transport of economically active individuals in the Slovak Republic are discussed in more detail in e.g. Mazúrová et al. (2021), Kollár and Mazúrová (2019). Based on the results of the analysis, it was found that the determinants that affect the travel mode choice of respondents include commuting time and monetary costs, income of respondents, education, and gender, type of employment and place of work. Our research so far has shown that commuters are most satisfied when they cycle or walk to work. The highest level of dissatisfaction is in relation to using public transport to commute to work. Given the current energy crisis, our aim is to stimulate a wider professional debate (also in Slovakia) on the benefits of public transport, cycling and other alternatives to commuting as a more environmentally, economically and health-friendly travel mode. These benefits should also be reflected by public policy makers and taken into account in spatial planning of infrastructure with respect to the climate and surface of Slovakia.

5   CONCLUSIONS

In view of the current post-pandemic developments and rising fuel prices, the issue of commuting is also a hotly debated topic and should therefore be given due attention in professional analyses and scientific research. Self-employed make up a substantial part of the workforce in Slovakia, yet research into their travel behavior is not given adequate attention in professional communities. The results of our analysis have shown that there are some differences between the commuting behavior of all workers and that of the self-employed. Although we cannot generalize our findings given the small sample of respondents, we can at least summaries our findings.

We can conclude that while time costs of commuting of self-employed do not differ compared to all respondents, there are significant differences in monetary costs. We also found out that the most common mode of transport used by all respondents is commuting by own car. Although our investigation has some limitations at this stage (e.g. we did not investigate the distances covered in commuting, the traffic situation, the level of infrastructure, etc.), the initial findings are a stimulus for further understanding and development of the issue also with regard to the world trends in people's mobility.

ACKNOWLEDGEMENT

This work was supported by the National Research Agency of Slovakia, project VEGA no. 1/0366/21 "Dependent Entrepreneurship in Slovakia – Reflection, Measurement and Perspectives" at the Faculty of Economics, Matej Bel University in Banska Bystrica, Slovakia.

REFERENCES

Albert, J.F., Casado-Díaz, J.M. & Simón, H. 2019. The Commuting Behaviour of Self-employed Workers: Evidence for Spain. *Papers in Regional Science* 98(6): 2455–2477.

Basmajian, C. 2010. Turn on the Radio, Bust Out a Song: The Experience of Driving to Work. *Transportation*, 37(1): 59–84.

Fujita, M. 1989. *Urban Economic Theory*. Cambridge: Cambridge University Press.

Gimenez-Nadal, J.I., Molina, J.A. & Velilla, J. 2018a. The Commuting Behavior of Workers in the United States: Differences Between the Employed and the Self-employed. *Journal of Transport Geography* 66(1): 19–29.

Giménez-Nadal, J.I., Molina, J.A. & Velilla, J. 2020. Commuting and Self-employment in Western Europe. *Journal of Transport Geography* 88: 1–13.

Kollár, J. & Mazúrová, B. 2019. Selected Issues of Commuting in Slovakia. *Economic and Social Challenges for European Economy, Čeladná, 3-5 September 2019*. Ostrava: Vysoká škola PRIGO.

Mazúrová, B., Kollár, J. & Nedelová, G. 2021. Travel Mode of Commuting in Context of Subjective Well-being – Experience From Slovakia. *Sustainability* 13(6): 1–17.

Ommeren, V. J. & Fosgerau B. 2009. Workers' Marginal Costs of Commuting. *Journal of Urban Economics* 65: 38–47.

Solá, A.G. 2016. Constructing Work Travel Inequalities: The Role of Household. *Journal of Transport Geography* 53: 32–40.

Slovak Business Agency. 2020. *Analýza Vybraných Aspektov Podnikania SZČO*. Bratislava: Slovak Business Agency.

Van Ommeren, J.N. & Van der Straaten, J.W. 2008. The Effect of Search Imperfections on Commuting Behavior: Evidence From Employed and Self-employed Workers. *Regional Science and Urban Economy* 38(2): 127–147.

Wheatley, D. & Wu, Z. 2014. Dual Careers, Time-use, and Satisfaction Levels: Evidence From the British Household Panel Survey. *Industrial Realtions Journal* 45(5): 443–464.

Wheaton, W.C. 1974. A Comparative Static Analysis of Urban Spatial Structure. *Journal of Economic Theory* 9: 223–237.

Economic and Business Management – Lent & Zhang (Eds)

Research on the new trend of low-carbon strategy of multinational corporations

Qi Fang & Yongjian Zong
School of Economics & Management, Nanjing University of Science & Technology, Nanjing, China

ABSTRACT: As an important part of the carbon emission process, the low-carbon strategy of multinational corporations plays a key role. In the process of low-carbon economy development, China should fully understand the new trend of low-carbon strategy of multinational corporations to realize China's carbon peak and carbon neutralization targets. This paper first summarizes the significance and necessity of multinational corporations' low-carbon transformation under the background of low-carbon economy and then analyzes the new trends of multinational corporations' low-carbon transformation from three aspects: carbon emission management, energy transformation and low-carbon technology. Finally suggestions are put forward on how to better realize low-carbon transformation from the perspectives of government and enterprises, which can promote the early realization of China's carbon peak and carbon neutralization targets.

1   INTRODUCTION

The Paris agreement adopted by the Paris Conference on climate change in 2015 established the long-term goal of global response to climate change, that is, to control the rise of global temperature within $2\,^{\circ}C$ based on the pre industrial level by the end of the 21st century, strive to control it within $1.5\,^{\circ}C$, achieve the peak of global greenhouse gas emissions as soon as possible, and achieve zero net greenhouse gas emissions in the second half of the 21st century [1]. Developed countries have passed the development stage with high-carbon energy as the main driving force. In this context, the development of low-carbon economy is an inevitable choice [2].

As an important carrier connecting the domestic and international double cycle, transnational corporations have broad development space and play an important role in global carbon emission reduction. Since the target of carbon peaking and carbon neutralizationity presented in China, Chinese government and enterprises have been making efforts to realize low-carbon transition.

2   LITERATURE REVIEW

2.1   *Multinational corporations and the low-carbon economy*

Xu Feng et al. (2022) proposed that green and low-carbon transformation could significantly improve the profitability of manufacturing enterprises, and increasing innovation investment and alleviating financing constraints were important mechanisms [3]. Vladislav Maksimov et al. (2019) found that multinational corporations with greater global connections in international diversification or international environmental certification had knowledge advantages in cultivating dynamic green capabilities, so the low-carbon strategy of multi-national corporations was more cutting-edge [4]. Wang Qi (2018) explained the important roles played by multinational corporations in international environmental cooperation in response to climate change [5].

Nemtinovay et al. (2022) pointed out that the use of carbon emission quota market would significantly bring economic entities and the whole society closer to low-carbon economy [6]. Therefore, China must make good use of carbon emission quota market to develop low-carbon economy. Hu Yufeng et al. (2022) found that the impact of low-carbon regulation tools was different. High carbon industries were more sensitive to low-carbon regulation tools, and the impact of carbon tax was more significant than carbon subsidies and carbon investment [7]. A phased and differentiated low-carbon regulation tool portfolio policy should be implemented.

2.2 *Digital economy*

Zhu Zhaoyi et al. (2022) summarized Israel's economic development experience and proposed that China should adhere to promoting innovative development, and create a low-carbon, green and sustainable development model [8]. Wang Shuo et al. (2022) pointed out that the current development mode of digital economy was the main booster to achieve the goal of carbon peak [9]. Enterprises need to accelerate digital transformation to promote carbon emission reduction. Wang Ruqi et al. (2022) found that there were obvious regional differences in the role of digital economy in promoting the development of regional real economy [10].

At this stage, China's government's mandatory control over digital carbon neutralizationization needs to be strengthened, and enterprises' digital carbon information disclosure is not active and insufficient. Therefore, the state should formulate mandatory low-carbon supervision system and safe harbor mechanism, and enterprises should strengthen the enthusiasm and scientificity of carbon information capture and disclosure of digital infrastructure.

3 THE SIGNIFICANCE OF MULTINATIONAL CORPORATIONS' LOW-CARBON TRANSFORMATION

3.1 *Enhance international competitiveness*

Soaring natural gas prices in 2021 led to a strong recovery of coal-fired power generation, which was the main reason for the "strong rebound" of carbon emissions in the energy sector. The high price of traditional energy and the rising cost of carbon emissions have largely increased the production and operating costs of multinational corporations and reduced their international market competitiveness. The energy-saving benefits brought by the implementation of low-carbon strategy are very significant. Multinational corporations can not only reduce carbon emission costs by using renewable energy and digital management to improve efficiency, so as to enhance their international competitiveness, but also form their core competitiveness by mastering advanced low-carbon technologies.

3.2 *Adapt to market demand*

For multinational corporations, especially those in the fields of electricity, transportation, construction and agriculture, which play a key role in realizing carbon emissions, if they do not meet the low-carbon requirements, they will be banned from market access. Take the transportation department as an example. In August 2021, the national highway traffic safety administration proposed a new standard. Among the vehicle models from 2024 to

2026, the fuel efficiency will be increased by 8% per year. In the context of low-carbon economy, the threshold of carbon emission is higher and higher. Multinational corporations have to implement low-carbon strategy in order to meet the needs of the market.

3.3 *Enhance brand image*

Research shows that green brand image plays a positive regulatory role in the relationship between environmental self-efficacy and green product purchase intention. With the enhancement of the green brand image of products, the positive impact of environmental self-efficacy on the purchase intention of green products has also been improved [11].

For multinational corporations, by implementing low-carbon strategy and producing high-quality green products, they can provide consumers with diversified choices. By deepening consumers' awareness of the green image of the brand, multinational corporations further strengthen the green attribute of brand products and improve consumers' Green Association and trust in the brand, so as to promote consumers to buy their own products.

4 ANALYSIS ON THE NEW TREND OF LOW CARBON STRATEGY OF MULTINATIONAL CORPORATIONS

4.1 *Further develop clear carbon emission targets*

Most multinationals have given their external assurance statements on carbon emissions in the corporate social responsibility section of their official website. At the same time, some multinational corporations have also formulated some specific quantitative indicators of carbon emissions, as shown in Table 1.

By comparing the changes of the carbon emission reduction targets of multinational corporations in Table 1, it can be found that the consistency of the carbon emission reduction targets formulated by multinational corporations in the past is poor. Nowadays, the carbon emission reduction targets of multinational corporations tend to be consistent. All multinational corporations have said that they want to achieve net zero emissions before

Table 1.   Changes of carbon emission reduction targets of 6 multinational corporations.

Corporations	Before	Now
Ericsson	From 2008 to 2013, the carbon footprint will be reduced by 40%.	Achieve net zero emissions throughout the value chain by 2040 and reduce emissions in the supply chain by 50% by 2030.
Intel	From 2007 to 2012, the absolute value of carbon emissions will be reduced by 20%.	Achieve an absolute reduction in carbon emissions by 2030.
IBM	From 2005 to 2012, carbon emissions will be reduced by 12% compared with 2005.	By 2030, net zero greenhouse gas emissions will be achieved through the use of feasible technologies.
Cisco	From 2006 to 2012, carbon emissions will be reduced by 25%.	It is committed to achieving net zero emissions by 2040.
Sony	From 2000 to 2015, the carbon emission of factories will be reduced by 30%.	Strive to reduce the environmental load to 0 by 2050.
Caterpillar	Reduce the absolute carbon emissions by 25% from 2006 to 2020.	Reduce greenhouse gas emission intensity by 50% by 2020.

Data source: sorted according to the corporate social responsibility and other relevant reports released on the official websites of multinational corporations.

19

2050 or earlier, which shows the determination of multinational corporations to achieve low-carbon transformation.

4.2 *Energy transformation*

Under the background of low-carbon global energy, the oil and gas industry is facing multiple pressures, such as the slowdown of traditional energy consumption, the increasingly strict carbon policy, the increasing carbon cost, the increasing risk of holding high-carbon assets, and the continuous suppression of oil and gas prices. The difficulties faced by traditional oil and gas production will further increase [12]. Coping with the change of carbon emissions is no longer a scientific problem limited to the field of environment, but also an important risk for the sustainable development of the industry.

Total, Shell Group and Norwegian oil company have realized the industrialization of new energy in some fields through various ways, and have a certain scale [13]. For example, Shell has been a "radical" in the development of new energy among international oil and gas companies in recent years. With its long-term accumulation in the field of new energy and recent frequent investment layout, shell has demonstrated its determination to transform energy. BP has the largest wind power business among international oil companies.

4.3 *Research and development of low carbon technology*

Representative low-carbon technologies include carbon capture, utilization and storage technology (CCUS), that is, the carbon dioxide emitted in the production process is purified and then put into the new production process, which can be recycled instead of simply stored. Compared with CCS, CCUS can recycle carbon dioxide, produce economic benefits and have more practical operability. Although CCUS is not economically feasible under the current carbon price and there are still difficulties in industrialization [14], it has been highly valued by countries and major energy companies all over the world, and has increased R&D efforts one after another. The investment and progress of multinational corporations in CCUS field is also the embodiment of their low-carbon development level. Chevron and other companies have carried out lots of research on CO_2 capture and storage, and have realized large-scale CO_2 geological storage.

5 SUGGESTIONS AND MEASURES FOR CHINESE GOVERNMENT AND ENTERPRISES

Coordinating the relationship between economic recovery and carbon emission reduction in the "post epidemic era" is a new challenge for the development of China's low-carbon economy. In order to achieve China's goal of carbon peak and carbon neutralizationization, Chinese government and enterprises can take the new trend of low-carbon strategy of multinational corporations as a reference for the path of low-carbon transformation.

5.1 *Government*

5.1.1 *Strengthen supervision*
When the government increases the punishment for enterprises adhering to the traditional production mode and enhances the supervision of third-party forces, enterprises prefer the low-carbon production mode [15]. Therefore, the government should not only optimize the carbon tax and low-carbon subsidy policies to attract enterprises to actively respond to the call for emission reduction, but also increase the punishment of enterprises that adhere to the traditional mode of production, so as to better urge enterprises to carry out low-carbon transformation. In terms of supervision, the government can not only supervise enterprises by itself, but also rely on the power of a third party. Third party forces can effectively complement the shortcomings of the government's single supervision.

5.1.2 *Establish and improve the carbon emission trading market*

In order to give further play to the guiding role of carbon emission trading, the government should vigorously improve the trading system of carbon emission trading market, such as formulating unified carbon quota trading standards and building a mature carbon emission trading market. In addition, in order to improve the transformation enthusiasm of enterprises, the government can also give certain price and tax concessions to enterprises using new energy and low-carbon production technology with the help of market-oriented regulation means, so as to support the low-carbon transformation of enterprises with market-oriented means.

5.2 *Enterprises*

5.2.1 *Cooperate with multinational corporations to strengthen technological innovation*

In the final analysis, the realization of China's goal of carbon peak and carbon neutralizationization needs the support of technological innovation. In general, multinational corporations have strong technical advantages and there is a huge space for cooperation with China at the industrial level. Chinese enterprises can cooperate with multinational companies for win-win results, carry out technology exchange and experience learning with an open and inclusive attitude, quickly solve technical shortcomings, improve internal defects, strive to create their own competitiveness, improve the strength of sustainable development.

5.2.2 *Digital transformation*

Enterprises have meaningless waste in many aspects. Such as in logistics, there are many invalid transportation and repeated transportation. Through digital transformation, carbon emissions in these processes can be reduced.

Chinese enterprises can promote the realization of China's goal of carbon peak and carbon neutralizationization through digital transformation. First, in the process of digital transformation, enterprises should set up specialized low-carbon management departments and personnel, build an independent and perfect governance structure and check and balance mechanism. By giving relevant managers or organizations certain decision-making power of carbon emission reduction actions and information disclosure, it is conducive to improve the carbon performance of enterprises, so as to strengthen the motivation of enterprises to carry out carbon information disclosure. Secondly, improve the carbon management process of the enterprise, pay attention to the impact of disclosure and do a good job of feedback management, so that the enterprise can timely capture the market dynamics and cooperate with the needs of stakeholders.

6 CONCLUSIONS

This paper analyzes the new trend of low-carbon strategy of multinational companies from three levels by combining the latest policies and summarizes the significance and necessity of multinational corporations' low-carbon transformation. As a country with huge carbon emissions, it is necessary for China to implement an efficient low-carbon strategy. Based on this, some suggestions are made for Chinese government and enterprises at the end of this paper.

The research content of this paper has been updated to a certain extent, but there are still some deficiencies due to data sources, limited research time and other reasons. The research stays at a more theoretical level and lacks relevant empirical research. Low-carbon development is an important aspect of China's sustainable development. Future research also needs to be deepened and expanded in combination with the latest policy environment and the international situation.

REFERENCES

[1] Cong, R. et al. 2022. Challenges and opportunities of China's oil and gas industry under the goal of carbon peak and carbon–Enlightenment Based on EU energy transformation. *Natural Gas and Oil* 40(02): 136–143.

[2] Hu, Y.F. et al. 2022. Differential Impact of Low-carbon Regulation Tools on Green Total Factor Productivity–Based on Empirical Evidence of Provincial and A-share Listed Companies in China. *Southern Finance* 2022(1): 68–78.

[3] Jia, J.T. & Zhang, M.R. 2022. Estimation of Regional Climate Comfort Along the "the Belt and Road" Under the Future Climate Scenario of the Paris Agreement. *Progress in Earth Science.*

[4] Liu, F.Y. & Li, X.R. 2022. Research on the Influence of Consumers' Initiative Personality on the Purchase Intention of Green Products–the Regulatory Effect of Green Brand Image. *Journal of Nanjing University of Technology (Social Science Edition)* 21(2): 68–80 + 112.

[5] Luo, F.Z. & Tang, J. 2020. Research on Evolutionary Game of Low Carbon Emission Reduction Strategy of Government and Enterprises Under the Supervision of the Third Party. *Ecological Economy* 36(4): 30–34.

[6] Maksimov, V. et al. 2019. Global Connectedness and Dynamic Green Capabilities in MNEs. *Journal of International Business Studies.*

[7] Nemtinova, Y. et al. 2022. The Market for Greenhouse Gas Emissions Quotas as an Incentive on the Way to a Low-carbon Economy. *IOP Conference Series: Earth and Environmental Science* 979(1): 28–31.

[8] Wang, C.Q. & Liu, C.X. 2022. Research on Sustainable Development of Enterprises Under the Background of Low-carbon Economy. *Modern Business* 2022(3): 141–143.

[9] Wang, N. et al. 2021. What Went Wrong? Learning From Three Decades of Carbon Capture, Utilization and Sequestration (CCUS) Pilot and Demonstration Projects. *Energy Policy* 2021:158.

[10] Wang, Q. 2018. Evaluation and Analysis of Japan's International Environmental Cooperation Mechanism to Deal With Climate Change: the Function of Non-state Actors. *International Forum* 20 (2): 27–32 + 77.

[11] Wang, R.Q. & Tao, S.G. 2022. How Digital Economy Affects the Development of Real Economy–Mechanism Analysis and Chinese Experience. *Discussion on Modern Economy* 2022(5): 15–26.

[12] Wang, S. & Wang, H.R. 2022. Research on the Strategy of Healthy Development of China's Digital Economy Under the Background of Double Carbon Goals. *Contemporary Economic Management* 2022 (2):1–10.

[13] Xu, F. et al. 2022. Research on the Impact of Green and Low-carbon Transformation on Enterprise Profitability Under the Goal of Carbon Peak and Carbon. *Macroeconomic Research* 2022(1): 161–175.

[14] Yu, H. et al. 2020. Strategic Transformation and Practical Results of Oil and Gas Industry From the Perspective of Global Low carbon. *Modern Chemical Industry* 40(10): 10–14.

[15] Zhu, Z.Y. et al. 2022. Practical Experience of Israel's Green Economy Development Under the Goal of Carbon Neutralizationization and Its Enlightenment to China. *International Trade* 2022(2): 14–21.

Economic and Business Management – Lent & Zhang (Eds)
© 2023 the Author(s), ISBN 978-1-032-24482-2

The influence of patent quality on export product quality of high-tech manufacturing enterprises in China

Jiawei Zuo & Yizhong Fu
School of Economics & Management, Beijing Forestry University, Beijing, China

ABSTRACT: China has grown into the largest global manufacturer. However, the quality of China's export products has always been questioned. "Big but not strong" has always been a puzzle for the development of China's trade. China should embark on the road of high-quality development; therefore, high-quality export is worthy of attention. China's high-tech manufacturing enterprises are at the forefront of innovation in core technology patents, bearing the R&D capability and mission to improve the quality of export products. Based on the heterogeneity of enterprises, this paper studied the influence and mechanism of patent quality on export product quality of High-tech manufacturing enterprises in China through the matching of industrial and enterprise customs patent data from 2000 to 2013. The results showed that patent quality had a significantly positive impact on the quality of export products of Chinese manufacturing high-tech enterprises, and government subsidies played a positive role in high-tech enterprises, and patent quality could improve the quality of export products of manufacturing high-tech enterprises by reducing production costs.

1 INTRODUCTION

Since the reform and opening up, especially after China's accession to the WTO, the expansion of export trade has always been the main driving force of China's rapid economic growth. China has been the world's largest exporter of goods for 12 consecutive years since 2009. In 2020, China's annual exports reached RMB17.9326 trillion yuan, up by 4.0 percent. However, the quality level of China's export products has been questioned for a long time, and "big but not strong" has always been a problem for the development of China's trade. Building China into a trading power means stronger competitiveness in foreign trade and better quality and efficiency in products. However, 13 of China Mainland's top 30 exporters in 2019 were contract manufacturers. In 2020, among China's top 100 foreign trade and export enterprises, small, medium, and micro enterprises were still the main force, and large and competitive trade-leading enterprises had not accounted for a high proportion. China's manufacturing industry cannot simply rely on the input of capital, labor, resources, and other factors to achieve wealth creation and extensive economic growth through economies of scale. It should emphasize quality and efficiency and keep up with the upgrading of demand. Innovation-driven development should be the new and sustainable driving force.

Innovation has become one of the most critical factors to determine China's sustainable economic growth (Tang W. et al. 2014). Patent is an important aspect reflecting a country's innovation activities at both macro and micro levels. Patent growth also plays a decisive role in the improvement of a country's independent innovation ability and economic growth (Hu & Jefferson 2009). Since 1984, when China formally promulgated the Patent Law, the number of patent applications and grants in China has seen explosive growth. According to the Report of the World Intellectual Property Organization (WIPO), after China overtook the United States in 2019 to become the largest source of international patent applications filed through WIPO, China continued to lead the world in the number of patent applications filed in 2020 with 68,720. However, the increase in the number of patents might not resemble the improvement of patent quality, and invention patents with high patent quality have a more obvious effect on the improvement of enterprise performance and economic growth, while the surge of patent data of utility models and industrial designs with low innovation degree may lead to "patent bubble" (Shen Y. et al. 2018). In China, both numbers of applications and granted invention patents only took 30 percent to 40 percent of the total amount of patent applications. According to the statistical analysis by Patsnap, a Chinese patent data statistics and analysis company, 90.43 percent of patents applied in the United States were invention patents, and numbers were 72.27%, 82.92%, 68.81%, and 80.5% in U.K., Japan, France, and Germany, respectively. And the number of patent applications did not imply the protection of intellectual property rights, only through patent authorization can a patent right be granted. As the forefront of R&D and the holder of a large number of core technologies, high-tech enterprises are at the forefront of patent innovation. How to further improve the export quality of Chinese manufacturing high-tech enterprises through independent innovation and realize the transformation of patents has become an urgent problem to be solved at present. Therefore, it is of great significance to study the influence of patent quality on the export product quality of high-tech manufacturing enterprises in China.

Considering previous opinions and theories, this paper used the analysis of Khandelwal (2010), B Shi and W. Shao (2014) to measure the quality of export products of high-tech manufacturing enterprises by using the KSW method at the level of micro-enterprise heterogeneity. This paper studied the influence and mechanism of patent quality on export product quality of China's manufacturing industry and obtained corresponding conclusions.

This paper first reviewed the relevant literature on patent quality and export product quality, listed the relevant definitions and measurement methods of the existing literature, and then gave a theoretical framework based on previous viewpoints. Regarding the research methods, this paper followed Khandelwal (2010) and B Shi & W. Shao (2014) to measure the quality of export products of high-tech manufacturing enterprises by using the ex-post projection method at the level of micro-enterprise heterogeneity. Then, through the matching of industrial and enterprise customs patent data from 2000 to 2013, empirical analysis and mechanism tests were carried out to study the impact of patent quality on the quality of Chinese manufacturing export products and the mechanism of action, and then the research conclusion was drawn.

2 LITERATURE REVIEW

2.1 *Concept and measurement of patent quality*

Some scholars defined patent quality from the perspective of review (Wagner 2009). Another scholar defined patent quality from the perspective of use, which can be further divided into technical innovation, economic benefit, and legal protection stability. From the perspective of micro-enterprises, Y. Jin (2019) identified high-tech enterprises as policy research objects, measured the patent quality of enterprises by the ratio of the number of invention patent applications to the total number of patent applications and the success rate of invention patent application authorization. J. Zhang et al. (2018) improved the patent width method and used the knowledge width method defined by the International Patent Classification Table (IPC) to measure patent quality and made an empirical analysis on whether patent subsidy and incentive policies could inhibit patent quality in China. Boeing et al. (2019) incorporated the data cited in ISR and the applicant's previous applications into the measurement range to construct FDS index to measure patent quality more comprehensively.

However, it was not easy to obtain information about the number of patent citations of Chinese enterprises. Therefore, some studies used patent authorization rate, patent withdrawal rate, patent renewal rate, number of patent applications, number of patent grants, and other indicators to measure patent quality.

Some scholars studied the impact of patent quality on business operations. Z. Zhao & C. Li (2020) used the average forward reference frequency of patents to measure the patent quality of enterprises and concluded that patent quality not only increased the enterprise value by improving the profitability of enterprises but also increased the enterprise value by increasing the stock price of enterprises. By studying listed companies, H. Li et al. (2021) concluded that the patent quality of enterprises enhanced the export competitiveness of enterprises by horizontally expanding the types of export products and vertically improving the quality of export products. Klette et al. (2004) focused on the relationship between technological innovation and products from the perspective of technological endogenous and believed that an enterprise could achieve growth through product innovation. The successful innovation of new products meant the expansion of the scale of the enterprise.

2.2 *Concept and measurement of export product quality of manufacturing industry*

Garvin (1984) analyzed the multiple meanings of quality from eight perspectives. In this paper, product quality was the same quantity of products, and all the features that might lead to the improvement of consumers' utility level could be summed up as product quality, which might include after-sales supporting services, brand characteristics, product visual design, durability, and so on.

The theoretical research on product quality in the field of international trade could be roughly divided into four categories. The first type of research explained the relationship between quality and international trade from the demand perspective, which could be traced back to the overlapping demand theory proposed by Linder (1961), and the standardized and mathematical expression of the overlapping demand theory by Fan (2005). The second type of research explained product quality and international division of labor from the perspective of supply. In the 1980s, the theory of vertical intra-industry trade was born, such as Falvey (1987), and Flam and Helpman (1987), based on product quality. The third type of research linked product quality with endogenous economic growth, extended the endogenous growth theory of product quality ladder to open conditions, and studied the impact of north-south trade on economic growth and economic convergence, such as Grossman and Helpman (1991,1992), etc. The fourth type of research was based on the theoretical framework of new-new trade, and studied the determining mechanism and influencing factors of export product quality from the enterprise level, which was also the most directly related to this paper. Melitz (2003) created the new trade theory, which emphasized the heterogeneity of production efficiency among enterprises and believed that only enterprises with high production efficiency would choose export. Recently, scholars have begun to pay attention to more dimensions of enterprise heterogeneity, and it is widely discussed that enterprise product quality heterogeneity and enterprises with high product quality have better export performance, Baldwin and Harrigan, 2011). This paper was based on the product quality heterogeneity model framework of Hallak (2006) and Hallak and Savadian (2009).

The main measurement method of product quality in international trade research is the unit export value method (Manova & Zhang 2012), ex-post projection method (Khandelwal 2010; Shi B. 2015), and the supply and demand information method (Feenstra et al. 2014). Unit export value method was too limited because in addition to quality factors, market supply and demand relationship, production costs, consumer preferences, and a series of other factors also affected the price of export products. Therefore, this article chose the latter calculation method to measure the quality of export products.

Some scholars believed that the knowledge accumulation and breadth of enterprises can bring higher economic benefits and a larger market. Some studies have shown that firms gained revenue from knowledge accumulation through vertical and horizontal approaches characterized by "creative destruction", that is, producing higher quality products and expanding product categories.

As for the influencing mechanism, Hallak (2009) believed that enterprises had heterogeneity of production efficiency and "quality" production capacity. Here, "quality" represented a series of factors that affected the use value of products, such as product technology content and product functionality. What determined the "quality" production capacity was the technological innovation ability of products. Shi (2013) studied on this basis and believed that consumer demand was also a key factor affecting product quality. What determines the optimal choice of consumers was the ratio of product price to product use value, commonly known as "cost performance ratio", and "cost performance ratio" could ultimately determine the quality of products in the market. However, as TFP was a very complex index, it cannot be well incorporated into the intermediary variable as an exact factor. Therefore, this paper considered the cost effectiveness of enterprises as the influencing mechanism to study the impact of patent quality on the export product quality of manufacturing enterprises.

Based on the literature, there were few empirical studies on the relationship between patent quality and export product quality of high-tech manufacturing enterprises. This paper tried to enrich the research in this aspect and promoted the research on the influence mechanism of patent quality on export product quality of high-tech manufacturing enterprises in China.

3 THEORETICAL MECHANISM

3.1 *Theoretical framework*

As for the measurement of export product quality, Khandelwal et al. (2013) were followed to measure the quality of export products. Product quality was introduced into the consumer CES utility function, and the expression of product quality is deduced through the utility function (see equation (1)).

$$U = \left[\int_{\omega \in \Omega} [q_\omega \lambda_\omega]^\rho d\omega \right]^{\frac{1}{\rho}} \tag{1}$$

where $0<\rho<1$ represented the degree of consumer preference diversification. The smaller the ρ value was, the greater the diversification choice tendency of consumers was. Ω was a collection of all products. $\sigma = \frac{1}{1-\rho}$ implied the elasticity of substitution between products, since $0<\rho<1$, it was easy to obtain $\sigma>1$. The greater the value of σ was, the greater the elasticity of substitution was and the fiercer the product competition was. ω indicated the product type. Assuming that each enterprise produced only one product category, therefore, ω also represented the enterprise. Ω indicated the set of product types. q represented the quality of product category ω. λ represented the number of product types ω. Given budget constraint, by assuming that the consumption budget being consumed was R, the consumer demand function for each product can be obtained from the utility maximization under consumer constraint.

$$\lambda_\omega = E\left(p_\omega^{-\sigma}\right)\left(q_\omega^{\sigma-1}\right)P^{\sigma-1} \tag{2}$$

Among which, P implied the composite price index:

$$P = \left[\int_{\omega \in \Omega} \left(\frac{p_\omega}{q_\omega} \right)^{1-\sigma} d\omega \right]^{\frac{1}{1-\sigma}} \tag{3}$$

It can be obtained that the demand for products produced by the enterprise was:

$$\lambda_{if\omega t} = p_{if\omega t}^{-\sigma} q_{if\omega t}^{\sigma-1} P_{ft}^{\sigma-1} E_{ft} \tag{4}$$

$\lambda_{if\omega t}$ was exports, $p_{if\omega t}$ was the product price, $q_{if\omega t}$ was product quality, P_{ft} was the composite price index of export destination country, and E_{ft} was the total consumption expenditure of export destination country.

Patent quality could improve the production efficiency of enterprises through technological improvement and total factor productivity improvement, and reduce the variable cost of enterprises. Patent quality would also be transformed into product quality through patents, so as to improve the quality production capacity of enterprises and reduce the fixed cost of enterprises. Based on this, the production cost of an enterprise (including variable cost and fixed cost) could be expressed as:

$$MC(q, \varphi) = \frac{c}{\varphi} \lambda^\alpha, \quad F(q, \xi) = F_0 + \frac{f}{\xi} \lambda^\beta \tag{5}$$

In which, MC was the marginal cost, and F represented fixed costs. φ represented enterprise productivity, which was used to describe enterprise marginal cost heterogeneity. ξ represented the fixed cost input efficiency of an enterprise, that is, the enterprise's ability to pay low fixed cost to produce high-quality products. It was used to describe the heterogeneity of fixed cost of an enterprise. The larger the value was, the lower the fixed cost of product quality of an enterprise; $\alpha(\alpha>0)$ and $\beta(\beta>0)$ represented the mass elasticity of marginal cost and fixed cost respectively. c and f were constants.

Given the demand function and cost function, the enterprise could obtain the product quality expression through the profit maximization behavior:

$$q(\varphi, \xi) = \left[\frac{1-\alpha}{\beta} \left(\frac{\sigma-1}{\sigma} \right)^\sigma \left(\frac{\varphi}{c} \right)^{\sigma-1} \frac{\xi}{f} \frac{E}{P} \right]^{\frac{1}{\beta'}} \tag{6}$$

in which, $\beta'=\beta-(1-\alpha)(\sigma-1)>0$, $0<\alpha<1$, $\beta>\beta'$. E/P implied the total quantity demanded by the market.

According to Equation (6), the quality of the firm's export products depends on the firm's productivity φ, and the firm's fixed-cost input efficiency ξ. It can be obtained by taking the first derivative of Equation (6).

$$\frac{\partial q(\varphi, \xi)}{\partial \varphi} = \frac{1}{\beta'} \left[\frac{1-\alpha}{\beta} \left(\frac{\sigma-1}{\sigma} \right)^\sigma \left(\frac{\varphi}{c} \right)^{\sigma-1} \frac{\xi}{f} \frac{E}{P} \right]^{\frac{1}{\beta'}-1} \frac{\sigma-1}{c} \frac{1-\alpha}{\beta} \left(\frac{\sigma-1}{\sigma} \right)^\sigma \left(\frac{\varphi}{c} \right)^{\sigma-2} \frac{\varsigma}{f} \frac{E}{P} > 0 \tag{7}$$

$$\frac{\partial q(\varphi, \xi)}{\partial \xi} = \frac{1}{\beta'} \left[\frac{1-\alpha}{\beta} \left(\frac{\sigma-1}{\sigma} \right)^\sigma \left(\frac{\varphi}{c} \right)^{\sigma-1} \frac{\xi E}{f P} \right]^{\frac{1}{\beta'}-1} \frac{1}{f} \frac{1-\alpha}{\beta} \left(\frac{\sigma-1}{\sigma} \right)^\sigma \left(\frac{\varphi}{c} \right)^{\sigma-1} \frac{E}{P} > 0 \tag{8}$$

Equations (7) and (8) indicate that improving the productivity and fixed-cost input efficiencyof enterprises is helpful in improving the quality of export products of enterprises. The higher the productivity and fixed cost input efficiency of the enterprise, the lower the variable cost and fixed cost paid by the enterprise, so there is more sufficient capital to invest in the upgrade of product quality, and the product quality is improved.

3.2 *The action mechanism between patent quality and export product quality of manufacturing enterprises*

Figure 1 showed the influence mechanism of patent quality on export product quality of manufacturing enterprises, including two paths. One mechanism was the knowledge accumulation. The increase in revenue that firms gained from knowledge accumulation was achieved by producing higher-quality products and expanding product categories. Theoretically speaking, if the breadth of knowledge contained in the knowledge accumulation of an enterprise was larger, the enterprise could be able to combine and apply more knowledge, and the quality improvement brought by each creative behavior would be larger, and the innovation degree of new products would be higher compared with the original products. In addition, the products transformed from patents with large knowledge width made it more difficult to realize relevant improvement and innovation, and the fewer alternative products, the quality of export products of enterprises would be improved. Then the higher patent quality meant the improvement of product quality. Therefore, this paper proposed Hypothesis 1: The improvement of enterprise patent quality could improve the export product quality of high-tech manufacturing enterprises.

Another mechanism was to reduce production costs. Patent quality could reduce production costs from three aspects: technological progress, optimization of production resources, and scale effect of enterprise innovation, to improve the quality of export products of manufacturing enterprises. Caldera et al. (2010) found that enterprises can reduce production costs through innovation. Patent was the concrete manifestation of innovation output. Patent quality reduced production costs through technological progress, making export products more competitive, so that enterprises had a greater competitive advantage to get market size expansion, and then improved enterprise sales and profits, and could also drive enterprises to pay attention to high innovation degree of invention patents, forming a virtuous circle, export product quality was improved. Second, high-quality patents put advanced equipment, raw materials, and other material products into the production process, which could effectively improve the efficiency of resource allocation in the production process, and then reduced the production cost of manufacturing enterprises, improved the efficiency of fixed input, and then improved the product quality of manufacturing enterprises. Finally, any innovation results would be shared and spread among different branches within the enterprise (X. Huang 2018). The improvement of patent quality brought the innovation scale effect and the decrease of production cost, thus increasing the enterprise's R&D investment and the probability of R&D success, and then improved enterprise productivity and the efficiency of fixed cost inputs such as information cost and adjustment cost

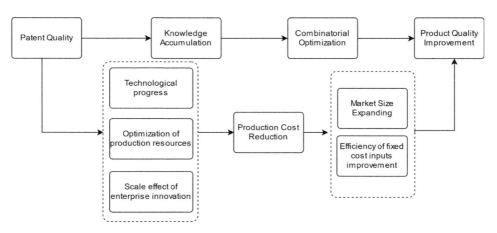

Figure 1.   Influence mechanism framework.

(Helsley & Strange 2007; Ito et al. 2015). It was concluded from formulas (7) and (8) that the quality of exported products was further improved. Therefore, this paper proposed *Hypothesis 2: Patent quality could reduce production cost, and then improve the quality of export products of high-tech manufacturing enterprises.*

4 METHODS

4.1 *Measuring the quality of export products of high-tech manufacturing enterprises*

This paper referred to the industry classification method of H. Gao (2012) and the industry classification of the national economy (GB/T4754-2017), and classified the high-tech industries as pharmaceutical manufacturing, general equipment manufacturing, special equipment manufacturing, transportation equipment manufacturing, electrical machinery and equipment manufacturing, communications equipment computer, and other electronic equipment manufacturing. Corresponding national economic industry classification (GB/T4754-2017) is C27, C34, C35, C37, C38, and C39 categories.

Taking the logarithm of the above Equation (4), the consumer demand was:

$$\ln \lambda_{if\omega t} = -\sigma \ln p_{if\omega t} + (\sigma - 1) \ln q_{if\omega t} + (\sigma - 1) \ln P_{ft} + \ln E_{ft} \tag{9}$$

Since $\sigma>1$, the higher the price of all products was, the lower the demand of consumers was. And the higher the quality of products was, with other things being equal, the higher the demand of consumers was. By controlling the total price index and preference information of the destination country over time, and including unobservable product quality information into the residual term, the econometric regression equation of Equation (9) can be obtained:

$$\ln \lambda_{if\omega t} = \chi_{ft} - \sigma \ln p_{if\omega t} + \mu_{if\omega t} \tag{10}$$

In equation (10), $\chi_{ft} = \ln E_{ft} - \ln P_{ft}$ was the dummy variable of export destination country – year. $\mu_{if\omega t} = (\sigma - 1)\ln q_{if\omega t}$ was the random disturbance term, including the quality of exported products. Direct estimation of the above formula by OLS may ignore the influence of product types and price endogeneity.

According to the practice of Khandelwal (2010), this paper added the GDP of each province representing the scale of domestic market demand into the above formula. In order to reduce the endogenous bias that may be caused by the correlation between product quality and price, the average price of exports by enterprise i to other countries was selected as the instrumental variable of the price of exports by enterprise i to f country, based on the ideas of Shi & Shao (2014). Selection of the average price of products ω of the enterprise i exported to other countries as instrumental variable of price of products exported by the enterprise to f country. Conclusively, the mass expression of the product can be obtained as in Equation (11).

$$quality_{if\omega t} = \frac{u_{if\omega t}}{\sigma - 1} = \frac{\ln q_{if\omega t} - \ln \widehat{q}_{if\omega t}}{\sigma - 1} \tag{11}$$

σ referred to the practice of Shi & Shao (2014), and took the value as 3. In order to conduct a summing analysis and facilitate calculation, the quality indexes of the above formula were standardized as in Equation (12).

$$rquality_{if\omega t} = \frac{quality_{if\omega t} - \min quality_{if\omega t}}{\max quality_{if\omega t} - \min quality_{if\omega t}} \tag{12}$$

In Equation (12), max and min, respectively, represented the maximum and minimum value of ω quality exported by all enterprises to all countries in all years, and the quality of exported products after standardization $rquality_{it}$, the value range was [0,1]. There was no measuring unit, so they could be summed up at the enterprise level, namely:

$$\text{exp\_quality}_{it} = \frac{value_{if\,\omega t}}{\sum_{if\,\omega t \in \Omega} value_{if\,\omega t}} rquality_{if\,\omega t} \tag{13}$$

exp_quality$_{it}$ represented the quality of exported products, $value_{if\omega t}$ represented the value of ω exported by enterprise i to country f in year t. Ω represented the set of products exported by enterprise i to all countries in year t.

4.2 The status of manufacturing high-tech enterprises export products

The results of instrumental variables were shown in Table 1, from which the quality of export products in enterprise-year can be obtained. There were 678054 observed values with an average value of 0.708 and the standard deviation of variables is 0.110.

Table 1. Conclusion of 2SLS.

2SLS	(1) IV	(2) IV
lnp	0.296***	0.296***
	(4021.00)	(4016.05)
lngdp		0.0361962***
		(39.79)
year	controlled	controlled
within R squ	0.377	0.377
Obs.	28717289	

According to the classification above, high-tech enterprises could be summed up at the micro level.

$$QUA_t = \sum_{img \in \Omega} w_{it} * quality_{it} \tag{14}$$

$quality_{it}$ shows the quality of exported products summed up to the enterprise year. w_{it} was the proportion of t annual exports of enterprise i in total exports of high-tech industry in t years. By taking the proportion of export volume as the weight, the quality trend chart of export products of high-tech enterprises in China was obtained in Figure 2.

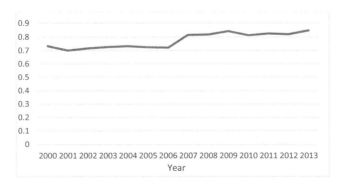

Figure 2. Current situation of export product quality in China's high-tech industries from 2000 to 2013.

As shown in Figure 2, from 2000 to 2013, the quality of export products of China's high-tech enterprises generally showed an upward trend. The high-tech industry grew 3.45% year-on-year in 2013. The high-tech industry had broad prospects for product quality growth and great potential in the future.

5 MODELLING

5.1 *Model construction*

The model constructed in this paper was as follows:

$$\exp\_quality_{it} = \alpha_0 + \alpha_1 invent\_A(invent\_B) + \theta X_{it} + \mu_{it} \qquad (15)$$

Table 2 showed the model variable meanings and data sources. $\exp\_quality_{it}$ was export product quality of high-tech enterprises. $invent\_A$ ($invent\_B$) was the core explanatory variable of patent quality. In order to evaluate the patent quality of enterprises objectively, the invention patent application rate ($invent\_A$) was adopted in this paper, that is, the ratio of the number of invention patent applications to the total number of patent applications was measured. On the other hand, the invention patent authorization rate ($invent\_B$) was adopted, that is, the ratio of the number of invention patents granted to the total number of patents granted. The authorization process for invention patents was relatively complex and the technical examination was more strict. Therefore, this index could better reflect the technical characteristics and real quality of patents.

Control variables X_{it} included the following ones:

Capital density ($kleatioit_{it}$) was measured as the logarithm of the ratio of net fixed assets to the number of employees.

Enterprise size ($size_{it}$) was expressed by logarithm of the average annual balance of the actual net fixed assets of the enterprise.

Government subsidies ($subration_{it}$) were expressed as the proportion of subsidies received by enterprises in total assets.

The length of life of the enterprise (age_{it}) was expressed as log of year of observation minus the year of firm establishment.

R&D efficiency ($research_{it}$) was described by three variables. The first one was the ratio of R&D output to R&D input (reff). The second one was whether the enterprise had a new

Table 2. Model variable meaning and data source.

	Variable name	Variable meaning	The data source
Dependent variable	$\exp\_quality_{it}$	Quality of export products	Customs database
Independent variables	$invent\_A$	Invention patent application rate	Industrial enterprise
	$invent\_B$	Invention patent grant rate	patent database
Control variables	$klratioit_{it}$	Capital density	Industrial enterprise
	$size_{it}$	Enterprise size	Database
	$subration_{it}$	Government subsidies	
	age_{it}	Length of life of the enterprise	
	$research_{it}$	R&D efficiency (measured by reff, dnew, waratiio)	
	$bcredit_{it}$	Financing constraints (measured by cfs, cash, captial)	
	lp	Total factor productivity	
	HHI	Herfindahl index	

31

product output value (dnew). It was selected due to the dropping data of reff and tried to describe R&D behavior more precisely. The paper also used the proportion of intangible assets in total assets (wzratio), considering that in general enterprise trademark rights, patent rights were taken as intangible assets. Therefore, intangible assets and corporate R&D behaviors had a stronger correlation.

Financing constraints ($bcredit_{it}$) was the ratio of current liabilities to total assets (cfs) in this paper. Enterprises could alleviate financing constraints through internal financing and external financing. With abundant cash flow, the enterprise was easy to implement financing constraints. This paper used the ratio of enterprise cash flow and the total assets (cash) to depict enterprise internal financing constraints. The greater the value was, the enterprise facing the smaller the degree of financing constraints. The change rate of the enterprise's paid-in capital (capital) could also represent the difficulty of internal financing of the enterprise.

Total factor productivity (lp): using OP method to calculate.

Industry-level variables: Herfindahl index (HHI), expressed as the sum of squares of market share of enterprises in the industry.

5.2 *Data source*

This paper mainly involved three types of data: the first one was the production data at the enterprise level; the second type was the data on import and export trade at the product level, which was used to calculate the quality of enterprises' export products; the third type was the data of enterprises' patent applications and grants in industrial and enterprise patent databases. Because the microdata was relatively large, and the data from industrial enterprise database in 2014 and 2015 had not been verified, the production data of enterprises in this paper were from the Database of Chinese industrial enterprises from 2000 to 2013. In this paper, the method of Brandtetal (2012) was referred to match the data of industrial enterprises. Before matching, the industry classification codes of the national economy and regional administrative codes were unified. The manufacturing samples with total output, sales, industrial added value, intermediate input, total fixed assets, annual average balance of net fixed assets missing, negative value, and zero value were excluded, and the manufacturing samples with employment shortage and less than 8 were excluded. The product trade data was from the Database of China Customs from 2000 to 2013. In order to be more scientific and accurate, the paper eliminated company names, names of the export destination countries, some small samples, and so on. The method of Yu (2015) was used to match the two sets of data. For the patent enterprise database, the industrial and enterprise patent data of high-tech enterprises were obtained according to the high-tech industry classification code, and then combined with the matched industrial and enterprise customs data through the unique organization code of the enterprise. The overall situation of the samples was shown in Table 3.

6 THE EMPIRICAL STUDY

6.1 *The empirical results*

In order to mitigate or eliminate the interference of institutional change and macroeconomic fluctuation on core causality, the model-controlled firm fixed effect η_i and year fixed effect η_t. In terms of reverse causality, this paper intends to take the average value of patent quality of other enterprises in the same industry as a tool variable, and adopt GMM method to control endogenous problems. Furthermore, the average value of patent quality of other firms in the same industry was taken as the instrumental variable of patent quality to reduce the endogeneity of firms.

Table 3. The situation of sample.

Variable	Mean	Variance	Minimum	Maximum
$exp\_quality_{it}$	0.6816	0.1343	0	1
Invent_A	0.4786	0.3033	0.0043	1
Invent_B	0.5978	0.3750	0.0048	1
in $COST_{it}$	11.8667	1.5775	0	18.7546
$klratioit_{it}$	4.2765	1.0369	−1.0664	8.0912
$size_{it}$	1.3504	1.0926	0	7.6251
$subratio_{it}$	0.6064	0.4885	0	1
age_{it}	2.3567	0.7820	0	5.0814
dnew	0.1533	0.3604	0	1
reff	2.0869	2.1854	0	11.1241
waratio	0.0268	0.0560	0	0.6654
cfs	0.4923	0.2296	−0.7711	6.0461
cash	0.0974	0.1389	−2.0916	7.5735
capital	0.0158	0.1608	−8.2868	3.6768
lp	9.7671	1.2563	3.9642	14.9536
HHI	0.2362	0.0344	0.2	0.3312

In Table 4, (1) and (2) were listed as the empirical results. In general, whether the application rate of an invention patent or the authorization rate of an invention patent, patent quality had a significant impact on the quality of export products, and the authorization rate of an invention patent had a greater impact on the export quality of high-tech manufacturing enterprises than the application rate of invention patent. Moreover, government subsidies and total factor productivity had obvious positive effects on export product quality. As can be seen from the R&D efficiency index, the R&D efficiency of enterprises was more obvious in the impact of invention patent authorization rate on export product quality, which also proved that patent authorization was more representative of patent quality than the number of applications.

Column (3) in Table 4 gives the GMM estimation results. Sargon test with P <0.05, Kleibergen-Paap RK LM, and Kleibergen-Paap Wald RK F test rejected the null hypothesis of insufficient and weak identification of instrumental variables. These indicate that there is a strong correlation between the instrumental variables and the potential endogenous variables, and the instrumental variables selected in this paper are relatively reasonable. And the patent quality coefficient is significantly positive, indicating that the results of the model are robust.

6.2 Influence mechanism analysis

Referring to the practice of H. Xu et al. (2020), this paper used ln $COST_{it}$ the logarithm of enterprise operating cost, as an alternative index of production cost. The model to test the cost effectiveness was as follows.

$$\ln COST_{it} = \varphi_0 + \varphi_1 invent\_A(invent\_B) + \varphi_2 X_{it} + \eta_i + \eta_t + v_{it} \tag{16}$$

$$exp\_quality_{it} = \lambda_0 + \lambda_1 invent\_A(invent\_B) + \lambda_2 \ln COST_{it} + \lambda_3 X_{it} + \eta_i + \eta_t + \rho_{it} \tag{17}$$

The explanatory variable of equation (16) was the logarithm of the enterprise's production cost. If patent quality can effectively reduce the enterprise's production cost, the coefficient of Patent Quality in equation (16) would be significantly negative. In equation (17), the index ln $COST_{it}$ was added on the basis of equation (15). In this case, the coefficient of Patent Quality represented the direct effect of Patent quality on the export quality of manufacturing

Table 4. Regression results.

		(1)		(2)		(3)	
Patent Quality	Invent_A	0.0065** (2.08)		0.0069** (2.17)		0.0058** (2.26)	
	Invent_B		0.0093*** (4.26)		0.0095** (2.31)		0.0083** (1.99)
$klratioit_{it}$				0.0059 (0.85)	0.0043 (0.62)	0.0028 (0.34)	0.0013 (0.18)
$size_{it}$				−0.0074 (−1.26)	−0.0023 (−0.35)	−0.0087 (−1.57)	−0.0053 (−0.77)
$subratio_{it}$				0.0577** (2.15)	0.1659** (1.96)	0.3386* (1.68)	0.1687** (1.98)
age_{it}				−0.0094* (−1.92)	−0.0099* (−1.73)	−0.0063 (−1.45)	−0.0122** (−2.35)
$research_{it}$	dnew			−0.0080 (−0.69)	0.0374** (2.53)	−0.0098 (0.77)	0.0349** (2.35)
	reff			0.0001 (0.02)	0.0064** (1.92)	0.0020 (0.73)	0.0057** (1.72)
	waratio			0.1669** (2.18)	0.1999** (2.04)	0.0816 (0.91)	0.2024** (2.08)
$bcredit_{it}$	cfs			0.0008 (0.04)	0.0161 (0.61)	0.0029 (0.13)	0.0075 (0.29)
	cash			0.0402* (1.79)	0.0371 (1.61)	0.0102 (1.19)	0.0194 (1.32)
	capital			0.0674* (1.65)	0.0340* (1.65)	0.0186 (1.35)	0.0328 (1.63)
lp				0.0251*** (4.12)	0.0264*** (3.91)	0.0268*** (4.56)	0.0077** (2.06)
HHI				0.0856 (1.19)	0.0209* (1.74)	0.0403*** (2.81)	0.0280* (1.68)
Fixed time		yes	yes	yes	yes	yes	yes
Fixed enterprise		yes	yes	yes	yes	yes	yes
LM						234.15	150.96
F						30.74	53.85
R^2		0.0556	0.0560	0.0697	0.1358	0.1378	0.1340
N		35897	35897	35897	35897	35897	35897

enterprises, while the coefficient of ln $COST_{it}$ represented the impact of production cost on the export quality of manufacturing enterprises after controlling Patent Quality.

As can be seen from Table 5, patent quality was related to the cost of production. Putting the cost of production in the model, the production cost was negatively related to the quality of enterprises to export products. With the higher cost of production enterprises to export products, the quality would be lower, which verified the mechanism mentioned above, that is, the higher the production efficiency of enterprises, the lower the cost of production, and export products quality would be higher.

In this paper, Sobel test was conducted to determine whether there was a mediation effect. The P value of Goodman-1(Aroian) was less than 0.05, indicating the mediation effect was established. In addition, Bootstrap was also used to test the intermediary variable of production cost. It can be seen from Table 6 that, judging from the 95% confidence interval, the same symbol in the confidence interval means that invent_A and invent_B were statistically significant at the level of 0.05, indicating the existence of the intermediary effect.

Table 5. Cost effect results.

		(16)		(17)	
ln $COST_{it}$				−0.0165**	−0.0157***
				(−2.45)	(−2.80)
Patent Quality	Invent_A	−0.0449***		0.0074***	
		(−3.99)		(2.66)	
	Invent_B		−0.0475***		0.0101**
			(−2.67)		(2.51)
Control variables		yes	yes	yes	yes
Fixed time		yes	yes	yes	yes
Fixed enterprise		yes	yes	yes	yes
R^2		0.7856	0.7873	0.1670	0.1687
N		35897	35897	35897	35897

Table 6. Bootstrap results.

		Observed Coef.	Bootstrap Std. Err.	z	P>|z|	Normal-based [95% Conf. Interval]
Invent_A	r(ind_eff)	−0.0043	0.0019	−2.27	0.023	[−0.0080,−0.0006]
	r(dir_eff)	0.0463	0.0122	3.79	0.000	[0.0223,0.0703]
Invent_B	r(ind_eff)	−0.0055	0.0023	−2.25	0.023	[−0.0082,−0.0006]
	r(dir_eff)	0.0579	0.0136	3.95	0.000	[0.0222,0.0700]

7 CONCLUSIONS AND FUTURE RESEARCH

In this paper, the influence of patent quality on manufacturing export product quality was investigated from the micro-enterprise level. The main conclusions were as follows: (1) The improvement of enterprise patent quality can improve the export quality of high-tech manufacturing enterprises. (2) Government subsidies play a positive role in high-tech enterprises. From the perspective of the number of patents granted, R&D efficiency has a significant impact on the export quality of high-tech manufacturing enterprises. (3) According to the mediating effect results, patent quality has an effect on export product quality by reducing the production cost of enterprises.

Despite some substantial contributions, this paper also had some limitations. First, this paper used the rates of invention patent application and authorization to measure patent quality. Some studies used patent reference frequency to measure patent quality. However, due to the difficulty in data acquisition, this paper was unable to utilize this measure. Therefore, the patent quality of future research could be checked by assessing the consistency of the empirical results from different patent measure ways. In addition, this paper did not study and analyze the segmented high-tech industries. In this respect, different industries and enterprise operation modes might draw different conclusions, which could be explored in future research.

REFERENCES

Baldwin R., Harrigan J. Zeros. 2011. Quality, and Space: Trade Theory and Trade Evidence[J]. *American Economic Journal: Microeconomics* 3(2): 60–88.
Boeing P., Mueller E. 2019. Measuring China's Patent Quality: Development and Validation of ISR Indices[R]. *ZEW Discussion Papers* No.19–017.

Brandt L., Johannes V.B., Zhang Y.F. 2012. Creative Accounting or Creative Destruction? Firm-level Productivity Growth in Chinese Manufacturing[J]. *Journal of Development Economics* 97(2): 339–351.

Caldera A. 2010. Innovation and Exporting: Evidence From Spanish Manufacturing Firms[J]. *Review of World Economics* 146(4): 657–689.

Falvey R. E., Kierzkowski H. 1987. Product Quality, Intra-industry Trade and (im) Perfect Competition[R].

Fan, C. S. 2005. Increasing Returns, Product Quality and International Trade. *Econometrica* 72: 151~169.

Feenstra R. C., Li Z., Yu M. 2014. Exports and Credit Constraints Under Incomplete Information: Theory and Evidence From CHINA[J]. *Review of Economics and Statistics* 96(4): 729–744.

Flam H., Helpman E. 1987. Vertical Product Differentiation and North-South trade[J]. *The American Economic Review* 1987: 810–822.

Gao H., Wang L. 2012. Analysis on the Standard of Defining the Scope of High, *Middle and Low Technology Industry*. Progress in Science and Technology and Countermeasures *29(13): 46–48.*

Garvin A D. 1984. What Does "Product Quality" Really Mean?[J].*MIT Sloan Management Review* 26(1): 25–43.

Grossman G. M., Helpman E. 1991. Quality Ladders and Product Cycles[J]. *The Quarterly Journal of Economics* 106 (2): 557–586.

Hallak J. C. 2006. Product Quality and the Direction of Trade[J]. *Journal of International Economics* 68(1): 238–265.

Hallak J. C., Sivadasan J. 2009. Firms' Exporting Behavior Under Quality Constraints[R]. *National Bureau of Economic Research*.

Helsley R. W., Strange W. C. 2007. Agglomeration, Opportunism, and the Organization of Production[J]. *Journal of Urban Economics* 62(1): 55–75.

Huang X., Jin Z., Yu L. 2018. Export, Innovation and Firm Markups: Based on Factor Intensity[J]. *World Economy* (5):125–146.

Hu A. G., Jefferson G. H. 2009. A Great Wall of Patents: What is Behind China's Recent Patent Explosion?[J]. *Journal of Development Economics* 90(1): 57–68.

Ito B., Xu Z., Yashiro N. 2015. Does Agglomeration Promote Internationalization of Chinese firms?[J]. *China Economic Review* 34: 109–121.

Jin Y., Wang P., Yuyuan Fu. 2019. Does Selective Industrial Policy Improve Patent Quality in China?– Experimental Research Based on Micro Enterprises[J]. *Industrial Economics Research* (06): 39–49.

Khandelwal, A. K. 2010. The Long and Short of Quality Ladders[J]. *Review of Economic Studies* 77(4): 1450–1476.

Khandelwal, A. K., P. K. Schott, and S. J. Wei. 2013. Trade Liberalization and Embedded Institutional Reform: Evidence from Chinese Exporters[J]. *American Economic Review* 103(6): 2169–2195.

Klette, Tor Jakob, and Samuel Kortum. 2004. Innovating Firms and Aggregate Innovation. *Journal of Political Economy* 112.5(2004): 986–1018.

Li H., Wang Y., Wu D. 2021. The Influence Mechanism of Patent Quality on Export Competitiveness: Based on the Perspective of Knowledge Breadth[J]. *The World Economy Research* 2021(01): 32–46+134.

Linder S. B. 1961. An Essay on Trade and Transformation[M]. *Stockholm: Almqvist & Wiksell*.

Manova K., Zhang Z. 2012. Export Prices Across Firms and Destinations[J]. *The Quarterly Journal of Economics* 127 (1): 379–436.

Melitz, M. J. 2003. The Impact of Trade on Intra-Industry Reallocations and Aggregate Industry Productivity. *Econometrica* 71(6): 1695–1725.

Shen Y., Huang H., Zhao L. 2018. Innovation And Innovation: a Review[J]. *Science Research Management* (4): 83–91.

Shi B. 2014. Heterogeneity of Export Product Quality of Chinese Enterprises: Measurement and Facts [J]. *Economics (Quarterly)* 13(01): 263–284.

Shi B. 2015. Whether FDI Improves the Quality of Domestic Enterprises' Export Products [J]. *International Business Studies* 36(02):5–20.

Shi B., Shao W., 2014. Chinese Enterprises' Export Quality Measurement and its Determinants: a Micro Perspective of Cultivating New Export Competitive Advantages[J]. *Management World* 2014(09): 90–106.

Wagner R P. 2009. Understanding Patent-quality Mechanisms[J]. *University of Pennsylvania Law Review* 157(6): 2135–2173.

Xu H., Jin Y., Wang H. 2020. Distance Between Banks and Firms and the Transformation and Upgrading of Export Trade[J]. *Economic Research Journal* 55(11): 174–190.

Yu, M. J. 2015. Processing Trade, Tariff Reductions and Firm Productivity: Evidence from Chinese Firms[J]. *Economic Journal* 125(6): 943–988.

Zhang J., Zheng W. 2018. Does Innovation Catch-up Strategy Inhibit Patent Quality in China?[J]. *Economic Research Journal* 53(05): 28–41.

Zhao Z., Li C. 2020. How Does Patent Quality Affect Firm Value?[J]. *Journal of Economic Management* 42(12): 59–75.

Impacts of economic policy uncertainty on foreign direct investment: Evidence from China provincial data

Qianshun Yuan

School of Economics and Management, Shanghai University of Political Science and Law, Shanghai, China

ABSTRACT: Foreign direct investment is bearing the brunt of the anti-globalization trend, particularly the rise in economic policy uncertainty. This study empirically examines the impact of Economic Policy Uncertainty (EPU) on foreign direct investment by using the Chinese provincial EPU index developed by Yu et al. (2021), which spans the years 2007 to 2017. This paper uses a system GMM estimation of a panel data model to alleviate the endogeneity problem. The findings show that the FDI reduces significantly when economic policy uncertainty increases.

1 INTRODUCTION

Since the start of economic reform and opening up in 1979, China has actively pursued foreign direct investment through the "bringing in and going out" strategy. According to the China Statistical Yearbook (2018), China's total foreign direct investment increased from $74.8 billion in 2007 to $131 billion in 2017. FDI has played a significant role in creating employment opportunities and fostering new advantages in international cooperation and competition over the last few decades, and it has become an important driving force for China's economic growth (Hu & Tan 2016).

Many policymakers and academics have focused on economic policy uncertainty (EPU) as an important factor influencing the flow of domestic and international capital. Due to policy uncertainty, expected returns on investment projects have become more difficult to predict. Because they have less knowledge of the policy environment and may be treated differently than domestic investors, foreign direct investors typically operate abroad for a long period of time (Bhattacharya et al. 2007). Many developed economies' economic policies have become more uncertain in recent years, particularly during and after the global financial crisis, as a result of unconventional monetary policy, Britain's withdrawal from the European Union, and global trade tensions. Most studies have shown that rising uncertainty has a negative impact on macroeconomic variables (Nguyen et al. 2019; Thanh B.N. 2019). The impact of economic policy uncertainty (EPU) on production and financial variables, in particular, has recently intrigued academic interest, with the availability of EPU measures proposed by Baker et al. (2016) (also see Bonaime et al. 2018; Drobetz et al. 2018; Hu et al. 2018). Global economic policy uncertainty has increased significantly, whereas foreign direct investment has decreased significantly. It indicates that short-term factors, including policy uncertainty, may have an impact on foreign direct investment, implying that there is a negative relationship between uncertainty and foreign direct investment. Foreign investors have limited knowledge and protection of the host country's laws and political institutions. Foreign investment is more politically sensitive than domestic investment (Aizenman 2006; Avom 2020; Dixit 2011). Noria et al. (2018) took Mexico as an example to study the negative impact of uncertainty on foreign direct investment. Mitsuo et al. (2020) studied that policy uncertainty in Japan affected foreign investment at the micro level. Canh et al. (2020) explored the negative impact of domestic economic policy uncertainty on foreign direct investment in 21 economies.

As a typical government-oriented country, China often changes and alters its economic policies to regulate the economy, which relies heavily on government regulation (Liu et al. 2020). The uncertainty of economic policy can negatively affect investor confidence in the host country, thereby hindering foreign investors' investment decisions. Therefore, analyzing the relationship between government policy and FDI has important implications for China. While the existing literature broadly demonstrates the impact of FDI on economic policy uncertainty, only a few studies consider it to be a major determinant of FDI in China. Zhang et al. (2019) also studied the impact of Chinese EPU on global economic markets but did not analyze the causal relationship between EPU and FDI. Zhang et al. (2022) studied the relationship between economic policy uncertainty and cross-border capital flow decisions of Listed Companies in China, but the source of news-based EPU often comes from only one newspaper, and the causal relationship of time changes is not identified. Su et al. (2022) studied that Chinese EPU can hinder China's FDI inflows, but ignored the heterogeneity and endogeneity issues.

This paper analyzes the specific relationship between EPU and FDI in China in 31 provinces from 2003 to 2017. Unlike other papers, this paper uses EPU measurement data of Chinese provinces proposed by Yu et al. (2021), which takes newspapers of each province as data and considers regional heterogeneity. From a methodological point of view, our research adopts the system Generalized Method (GMM) econometric method of moments. This econometric approach allows us to have a dynamic model specification that captures the complete heterogeneity of countries and addresses internal issues.

The rest of the paper is arranged as follows: Section 2 illustrates the econometric methodology and data. Section 3 discusses the empirical results. Finally, Section 4 concludes.

2 METHODOLOGY AND DATA

2.1 *Model specification*

This paper adopts the system GMM technique, which can address the problem of missing variable bias and heteroskedasticity and produces estimated reliability (Abdouli et al. 2017; Omri et al. 2014). We use a one-year lag for all explanatory variables except the EPU index, referring to the articles of Sun et al. (2002) and Hsu et al. (2018). Meanwhile, in order to eliminate the drastic fluctuation and heteroscedasticity of the time series, we take logarithms of all of the explanatory variables except for openness, investment, infrastructure, and innovation. We also use system GMM estimates as a robustness check and the lagged level of the dependent variables as instrumental variables. In the empirical analysis, our model is given as follows:

$$\ln FDI_{it} = \alpha_{it} + \ln FDI_{it-1} + \beta_1 \ln EPU_{it} + \beta_2 \ln Market_{i,t-1} + \beta_3 Openness_{it-1}$$

$$+ \beta_4 Investment_{it-1} + \beta_5 \ln Wage_{it-1} + \beta_3 \ln GDP_{it-1} \qquad (1)$$

$$+ \beta_7 Infrastructure_{it-1} + \beta_8 Innovation_{it-1} + \varepsilon_{it}$$

In this equation, the explained variable $\ln FDI_{it}$ represents the amount of foreign direct investment of province i in year t. The interpretation of the key variable is $\ln EPU_{it}$, measured by the EPU index of province i in year t. α_{it} and ε_{it} represent constant and error term respectively. The descriptive statistics of all the variables are summarized in Table 1.

Table 1. Descriptive statistics of primary variables.

Variable	Description	Observations	Mean	Std
lnFDI	The natural logarithm of the foreign direct investment flow in a province	341	7.95	1.528
EPU1	Chinese provincial EPU index constructed by Yu et al. (2021)	341	4.447	0.481
EPU2	The standardization of China's provincial EPU index constructed by Yu et al. (2021)	341	20.83	14.456
lnMarket	The natural logarithm of per capita GDP	341	10.319	0.57
Openness	The ratio of the total imports and exports to provincial real GDP	341	0.333	0.374
Investment	The ratio of the government expenditure to provincial real GDP	341	0.264	0.193
lnWage	The natural logarithm of the average wage of urban employed persons	341	10.556	0.432
lnGDP	The natural logarithm of provincial real GDP	341	8.923	1.053
Infrastructure	The ratio of the length of roads to the total area	341	0.828	0.487
Innovation	The ratio of the patent approvals in a province to the total patent approvals in China	341	0.032	0.046

2.2 Data

This study is based on the panel data of 31 provinces in China from 2007 to 2017, excluding Hong Kong, Macao, and Taiwan. In this empirical analysis, we use the province-level EPU index proposed by Yu et al. (2021).[1] They constructed the annual index for China's 31 provinces from 2000 to 2017 by conducting keyword searches in local newspapers. In addition, we also adopt the standardization of the Chinese provincial EPU index (EPU2) proposed by Yu et al. (2021) for robustness tests. The data for all other variables is mainly from the official website of the China Statistics Bureau and the China Statistical Yearbook 2008–2018. The data denominated in US dollars, such as FDI and total import and export volume, are translated into RMB based on the annual average exchange rate of the year, and the actual values of FDI, GDP and wages are calculated based on the year 2000.

3 EMPIRICAL RESULTS

In this study, a panel data is used to empirically analyze the impact of economic policies uncertainty on foreign direct investment. Table 2 shows the empirical results and the test results of the corresponding system GMM model. Economic policy uncertainty is a problem for companies or investors involved in cross-border capital investment (Zhang et al. 2022). Columns 1-3 in Table 2 show that EPU1 and lnMarket have stable statistical significance in the system GMM model. It indicates that EPU1 and market size are important factors influencing FDI inflow in provinces. For every 1% increase in real local GDP per capita, FDI inflows will increase by 0.657%. As a proxy variable of economic policy uncertainty, EPU1 has a statistically significant negative impact on FDI inflow. It suggests that the economic policy stability of the host province is important in cross-border investment decision-making. This finding is consistent with Choi et al. (2021) research on China and that of other countries: increased policy uncertainty will significantly reduce foreign direct investment. With the gradual growth of per capita GDP and the support of the government's stable economic policies, the scale of FDI inflow will increase. However, the impact of the

[1]The EPU index can be downloaded from http://cedcdata.cufe.edu.cn/cedc/metadata/list.html

Table 2. Regression results.

VARIABLES	(1) Fix effect	(2) Random effect	(3) System GMM	(4) Fix effect	(5) Random effect	(6) System GMM
L.lnFDI			0.472***			0.523***
			(0.133)			(0.0752)
EPU1	−0.0367**	−0.0530***	−0.349**			
	(0.0175)	(0.0193)	(0.151)			
EPU2				−0.00209***	−0.00256***	−0.00858**
				(0.000743)	(0.000653)	(0.00392)
lnMarket	−0.168	0.252	0.657*	−0.182	0.165	0.613***
	(0.320)	(0.313)	(0.363)	(0.318)	(0.310)	(0.202)
Openness	−0.361	−0.0561	0.188	−0.355	−0.0934	0.178
	(0.265)	(0.246)	(0.156)	(0.263)	(0.245)	(0.128)
Investment	−0.0342	0.0150	−0.703	−0.0462	0.0318	−0.667*
	(0.648)	(0.526)	(0.533)	(0.644)	(0.528)	(0.341)
lnWage	−0.612	−0.362	−0.140	−0.584	−0.329	−0.165
	(0.436)	(0.307)	(0.386)	(0.438)	(0.303)	(0.208)
lnGDP	1.866***	1.038***	0.246	1.849***	1.096***	0.250*
	(0.356)	(0.129)	(0.152)	(0.357)	(0.118)	(0.123)
Infrastructure	0.186	0.609**	0.220	0.195	0.580**	0.172
	(0.609)	(0.265)	(0.207)	(0.602)	(0.273)	(0.140)
Innovation	0.995	1.822	2.041	1.180	1.841	1.648*
	(1.499)	(1.713)	(1.486)	(1.487)	(1.687)	(0.929)
Constant	−0.396	−0.401	−1.832	−0.534	−0.518	−2.878***
	(0.948)	(1.154)	(1.169)	(0.942)	(1.133)	(0.681)
Observations	341	341	310	341	341	310
R^2 within	0.720	0.688		0.721	0.696	
R^2 between	0.645	0.797		0.645	0.775	
R^2 overall	0.644	0.788		0.644	0.769	
Hansen J statistics (p-value)	0.152	0.120				
ar(1) test (p-value)			0.053			0.018
ar(2) test (p-value)			0.115			0.128

Notes: Robust standard errors in parentheses. *Significant at 10% level; **significant at 5% level; ***significant at 1% level.

epidemic and the turmoil in the international situation have increased EPU volatility. The sharp increase in EPU is a signal of declining foreign direct investment.

As a robustness test, we also adopt the standardization of the Chinese provincial EPU index (EPU2) proposed by Yu et al. (2021). The definition of EPU2 is shown in the variable section. The regression results in columns 4–6 of Table 2 show that the coefficients of EPU2 are significant at the statistical level. These results indicate that our previous conclusions are robust and further confirm that EPU has a significant negative impact on FDI in China. For sensitive cross-border investments, economic policy influences investment decisions through changes in the domestic or foreign economic environment.

4 CONCLUSIONS

This paper studies the impact of regional economic policy uncertainty on foreign direct investment based on the provincial-level panel data from 2007 to 2017. The empirical results show that increased economic policy uncertainty has a significant negative impact on foreign direct investment. It suggests that the host government needs to deal with the negative impact of EPU on FDI by innovating the regulatory system of economic policies and strengthening capacity. A stable economic policy-making mechanism plays an important role in reducing the negative impact of EPU on FDI. Our research results suggest that in the case of China, economic policy uncertainty is inhibitory to FDI. In other words, policymakers must make extra efforts to reduce decision-making uncertainty and provide a stable policy environment to attract foreign investment. At the same time, the findings of this study indicate that in the case of China, economic policy uncertainty inhibits FDI in this period. In other words, policymakers must make extra efforts to reduce decision-making uncertainty and provide a stable policy environment to attract foreign investment.

There are some limitations to our study. This paper only studied the data from 2007 to 2017, and could not see the impact of EPU on FDI in the long term. Moreover, this paper only considers the regression relationship between EPU and FDI and ignores the mediating effect in the relationship between EPU and FDI. In the future, we will focus on the mediating variable of EPU affecting FDI and find out its internal influencing mechanism.

REFERENCES

Abdouli, M., Hammami, S. 2017. Investigatingthecausality Linksbetween Environmental Quality, Foreign Direct Investment and Economic Growth in MENA Countries. *Int Bus Rev* 26(2): 264–278.

Aizenman, J., M. M. Spiegel. 2006. "Institutional Efficiency, Monitoring Costs and the Investment Share of FDI." *Review of International Economics* 14 (4): 683–697.

Avom, D., Njangang, H. and Nawo, L. 2020. World Economic Policy Uncertainty and Foreign Direct Investment, *Economics Bulletin* 40(2): 1457–1464.

Baker, S. R., N. Bloom, and S. J. Davis. 2016. Measuring Economic Policy Uncertainty. *Quarterly Journal of Economics* 131 (4): 1593–1636. doi:10.1093/qje/qjw024.

Bhattacharya, U., N. Galpin, B. Haslem. 2007. The Home Court Advantage in International Corporate Litigation. *J. Law Econ.* 50: 625–659.

Bonaime, A., Gulen, H., & Ion, M. 2018. Does Policy Uncertainty Affect Mergers and Acquisitions? *Journal of Financial Economics*. 129(3): 531–558, doi:https://doi.org/10.1016/j.jfineco.2018.05.007.

Canh, N.P., Binh, N.T., Thanh, S.D., Schinckus, C. 2020. Determinants of Foreign Direct Investment Inflows: The Role of Economic Policy Uncertainty. *International Economics*, doi:https://doi.org/10.1016/j.inteco.2019.11.012.

Choi, S., D. Furceri, C. Yoon. 2021. Policy Uncertainty and Foreign Direct Investment. *Review of International Economics* 29(2): 195–227.

Drobetz, W., El Ghoul, S., Guedhami, O., & Janzen, M. 2018. Policy Uncertainty, Investment, and the Cost of Capital. *Journal of Financial Stability* 39: 28–45, doi:https://doi.org/10.1016/j.jfs.2018.08.005.

Dixit, A. 2011. International Trade, Foreign Direct Investment, and Security. *Annual Review of Economics* 3(1): 191–213.

Hsu M., J. Lee, L. G. Roberto, Y. Zhao. 2018. Tax Incentives and Foreign Direct Investment in China. *Applied Economics Letters*. DOI:10.1080/13504851.2018.1495817.

Hu, C., Y. Tan. 2016. Export Spillovers and Export Performance in China. *China Econ. Rev.* 41: 75–89.

Hu, S., & Gong, D. 2018. Economic Policy Uncertainty, Prudential Regulation and Bank Lending. *Finance Research Letters*. doi:https://doi.org/10.1016/j.frl.2018.09.004

Liu, G. and Zhang, C. 2020. Economic Policy Uncertainty and Firms' Investment and Financing Decisions in China. *China Economic Review*. Vol. 63, doi: 10.1016/j.chieco.2019.02.007.

Mitsuo, M. and Naoto, R. 2020. To What Degree does Policy Uncertainty Affect Foreign Direct Investment? Micro-evidence from Japan's International Investment Agreements INADA, *RIETI Discussion Paper Series* 20-E-022.

Nguyen T. B., Strobel, J., Lee, G. 2019. A New Measure of Real Estate Uncertainty Shocks. *Real Estate Economics.*

Noria, G. L., and Fernández, J. J. Z. 2018. The Effect of Uncertainty on Foreign Direct Investment: The Case of Mexico. *Estudios Económicos* 33(1):117–149.

Sun, Q., W. Tong, and Q. Yu. 2002. Determinants of Foreign Direct Investment across China. *Journal of International Money and Finance* 21(1): 79–113, doi:10.1016/S0261-5606(01)00032-8.

Su, C.W., Meng, X. L., Tao, R. and Umar, M. 2022. Policy Turmoil in China: a Barrier for FDI flows? *International Journal of Emerging Markets* 17(7): 1617–1634, https://doi.org/10.1108/IJOEM-03-2021-0314.

Thanh, B. N. 2019. Macroeconomic Uncertainty, the Option to Wait and IPO Issue Cycles. *Finance Research Letters.*

Yu, J., X. Shi, D. Guo, and L. Yang. 2021. Economic Policy Uncertainty (EPU) and Firms' Carbon Emissions: Evidence Using a China Provincial EPU Index. *Energy Economics.* 94: 105071, doi:10.1016/j.eneco.2020.105071.

Zhang, D., Lei, L., Ji, Q. and Kutan, A.M. 2019. Economic Policy Uncertainty in the US and China and their Impact on the Global Markets. *Economic Modelling* 79: 47–56.

Zhang, L and Colak, G. 2022. Foreign Direct Investment and Economic Policy Uncertainty in China. *Economic and Political Studies.* DOI: 10.1080/20954816.2022.2090096.

The comparative research on the digital inclusive finance and traditional rural finance in China: An investigation based on the perspective of agricultural total factor productivity

Zhaojun Sun & Yueli Xu
Department of Economics and Trade, Guangdong University of Foreign Studies, Guangzhou, China

Liping Sun*
Guangdong Institute for International Strategies, Guangdong University of Foreign Studies, Guangzhou, China

ABSTRACT: Both traditional rural financial institutions and emerging digital inclusive financial institutions have significance in development of finance. Previous studies have shown that compared with traditional rural finance, the development of digital inclusive finance is more helpful to solve the problems of information asymmetry and financial market friction. However, few previous studies have compared digital inclusive finance and traditional rural finance from the perspective of agricultural total factor productivity (ATFP). This paper calculates China's ATFP by using DEA Malmquist index method across the 31 provinces over the period 2011–2020 to do the comparative research between TRF and DIF. The results show that digital inclusive finance has significantly improved ATFP. Moreover, by using the sub-indicators of digital inclusive finance for robustness test, the results are still in line with the above conclusions.

1 INTRODUCTION

Compared with cities, there are serious financial frictions in the rural credit market, which aggravates the difficulty of farmers' financing, and has always been an important factor hindering the solution of the three rural issues. Therefore, the development trend of the credit market in backward and underdeveloped areas is not optimistic. For a long time, the imbalance and lack of rural land property rights have restrained the process of "property right ownership" of rural land, resulting in the lack of appropriate collateral for farmers and strong financing constraints (Cai 2017; Chen 2015; Field 2006; Kemper 2015; Li 2015; Swamy 2020). In particular, the current limited liability credit system based on personal assets makes low-income families face severe formal credit rationing and it is difficult to achieve the ideal investment scale (Kochar 1997; Yuan 2016; Zhou 2017).

In recent years, in order to better promote rural revitalization, China's agriculture has entered the construction stage of "three systems" of industry, production, and operation. In addition, the structure of agricultural industrial chain and value chain is facing new

---

*Corresponding Author:

DOI: 10.1201/9781003278788-7

problems. In order to accelerate the construction of modern agriculture and countryside, the corresponding financial and insurance policies also need to be improved (Madden 1997). The main way to improve ATFP is for farmers to obtain financing. To a certain extent, the development of DIF will have an impact on traditional rural financial services. It will not only affect farmers' financing status but also have a chain reaction on ATFP.

2 THE BACKGROUND IN CHINA

2.1 *Traditional rural finance*

In 2010, China successively issued several policies, such as the opinions of the CPC Central Committee and the State Council, on strengthening the overall planning of urban and rural development and further consolidating the foundation of agricultural and rural development, the guiding opinions on comprehensively promoting the innovation of rural financial products and services, the opinions on strengthening the cooperation between agriculture-related credit and agriculture-related insurance, and the construction of rural inclusive financial system. In 2015, a new financial business format emerged, including Internet Finance and mobile finance represented by the financial sector of P2P online loans and agriculture-related loan of e-commerce platforms. So far, a relatively perfect "government, business, small and mutual" financial system has been formed, namely policy financial institutions, commercial financial institutions, small and medium-sized financial institutions, and rural mutual aid cooperatives. Financial leasing companies, microfinance companies, and professional cooperative organizations also developed rapidly at this stage.

2.2 *Digital inclusive finance*

In recent years, digital Inclusive Finance has developed rapidly, and platforms such as agriculture-related P2P online loan, e-commerce credit, and agriculture-related crowd-funding have sprung up, breaking through the original limitations of the traditional financial model. The availability and quality of financial services have been further improved. In 2017, the average total index of family Inclusive Finance in China was 0.575 (Yin 2019). The family-inclusive finance index jumped to the middle and upper level, which means it has been significantly improved. By the end of 2019, China's banks had handled 223.388 billion e-payment services, 719.998 billion online payment services related to other non-bank payments, and the proportion of the overall transaction scale of mobile payment had increased to 62.8%. The emergence and development of digital inclusive finance effectively cater to the national strategy and brings dawn to the solution of the three rural issues. The development report on China's financial technology and digital Inclusive Finance (2020) points out that looking forward to 2021 from the perspective of 2020, rural digital inclusive financial services will be more accurate. The advent of the big data era and the development of Internet technology have ushered in a new transaction mode in the financial field and further expanded the scope of financial services. Even in remote and backward areas, the availability and durability of services have been improved (Diniz 2012; Xie 2012). The results show that the rapid development and promotion of Internet technology have effectively promoted the growth of financial services and economic development (Ghosh 2016; Madden 2014; Zhou 2018). The three-level index system of digital Inclusive Finance is shown in Figure 1.

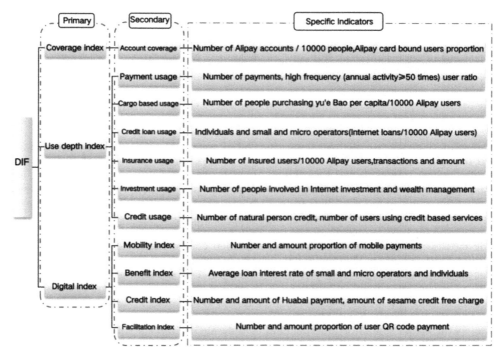

Figure 1. Indicators of different dimensions of DIF*.
*The DIF index used here is from Peking University. For details, please refer to the article of Guo Feng (2020). In this paper, DIF is the abbreviation of digital inclusive finance.

3 DESCRIPTION AND ANALYSIS OF ATFP IN CHINA

3.1 *Total factor productivity in China*

Relevant data show that by 2020, China's GDP had reached 101.6 trillion yuan, a yearly increase of 2.3%, of which the added value of the primary industry was 7.78 trillion yuan, a yearly increase of 3.0%, and the GDP of the primary industry accounted for 9.2% of the total GDP. Comparing the GDP of agriculture, forestry, animal husbandry, and sideline fisheries from 2011 to 2020, it is found that the GDP has increased year by year in recent 10 years, but occasionally decreased in terms of yearly growth rate.

3.2 *Selection of input indicators*

On the selection of ATFP input indicators, this paper has drawn lessons from previous literature, the relevant agricultural statistics and the theory of production factors. Referring to the practice of Wang (2020), starting from the four aspects of land, capital, labor force, and entrepreneurial talent, selecting the land area input of crop sowing (belonging to land input), agricultural land irrigation input indicators, agricultural machinery and equipment input, pesticide use (to be used), agricultural chemical fertilizer application input (the above four items belong to capital input) and agricultural labor input (belong to labor input) as input indicators.

3.3 *Selection of output indicators*

In the selection of output indicators, this paper selects the GDP of the primary industry, that is, the GDP of agriculture, forestry, animal husbandry, sideline fisheries, as one of the output indicators. On this basis, excluding the impact of intermediate consumption, the added value of the primary industry is selected as another index of output, and the second index can more accurately represent the real agricultural production. It should be noted that the selection time range of input indicators and output indicators is 2011–2020.

4 EMPIRICAL ANALYSIS

4.1 *Model of two types of financial organizations on ATFP*

At present, there are two methods to measure ATFP: one is the method of parametric model and the other is the method of nonparametric model. The methods of parameter model mainly include transcendental logarithmic function method, Solow residual method, algebraic index method, and Cobb-Douglas (C-D) production function method. The C-D production function method is evolved from the Solow residual method. This method is mostly used in the previous research on total factor productivity. However, the parameter method is mostly used for large sample data and has high requirements for model construction and a little carelessness will lead to errors. Nonparametric model methods include stochastic frontier analysis (SFA), Malmquist index method, and data envelopment analysis (DEA). This paper will use the literature of Alireza (2011) for reference and use the DEA Malmquist method to calculate China's ATFP from 2011 to 2020. This paper uses the DEA Malmquist method to calculate ATFP and decomposes it into two indicators: technological progress and technical efficiency. Since this paper mainly investigates the impact of DIF on ATFP, it is set as the main explanatory variable and considering that ATFP will be affected by time continuity. Therefore, the dynamic characteristics of the model should be considered. Finally, the model is set as follows:

$$ATFP_{it} = \alpha_1 + \beta_{11}ATFP_{it-1} + \beta_{12}ATFP_{it-2} + \gamma_1 TRF_{it} + \delta_1 DIF_{it}$$

$$+ \sum \varphi_i^1 Lncontrols_{it} + \mu_{it}^1 \tag{1}$$

$$Techpro_{it} = \alpha_2 + \beta_{21}Techpro_{it-1} + \beta_{22}Techpro_{it-2} + \gamma_2 TRF_{it} + \delta_2 DIF_{it}$$

$$+ \sum \varphi_i^2 Lncontrols_{it} + \mu_{it}^2 \tag{2}$$

$$Techeff_{it} = \alpha_3 + \beta_{31}Techeff_{it-1} + \beta_{32}Techeff_{it-2} + \gamma_3 TRF_{it} + \delta_3 DIF_{it}$$

$$+ \sum \varphi_i^3 Lncontrols_{it} + \mu_{it}^3 \tag{3}$$

In this expression, ATFP represents the change rate of ATFP, Techpro represents the rate of change in technological progress, Techeff represents the rate of change in technical efficiency, TRF represents the development level of traditional rural finance, DIF represents the figures inclusive financial index, $\sum \varphi_i$Controls$_{it}$ represents the variables that need to be controlled in the model, μ_{it} represents random interference term. Except for a series of control variables, other variables exist in the form of ratio, so that only the control variables are logarithmicized in the model to reduce the deviation caused by different orders of magnitude.

$$ATFP_{it} = \alpha_1 + \beta_{11}ATFP_{it-1} + \beta_{12}ATFP_{it-2} + \gamma_1 DIF_{it} + \sum \varphi_i^1 Lncontrols_{it} + \mu_{it}^1 \quad (4)$$

$$Techpro_{it} = \alpha_2 + \beta_{21}Techpro_{it-1} + \beta_{22}Techpro_{it-2} + \gamma_2 DIF_{it} + \sum \varphi_i^2 Lncontrols_{it} + \mu_{it}^2 \quad (5)$$

$$Techeff_{it} = \alpha_3 + \beta_{31}Techeff_{it-1} + \beta_{32}Techeff_{it-2} + \gamma_3 DIF_{it} + \sum \varphi_i^3 Lncontrols_{it} + \mu_{it}^3 \quad (6)$$

The variable symbols in the formula are the same as those in formulas (4), (5), and (6). Since this paper tends to make a comparative study of Chinese traditional rural finance and digital Inclusive Finance, it is necessary to set up a model including two explanatory variables of TRF and DIF at the same time. According to previous literature and preliminary regression results, it is found that traditional rural finance has little impact on ATFP, which is limited to space. Therefore, the following will mainly show the impact of DIF on ATFP.

4.2 Estimation results

Based on previous studies, this paper makes a comparative study on digital Inclusive Finance and traditional rural finance and makes an empirical test with ATFP as the starting point. Corresponding to the benchmark regression models of equations (1), (2), and (3), Table 1 reports the preliminary regression results of digital Inclusive Finance and traditional finance on ATFP, technical efficiency, and technological progress rate. The results shown in the table are as follows:

Table 1.   Empirical results of DIF and TRF on agricultural total factor productivity.

	ATFP	Techeff	Techpro
Lag phase I	0.0238**	0.0196**	0.0174**
	(0.0092)	(0.0075)	(0.0067)
DIF	0.0553***	0.0699***	0.0283***
	(0.0171)	(0.0122)	(0.0098)
TRF	0.0011	0.0026	0.0043
	(0.0009)	(0.0078)	(0.0035)
Ain	0.0295***	0.0271***	0.0219***
	(0.009)	(0.0035)	(0.0032)
Dis	−0.1536**	−0.0145*	−0.0158**
	(0.0627)	(0.0086)	(0.0061)
Urb	0.0205***	0.0265**	0.0204**
	(0.0041)	(0.0102)	(0.0078)
Ind	0.8437***	0.1611***	0.0964***
	(0.1952)	(0.0238)	(0.0201)
Edu	−0.0143	−0.0067	−0.0056
	(0.0291)	(0.0037)	(0.0545)
Year	YES	YES	YES
Region	YES	YES	YES
N	310	310	310

Note: the statistical results *, **, *** in the table are significant at the levels of 10%, 5% and 1%, respectively. The data reported in "()" is robust standard error (std.err.)

First of all, digital Inclusive Finance (DIF) has a significant positive impact on ATFP, and the agricultural technical efficiency (techeff) and agricultural technical progress rate (techpro) decomposed by ATFP are also significant at the level of 1%. Moreover, this paper finally uses agricultural fixed investment (Ain), crop-affected area (Dis), industrialization level (Ind), urbanization level (Urb), and per capita education level (Edu) as control variables for the empirical test. The results show that agricultural fixed investment has a significant positive impact on ATFP, indicating that with the continuous increase of agricultural fixed investment, ATFP will also be improved, which is consistent with the economic reality. Looking at the level of urbanization and industrialization, the effect is also significant at the 1% level. Although the significant level of urbanization rate, technical efficiency, and technological progress rate is not high, it has also reached the significant level of 5%. The last control variable is the level of education. This paper uses the number of years of education per capita as the measurement data of the level of education. It is found that the level of education has a negative impact on ATFP. It may be because talents with high education levels are more inclined to engage in secondary and tertiary industries. This paper uses SYS -GMM and 2SLS for the robustness test. The specific test results are shown in Table 2.

Table 2.　Robustness test (SYS -GMM).

	(1) ATFP	(2) techeff	(3) techpro	(4) peff	(5) seff
DIF	0.0272***	0.0139**	0.0102**		
	(0.0080)	(0.0050)	(0.0036)		
DIF·Decomposition				0.0083**	0.0091**
				(0.0030)	(0.0033)
Ain	0.0386***	0.0226***	0.0207***	0.0212***	0.0224***
	(0.0042)	(0.0015)	(0.0014)	(0.0015)	(0.0015)
Dis	−0.0336**	−0.0317***	−0.0313***	−0.0304***	−0.0319***
	(0.0165)	(0.006)	(0.0057)	(0.0058)	(0.0060)
Urb	0.0417***	0.0256***	0.0240***	0.0241***	0.0254***
	(0.0083)	(0.0030)	(0.0028)	(0.0029)	(0.0030)
Ind	0.2060***	0.1352***	0.1162***	0.1164***	0.1339***
	(0.0791)	(0.0287)	(0.0275)	(0.0276)	(0.0285)
Edu	−0.1007**	−0.0539***	−0.0465**	−0.0480***	−0.0532**
	(0.0465)	(0.0169)	(0.0161)	(0.0162)	(0.0168)
Year	YES	YES	YES	YES	YES
Region	YES	YES	YES	YES	YES
Adjust-R^2	0.5038	0.6615	0.6599	0.5608	0.60 17
N	310	310	310	310	310
AR (1)	0.000	0.000	0.000	0.000	0.000
AR (2)	0.516	0.215	0.158	0.298	0.173
Hansen -J	0.425	0.287	0.986	0.719	0.667

Note: the statistical results *, **, *** in the table are significant at the levels of 10%, 5%, and 1%, respectively. The data reported in "()" is robust standard error (std.err.), AR (1) and AR (2) tests list the P values of the first-order and second-order autocorrelation tests of the first-order difference of the model residual term respectively, and the Hansen test lists the P values of the over-identification of instrumental variables.

5　CONCLUSIONS AND POLICY IMPLICATIONS

According to the relevant research basis of traditional rural finance and DIF, it is considered that digital Inclusive Finance has a positive impact on China's total factor productivity. In order to verify this conjecture, in the following paper, an empirical model is constructed to test, and the robustness is tested by using secondary indicators. The results show that the development of China's digital Inclusive Finance has a significant positive impact on ATFP. It is found that it mainly affects China's ATFP through the path of the coverage breadth and usage depth, which the indicators of digitization degree and usage depth are followed by. However, this paper only makes a relatively basic and simple analysis of digital Inclusive Finance and traditional rural finance, and further excavation and discussion are needed in the follow-up. There are many rising spaces in other data collection, variable selection, theory and method, demonstration, and test.

Combined with the above research, this paper puts forward the above relevant policy suggestions: First, "food is the most important thing for the people" and informatization is the key to responding to the theme of China's high-quality development. The relevant research on digital inclusive finance needs to be further deepened, and digital inclusive finance needs to be better applied to agricultural development, and carry out targeted digital inclusive financial services in rural areas; Second, the trend of agricultural technical efficiency and technological progress rate is unstable. It is necessary to optimize and upgrade the industrial structure and resource allocation in order to promote the coordinated and sustainable development of agriculture and rural areas; Third, strengthen the training and management of agricultural financial literacy and agricultural innovative technology, so that agricultural owners can better carry out agricultural production and work, and further improve ATFP. Last but not the least, the government needs to improve and perfect the supporting policies and measures for agricultural and rural development, give full play to the strong leadership role of government departments, and make agricultural development "have laws and rules to follow".

FUNDINGS

This work was supported by the Graduate Research Innovation Project of GDUFS (Fund no. 22GWCXXM-017).

REFERENCES

Chen. 2015. Innovations in Financing of Agri-food Value Chains in China and India. *China Agricultural Economic Review* 7(4): 616–640.

Diniz, E., R. Birochi, and M. Pozzebon, 2012. Triggers and Barriers to Financial Inclusion: The Use of Ict-based Branchless Banking in an Amazon County. *Electronic Commerce Research and Applications* 11(6): 484–494.

Guangsu Zhou, Qi Liang. 2018. Internet Use, Market Friction and Household Risk Financial Asset Investment. *Financial Research* 1: 84–101.

Ghosh, S. 2016. Does Mobile Telephony Spur Growth? Evidence from Indian States. *Telecommunications Policy* 40(10-11): 1020–1031.

Field E. 2006. Do Property Titles Increase Credit Access Among the Urban Poor? Evidence from a Nationwide Titling Program. *Working paper*.

Kemper N. 2015. Property Rights and Consumption Volatility: Evidence from a Land Reform in Vietnam. *World Development* 71: 107–130.

Kochar A. 1997. An Empirical Investigation of Rationing Constraints in Rural Credit Markets in India. *Journal of Development Economics* 53(4): 339–371.

Li, Rui, Qinghai Li, Shao'an Huang, and Xi Zhu, 2015. The Credit Rationing of Chinese Rural Households and Its Welfare Loss: An Investigation Based on Panel Data. *China Economic Review* 17–27.

Madden, G. G., and S. J. Savage. 1997. CEE Telecommunications Investment and Economic Growth. *Information Economics and Policy* 10(2): 173–195.

Ping Xie, Chuanwei Zou. 2012. Research on Internet Financial Model. *Journal of Financial Research* (390): 11–22.

Swamy, V., and M. Dharani, 2020. Analyzing the Agricultural Value Chain Financing: Approaches and Toolsin India. *Agricultural Finance Review* 76(2): 211–232.

Yuan, Y. and Xu, L. H. 2016. Are Poor Able to Access the Informal Credit Market? Evidence from Rural Households in China. *China Economic Review* 33(2): 232–246.

Economic and Business Management – Lent & Zhang (Eds)
© 2023 the Author(s), ISBN 978-1-032-24482-2

A comparative study on policies of intelligent equipment industry between China and foreign countries based on content analysis of policy texts

Shunlong Zhao & Zhonglin Fei
School of Economics and Management, Nanjing Tech University, Nanjing, Jiangsu Province, China
Jiangsu Industrial Technology Innovation Research Center, Nanjing, Jiangsu Province, China
Jiangsu Science and Technology Policy Think Tank, Nanjing, Jiangsu Province, China

Lin Li & Weiguo Huang
School of Economics and Management, Nanjing Tech University, Nanjing, Jiangsu Province, China

ABSTRACT: This article constructs a two-dimensional analytical framework of the intelligent equipment industry policy from policy instruments and industrial innovation chain. To compare the policy instruments taken in different countries, the article collects policy texts related to intelligent equipment industry during 2010 to 2018 from typical countries such as China, Germany, the United States, and Japan. The content analysis method is taken for coding the policy texts with the Nvivo software. The research findings show that, compared with other countries, China uses the most environmental policy instruments and the least supply policy instruments; furthermore, the types of policy instruments are diverse but scattered. Talent policy instruments are not drawn enough attention, the industrialization stage is obtained more emphasis than the basic or applied research stage, more subsidy or outsourcing policy instruments are taken in the industrialization stage, while the trade control policy instruments are rarely taken. According to the above findings, the article puts forward several policy suggestions for developing intelligent equipment industry in China.

1 INTRODUCTION

Compared with the intelligent manufacturing strategy implemented by relevant countries such as the "Industrial Internet" of the United States, Japan's "Revitalization Strategy" and Germany's "Industry 4.0," China's "Intelligent Manufacturing" industry concept has the largest scope. In addition to industrial network foundation and internet application, information physical integration system, intelligent factory, and production, it also includes high-end CNC machine tools, industrial robots, additive manufacturing, and other intelligent manufacturing equipment and intelligent core devices, intelligent logistics, and storage equipment.

Leading countries such as the United States, Germany, and Japan have obvious advantages in the intelligent equipment industry, especially in the fields of robots, machine instruments, and automation. Currently, China has made great progress in intelligent equipment manufacturing technology and has gradually formed an intelligent equipment industry system. Industrial areas have appeared in the Bohai Rim region, Pearl River Delta region, and Yangtze River Delta.

Freeman & Soete (1997) argued that public policies affect industrial technological innovation and the development of emerging industries during the rise of industries in developed

DOI: 10.1201/9781003278788-8

and newly industrialized countries. Rodrik (2008) argues that industrial policy measures such as public R&D, industrial subsidies, and tax incentives for the development of specific industries should be taken seriously. Policy intervention is necessary because of the information and coordination externalities of industrial activities. The success of "economic restructuring" also depends on policy intervention. Therefore, whether the existing industrial policies meet the needs of industrial activity, whether they are conducive to industrial development, and whether they can be adjusted and improved to make them more effective have always been a great concern to government authorities, industry, and related scientific research institutions.

After collecting the coding policy texts related to the intelligent equipment industry from China, the United States, Germany, and Japan, this study statistically compares the frequency of policy instruments used in each phase of industrial innovation in different countries. Through this comparison, we can find the current status of China's intelligent equipment industry policy, learn from the experience of leading countries, and improve China's industrial policy measures in this industry.

2 LITERATURE REVIEW

Regarding the definition of policy instrument, Owen (2004) argued that public policy instruments were the mechanisms and ways by which the government uses certain means to regulate its behaviors. Policy instruments were defined as methods, approaches, or certain measures adopted by decision-makers and executors to achieve goals (Shen et al. 2015). As for the classification of policy instruments, Rothwell & Zegveld (1981) divided the policy instruments into three categories: supply, demand, and environment. While Woolthuis, Lankhuizen & Gilsing (2005) divided policy instruments into four categories: information, authority, organization, and finance according to the different resources used by governments. In recent years, research on policy instruments are also increasing. Jacobsson & Bergek (2011) argued that current policies could be divided into creative policies and destructive policies. If the intensity of government administrative intervention is the standard, policy categories can be classified into mandatory, hybrid, and voluntary (Ding et al. 2019). Among the above-mentioned categories, the classification mode proposed by Rothwell & Zegveld (1981) is the most common one which is suitable for various countries. Furthermore, it could be better combined with the industrial innovation chain, so this study also introduces this classification mode.

Kline & Rosenberg (1986) proposed that in a series of links such as basic research and development, demonstration, commercialization, and market accumulation, the cooperation in knowledge flow or among various industrial innovation participants is periodical. The technological innovation chain is a chain structure formed by the flow of technical knowledge of various organizations participating in innovation activities (Peng et al. 2012). Policy support is vital for a new technology to cross all "death valleys" (Wu et al.2008). As an emerging industry, the intelligent equipment industry depends on technological innovation highly. It is more reasonable to consider the demands of policy instruments in different stages of innovation chain than to apply the whole policy toolkit at every stage.

3 TWO-DIMENSIONAL ANALYTICAL FRAMEWORK OF THE INTELLIGENT EQUIPMENT INDUSTRY POLICY

Based on the classification of innovation policy given by Rothwell & Zegveld (1981), intelligent equipment industrial policy could be divided into three categories: supply, demand, and environment, and each category conclude several policy instruments. The supply-side policy is the provision of financial, information, manpower, and other resources assistance.

It usually works in the early phase of the innovation process. Demand-side policy refers to the government purchase or contracts to provide markets for new products, reduce market risks, and drive technological innovation. It generally works at the later phase of the innovation process. Environmental policies are those which establish the legal and fiscal frame-

Table 1. Definition of policy instruments.

Instrument category	Instrument name	Definition
Supplypolicy	Direct investment	Encourage scientific research and technology activities through direct investment such as special funds.
	Scientific infrastructure	R&D laboratories, R&D bases, R&D centers, research associations, high-tech parks, etc.
	Information	Information networks and centers, libraries, advisory and consultancy services, data bases, and liaison services.
	Talent cultivation	Various talent development plans, general education, universities, technical education, trainee program, continuing and further education, and retraining.
	Public service	Service supporting facilities such as medical care, transportation, communication, professional consulting service agencies, etc.
Demand policy	Government procurement	Central or local government purchases and contracts, public corporations R&D contracts, and prototype purchases.
	Financial subsidies	Price subsidies, enterprise loss subsidies, and other measures to stabilize prices and support industrial development.
	Trade barrier	Various import and export control measures such as tariffs and trade agreements.
	Public service outsourcing	Private enterprises and capital cooperate with the government to participate in the construction of public infrastructure.
Environmental policy	Taxation	Tax deductions and deductions, preferential tax rates, accelerated depreciation, etc.
	Financial	Grant loans, subsidies, financial sharing arrangements, provision of equipment buildings or services, loan guarantees, and export credits.
	Political	Planning, regional policies, honor or awards for innovation, encouragement of mergers of joint consortia, and public consultation.
	Legal regulatory	patents, industrial standards, environmental and health regulations, supervisory agencies, and monopoly regulations.

work for industry operations. As shown in Table 1, there are various policy instruments under each category.

According to the innovation chain given by Grubb (2004), this study divides the intelligent equipment industry innovation chain into four stages: Stage I—basic research and development, technological research; Stage II—development and demonstration; Stage III—market demonstration and commercialization; Stage IV—market accumulation. Fei & Wei (2013) argue that in the nonlinear circular innovation chain, innovation stakeholders have different demands for industrial policies, which is caused by the characteristics of different stages and the interactive feedback among innovation elements. Murphy & Edwards (2003) believe that the maturity and commercialization of technology do not simply rely on increasing public R&D investment. There are great differences in the needs of the public sector and the private sector, the policy instruments of capital investment play a greater role in the early stage than in the later one of innovation chain. To analyze the application of specific policy instruments at different stages, a two-dimensional analytical framework of the intelligent equipment industry policy should be constructed before carrying out the policy text analysis, as shown in Figure 1.

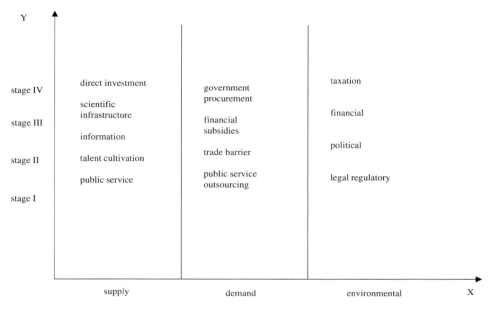

Figure 1.   Two-dimensional analytical framework of the intelligent equipment industry policy.

4   RESEARCH METHODS AND ANALYSIS PROCESS

4.1   *Research method*

4.1.1   *Policy text selection and coding*

Currently, China, Germany, the United States, and Japan lead the intelligent equipment industry. China is one of the few developing countries with advanced development in the intelligent equipment industry. This article takes the above countries as samples for comparative study.

The selection of policy texts follows the following principles: (1) Openness. Taking public documents such as notices, instructions, plans, initiatives, announcements, and guidelines published on relevant websites of different countries. (2) Authority. All the documents are downloaded from the official websites of government authorities. (3) Representativeness. Only policies that explicitly mention the intelligent equipment industry are selected. In addition, due to the different uploading times of policies in different countries, this article only selects the policy texts published by official websites from 2010 to 2018 for research to ensure a balanced sample size.

Considering the principles of openness, authority, and representativeness, the policy texts explicitly referring to the "intelligent manufacturing" industry published on official websites from 2010 to 2018 were searched and screened. Chinese policy texts are selected from official websites such as the State Council, the Ministry of science and technology, and the Ministry of industry and information technology. The text of German policy is selected from the website of the German federal government and its sub websites. The U.S. policy text is selected from the website of the White House Science and technology policy office and the website of the National Science Foundation. Japanese policy texts are selected from websites such as the Ministry of economy, industry, culture, science and technology, the Ministry of education, the Ministry of education and science, and the Department of science and technology of Japan.

A total of 45 pieces of intelligent equipment industrial policy texts from China, Germany, the United States, and Japan were selected in this study. Nvivo software is used to encode them, which replicated that there are 22 Chinese texts with 299 codes; 11 American texts with 302 codes; 6 German texts with 211 codes; 6 Japanese texts with 266 codes.

4.1.2 *Content analysis and comparison*
After coding, under the two-dimensional analytical framework, the frequencies of application of intelligent equipment industry policy instruments on four stages of innovation chain in China, Germany, the USA, and Japan are counted.

4.2 *Analysis process*

4.2.1 *Distribution of policy instruments in the innovation chain*
Table 2 shows that most policy instruments are applied in Stage III (32.5%), followed by Stage I (26.1%) and Stage II (24.7%). The frequency of policy instruments applied in Stage IV is the least (16.7%). The proportions of the three categories of policy instruments are environmental-side (60.2%), supply-side (37.6%), and demand-side (2.2%).

Table 2 shows that from 2010 to 2018, the intelligent equipment industry policies of China, Germany, the USA, and Japan are mainly aimed at the research and development stages (including applied and basic research) and commercialization stages. However, fewer policy instruments are applied in the market accumulation stage. The results sound reasonable because in most countries intelligent equipment industry is an emerging industry and is in the early stage of the industry life cycle. In this stage, government intervention usually dominates over market mechanisms. Once the industrial innovation enters the later stage, the market adjustment will become effective.

Further analyzing the application of various types of policy instruments, "political" is the most regular policy instrument in all stages of the industrial innovation chain, especially in Stages II and III, as 14.5% and 13.2%, respectively. Policy instruments such as "legal regulatory," "scientific infrastructure," and "talent cultivation" are the second most applied

Table 2. Statistics on the distribution of policy instruments in the innovation chain.

Instrument category	Instrument name	Stage I	Stage II	Stage III	Stage IV	Total
Supply policy	Public service	16	12	23	12	63
	Scientific infrastructure	42	32	38	13	125
	Talent cultivation	63	10	39	1	113
	information	9	18	13	9	49
	Direct investment	27	5	14	9	55
Environmental policy	Legal regulatory	22	27	46	40	135
	Financial	3	2	17	15	37
	Political	98	156	142	56	452
	Taxation	0	1	9	15	25
Demand policy	Trade barrier	1	0	0	5	6
	Public service outsourcing	0	0	1	0	1
	Financial subsidies	0	0	7	3	10
	Government procurement	0	4	1	2	7
Total		281	267	350	180	1078

instruments. Among them, "legal regulatory" is mainly applied to Stages III and IV accounting for 4.3% and 3.7%, respectively. "Scientific infrastructure" is mainly applied to Stages I, II, and III, accounting for 3.9%, 3.0%, and 3.5% respectively. "Talent cultivation" is mainly applied to Stages I and III, accounting for 5.8% and 3.6%, respectively.

4.2.2 *Distribution of policy instruments in different countries*

Table 3 shows the application of policy categories in China, Germany, the United States, and Japan. Environmental policies occupy the largest proportion (more than 50%) in all countries, especially in China which is nearly 70%. Japan and Germany apply for more S-side policies than the other two countries, accounting for 42.48% and 40.76% of all policy instruments, respectively. China applied the least S-side policy among all countries, only accounting for 30.43% of all its policy instruments. While D-side policy is the most applied category in China, the same situation is in the USA.

Table 3.   Statistics on the distribution of policy instruments in different countries.

Instrument category	Instrument name	China	Germany	USA	Japan	total
Supply policy	Public service	21	12	17	13	63
	Scientific infrastructure	35	32	20	38	125
	Talent cultivation	14	27	39	33	113
	Information	6	10	11	22	49
	Direct investment	15	5	28	7	55
Subtotal		91	86	115	113	405
Environmental policy	Legal regulatory	46	33	23	33	135
	Financial	20	3	3	11	37
	Political	126	87	141	98	452
	Taxation	7	0	11	7	25
Subtotal		199	123	178	149	649
Demand policy	Trade barrier	0	1	2	3	6
	Public service outsourcing	1	0	0	0	1
	Financial subsidies	8	0	0	1	9
	Government procurement	0	1	7	0	8
Subtotal		9	2	9	4	24
total		299	211	302	266	1078

Further analysis of detailed instruments in Table 4 shows that China and USA apply 11 types of policy instruments, and the distribution of various types is comparatively scattered. The top three instruments in China are "political" (42.14%), "legal regulatory" (15.38%), and "scientific infrastructure" (11.71%), accounting for 69.23% in total. While the top three in the USA are "political" (46.69%), "talent cultivation" (12.92%), and "direct investment" (9.27%), accounting for 68.88% in total. Germany's application of policy instruments is the most concentrated, with 10 of the 13 instruments, "political" (41.23%), "legal regulatory" (15.64%), and "scientific infrastructure" (15.17%) occupy 72.04% of all the instruments. Japan also applies 11 types of policy instruments, "political" (36.84%), "scientific infra-structure" (14.28%), "talent cultivation," and "legal regulatory" (both are 12.41%) are the top four instruments, with a total of 75.94%. To sum up, China, Germany, and Japan put more emphasis on "scientific infrastructure" and "legal regulatory," while "direct

Table 4. Statistics on the percentage of distribution of policy instruments.

Instrument category	Instrument name	China	Germany	USA	Japan	Total
Supply policy	Public service	7.02%	5.69%	5.63%	4.89%	5.84%
	Scientific infrastructure	11.71%	15.17%	6.62%	14.28%	11.60%
	Talent cultivation	4.68%	12.80%	12.92%	12.41%	10.48%
	Information	2.01%	4.74%	3.64%	8.27%	4.55%
	Direct investment	5.02%	2.37%	9.27%	2.63%	5.10%
	Subtotal	30.44%	40.77%	38.08%	42.48%	37.57%
Environmental policy	Legal regulatory	15.38%	15.64%	7.62%	12.41%	12.52%
	Financial	6.69%	1.42%	0.99%	4.14%	3.43%
	Political	42.14%	41.23%	46.69%	36.84%	41.93%
	Taxation	2.34%	0.00%	3.64%	2.63%	2.32%
	Subtotal	66.55%	58.29%	58.94%	56.02%	60.20%
Demand policy	Trade barrier	0.00%	0.47%	0.66%	1.13%	0.56%
	Public service outsourcing	0.33%	0.00%	0.00%	0.00%	0.09%
	Financial subsidies	2.68%	0.00%	0.00%	0.37%	0.84%
	Government procurement	0.00%	0.47%	2.32%	0.00%	0.74%
	Subtotal	3.01%	0.94%	2.98%	1.50%	2.23%
	Total	100.00%	100.00%	100.00%	100.00%	100.00%

investment" in science and technology is highly valued in the USA (China is the second one in this respect), and "legal regulatory" is undervalued compared to other countries.

As for the distribution of policy instruments in each stage of the industrial innovation chain (Table 5), in China and Japan, most instruments are applied to Stages III and IV,

Table 5. Statistics on the distribution of policy instruments in each stage of the industrial innovation chain.

Name	China				Germany				USA				Japan				Total
	I	II	III	IV	I	II	III	IV	I	II	III	IV	I	II	III	IV	
Public Service	3	3	10	5	3	4	0	5	6	4	7	0	4	1	6	2	63
Scientific Infrastructure	5	4	21	5	12	7	8	5	10	7	1	2	15	14	8	1	125
Talent Cultivation	3	0	11	0	23	1	2	1	25	4	10	0	12	5	16	0	113
Information	1	0	1	4	2	4	3	1	0	6	3	2	6	8	6	2	49
Direct Investment	2	1	9	3	4	0	0	1	18	4	3	3	3	0	2	2	55
Legal Regulatory	2	0	24	20	8	9	2	14	9	8	2	4	3	10	18	2	135
Financial	1	1	8	10	2	0	1	0	0	0	1	2	0	1	7	3	37
Political	8	32	65	21	31	28	17	11	39	69	19	14	20	27	41	10	452
Taxation	0	0	5	2	0	0	0	0	0	1	1	9	0	0	3	4	25
Trade Barrier	0	0	0	0	1	0	0	0	0	0	0	2	0	0	0	3	6
Public Service Outsourcing	0	0	1	0	0	0	0	0	0	0	0	0	0	0	0	0	1
Financial Subsidies	0	0	7	1	0	0	0	1	0	0	0	0	0	0	0	1	10
Government Procurement	0	0	0	0	0	0	0	0	0	4	1	2	0	0	0	0	7
Total	25	41	162	71	86	53	33	39	107	107	48	40	63	66	107	30	1078

which exceed 50% of all instruments applied. On the contrary, Germany and the United States, whose policy instruments are mainly applied to Stages I and II, account for more than 65% in total. Even though China and Japan apply more policy instruments to the later stage of the innovation chain, there are still some differences in the types of instruments applied. For example, on the S-side, "scientific infrastructure" is the most applied one in China, whereas in Japan it is "talent cultivation"; in the environmental category, China applies "political" 5% more than Japan does; and in Stage III, Japan seldom applies D-side policy, while China is the only one who applies "financial subsidies." Germany and the United States apply the most policy instruments in Stage I, accounting for 40.76% and 35.43%, respectively, but there are still differences. In Germany, "scientific infrastructure" and "talent cultivation" are more applied to Stage I, whereas in the United States, they are "talent cultivation" and "direct investment."

5   COMPARATIVE ANALYSIS RESULTS

According to the above results, current industrial policies in China related to intelligent equipment have the following features compared with Germany, the United States, Japan, and other countries.

5.1   *China prefers more environmental policies than demand-side policies*

Compared with other countries, China applies the most environmental policy instruments and the least supply policy instruments.

Among the three policy categories, an environmental policy, which has an indirect effect on promoting industry development, is the most important policy category in all countries. However, compared with other countries, the application of environmental policy in China is accounting for nearly 70% of all policy instruments. High valuing of the political and legal regulations from the government and undervaluing of the fiscal or market incentives which belong to demand-side are distinguished in China.

All the above countries tend to promote industrial innovation and increase the spillover effect of knowledge through supply-side policy. While the proportion of S-side policy in all categories in China is the lowest one among all countries.

D-side policy occupies the least proportion in all countries, but the remarkable thing is China and the United States apply "financial subsidies" and "government procurement" respectively, which shows their interest in pulling industrial innovation by creating new markets and increasing new demands.

5.2   *China's policy instruments application are diverse but scattered*

If the application of policy instruments is scattered, the overall effect will be weakened. Different from the relatively concentrated application in Japan and Germany, China applies 11 of the 13 types of policy instruments, and the frequency of each instruments application is relatively low. The first three high frequencies of application account for about 69% in total. While in Germany, which applies 10 types of policy instruments, the top three high-frequency application account for more than 72%.

5.3   *China does not set enough value on talent and information*

Unlike other countries that set enough value on "talent cultivation" (nearly 13% of all their policy instruments), the proportion of this instrument in China only occupies 4.68%, far less than that of other countries. Meanwhile, the proportion of "information" ranks last among the four countries, accounting for only about 2%. Furthermore, the proportion of "public services," "subsidies," and "financial" is about 3% higher than that of other countries.

5.4 *China places more emphasis on the later stage of innovation chain than on the early stage*

China's current intelligent equipment industry policy instruments are mainly aimed at Stage III-market demonstration and commercialization, which is similar to Japan's. However, the policy instruments applied at this stage account for 54% of the application frequency of all instruments, which is the highest among all countries, even exceeding 10% than that of Japan. Meanwhile, the proportions of policy instruments applied in Stage I and Stage II are the lowest in all countries, only about 8% and 14%, respectively, which are far lower than Germany (41% and 25%), the United States (35% and 35%), and Japan (24% and 25%).

5.5 *China uses more subsidies and public service outsourcing in Stage III*

China is the only country that uses "financial subsidies" in Stage III, accounting for 2.34% of all the applications of policy instruments. The United States only uses a small amount of "government procurement" in this stage, and both Germany and Japan hardly use D-side policy in Stage III. China is also the only country using "public service outsourcing" in this stage, accounting for 0.33%. Although Japan also applies more S-side policy in this stage, the emphasis is more on "talent cultivation," compared to China's "scientific infrastructure construction."

5.6 *China rarely uses the commercial regulation*

China is the only country that does not use "commercial regulation." The proportion of this policy instrument in Germany is 0.47% and is applied all in Stage I. Japan is the county that uses this instrument the most, accounting for nearly 80% of all D-side policies it uses, and mostly in Stage IV, a similar situation in the USA. With the development of certain industries, the lack use of commercial regulation is not a good thing.

6 POLICY SUGGESTIONS

Based on the above analytical results, this article puts forward the following policy suggestions on developing the intelligent equipment industry in China for reference.

First of all, relative enterprises, research institutions, and government authorities in China should analyze the current stage of the innovation chain in certain technological fields. Later, they should concentrate on suitable policy instruments to meet the innovation demands rather than taking every possible instrument under different stages or circumstances. It's significant for increasing the efficiency of policy application because spreading critical resources across many different areas will lead to the waste.

Second, compared with Stage III and IV, China should focus more on Stages I and II. On the one hand, foundational and technological R&D is always the basis of emerging industries. On the other hand, in these stages incentives from government authorities through policy application will have more effect on the promotion of industrial development.

Third, compared with environmental policy and demand-side policy, China should set more value on supply-side policy, especially on talent and information. These advanced productive factors are harder to obtain than infrastructure and direct investment because they require long-term accumulation. Although directly introducing skills or technologies from the outside typically produces quick results,, there are risks of unstableness, inadaptability, and insecurity.

Finally, even in Stages III and IV, the demand-side policy will become more effective, China still needs to place more emphasis on commercial regulation and let more innovation stakeholders be involved in policy initiatives, but not to play a sole party to pull the innovation through government procurement, public service outsourcing, financial subsidies, etc. Because in the later stage of the innovation chain, the industry market has become mature, more and more resources from private sectors will tend to enter it. Relative free market competition could save a lot of public resources investment.

REFERENCES

Ding, G., Deng, Y. L. & Lin, S. S. 2019. A Study on the Classification of China's Provincial Carbon Emissions Trading Policy Instruments: Taking Fujian Province as an Example. *Energy Reports* 5, 1543–1550.

Freeman, C. & Soete, L. 1997. The Economics of Industrial Innovation, 3rd edn, Pinter, London. *Innovation & Small Business Volume.*

Fei, Z. L. & Wei, W. 2013. Government Policies to Support Strategic Emerging Industries – Based on the Consideration of Industrial Life Cycle. *Scientific and Technological Progress and Countermeasures* 30(003), 104–107.

Grubb, M. 2004. Technology Innovation and Climate Change Policy: An Overview of Issues and Options. *Keio Economic Studies* 41(2): 103–132.

Jacobsson, S. & Bergek, A. 2011. Innovation System Analyses and Sustainability Transitions: Contributions and Suggestions for Research. *Environmental Innovation & Societal Transitions* 1(1), 41–57.

Kline, S. J. & Rosenberg, N. 1986. An overview of innovation. Studies On Science and The Innovation Process: *Selected Works of Nathan Rosenberg.*

Murphy, L. M. & Edwards, P. L. 2003. Bridging the Valley of Death: Transitioning From Public to Private Sector Financing. Golden, CO: *National Renewable Energy Laboratory.* May.

Owen, E. H. 2004. Public Management and Administration: An Introduction. *Renmin University of China Press.*

Peng, S., Gu, X. & Wu, S. B. 2012. Structure, Formation and Operation of Technological Innovation Chain. *Scientific and Technological Progress and Countermeasures* 029(009), 4–7.

Rothwell, R. & Zegveld, W. 1981. Industrial Innovation and Public Policy: Preparing for the 1980s and the 1990s. *American Political Science Review* 76(3), 699.

Rodrik, D. 2008. One Economics, Many Recipes: Globalization, Institutions, and Economic Growth. *Princeton University Press.*

Shen, L., He, B., Jiao, L., Song, X. & Zhang, X. 2015. Research on the Development of Main Policy Instruments for Improving Building Energy-efficiency. *Journal of Cleaner Production.*

Woolthuis, R. K., Lankhuizen, M. & Gilsing, V. 2005. A System Failure Framework for Innovation Policy Design. *Technovation* 25(6), 609–619.

Wu, X. B. & Wu, D. 2008. On the Systematic Evolution of Innovation Chain and its Policy Implications. *Research on Dialectics of Nature* (12), 58–62.

Economic and Business Management – Lent & Zhang (Eds)

Analysis of Guangdong carbon emissions trading market: New evidence using quantile-on-quantile regression approach

Zhenting Gong & Yanbei Chen
Zhanjiang Preschool Education College, Zhanjiang, China

YungLieh Yang
Ling Tung University, Taiwan, China

ABSTRACT: The relationship between the China carbon trading market and stock markets remains unsettled in the previous literature. This article proposes two quantitative methods (the quantile regression and the quantile-on-quantile regression models) to quantify the impact among them by taking the carbon-emissions trading market of Guangdong Province as an empirical example. First, the quantile regression is applied to evaluate the impacts of the Shanghai and Shenzhen stock market and the European carbon trading futures market on the China carbon-trading market under different quantiles points, respectively. The result reveals that no matter what the European carbon trading futures market and Shanghai and Shenzhen stock markets under bearish conditions and bullish conditions market states, they always have a positive impact on the China carbon trading market. Second, taking into account extreme observations, the novel model quantile-on-quantile regression is used to provide more in-depth information on the impact's intricate characteristics. The findings indicate that the China carbon trading market is insensitive to the European carbon trading futures market across all their quantiles combination. However, the China carbon trading market is sensitive to the Shanghai and Shenzhen stock market changes, especially while the Shanghai and Shenzhen stock markets under bullish market condition positively affect the China carbon trading market in the upper quantiles. Furthermore, when the Shanghai and Shenzhen stock markets are in the bearish state and the China carbon trading market is recovering from the bearish state, the impact of the Shanghai and Shenzhen stock market will become slighter. Finally, this paper hopes to show that the investors should take the different quantiles condition of the markets into account when they adjust their investment plans and asset portfolios.

1 INTRODUCTION

As a developing country, China must establish a long-term carbon-constraint mechanism in accord with its current economic development and potentially huge energy use. Ever since the Kyoto Protocol, under the 2014 United Nations Framework Convention on Climate Change, China has explicitly stated its carbon-emission-reduction targets. China has promised that by 2030, carbon emissions per unit of GDP will fall by 60–65% compared with 2005 (Li et al. 2021). Aiming to mitigate the excessive carbon emissions issue, emissions trading systems (ETS) are adopted as effective market mechanisms, from which the carbon price is formed by the supply and demand of carbon emission allowances. The National Development and Reform Commission of China has embarked on one of the largest endeavors in climate economics ever, having established, since 2011, seven carbon-trading

DOI: 10.1201/9781003278788-9

pilots in Beijing, Tianjin, Shanghai, Chongqing, Guangdong, Hubei, and Shenzhen to explore the establishment of a carbon-trading mechanism.

Moreover, carbon emissions in trading schemes are characterized by the ability to be capped, priced, and traded. These allowances indicate a cost of emissions reduction and can be traded between companies, so they have a market value (Wen et al. 2020). Furthermore, the carbon price depends on marginal abatement costs and marginal revenues, especially when the latter is related to the forecasts of production growth, which is associated with economic activity. According to the previous study, there is a positive relationship between economic growth and energy needs. Additionally, the rise in energy needs will lead to higher carbon emissions, resulting in higher carbon prices. However, on the flip side, high carbon prices will cause an increase in enterprises' production costs, thereby suppressing economic growth. Due to the intricate relationship between carbon emissions and economic growth, the stock market seems to be a suitable indicator because stock prices are sensitive to the performance of both the economy and enterprise (Jiang et al. 2022). Although study related to the topic of the relationship between the carbon trading market and the stock markets is increasing, studies related to China's carbon trading market are few, let alone any that apply non-linear models of quantile regression (QR) and the novel quantile-on-quantile regression (QQ) to explore the relationship between stock markets and China's carbon trading market.

Following the introduction, this article will organize as follows: The second section conducts a review of relevant studies. The description of data applied in the study and the quantitative methodology, namely, the quantile-on-quantile regression model are placed in the third section. The fourth section provides a series of tests, especially the quantile-on-quantile regression (QQ) estimates, and analyzes the results of them in detail. The last section will propose corresponding conclusions based on the analysis above. We hope that the findings of this paper will be of interest to policymakers and stakeholders.

2 LITERATURE REVIEW

Traditional econometric methods are incapable of resolving the relationship's complexity and may conceal some intriguing traits. Instead, quantile-on-quantile regression approach researchers might present the nonlinear relationship in an ad hoc manner (Han et al. 2019).

In the context of a deteriorating environment, domestic and foreign scholars are increasingly researching carbon-emission issues from three main aspects. First, some focus on renewable energy. Applying the quantile-regression model, Zheng et al. (2021) measure the impact of renewable energy generation in China on its carbon emissions to determine how promoting the usage of renewable energy might assist China to reduce its carbon emissions. Yu et al. (2020) propose a panel quantile-regression model to assess whether China's renewable energy development has effectively contributed to a decrease in carbon emissions. Khan et al. (2020) applied panel quantile-regression to examine the heterogeneity of renewable-energy consumption, carbon dioxide emission, and financial development in 192 countries. They pointed out that the impact of renewable energy consumption on carbon emission is negative, while financial development has an increasing influence on carbon emission. Second, some research focuses on the issue of the relationship between China's carbon-emissions trading and stock markets. Wen et al. (2020) chose the Shenzhen pilot as an example and applied the difference-in-differences (DID) method to analyze quantitatively the impact of carbon emissions regulation on the stock returns of companies; in their findings, the coefficient of carbon risk factor is significantly positive and can be explained by the fact that companies participating in the carbon market have higher carbon exposures. Jiang et al. (2022) examined the nonlinear dependence between the carbon market and the stock market in China under normal and extreme market conditions by employing two novel nonlinear approaches. Ren et al. (2022) use the quantile Granger causality test and the quantile-on-quantile regression techniques to determine the influence of crude oil price on carbon pricing throughout the carbon-oil distribution. Third, some people concentrate on the causes of carbon emissions. Dong et al. (2018) employed structural decomposition analysis (SDA) and quantile regression to investigate the factors that drive changes in CEI in China. Xu and Lin (2020) used the quantile regression model to investigate drivers of CO2 emission in China's heavy industry. The empirical results of their study show that the influence of economic growth exerted on the heavy industry's CO2 emissions is quite various in different quantiles.

In short, based on the aforementioned discussion, literature on carbon issues is relatively abundant. Furthermore, one can easily see that the QR method is popular in their studies. However, studies that apply the QQ approach to analyze carbon issues are still scarce. Aiming to enrich the previous literature, this paper uses the comprehensive QQ approach to analyze the relationship between the China carbon trading market and stock markets.

3 DATA AND METHODOLOGY

3.1 *Data source*

The article takes the carbon trading price represented by the closing price in Guangdong province as an explained variable, while the foreign carbon trading price and the China stock market index as explanatory variables. The variables mentioned above are daily data, from August 6, 2018, to December 14, 2021. Their definitions are provided in Table 1.

Table 1. Variables' definition.

Variable	Symbol	Definition	Source
Carbon trading price	GDEA	Guangdong carbon trading market's closing price and logarithmic	Wind
Foreign carbon trading price	EUA	European carbon trading futures market's closing price and logarithmic	
Stock market index	CSI300	Shanghai and Shenzhen stock markets index and logarithmic	Investing.com

3.2 *Methodology*

Due to the complicated relationship between the carbon trading market and the stock markets, in this paper, the quantile-on-quantile methodology (QQ) is used to determine the influence that various quantiles of the foreign carbon-trading price (EUA) and the China stock market index (CSI300), respectively, have on the different quantiles of the Guangdong carbon-trading market (GDEA). Due to the complex relationship between the carbon trading market and the stock markets, here we propose the quantile-on-quantile method to estimate the effect of different quantiles of foreign carbon-trading price (EUA) and the China stock market index (CSI300) on different quantiles of the Guangdong carbon trading market (GDEA).

The conventional method of quantile regression is only able to determine the influence that the X variable has on the different quantiles of the Y variable but cannot reveal the intricate characteristics of the impact that account for extreme data (Han, Liu, and Yin, 2019). The QQ approach is modified on conventional quantile regression (Adebayo et al. 2021) and is capable of capturing the dependency between the ranges of the Y variable's distribution and the X variable's distribution, as well as revealing two subtle aspects in the Y-X connection (Sim & Zhou 2015). In short, the QQ approach could provide a lens for the complicated relationship in the Y–X relationship. In the context of this study, The following equation may be used as a starting point for the QQ model:

$$E_t = \beta^\theta(X_t) + u_t^\theta \tag{1}$$

where E_t is defined as the GDEA, X_t represents the independent variables, here referring to EUA and CSI300, the θth quantile of the conditional distribution of the X_t is denoted by the symbol θ, and u_t^θ is shorthand for an error term that has an θ-quantile of zero. The relationship between X_t and E_t is unknown, as no preceding information exists, the function $\beta^\theta(X_t)$ is allowed to be unknown. Equation (1) is then assessed in the neighborhood of X^τ applying local linear regression to analyze the relationship between the θth quantile of E_t and the τth quantile of X_t, which is symbolized by the symbol X^τ. Given that $\beta^\theta(X_t)$ is a parameter whose value is not known, it is possible to linearize this function by performing a Taylor expansion of the first order around the quantile X^τ:

$$\beta^\theta(X_t) = \beta^\theta(X^\tau) + \beta^{\theta'}(X^\tau)(X_t - X^\tau) \tag{2}$$

In Eq. (2), $\beta^{\theta'}$ represents the partial derivative of $\beta^\theta(X_t)$ with respect to X_t. This concept is also known as the marginal effect, meanwhile, it is similar in interpretation to the slope coefficient in a linear regression model. A prominent feature of Eq. (2) is that the parameters $\beta^\theta(X^\tau)$ and $\beta^{\theta'}(X^\tau)$ are doubly indexed in θ and τ. Given that $\beta^\theta(X^\tau)$ and $\beta^{\theta'}(X^\tau)$ are functions of θ and X_t while the X_t is a function of τ, which means $\beta^\theta(X^\tau)$ and $\beta^{\theta'}(X^\tau)$ are both functions of θ and τ. Therefore, by re-denoting $\beta^\theta(X^\tau)$ and $\beta^{\theta'}(X^\tau)$ as $\beta_0(\theta, \tau)$ and $\beta_1(\theta, \tau)$, respectively, Eq. (2) could be rewritten as follow:

$$\beta^\theta(X_t) \approx \beta_0(\theta, \tau) + \beta_1(\theta, \tau)(X_t - X^\tau) \tag{3}$$

By substituting Eq. (3) in Eq. (1), we can obtain the following equation:

$$E_t = \beta_0(\theta, \tau) + \beta_1(\theta, \tau)(X_t - X^\tau) + u_t^\theta \tag{4}$$

Notice that the independent variable X here refers to EUA and CSI300; thus the notations X in Eq. (4) should be distinguished as follow.

$$E_t = \beta_0(\theta, \tau) + \beta_1(\theta, \tau)(EUA_t - EUA^\tau) + u_t^\theta$$
$$E_t = \beta_0(\theta, \tau) + \beta_1(\theta, \tau)(CSI300_t - CSI300^\tau) + u_t^\theta \tag{5}$$

4 EMPIRICAL ANALYSIS

Table 2 provides statistical descriptions of the variables in this work. The median and mean numerical values of the GDEA and EUA are close to 3, although the CSI300 is somewhat

Table 2. Summary statistics.

	GDEA	EUA	CSI300
Mean	3.305	3.394	8.345
Median	3.325	3.260	8.309
Max	3.964	4.487	8.667
Min	2.485	2.724	7.995
Std. dev.	0.303	0.389	0.168
Skewness	−0.256	0.860	−0.179
Kurtosis	2.617	2.639	1.856
Obs	758	758	758

higher. When it comes to skewness and kurtosis index, the former determines the degree to which the distribution is asymmetric, whereas the latter determines how steep it is. Their numerical value is about 0 and 2, respectively.

4.1 Pre-tests

Before conducting more analysis, it is necessary to confirm if the series possesses the necessary properties. This study used Fuller's (1979) ADF test to evaluate if the variables were stationary. All series are nonstationary at level, although their first-order differences are substantially stationary, as shown in Table 3.

Table 3. Summary statistics.

Variable	GDEA	EUA	CSI300
Level			
ADF t-Statistic	−1.019	−0.113	−1.336
First difference			
ADF t-Statistic	−34.039***	−28.599***	−27.195***

Note: * $p < 0.1$, **$p < 0.05$, *** $p < 0.01$.

Nelson and Plosser (1982) argue that many economic variables are not stationary and that treating the data purely by differencing to a stationary series would deprive the data of important information embedded in their economic theory, but if the original unstable series could be tested for cointegration, rather than being treated by differencing to a stationary series, it would have the advantage of avoiding the loss of economic significance while considering the underlying conditions of the regression. Thus, before statistical analysis, the Johansen cointegration test was used to test the presence of cointegration between series and the results presented in Table 4. It indicates that the series is in long-run equilibrium, so the subsequent statistical analysis will be conducted using the original order data.

Table 4. Johansen cointegration test.

		Johansen MLE estimates (GDEA ~ EUA)			
NULL:		Trace Statistic	Crit 90%	Crit 95%	Crit 99%
r <= 0	GDEA	17.573	16.162	18.398	23.148
r <= 1	EUA	3.572	2.705	3.841	6.635
		Johansen MLE estimates (GDEA ~ CSI300)			
NULL:		Trace Statistic	Crit 90%	Crit 95%	Crit 99%
r <= 0	GDEA	16.668	16.162	18.398	23.148
r <= 1	CSI300	6.052	2.705	3.841	6.635

4.2 The result of Quantiles regression approach

Empirical analysis is conducted using the 5th, 10th, 25th, 50th, 75th, 90th, and 95th quantiles, which are indicative of the majority of extant research. Because the quantile regression applies several different quantile functions to estimate the model, it offers a lens through which we can investigate the impact that informative factors have on the variables that they

Table 5. Empirical results of QR.

| Variables | OLS | Quantiles levels | | | | | | |
		Q0.05	Q0.1	Q0.25	Q0.5	Q0.75	Q0.9	Q0.95
EUA	0.65***	0.85***	0.81***	0.77***	0.62***	0.51***	0.41***	0.39***
CSI300	1.53***	1.55***	1.36***	1.22***	1.61***	1.74***	1.82***	1.77***

Note: *p < 0.1, **p < 0.05, ***p < 0.01

are supposed to explain at a variety of quantile points (Xu & Lin 2020). Table 5 summarizes the findings of QR and OLS. All two models' results had p-values less than 0.01. Both the EUA and CSI300 positively impact GDEA, according to the estimations results of QR; the former becomes weakened across quantiles, while the greatest positive coefficient value of the latter comes at the 90th quantile.

In addition, Figure 1 provides a visual representation of the findings of quantile regression. The estimation of the QR is represented by the black line, and the 95% confidence interval is depicted by the gray region in the figure. Along the vertical axis, there are the calculated coefficients of variables. Quantile values are depicted along the horizontal axis. The parallel continuous red line is the OLS estimate, whereas the dashed red line represents the 95% confidence interval. In addition, Figure 2 displays the quantile regression (fit) findings at various quantile levels. The continuous blue line shows the OLS linear, whereas the dashed lines show quantiles from the lowest to the highest quantiles.

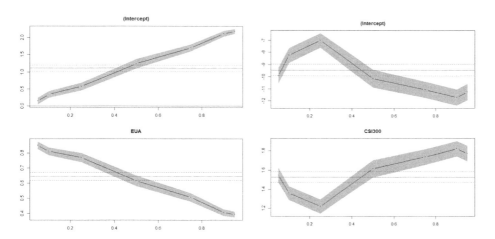

Figure 1. Quantile regression coefficients with 95% confidence intervals.

4.3 The result of Quantile-on-Quantile regression approach

Figure 3 depicts a graphical representation of the QQ results. The figure depicts the slope estimates $\hat{\beta}_1(\theta, \tau)$, which captures the impact of the τth quantile of EUA (CSI300) on θth quantile of GDEA for a variety of possible combinations.

The z-axis displays the slope coefficients, while the x and y-axes display the quantiles of EUA (CSI300) and GDEA, respectively. The one on the left is the impact of EUA on GDEA, while the one on the right is CSI300 on GDEA.

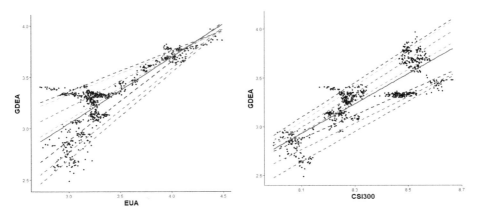

Figure 2.   Quantile regression fit findings at various quantile points.

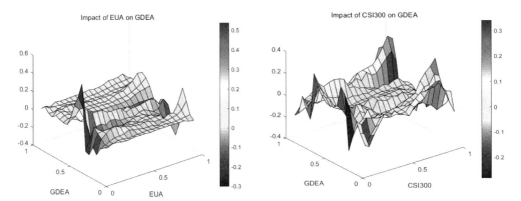

Figure 3.   The estimates of QQR.

In all quantiles (0.01–0.95) of the combination of EUA and GDEA, most of the effect of EUA on GDEA is positive, and it produces a flat-looking figure; more specifically, the obtained slope coefficients take positive and similar values for the majority of quantiles. The influence is especially more strong in the middle tail (0.5–0.75) of GDEA and the lower quantiles of EUA (0.05–0.25), and its sign turns from positive to negative between the lower quantiles of EUA (0.1–0.25) and the lower quantiles of GDEA (0.25–0.5). As for the combination of CSI300 and GDEA, the figure is quite different where the GDEA is sensitive to CSI300's changes. The slope estimates are at the highest between the upper quantiles (0.9–0.95) of GDEA and the upper quantiles of CSI300 (0.9–0.95), which indicates that the CSI300 under bullish market conditions positively affects the GDEA while it is in the upper quantiles. A similar impact can also be seen between the upper quantiles of CSI300 (0.9–0.95) and the lower quantiles of GDEA (0.25–0.5). The estimated slope coefficient falls drastically in the area that combines the lower quantiles of CSI300 (0.1–0.25) and the median quantiles of GDEA (0.25–0.5).

4.4   *The result of robustness check*

Comparing the results of QQ estimates with those of QR reveals that the findings of QQ estimates are roughly compatible with those of QR.

The QQ method regresses the θth quantile of the EUA (CSI300) against the τth quantile of GDEA; hence, its parameters may be described by θ and τ. Because the QR parameters can only be described by θ, the QQ method may be referred to as the "decomposition" of the QR estimates (Sim & Zhou 2015). Based on this approach, approximate QR estimates should be derived from QQ estimates. The effect of EUA (CSI300) on GDEA may be expressed by noting the slope coefficient of QR as $\gamma_1(\theta)$.

$$\gamma_1(\theta) \equiv \widehat{\bar{\beta}}_1(\theta) = \frac{1}{S} \sum \widehat{\beta}_1(\theta, \tau) \qquad (6)$$

where S = 19 is the number of quantiles θ = [0.05, 0.10, ... , 0.95].

As shown in Figure 4, the parameters that were figured out for the QR model are shown in this figure in the form of black lines. The average QR estimations may be found across all GDEA quantiles and are denoted by the red dashed lines. The one on the left is the estimate of EUA on GDEA, whereas the one on the right is CSI300 on GDEA.

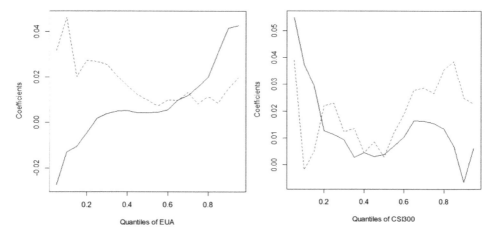

Figure 4.   Analyzing the Differences Between QQ and QR.

5   CONCLUSIONS

China has made a great effort in low-carbon development since 2011, as the conception of decreasing carbon emissions has become a core issue of human concern. The adoption of steps to decrease carbon emissions, especially in China, the world's biggest energy user and carbon emitter, will unquestionably affect carbon-reducing around the globe. The goal of this study is to collect fresh data using the innovative quantile-on-quantile regression approach to examine the influence of the stock market and the overseas carbon-trading market on the Guangdong carbon-trading market. The empirical analysis yielded the following set of results:

The QR approach estimation result shows that both the EUA and CSI300 have a positive impact on GDEA; in other words, no matter what the EUA and CSI300 market under bearish or bullish market conditions, they always have a positive impact on China carbon trading market. The influence of EUA on GDEA becomes weakened across quantiles, while the CSI300 acquires its greatest positive effect on GDEA at the 90th quantile. Furthermore, the latter indicates that when the Shanghai and Shenzhen stock markets are in bullish condition, the positive influence on China's carbon trading will become stronger than the others. As for the QQ approach estimation result, although most of the effect of EUA on GDEA appears to be positive across quantiles, it does provide more detailed information compared to the QR result, showing a flat-looking figure. The result indicates that China's carbon trading market is insensitive to the European carbon trading futures market across all the quantiles combination of them. On the contrary, the findings show that the GDEA is sensitive to CSI300 changes, while the CSI300 under bullish market conditions positively affects the GDEA while it is in the upper quantiles. Moreover, when it comes to the area between the lower quantiles of CSI300 (0.1–0.25) and the median quantiles of GDEA (0.25–0.5), the estimated slope coefficient falls drastically. It can be interpreted as when the Shanghai and Shenzhen stock markets are in a bearish condition and the China carbon trading market recovers from a bearish condition, the impact coming from the CSI will become slighter.

For whoever may be concerned, the investors can refer to the conclusion this paper sets out. When they adjust their investment portfolio or manage risk hedging, we hope that the estimation result and the impact of EUA and CSI300 on GDEA under different quantile conditions could provide some useful information.

ACKNOWLEDGMENT

This research is supported by Zhanjiang Philosophy and Social Science Planning Youth Project 2022 granted: ZJ22QN02.

REFERENCES

Adebayo, T.S. *et al.* 2021. The Asymmetric Effects of Renewable Energy Consumption and Trade Openness on Carbon Emissions in Sweden: New Evidence From Quantile-On-Quantile Regression Approach, *Environmental Science and Pollution Research* 1–12.

Dong, F. *et al.* 2018. Drivers of Carbon Emission Intensity Change in China, *Resources, Conservation and Recycling* 129: 187–201. doi:10.1016/j.resconrec.2017.10.035.

Fuller, D.W.A. (1979) 'Distribution of the Estimators for Autoregressive Time Series With a Unit Root', *Journal of the American Statal Association* 79(366): 355–367.

Han, L., Liu, Y. and Yin, L. 2019. Uncertainty and Currency Performance: A Quantile-on-Quantile Approach, *The North American Journal of Economics and Finance* 48: 702–729. doi:10.1016/j.najef.2018.08.006.

Jiang, Y., Liu, L. and Mu, J. 2022. Nonlinear Dependence Between China's Carbon Market and Stock Market: New Evidence From Quantile Coherency and Causality-in-Quantiles, *Environmental Science and Pollution Research [Preprint]*. doi:10.1007/s11356-022-19179-x.

Khan, H., Khan, I. and Binh, T.T. 2020. The Heterogeneity of Renewable Energy Consumption, Carbon Emission and Financial Development in the Globe: A Panel Quantile Regression Approach, *Energy Reports* 6: 859–867. doi:10.1016/j.egyr.2020.04.002.

Li, Y. *et al.* 2021. Energy Structure, Digital Economy, and Carbon Emissions: Evidence From China, *Environmental Science and Pollution Research* 28(45): 64606–64629. doi:10.1007/s11356-021-15304-4.

Ren, X. *et al.* 2022. Information Spillover and Market Connectedness: Multi-Scale Quantile-on-Quantile Analysis of the Crude Oil and Carbon Markets, *Applied Economics* 1–21. doi:10.1080/00036846.2022.2030855.

Sim, N. and Zhou, H. 2015. Oil Prices, us Stock Return, and the Dependence Between Their Quantiles, *Journal of Banking & Finance* 55: 1–8. doi:10.1016/j.jbankfin.2015.01.013.

Su, X. *et al.* 2019. Quantile Regression Analysis of Guangdong Carbon Trading Market, *Reports on Economics and Finance* 5(1): 81–87. doi:10.12988/ref.2019.944.

Wen, F., Wu, N. and Gong, X. 2020. China's Carbon Emissions Trading and Stock Returns, *Energy Economics* 86: 104627. doi:10.1016/j.eneco.2019.104627.

Xu, B. and Lin, B. 2020. Investigating Drivers of CO2 Emission in China's Heavy Industry: A Quantile Regression Analysis, *Energy* 206: 118159. doi:10.1016/j.energy.2020.118159.

Yu, S. *et al.* 2020. Does the Development of Renewable Energy Promote Carbon Reduction? Evidence From Chinese Provinces, *Journal of Environmental Management* 268: 110634. doi:10.1016/j.jenvman.2020.110634.

Zheng, H., Song, M. and Shen, Z. 2021. The Evolution of Renewable Energy and its Impact on Carbon Reduction in China, *Energy* 237: 121639. doi:10.1016/j.energy.2021.121639.

The impact of trade facilitation on China's cross-border e-commerce exports

Hehua Li & Lu Liu

School of Economics and Management, Shanghai Polytechnic University, Shanghai, China

ABSTRACT: From the standpoint of trade facilitation, this paper investigates its impact on China's cross-border e-commerce exports. First, five primary indexes and fifteen secondary indexes are selected to construct the trade facilitation index system. The Delphi method and AHP are used to calculate index weight, and the trade facilitation level of each country is calculated from 2013 to 2019. It is discovered that there are obviously varies in all nation's level of trade facilitation. The highest trade facilitation index is Singapore, which is as high as 0.958790, and the lowest is the Philippines, which is as low as 0.485289. Then, the trade facilitation index is introduced into the extended gravity model as the core explanatory variable, and the panel data is regressed with fixed effects using Stata16.0. According with findings, trade facilitation is significantly more important to China's cross-border e-commerce exports than economic size, total population, distance, or the signing of free trade agreements. For every 1% increase in trade facilitation, China's cross-border e-commerce exports will raise by 1.803%. Finally, comprehensive recommendations are proposed based on the research results.

1 INTRODUCTION

In recent years, affected by the situation in Russia and Ukraine, the new crown epidemic and international trade deterioration, the growth of global trade in 2022 is expected to drop from 4.7% in October last year to 2.4%–3%. Under this context, it is particularly important to study trade facilitation level in various countries and how to fully utilize trade facilitation for the development of China's cross-border e-commerce, making way for China to further deepen the trade facilitation mechanism and promote cross-border trade development.

2 LITERATURE REVIEW

In terms of research on trade facilitation, YAN Qiumei (2010) analyzed the current situation and problems of global facilitation, and believed that it was of great significance to improve China's trade competitiveness. By analyzing the connotation of trade facilitation, ZHANG Zengfu (2021) selected four indexes of cross-border logistics, regulatory environment, cross-border payment and cross-border customs clearance as the evaluation indexes of trade facilitation; FU Shuyi (2021) selected four indexes of Internet surroundings, customs surroundings, infrastructure and regulatory surroundings as the evaluation indexes of trade facilitation;

In terms of research on cross-border e-commerce, according to Shu Jie (2021), factors affecting cross-border e-commerce export volume include a country's GDP, the distance between the two countries, and total population. Zhang Jianglin (2012) believes that credit problems, delays in customs clearance, and lag in cross-border logistics in cross-border

DOI: 10.1201/9781003278788-10

payments are all obstacles to the development of cross-border e-commerce. Ma Shuzhong (2019) used the gravity model to demonstrate how the Internet can boost cross-border e-commerce exports.

In terms of research on the relationship between trade facilitation and cross-border e-commerce, Chen Ruohong (2017) took the "Belt and Road" countries as a research perspective, believing that the problem of trade inconvenience was the reason for the further development of cross-border e-commerce. Wang Junjuan (2021) discovered that China's cross-border e-commerce has a trade facilitation result, with the export effect being stronger than the import effect.

Based on the research results of the above scholars, it can be seen that: First, there are minor differences in the choice and computation of trade facilitation indexes; Second, trade facilitation policies and measures can have a beneficial effect on cross-border e-commerce. Since there is currently no unified standard system for quantifying the level of trade facilitation, it is necessary for us to establish a trade facilitation evaluation system and carryout level measurement to study its specific impact on cross-border e-commerce trade. Third, there have been few research into the relationship between the two. To some extent, such the article adds to the existing research on the impact of trade facilitation on cross-border e-commerce exported.

3 INNOVATIONS

First, this paper selects the data from 2008 to 2019, and uses the latest data for the data selection of trade facilitation indexes, which can obtain the latest research results. Furthermore, given the preceding context, how to improve trade facilitation level in later stages to foster the development of China's cross-border e-commerce, restore production, and strengthen livelihoods is of critical practical importance.

Second, in research method, the above article adopts different research approach, including qualitative, quantitative, and empirical analysis, resulting in research that is both theoretical and practical in nature. In the measurement of trade facilitation level, this article utilizes Wilson's research findings to assess a country's trade facilitation level across five dimensions: infrastructure, customs environment, institutional environment, e-commerce, and financial services.

Third, in the empirical analysis on the handling of panel data geographic location and economic scale, this article utilizes oil prices multiplied by geographic distance to represent DIS_{ij} and $GDP_i * GDP_j$ to represent the economic scale of the 2 nations, making the empirical model selection and results more reliable.

4 CALCULATION AND ANALYSIS OF FACILITATION DEVELOPMENT LEVEL

4.1 *Construction of trade facilitation index system*

Wilson (2003) is cited within that article to select 5 indexes as primary indexes of trade facilitation and the corresponding 15 secondary indexes. Among them, Infrastructure includes four secondary indexes: aviation infrastructure, road infrastructure, port efficiency, and railway infrastructure; The customs environment includes three secondary indexes: the buyer's complexity, the trade tariff and the prevalence of NTBs; The legal and institutional environment includes three secondary indexes: judicial independence, efficiency of legal framework in resolving disputes, and burden of government regulation; E-commerce includes three secondary indexes: The amount of mobile phone subscribers per 100 individual, fixed broadband subscribers per 100 individual, and Internet subscribers per 100 individual; Finance includes two secondary indexes: venture capital availability and soundness of the bank. Among them, the secondary indexes of e-commerce have marks ranging from 1 to 100, while the other secondary indexes have marks ranging from 1 to 7.

4.2 Determining trade facilitation index weights

This article uses Delphi to get expert opinions and integrates them, and AHP is used to establish a hierarchical model, input data and calculate the weights of indexes at all levels, which have passed the consistency test. The results are shown in Table 1.

Table 1. Weights of the trade facilitation system.

	Primary index (weight)	Secondary index (weight)
Trade Facilitation Development Level Measurement (TFI)	Infrastructure (0.3537)	Port efficiency (0.0984) Aviation infrastructure (0.1398) Railway infrastructures (0.0578) Road infrastructure (0.0578)
	Customs environment (0.2056)	Trade tariff (0.0822) Prevalence of NTBs (0.0822) Buyer's Complexity (0.0411)
	Regulatory and institutional environment (0.1942)	Judicial independence (0.0505) Efficiency of legal framework in resolving disputes (0.0801) Burden of government regulation (0.0636)
	E-commerce (0.1402)	Mobile phone subscribers per 100 individual (0.0578) Fixed broadband subscribers per 100 individual (0.0364) Internet subscribers per 100 individual (0.0459)
	Finance (0.1063)	Venture Capital Availability (0.0709) Soundness of the bank (0.0354)

4.3 Data processing of trade facilitation indexes

We discovered that the mark ranges of the secondary indexes differ, and there is no quantitative comparison. Therefore, this paper uses formula (1) to standardize the secondary indexes.

$$Y_{ij} = \frac{X_{ij}}{X_{\max}} \quad (0 < Y < 1) \tag{1}$$

Among them, Y_{ij} denotes new value obtained after normalization, X_{ij} denotes original value before processing, and $X_{\max}$ denotes largest original value. Then, the evaluation index of trade facilitation is calculated by formula (2).

$$TFI = \sum_{i=1,2,3,4}^{j=1,2,3,4} W_{ij} Y_{ij}. \tag{2}$$

Among them, TFI denotes evaluation index of trade facilitation, and W_{ij} denotes weight of every secondary index ($i = 1,2,3,4,5; j = 1,2,3,4$).

4.4 Calculation and analysis of trade facilitation levels

Trade facilitation level can be calculated using the above analysis, and the results are shown in Table 2. By sorting out nations that have signed free trade agreements with China and the main trade exporting countries, the research objects of this paper are finally determined as: South Korea, ten ASEAN countries, Japan, Australia and New Zealand. However, while compiling the data, it was discovered that the indexes for 2020 had not updated, and the indexes data for Myanmar and Brunei were missing. Therefore, this article will select 12 countries except Myanmar and Brunei for analysis from 2013 to 2019.

It can be seen from Table 2 that Singapore, Japan and New Zealand are among the countries with high level of trade facilitation. Nations like Laos and Cambodia rank near the bottom of the trade facilitation index, stifling ASEAN trade development. The consequence trade facilitation index results are used in the empirical analysis in the next section.

Table 2. 2013–2019 Trade facilitation index results.

Country	2013	2014	2015	2016	2017	2018	2019
Singapore	0.874686	0.872358	0.857586	0.878574	0.879048	0.958790	0.881183
Japan	0.773705	0.783691	0.765220	0.786685	0.787510	0.875062	0.831443
New Zealand	0.789270	0.790582	0.749808	0.765819	0.772439	0.842261	0.773091
South Korea	0.763538	0.728850	0.722430	0.751762	0.766525	0.786715	0.810044
Australia	0.744499	0.720359	0.707981	0.716528	0.730538	0.804052	0.717580
Malaysia	0.720125	0.765463	0.766675	0.765762	0.766150	0.805992	0.791769
Indonesia	0.584719	0.582254	0.608029	0.582081	0.628382	0.685510	0.662564
Thailand	0.620503	0.619728	0.643311	0.516092	0.667493	0.684058	0.684928
Vietnam	0.547405	0.529963	0.561738	0.572330	0.565925	0.590536	0.645375
the Philippines	0.509021	0.525376	0.532777	0.485289	0.486447	0.592185	0.576226
Laos	0.569673	0.538371	0.528581	0.527023	0.531581	0.548948	0.567842
Cambodia	0.555504	0.518361	0.512029	0.537656	0.536992	0.543205	0.603241

5 EMPIRICAL ANALYSIS

5.1 Setting of gravity model and data source

Tinbergen introduced the gravity model initially, believing that trade flow between 2 nations is positively associated with economic scale and negatively associated with distance between 2 nations. Subsequently, scholars at home and abroad continued to expand the model, added population as a variable, which provided a new ideas for international trade and was widely used. The basic formula of the gravitational model is shown in formula (3):

$$M_{ij} = \beta_0 GDP_i GDP_j DIS_{ij} A_{ij}, \quad M_{ij} \tag{3}$$

Among them, M_{ij} denotes the trade volume between the 2 nations, GDP_i denotes the GDP of nation i, GDP_j denotes the GDP of nation j, DIS_{ij} denotes the distance between the 2 nations, and A_{ij} stands for other variables that affect trade flows.

Draws on research results of scholars, this paper employs the lengthened gravity model. In model, China's cross-border e-commerce exports to country j is used as explained variables, and explanatory variables are whether or not to sign a free trade agreement, development level of trade facilitation, distance, GDP and population. Variables logarithm is used to reduce heteroscedasticity, and the regression model of empirical analysis is obtained as formula (4)

$$\ln EX_j = \beta_1 + \beta_2 \ln TFI_j + \beta_3 DIS_{ij} + \beta_4 \ln P_j + \beta_5 \ln GDP_i * GDP_j + \beta_6 FTA_j + \varepsilon_{ij} \quad (4)$$

The expected symbols, descriptions and data sources of the variables are shown in Table 3.

Table 3. Anticipated signs, descriptions and data sources for variables.

Variables	Anticipated Sign	Data Sources	Descriptions
EX_j	/	UNCTAD database	China's cross-border e-commerce exports to nation j
TFI_j (core)	+	Calculated above	development level of trade facilitation in nation j
DIS_{ij}	−	CEPII database, U.S. Energy Information Administration	The distance between the capitals of the two countries multiplied by the price of Brent crude oil for that year
P_j	+	World Bank Database	The total population of nation j
$GDP_i * GDP_j$	+	World Bank	two nations' economic scale
FTA_j	+	China Free Trade Zone Service Network	whether or not to sign a free trade agreement with nation j, the value of signing is 1, otherwise it is 0
ε_{ij}	/	/	random error distractor

5.2 Outcome of practice

5.2.1 Data verification

This article utilizes ADF to determine whether the sequence is stationary. The results show that $\ln EX_j, \ln TFI_j, \ln GDP_i * GDP_j, DIS_{ij}, \ln P_j$ are all stationary series, so regression analysis can be carried out. In addition, to prevent variables heteroscedasticity from affecting the experimental results, the WALD test is done to evaluate whether there's any heteroscedasticity. The findings demonstrate that $P = 0.0000$, indicating heteroscedasticity. At this time, the classic Hausman test is no longer applicable, and a robust Hausman test is required.

5.2.2 Model selection

Before regression, a particular model must be chosen. F and LM tests were used to exclude the mixed-effects model within article, and the robust Hausmann test was used to select the fixed-effects model or the random-effects model. The results are shown in Table 4.

Through the above test, it can be seen that $P = 0.0000 < 0.005$, the null hypothesis is rejected, so the fixed model is used for regression analysis.

Table 4. Robust hausman test results.

Variable	Chi2	P value	Result
$\ln EX_j$	40.580	0.0000	fixed effects model

5.2.3 Regression results

Given the previous analysis, this paper employs Stata16.0 software to perform regression of the fixed effect model, with the results shown in Table 5.

Table 5. Regression results.

Variable	Ln EX
Ln TFI	1.803***
	(3.51)
Ln GDP	0.554***
	(8.34)
dis	−0.000***
	(−4.61)
Ln P	0.403***
	(3.75)
FTA	0.813***
	(8.49)
Constant	−7.582***
	(−6.62)
R-squared	0.994

Note: ***, **, * represent passing the significance test at the levels of 0.01, 0.05 and 0.1, respectively.

Table 5 demonstrates that R^2 is 0.994, indicating that the above variables can well explain the impact on cross-border e-commerce exports. Therefore, the regression equation of the model is:

$$\ln EX_j = -7.582 + 1.803 \ln TFI_j + 0.403 \ln P_j + 0.554 \ln GDP_i * GDP_j + 0.813 \, FTA_j \quad (5)$$

From the regression results, it can be seen that:

1) The TFI_j coefficient is 1.803, illustrating that the exporting country's TFI and the export volume of China's cross-border e-commerce play a promoting role, which is consistent with the analysis conducted prior to the empirical study. When all other factors remain constant, ever other 1% increase in a trading partner's trade facilitation level increases China's cross-border e-commerce exports to that country by 1.803%. Compared with other factors, its coefficient is the largest, indicating that the trade facilitation level has greatest impact on it.

2) The $GDP_i * GDP_j$ coefficient is 0.554, illustrating that the two nations' economic scales have a stimulatory effect on China's cross-border e-commerce exports, which is in line with the theoretical analysis before the empirical study. When all other factors remain constant, China's cross-border e-commerce exports to the country will increase by 0.554% for every 1% rise in the two nations' economic scale.

3) The DIS_{ij} coefficient is 0, which contradicts the analysis prior to the empirical evidence, indicating that the distance between the two countries is just no longer an impediment to cross-border e-commerce export.

4) The P_j coefficient is 0.403, which is consistent with the analysis conducted prior to the empirical study. When all other factors remain constant, the value of cross-border e-commerce will rise by 0.403% for each 1% increment population. Population growth leads to an increase in online consumers, which boosts China's cross-border e-commerce exports.

5) The TFA coefficient is 0.813, which is consistent with the analysis conducted prior to the empirical evidence. China's cross-border e-commerce exports rise by 0.813% per each 1% rise in FTA.

6 CONCLUSIONS AND SUGGESTIONS

First, Trade facilitation level varies dramatically between nations. Countries such as Singapore and South Korea have relatively high level of trade facilitation. Countries such as Laos and Cambodia have relatively low levels of trade facilitation, and their index ranks at the bottom, seriously hindering the development of ASEAN's international trade. This demonstrates that China should prioritize emerging markets. Developed countries such as Singapore and Japan have a relatively high degree of trade facilitation, with mature markets and less room for expansion. Cross-border e-commerce companies can adjust their strategies in a timely manner and set their sights on emerging markets with low trade facilitation such as Laos and Cambodia with huge development potential.

Second, when comparison to other factors, the coefficient of trade facilitation level is the highest, meaning that it is necessary to actively promote the improvement of this indicator in order to promote the increase of cross-border e-commerce exports. Similar to old-fashioned international trade, economic scale of the 2 nations in trade is positively associated with China's cross-border e-commerce exports; but unlike old-fashioned international trade, the distance between the 2 nations is no elongated an impediment to China's cross-border e-commerce exports; Free trade agreements signed with China and the larger the population, the better it will be for Chinese cross-border e-commerce exports.

Third, China should enhance trade facilitation levels at the current stage in light of China's current development status. The infrastructure for cross-border trade should be improved to create a better environment for port trade. By improving customs management level, a fast and efficient customs clearance atmosphere should be created. System construction should be strengthened to build a fairer and more transparent trade system.

REFERENCES

Chen Ruohong. 2017. Promote the Development of Cross-Border Ecommerce with Agreementon Trade Facilitation - From the Perspective of the Belt and Road Initiative Partner Countries[J]. *Area Studies and Global Development* 1(01): 37–48+155.

Fu Shuyi. 2021. Research on the Impact of Trade Facilitation on China's Cross-border E-commerce Export [D]. *Jiang xi University of Finance Economics* 2021.000143.

Ma Shuzhong, Fang Chao, Zhang Hongsheng. 2019. Can Cross-border E-commerce Declare the Death of Distance[J]. *Finance & Trade Economics* 40(08): 116–131.

Shu Jie. 2021. An Empirical Study on the Effects of Trade Facilitation on China's Cross-border E-commerce Export[D]. *University of International Business and Economics*, DOI: 10.27015/d.cnki.gdwju.2021.000010.

Wang Junjuan. 2021. The Trade Facilitation Effect of China's Cross-Border E-Commerce Development - Based on the Empirical Analysis of Countries Along the "Belt and Road"[J]. *Journal of Commercial Economics* 2021(02): 70–73.

Wilson, John S., Mann, Catherine L., Otsuki, Tsunehiro. 2003. Trade Facilitation and Economic Development[J]. *World Bank Economic Review* 17(3).

Yan Qiumei. 2010. The Development Status of International Trade Facilitation and China's Counter-measures[J]. *Commercial Times* 2010(33): 42–43.

Zhang Zeng-fu, Zhang Ying-jie. 2021. Research on the Mechanism of Trade Facilitation Affecting Cross-Border E-commerce Export[J]. *Journal of Guiyang University Natural Sciences* 16(02): 35–38.

Zhang Jianglin. 2012. Research on the difference between technology transactions and economic growth in different regions of my country [D]. *Capital University of Economics and Business.*

Economic and Business Management – Lent & Zhang (Eds)
© 2023 the Author(s), ISBN 978-1-032-24482-2

Analysis on the influence of Chinese enterprises' overseas investment under green development

Qianqian Chen & Yongjian Zong
School of Management & Economics, Nanjing University of Science & Technology, Nanjing, China

ABSTRACT: Green and low-carbon development is not only the main trend of international social and economic development, but also an important research topic of Chinese enterprises' overseas investment. Given a global market outlook, green investment is leading a new change trend. Chinese enterprises must face up to the international environment and make reasonable overseas investment under the guidance of policies, market incentives and other mechanisms. Supported by the theories of green development, low-carbon economy and green investment, this paper summarizes the latest policies and the current situation of overseas investment of Chinese enterprises. Besides, it analyzes the influence mechanism of overseas investment of Chinese enterprises from four aspects: government regulation, market incentive, social governance and legal system. Finally, it puts forward relevant policy suggestions for Chinese enterprises' overseas investment under the background of green development from the perspectives of government and enterprises. The government should take action in terms of policy innovation, incentive mechanism, top-level design, and legislative constraints. At the same time, enterprises should also transform and upgrade from the levels of strategy, innovation, social responsibility, and legal awareness. This paper provides theoretical support for the Chinese government and enterprises to further promote overseas green investment.

1 INTRODUCTION

Green development has become a key factor in the progress of the times and plays the role of "Guardian" of sustainable economic development. From the response measures taken by countries all over the world, in the context of green development, technology and institutional innovation are the key factors, and government leadership and enterprise participation are the main forms of implementation. Nowadays how to achieve sustainable development has become a common challenge for all countries, especially in the post epidemic era. As the largest foreign investor, China will actively promote the green recovery of the world economy. With "carbon peaking and carbon neutrality goals" as the direction, all industries are actively looking for their own way of sustainable development. More and more enterprises integrate the concept of green development into production and operation (Qi 2022). Based on the current situation of green development and overseas investment, this paper explores its impact on Chinese enterprises' overseas investment from government regulation, market incentive, social governance and legal system.

This paper mainly adopts the literature analysis method, through comparing the relevant literature on green development and foreign investment, makes a targeted summary

DOI: 10.1201/9781003278788-11

according to the research direction. The article also uses the qualitative analysis method to summarize the development trend of Chinese enterprises' overseas investment. With the latest international policy and domestic situation, this paper has a certain theoretical value for enriching the research in this field. Besides, with the "carbon peaking and carbon neutrality goals", many enterprises quickly carry out strategic layout or accelerate the realization of low-carbon transformation. Therefore, the research of this paper has a certain practical guiding role for Chinese enterprises on how to optimize overseas investment. This paper is divided into six sections. Section 1 describes the research background, significance, methods. Section 2 mainly summarizes the relevant literature. Section 3 is the current situation analysis. Section 4 discusses the impact mechanism. Section 5 puts forward relevant suggestions. Section 6 proposes the conclusions.

2 LITERATURE REVIEW

The contradiction between rapid economic development and the intensification of environmental crisis has become an inevitable challenge for mankind. Debbrama & Choi (2022) proposed that green governance was the key to achieve the agreed goals of local and global governments. The Chinese government had made continuous exploration for green development, launched programs such as "new infrastructure construction" and "China's carbon neutrality commitment", and demonstrated China's determination and confidence in promoting "green development cooperation" to the international community. Under the background of green development, enterprises, as the subjects participating in the market, must implement this concept in order to achieve sustainable development. Throughout the relevant research of domestic and foreign scholars on enterprise green investment, they generally support it. Y ITO (2013) believed that enterprise green investment could achieve a win-win situation of economic growth and environmental protection. Chen (2018) believed that green investment was an investment that comprehensively considers economic growth and ecological balance. Chen et al. (2021) found that green investment could help reduce environmental violations, which in turn helped strengthen the impact of green investment on improving the long-term performance of enterprises. With the continuous extension of green development theory, many scholars have also conducted a lot of research on the green investment behavior of enterprises. Chen (2019) pointed out from the perspective of "efficiency" that the efficiency of enterprise green investment played a leading role in realizing sustainable development and maximizing enterprise social value. Rokhmawati (2021) proposed that greenhouse gas emission reduction was a successful factor for enterprises to achieve competitiveness. Mendolagine et al. (2021) proved that green FDI enhanced the overall positioning of multinational enterprises.

The concept of green investment will inevitably affect the overseas investment decision-making and efficiency of Chinese enterprises to a certain extent. Cheng et al. (2020) pointed out that the Chinese government was building a green the Belt and Road, expanding overseas investment. Zhang (2022) have proved that the green credit policy could improve the efficiency of enterprises' foreign investment. The global economy is in the early stages of green transformation. Many enterprises have begun to green their investment efforts. China has been constantly improving the top-level design of green development, which puts forward more specific requirements for Chinese enterprises' overseas green investment. The research on green development in the existing literature mostly focuses on the field of agriculture, and there are relatively few literatures in the related fields combined with foreign direct investment of enterprises. Therefore, combined with the latest international policies and domestic situation, it is of great theoretical and practical significance to study the overseas investment environment of Chinese enterprises under the background of green development.

3 ANALYSIS ON THE CURRENT SITUATION

To analyze the impact of green development on China's overseas enterprise investment, this paper focuses on the current green development policies at home and abroad and the current situation of Chinese enterprise overseas investment. It is very important to fully grasp the current situation so as to clarify the influence relationship between the two and analyze the deep-seated influence mechanism.

3.1 Current situation of green development policy

Green development has become the wind vane of global governance. At the global level, the integration of existing resources and the formulation of globally unified sustainable development reporting standards have been included in the discussion process. The successful experience of environmental policy innovation in developed countries can provide useful enlightenment for China's green practice. Federal Climate Protection Law of Germany in November 2019 provided a strict legal framework for achieving emission reduction targets (Yu 2022). The 25-year plan for improving the environment in the UK is one of a series of environmental policies that the UK plans to implement after Brexit (Zhang et al. 2021). Throughout the evolution of China's green development policy, it is a continuous improvement trend from shallow to deep and from wide to fine. China put forward the concept of building a community with a shared future for mankind, actively guided international cooperation on climate change, took green as the background of international cooperation, and issued the guiding opinions on promoting the construction of the green "the Belt and Road" (Li et al. 2020). Looking forward to the future, China will build a capital green environmental and economic policy system under the guidance of the long-term goals of carbon peaking in 2030 and carbon neutrality in 2060.

3.2 Current situation of overseas green investment of Chinese enterprises

Chinese enterprises are an important part of international investment. In 2020, the flow of China's foreign direct investment reached US $153.71 billion, 5.8 times that of 2007. Despite the impact of the COVID-19 in 2019, China's foreign investment in 2020 still achieved positive growth. China's foreign direct investment has shifted from pursuing "quantity" to pursuing "quality". For example, the proportion of mining industry decreased from 19.35% in 2011 to 3.99% in 2020. The information transmission, computer service and software industry increased from 1.04% in 2011 to 5.98% in 2020. The environmental behavior evaluation system of enterprises based on the principle of ESG was gradually established. Various evaluation indexes are closely related to the green investment of enterprises (Zhang 2021). According to the data, by the end of June 2021, 1112 A-share listed companies had disclosed ESG related reports, compared with 638 in 2012. It further proved that the green transformation of Chinese enterprises' foreign investment in recent years had achieved certain results.

3.3 Impact of green development on overseas investment of Chinese enterprises

Since the Chinese government put forward the "going global" strategy in 2000, the scale of China's foreign investment and cooperation has increased rapidly. As the main body of the "going out" strategy, Chinese enterprises have handed over satisfactory answers to the green development of overseas investment by strengthening internal governance and paying attention to maintaining the harmonious development of the host country's economy, society and environment. Especially in environmental and ecological protection and green management, it has been widely recognized by the host country and the international community. As shown in Table 1, according to the different development stages of China, the

Table 1. Main policy documents of China's foreign direct investment.

Year	Policy Document	Content Target
2004	Interim Measures for the administration of the approval of overseas investment projects; Provisions on the approval of overseas investment in Enterprises	Establish approval management mode
2009	Measures for the administration of overseas investment	Standardize approval management
2013	Guidelines for environmental protection of foreign investment and cooperation	Standardize investment and environmental protection behavior
2014	Measures for the administration of approval and filing of overseas investment projects; Measures for the administration of overseas investment (New)	Establish filing management mode
2017	Guidance on further guiding and regulating the direction of overseas investment	Standardize investment direction
2018	Measures for the administration of overseas investment of enterprises; Interim Measures for foreign investment filing (Approval) report	Standardize filing management; Establish the supervision mode of project report
2021	Guidelines for green development of foreign investment	Establish the green direction of investment

Source: According to the relevant information on the websites of the national development and Reform Commission and the Ministry of Commerce.

national development and Reform Commission and the Ministry of Commerce issued a series of targeted policies according to the foreign direct investment projects, and issued relevant documents to guide the development of overseas investment of Chinese enterprises in accordance with the international market situation and domestic development status.

The global competitiveness report pointed out that there was a significant correlation between active environmental policies and a country's competitiveness. The positive effects of environmental policy innovation and the positive trend of competitive potential energy were considerable, so it was actively promoted by green development countries (Xu 2021). The guidelines for green development of foreign investment issued in July 2021 shows that China is actively building an economic system in line with the concept of green development, promoting the sustainable development of overseas investment cooperation, paying more attention to the green rules in international trade and investment, and actively participating in international environmental governance and fulfilling international responsibilities.

4 ANALYSIS ON THE INFLUENCE MECHANISM

To sum up, we can see that under the background of green development, the overseas investment of Chinese enterprises will inevitably be affected. This paper makes a specific analysis from four perspectives: government regulation, market incentives, social governance and legal systems.

4.1 *From the perspective of government regulation*

The policy norms formulated by the government can play a good role in regulating and guiding the foreign investment behavior of enterprises, and provide policy impetus for the green development direction of foreign direct investment of enterprises. In the long run, the government's strict implementation of environmental policies can urge investors to pay attention to the environmental impact of investment. At present, the Chinese government encourages enterprises to formulate green development strategies and is striving to build a world-class enterprise in the field of green economy with high-level global resource integration ability, overall potential and industrial leading power.

4.2 *From the perspective of market incentive*

Under the constraints of the government's market incentive environmental policies, such as environmental tax, emission reduction subsidies and carbon emission trading, it has gradually strengthened the environmental awareness of multinational investors, so as to stimulate the technological innovation of multinational enterprises. The technological innovation of enterprises can offset the cost of implementing environmental policies. In this process, it can not only improve the self-value of Chinese enterprises, but also establish a good international image of enterprises, and publicize the concept of green development to consumers in the broad market. The formation of this virtuous circle makes the "greening" of overseas investment of enterprises develop in depth.

4.3 *From the perspective of social governance*

Corporate social responsibility is reflected in increasing the competitiveness of enterprises, improving the overseas image of enterprises and so on, which can promote the international operation of enterprises (Jia 2021). Corporate social responsibility has a significant positive correlation with the overseas image of Chinese products. In the process of "going global", enterprises should tell Chinese stories, fulfill social responsibilities, and establish a good Chinese corporate image in promoting local employment and environmental protection. Under the international background of green development, corporate social responsibility has also received extensive attention, which is not only related to the sustainable development of overseas investment of Chinese enterprises, but also related to the shaping of the image of China's big country.

4.4 *From the perspective of legal system*

From a macro perspective, the establishment of environmental protection legal system can alleviate the dilemma of the decline of economic competitiveness caused by the singleness of environmental policy, and promote the improvement of international environmental standards. From a micro perspective, it can promote the implementation of environmental policies by enterprises. China has signed relevant legal documents with the host country to implement the principle of sustainable development in the field of investment. In terms of domestic legislation, China's Guide to environmental protection for foreign investment and cooperation is specifically aimed at environmental protection in overseas investment, hoping to strengthen the guidance of environmental protection for "going global" enterprises.

5 SUGGESTIONS

China's foreign investment is gradually moving towards dark green. In recent years, the government has always followed up the top-level design of green development and put forward detailed requirements for overseas green investment of Chinese enterprises.

5.1 *Government perspective*

It brings challenges to the development of enterprises, but also needs our government's continuous optimization policy. Firstly, closely follow the international development trend and guide the innovation of environmental policies. Our government should pay close attention to international environmental requirements, and actively participate in international environmental agenda and cooperation. China should formulate policy design in line with its own national conditions. Second, improve the evaluation system of foreign-funded projects and establish a green investment incentive mechanism. It is necessary to incorporate the requirements of green development into the evaluation system of foreign-funded projects, and vigorously support foreign-funded projects of enterprises with strong sustainable development ability. Third, improve the top-level design of green investment and improve the participation of market participants. This requires the government to actively adopt public opinion and strengthen market research to provide practical convenience and mechanism. Fourth, strengthen the constraints of environmental protection legislation and formulate systematic laws and regulations. At present, Britain, France, Germany and other countries around the world have passed relevant legislation on "carbon neutrality". China needs more institutional and legal arrangements to ensure that domestic environmental standards are in line with international standards.

5.2 *Enterprise perspective*

The global agreement on carbon emissions has put forward new requirements and expectations for Chinese enterprises' overseas green investment. Chinese enterprises can focus on the following aspects to transform. Firstly, implement the green development policy and establish a green investment transformation strategy. Enterprises should grasp the development direction of international investment and pay close attention to the environmental protection policies of various countries. Secondly, actively seek innovative projects to improve the market competitiveness of enterprises. Enterprises must pay attention to whether the foreign-funded projects comply with the green and environmental protection production mode and the local carbon emission requirements. Thirdly, establish the awareness of environmental protection of enterprises and actively undertake social responsibility. Multinational corporations should carefully examine the investment review policies of the host country and actively disclose environmental information. A good reputation can accumulate intangible assets for Chinese enterprises. Finally, enhance the legal awareness of enterprises and strictly abide by relevant regulations. Enterprises should adjust their operation and investment strategies in time. By establishing an early warning mechanism, enterprises can audit overseas investment projects with higher standards and requirements.

6 CONCLUSIONS

Combined with the latest policies and data, this paper analyzes the current situation of China's green development and overseas investment of Chinese enterprises, and summarizes the domestic and foreign literature on the relationship between them. This paper summarizes the impact mechanism of green development on Chinese enterprises' overseas investment from four aspects: government regulation, market incentive, social governance and legal system. It is concluded that the international background of green development has had a profound impact on the overseas investment of Chinese enterprises. As the largest foreign investor at present, China will actively promote the green recovery of the world economy in the post epidemic era. Based on this, this paper proposes targeted policies and suggestions for overseas green investment of Chinese enterprises from the perspectives of government and enterprises. On the one hand, the government should keep up with international trends, constantly improve the incentive mechanism, update the top-level design, and strengthen legislative constraints to firmly grasp the key factor of institutional innovation. On the other hand, enterprises should also play the role of the main body of implementation and formulate advanced strategies to speed up transformation and upgrading.

This paper explores the impact of green development on Chinese enterprises' overseas investment, and the research content is updated to a certain extent. However, due to the limited data sources and research time, the research still has some deficiencies. The research stays at a more theoretical level and lacks relevant empirical research. Green development and overseas investment of enterprises are important aspects in the construction of China's sustainable development. Future research also needs to be deepened and expanded in combination with the latest policy environment and international situation.

REFERENCES

Amendolagine, V., Lema R. & Rabellotti R., 2021. Green Foreign Direct Investments and The Deepening of Capabilities for Sustainable Innovation in Multinationals: Insights From Renewable Energy. *Journal of Cleaner Production* 310(1): 127381.

Cheng, C. & Ge, C., 2020. Green Development Assessment for Countries Along the Belt and Road. *Journal of Environmental Management* 263: 110344. (in Chinese)

Chen, D. & Chen A.Z., 2018. GVC Embedding, Political Connection and Environmental Protection Investment – Evidence from Chinese Private Enterprises. *Journal of Shanxi University of Finance and Economics* 40(02): 69–83 (in Chinese)

Chen, Y. & Ma, Y., 2021. Does Green Investment Improve Energy Firm Performance? *Energy Policy* 153(1): 112252. (in Chinese)

Chen, Y.T., 2019. Research on the Corporate Green Investment Efficiency: Measurement, Determinants and Impression Management. *Southwest University of Finance and Economics.* (in Chinese)

Debbarma, J. & Choi, Y., 2022. A Taxonomy of Green Governance: A Qualitative and Quantitative Analysis Towards Sustainable Development.

Ito, Y. Managi, S. Matsuda, A., 2013. Performances of Socially Responsible Investment and Environmentally Friendly Funds. *Journal of Operational Research Society* 64(11): 1583–1594.

Jia, H., 2021. Research on State Responsibility for Environmental Protection of International Investment. *China University of Political Science and Law.* (in Chinese)

Liu Y., 2021. Research on Xi Jinping's the People Centered Concept of Green Development. *Donghua University of Technology* (in Chinese).

Li, L.P., Liu, J.M., Huang, X.H., Li, Y.Y. & Jiang, H.H., 2020. A Review of International Environmental Policy Research. *Environment and Sustainable Development* 45(01): 119–122 (in Chinese)

Rokhmawati, A., 2021. The Nexus Among Green Investment, Foreign Ownership, Export, Greenhouse Gas Emissions, and Competitiveness. *Energy Strategy Reviews* 37(1): 100679.

Qi, L., 2022. "Carbon Peaking and Carbon Neutrality Goals" Vision Leads Listed Companies to Build Green Competitiveness in the Future. *Chinas Foreign Trade* (03): 64–65. (in Chinese)

Xu, S.B., 2021. Research on the Impact of Corporate Social Responsibility on Enterprises' Foreign Direct Investment. *Jiangxi University of Finance and Economics.* (in Chinese)

Yu, W.J., 2022. Path Selection and Enlightenment of Green Development in Germany – Policy Practice Based on the Roadmap of "Carbon Neutrality". *Financial Expo* (04): 55–57 (in Chinese)

Zhang, J.J., Luo, Y.C. & Ding, X.H., 2022. Can Green Credit Policy Improve the Overseas Investment Efficiency of Enterprises in China? *Journal of Cleaner Production* 340. (in Chinese)

Zhang, H.Y., Lu, Y.L. & Cao, D., 2021. Policy Interpretation and Enlightenment of Green Future: 25-year Plan for Improving the Environment in the UK. *Environment and Sustainable Development* 46(06): 63–68 (in Chinese)

Zhang, T., 2021. Research on the Impact of Environmental Regulations on Corporate Green Investment. *China Mining University.* (in Chinese)

Economic and Business Management – Lent & Zhang (Eds)
© 2023 the Author(s), ISBN 978-1-032-24482-2

Happy of getting or tired of losing? The effect of the target framework effect of commodity information on consumers' willingness to buy

Juzhu Li, Wei Gao & Junlin Chen
School of Business and Tourism, Sichuan Agricultural University, Chengdu, People's Republic of China

ABSTRACT: Commodity information is often expressed in different framework forms. Studies have shown that different framework forms may affect consumers' perception quality of commodities, and different cognitive needs are greatly affected by the framework effect. Previous studies have found that the interaction of attribute frameworks and cognitive needs has an impact on perceived quality, but there are few studies on the effects of target frameworks. In this paper, through 2×2 inter-group experiments, we explored the effect of goal frame and cognitive demand on purchase intention.

1 INTRODUCTION

Today's era is the era of information. When people are shopping online, product information could directly affect people's willingness to buy. And commodity information can be displayed to consumers in different frame forms, and different frame forms will be processed into different information in people's brains. Thus what kind of frame form the commodity can be used as information transmission to enhance people's purchase intention has become the focus of current research.

The framing effect means that people have different decision-making judgments due to different ways of describing the same fact objectively [1]. The research of Levin et al. [2] found that frame effects can be divided into three categories: attribute frame effects, risk frame effects and target frame effects. At present, many studies have shown that the framing effect often plays a role when people make decisions, but the framing effect does not exist in all situations. Scholars Yu Huihui et al. [3] found that gender, personality characteristics, cognition and other factors may have an impact on it. Liu Hanhui et al. [4] investigated the specific influence of personality characteristics on the framing effect through experimental methods. Lewei et al. [5] conducted experiments with eye trackers and found that individuals with different cognitive needs have different strengths of attribute frame effects. Individuals with high cognitive needs have weaker attribute frame effects, while individuals with low cognitive needs have stronger attribute frame effect. But at present, there are few studies on the relationship between goal frame effect and cognitive needs. Will individuals with different cognitive needs produce different goal framing effects? Faced with different frameworks and different cognitive needs, will consumers' purchase intentions differ? There is no definite answer to these questions, but they have theoretical and practical significance and are worthy of our in-depth study.

2 THEORETICAL FRAMEWORK AND ASSUMPTIONS

Purchase intention is a manifestation of consumer psychology before making a purchase decision, which refers to the possibility of consumers buying a certain product [6].

DOI: 10.1201/9781003278788-12

Nowadays, the competition in online shopping is fierce, and businesses are paying more and more attention to consumer psychology. Shopping websites often have product descriptions such as "Purchasing this product during the event period will give you a 5 yuan cash red envelope" or "If you miss this event, you will lose the 5 yuan cash red envelope discount". This is the target framework. The experiment conducted by Mayerowitz and Chaikn [7] on persuading women to accept breast self-examination is a typical example of the target frame effect. The results of this experiment show that negative target frame information is more convincing. Under this framework, subjects are more inclined to undergo breast examinations. On shopping websites, in addition to pictures, the most intuitive representation of the product is the text description of the product. If the merchant adds the text description of the product to the target frame, it will affect the consumer's willingness to buy.

However, there are some differences between the actual situation and the theory, and the framing effect does not always occur. Cheng Yanrong [8] found that for college students' purchasing attitude, willingness to pay and purchase intention, the goal frame effect did not have a significant impact on them. Scholars such as Wen Guichan [9] pointed out that factors such as experience, personality traits, calculation ability, and cognition would have an impact on the frame effect.

Some people who are good at thinking may find that the information described by the positive and negative frames reflects the same objective facts. This type of group that is good at thinking can also be called a group with high cognitive needs. In 1982, Cacioppo and Petty [10] proposed that cognitive needs are the tendency of individuals to participate and enjoy thinking. Individuals with high cognitive needs tend to explore, think and truthfully reflect information when they understand the stimuli, relationships and events in the world; conversely, individuals with low cognitive needs rely more on other people, heuristic cognitions or social comparison processes. Furthermore, this article proposes the following hypotheses:

H1: When the same product is described in the positive and negative target frameworks, the individual's cognitive needs will have an impact on the purchase intention.

H1a: For individuals with high cognitive needs, the difference between the purchase intention of goods under the positive goal framework and the negative goal framework is small.

H1b: For individuals with low cognitive needs, there is a big difference between the purchase intention of goods under the positive goal framework and the negative goal framework, and individuals under the negative framework have stronger purchase intentions.

3 RESEARCH METHODS

3.1 *Research participants*

This study conducted a survey on people of all ages through an online platform, and eliminated incomplete questionnaires or obvious errors in the questionnaire information. In the end, a total of 291 effective experiment participants were obtained, including 74 boys and 217 girls, who participated before the experiment. None of them knew the specific content of the experiment.

3.2 *Experimental design*

In order to prevent subjects from accepting different frames of the same information, the experimental results will be inaccurate, so one subject in this experiment only uses one of the two target frames. The experiment is an inter-group experimental design of 2 (positive target frame, negative target frame) × 2 (high cognitive demand, low cognitive demand), and the dependent variables are perceived value and purchase intention.

3.3 *Measuring tools*

In this study, a scale developed by Cacioppo and Petty in 1982 and modified and simplified into 18 questions in 1984 was used to measure cognitive needs. The internal consistency coefficient of the scale was 0.89 and the half-point reliability was 0.9. The scale for measuring perceived value was adapted from the scale of Wang [11] and others, and the scale for measuring purchase intention was adapted from the scale of Zeithhaml [12] and others. Both scales have been widely used in many subsequent studies use. The scales in the questionnaire in this study are all measured by the Likert five-point method, "strongly disagree=1, disagree=2, not necessarily=3, agree=4, strongly agree=5".

4 VARIABLE MEASUREMENT

Before performing hypothesis testing, analyzed reliability and validity. The SPSS was used to measure the reliability of purchase intention, the result was that the Cronbach's α coefficient is 0.836, which was greater than the acceptable standard of 0.700, indicating good reliability. At the same time, a confirmatory factor analysis was performed on the variables. The Chi-square degree of freedom ratio was 2.405, which was less than 3, and the GFI was 0.939, which was greater than the minimum standard of 0.85 and the NFI was 0.946, which was greater than the minimum standard of 0.85, and the RMSEA was 0.069, less than 0.1, RMR was 0.04, less than 0.05, indicating that the model fit well. The standardized factor loading values of all question items were between 0.675–0.892, exceeding the minimum standard of 0.500, which indicated that each variable had good aggregate validity.

5 RESULT ANALYSIS

For the convenience of analysis, this study adopts a dichotomy. According to the average number of cognitive needs, the subjects were divided into high cognitive needs group and low cognitive needs group.

5.1 Test of the direct effect of target framework and cognitive demand on purchase intention

Using the analysis of variance, the results of the main effects test are shown in Table 1.

Table 1. The main effect test of target framework and perceived demand on purchase intention.

Type	df	Mean square	F	P
Target frame	1	0.187	0.254	0.615
Perceived need	1	0.061	0.083	0.773
Target framework * Perceived needs	1	5.064	6.890	0.009

The results showed that the direct effect of the target frame effect was not significant, M negative = 3.63, M positive = 3.54, F = 0.254, p = 0.615 > 0.05. The direct effect of cognitive needs was not significant, Mlow = 3.58, Mhigh = 3.60, F = 0.083, p = 0.773 > 0.05. The interaction between goal framework and cognitive needs is significant, F = 6.890, p = 0.009 < 0.05. Using single-factor analysis of variance, the grouping results of high cognitive needs were shown in Table 2.

Table 2. The impact of the target framework of high and low cognitive needs on purchase intention.

Type	F	p
High	1.553	0.215
Low	7.103	0.008

Comparing the results of high grouping and low grouping, it was found that when individuals with high cognitive needs face the positive and negative frames, there was little difference in purchase intention, $p = 0.215 > 0.05$. However, when individuals with low cognitive needs face in the two frameworks, the purchase intention was quite different, $p = 0.008 < 0.05$. And individuals under the negative framework had stronger purchase intentions, M negative $= 3.72 >$ M positive $= 3.40$. From this result, H1 was established.

6 CONCLUSIONS

This research used the method of online scenario experiments to explore the influence of individuals with different cognitive needs on the purchase intention of goods under the effect of the target framework. The results showed that individuals with high cognitive needs were less affected by the framing effect, and individuals with low cognitive needs were more affected by the framing effect. It can be seen that the interaction between cognitive needs and the target frame is significant.

This article enriches the theoretical basis of frame effects through scenario experiments, and discussing target frames. But there are some limitations in the article that need to be improved. First, this article only discussed the impact of cognitive needs on the goal framework, and did not discuss other personality characteristics and cognitive efforts triggered by cognitive needs. The research perspective and depth needed to be expanded. Second, the experimental materials that were only used was yogurt as a food and failed to conduct research on other commodities. Later, other commodities can be used as experimental materials for research.

REFERENCES

[1] Cheng Yanrong. 2013. An Empirical Study on the Impact of Frame Effect and Cognitive Needs on College Students' Purchase Decisions[D]. *Southwest University*.

[2] Cacioppo J.T., Petty R.E., Sidera J.A. 1982. The Effects of a Salient Self-schema on the Evaluation of Proattitudinal Editorials: Top-down versus bottom-up message processing[J]. *Journal of Experimental Social Psychology* 18(4): 324–338.

[3] Han Rui, Tian Zhilong. Research on the Impact of Promotion Types on Consumer Perception and Behavioral Intentions[J]. *Management Science* 2005(02): 85–91.

[4] Levin I.P., Schneider S.L., Gaeth G.J. 1998. All Frames Are Not Created Equal: A Typology and Critical Analysis of Framing Effects[J]. *Organizational Behavior and Human Decision Processes* 76.

[5] Le Wei, Han Xiao, Yin Hongjuan. 2018. Product Perception Quality Difference Measurement Under the Attribute Framework: Based on eye Tracking Technology[J]. *Chinese Journal of Management Engineering* 32(04): 88–94.

[6] Liu Hanhui, Zhou Hongyu, Che Hongsheng. The Influence of Personality Characteristics on Decision-Making Under Different Types of Frameworks[J]. *Psychological Sciencetab* 2010(4): 823–826.

[7] Meyerowitz B.E., Chaiken S. 1987. The Effect of Message Framing on Breast Self-Examination Attitudes, Intentions, and Behavior[J]. *Journal of Personality and Social Psychology* 52(3): 500–510.

[8] Tversky A., Kahneman D. 1981. The Framing of Decisions and the Psychology of Choice[J]. *Science* 211(4481): 453–458.

[9] Yu Huihui, Xu Fuming, Huang Baozhen, et al. 2012. Individual Differences in Framing Effects[J]. *Advances in Psychological Science*.

[10] Wen Guichan, Xu Fuming, Yu Huihui, et al. 2011. The Psychological Mechanism and Influencing Factors of the Characteristic Frame Effect[J]. *Advances in Psychological Science* 19(012): 1822–1833.

[11] Wang Y., Lo H.P., Chi R., et al. 2004. An Integrated Framework for Customer Value and Customer-Relationship-management Performance: A Customer-based Perspective From China[J]. *Journal of Service Theory & Practice* 14(2): 169–182.

[12] Zeithaml V.A., Berry L.L., Parasuraman A. 1996. The Behavioral Consequences of Service Quality[J]. *Journal of Marketing* 60(2): 31–46.

Economic and Business Management – Lent & Zhang (Eds)

Innovative research on supply chain financing model for SMEs under blockchain technology

Yufan Lu

Shanghai Polytechnic University, Shanghai, China

ABSTRACT: With the rapid development of the economy, the number of SMEs has increased and so has their demand for capital, which highlights the risks and limitations faced by SMEs in financing through the traditional supply chain finance model. Based on this, this paper takes "blockchain technology and the financing model of supply chain finance" as the core, and through a specific analysis of the basic principles of blockchain technology, finds the best fit between blockchain technology and the financing model of supply chain finance, and deeply integrates the two, to build a new model of supply chain finance, namely the "swap financing model", thereby alleviating the problems of enterprises in financing and promoting the rapid development of the economy.

1 INTRODUCTION

With the rapid development of China's economy and society, small and medium-sized enterprises have gradually become an important part of China's economic production, occupying a certain share of the market competition. At the present stage, SMEs in China have accounted for more than 96% of the total number of enterprises in China, accounting for more than 60% of China's GDP and making a great contribution to China's employment rate; however, the occupancy rate of their financial resources in the country is less than 20%. In this paper, we analyze the traditional supply chain finance models of SMEs, namely accounts receivable financing, bonded warehouse financing, and finance through warehouse financing, and further analyze the whole business operation process of these models in detail. The existence of these risks has to a certain extent hindered the development of SMEs, and at the same time, this mode of financing has to a certain extent the limitations of the participating parties, which have great drawbacks in solving the practical operation of some specific logistics areas and seriously affect the operational efficiency of SMEs financing. Therefore, SMEs urgently need a better financing model to alleviate the problems they face in terms of financing. Based on this, this paper proposes an innovative supply chain financial financing model by integrating blockchain technology, which is mainly applied to the participation of multiple SMEs in the supply chain, so as to solve some problems caused by the traditional supply chain financial financing model, thus further alleviating the financing difficulties of SMEs and promoting the healthy development of the economy.

2 LITERATURE REVIEW

2.1 *Foreign literature review*

For some foreign scholars, in supply chain finance models: By examining this aspect of financial supply chain management and the development of supply chain models, Mehdi

Fathollah (2019) suggests that through the coordination and integrity of inventory, information, and financial flows in the supply chain, financial risks can be addressed, providing a more stable value stream for the supply chain and creating better conditions for the individual members of the supply chain. Mohamed Abdel-Basset, Rehab Mohamed, Karam Sallam, and Mohamed Elhoseny (2020) proposed a novel decision model for supply chain finance in an uncertain environment to further investigate sustainable supply chain finance, leading to the conclusion that financial attributes and product service management are the most important indicators for improving firm performance and access to sustainable supply chain finance.

In blockchain technology: Zunli Zhang and Xinyi Li (2019) analyzed the pain points of supply chain finance from the phenomenon of "information silo", combining the traditional supply chain finance model with blockchain technology to promote supply chain finance in the era of digital visualization. By exploring the application of blockchain technology in the supply chain, Rijanto Arief (2021) used TAM theory to analyze 30 blockchains in the supply chain to conclude that perceived usefulness drives the adoption of supply chain finance and solves some of the practical problems in supply chain finance.

2.2 *Domestic literature review*

For some domestic scholars, in supply chain finance models: Xiaolong Liang (2018), on the basis of an accurate understanding of the current situation of supply chain finance, studied the risk prevention of supply chain finance, fully understand the potential risks involved, formulate effective risk prevention measures to avoid risks in operation and promote the healthy and sustainable development of China's economy. Jiangbo Qin (2021) proposed countermeasures for the development of supply chain finance by studying in the context of a new coronavirus, arguing that first, China's supply chain finance policy system should be improved, innovation in supply chain finance products should be promoted, where the management of practitioners should be strengthened and technology should be used to anchor the development of supply chain finance.

In blockchain technology: Chenglong Jiang (2020) combined industry and finance, departing from the traditional development model of finance based on finance and forming a development pattern of coming from industry and going to finance by studying the specific application of blockchain technology in supply chain finance. Yanming Feng and Da Zhang (2022), based on summarizing and analyzing the three traditional financing models of supply chain finance and their problems, discussed the characteristics of blockchain technology and its ways and effects on optimizing the financing model of supply chain finance, highlighted the imperfections of the current blockchain technology, and proposed problems and measures that need to be further studied and solved at present.

2.3 *Summary*

From the above-mentioned literature, we find that most scholars focus on the various risks associated with the supply chain financing model, and thus propose specific solutions to them. The blockchain research mainly focuses on the specific application of blockchain technology in the traditional supply chain financial financing model, and optimizes the traditional supply chain financial financing model by analyzing the theoretical basis of blockchain and other advantages, but ignores some fundamental problems of the traditional financing model in the financing process and it is less involved in optimizing the whole process. This paper fills this gap by proposing a specific and innovative financing model, namely the "swap financing model," which will make it easier and more efficient to address the various risks involved in the financing process of SMEs.

3 THE CONSTRUCTION OF A "SWAP FINANCING MODEL"

3.1 *Presentation of the swap financing model*

Currently, SMEs mainly use the three traditional financing modes: accounts receivable financing model, bonded warehouse financing model, and the warehouse financing model. With the increase in the number of SMEs, the amount of financing is increasing, which makes the problems of SMEs in the financing process also gradually highlighted. After specific analysis of the entire business operation process of the traditional supply chain financing mode, it is found that there are some inevitable risks in this process, such as credit risk, operational risk, collateral risk, etc. The existence of these risks has, to a certain extent, hindered the rapid development of SMEs, while this financing model also has the disadvantage of limited participation. In other words, when there is more than one SME in the supply chain for financing, the SME and the commercial bank will execute multiple financing and guarantees at one end of the supply chain, which will multiply the financing risk in the supply chain and greatly increase the risk borne by the bank, thus reducing the efficiency of financing and increasing the financing risk, as well as increasing the total cost of society, which is not conducive to the rapid development of the economy. Therefore, this paper addresses the various risks and limitations of the traditional supply chain financing model and builds an innovative supply chain financing model—"Swap Financing Model."

3.2 *Financing options for swap financing models*

The "swap financing model" is mainly applicable to the supply chain finance financing model with the participation of multiple financing entities. In the financing process of supply chain finance for SMEs, when there are multiple participating parties, we generally regard these participating parties as a supply chain, from the most upstream enterprises producing raw materials to the most downstream enterprises selling them, forming a blockchain. Using blockchain technology, each enterprise in the supply chain shares information about its products on the blockchain, and each enterprise in the chain is required to register its enterprise information for enterprise real name authentication. In this process, the bank mainly acts as a guarantor in the middle, ensuring the authenticity and validity of each registered enterprise's information and then guaranteeing the enterprise. After the enterprise's information has been audited by the bank, it will open the enterprise's blockchain application rights, so that the enterprise can track the progress of the whole process, from production to sales, of the relevant products in a certain chain of blockchain. In this process, the logistics enterprise mainly acts as a supervising party. When the upstream enterprise delivers to the downstream enterprise, it is first sent to the warehouse of the logistics enterprise, which audits the quality of the goods and supervises the whole process of delivery of goods.

Financing applications can be made after ensuring that every business in the supply chain is registered with real names and has the right to share information on the blockchain. In this paper, this new financing model is called the "swap financing model," which means that each enterprise in the supply chain uses credit as security and the products in the chain as collateral for swap financing. The financing process does not require the provision of actual funds, but only the signing of a swap agreement between two adjacent parties, and the repayment of the financing amount will be made layer by layer when the seller at the last end of the chain obtains the funds, finally completing the entire transaction process from the production end to the sales end of the products.

3.3   *The main operational processes of the swap financing model*

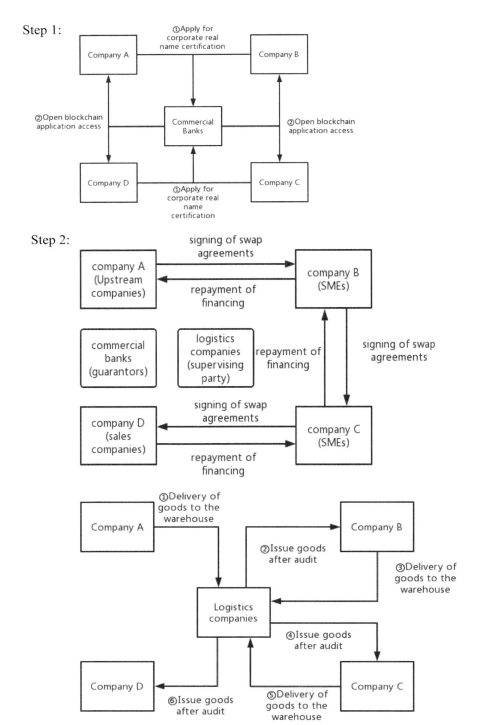

Figure 1.   The main operational processes of the swap financing model.

1. Quadrilateral SMEs first apply to banks for the terms of swap financing;
2. Commercial banks examine the application materials and corporate finance of the applied enterprises, register the accounts of the audited enterprises, open blockchain application privileges, and guarantee the financing of the applied enterprises;
3. The entry of an enterprise into its own account in the blockchain means that it has met the conditions for swap financing and can trade and cooperate in the supply chain to which it belongs for all relevant products;
4. When upstream and downstream SMEs cooperate in the sale and purchase of traded products, adjacent upstream and downstream suppliers enter into swap agreements to trade products;
5. Upstream enterprises first send the relevant products to the logistics enterprises they cooperate with, and the logistics enterprises audit the product quality and other relevant information of the products and then send them to the downstream enterprises after the audit is passed;
6. Repayment of the financing will begin sequentially when the sales proceeds from the last selling firm arrive, until the top firm receives the financing proceeds.

The "swap agreement" mainly refers to the swap of collateral (products sold) of the upstream enterprise and the credit and compensation of the downstream enterprise, whereby the upstream enterprise sells raw materials, or primary or secondary processed products to the downstream SME, and the downstream SME uses the credit and compensation as security to obtain nominal financing from the upstream enterprise for the purchased products, and so on, until the final selling enterprise obtains the funds and then repays them in turn. Commercial banks are responsible for verifying and reviewing the information and creditworthiness of the companies registered in the blockchain, providing a simple credit rating for their companies and, in some cases, providing a degree of guarantee for SMEs.

3.4 *Advantages of swap financing*

1. It makes up for the limitations of the traditional supply chain finance model by extending supply chain financing to multiple entities, solving the duplication of financing when there are multiple entities in the traditional financing process, improving the efficiency of financing, and enhancing the liquidity of commercial banks, thus saving more funds for other investment and financing.
2. It uses the advantages of blockchain technology in greater depth and connects the financing of supply chain finance with blockchain perfectly, making it possible for each participating body in the supply chain to track and query the project in real-time and to grasp the project at any time and from anywhere, reducing the risk of enterprises, increasing the transparency of information, and improving the trust of each enterprise in the supply chain.
3. It changes the way of traditional financing in which commercial banks act as financiers, through cooperation between enterprises, using commodities as collateral, signing swap contracts, and using legal terms to hold each other in check. Then, repaying them layer by layer after the terminal seller has obtained the funds, in which each enterprise in the supply chain is nominally equivalent to a financier, and the bank is only a supervisor and guarantor in the middle, not providing them financing as in the traditional financing model. This not only improves the liquidity of commercial banks but makes banks having more funds to invest in higher quality, less risky projects, reducing to a certain extent the investment risk of commercial banks. At the same time, this model treats all enterprises in a supply chain as a whole, so that their interests are related to a certain extent, which can increase the attention and responsibility of each subject to the product, and the interests

of each participating subject are closely related, reducing the risk of default and credit risk in supply chain business.

4. As each enterprise in this financing model must undergo strict vetting by banks before it can enter, the threshold is relatively high and the enterprise must have a certain credit rating. Therefore, each enterprise in the blockchain belongs to a relatively high-quality enterprise with a relatively high-credit rating. Its advantages are to have a wider choice of companies in the supply chain to cooperate on projects, and the quality of the companies is also higher, which makes the financing process of supply chain finance smoother and greatly reduces the risks involved in the financing process.

3.5 *Problems solved by the swap financing model*

After analyzing the business processes of traditional supply chain financing models, it is found that they generally have the problems of credit risk, operational risk, collateral risk, and limitations of the participating parties.

In this paper, an innovative supply chain financing model, namely the Swap Financing Model, is developed to better address the problems of the traditional model, as shown in Table 1.

Table 1. The specific applications of the swap financing model.

Risk problems	Solutions
Credit risk	Information is shared in real-time through blockchain technology, thus ensuring the timeliness and authenticity of information. At the same time, commercial banks, as guarantors, have more information about the companies in the supply chain, which can greatly alleviate the credit risk in the process of supply chain finance.
Operational risk	Blockchain-based online internet applications avoid the operational errors associated with traditional offline manual credit granting and, to a certain extent, improve the efficiency of financing.
Collateral risk	In the swap financing process, its partner logistics companies act as the main supervisors to monitor the products traded in real-time, while the existence of blockchain technology makes the information on collateral products more transparent, which greatly reduces the problem of collateral risk that exists in traditional supply chain financing.
Limitations of the participating parties	It breaks the limitations of the traditional supply chain finance model which is applicable to two-party enterprise financing. Swap financing models can be directly applied to more than three parties with multiple SME participants.

4 CONCLUSIONS

The emergence of the supply chain finance model has, to a certain extent, alleviated the problems of financing difficulties and expensive financing for SMEs, injected important financial support into SMEs, and promoted their rapid development. However, due to the problems and limitations of the traditional supply chain finance model, such as credit risk and operational risk, these problems have become a stumbling block for SMEs on the road to development. Therefore, based on blockchain technology, this paper mainly applies its distributed technology, smart contract technology, decentralization feature, and federated chain technology to build a new supply chain financing model, namely "swap financing model." Ultimately, the problem of difficult financing for enterprises can be effectively solved, allowing enterprises to have access to more financing opportunities and channels, thus laying a good foundation for enterprises to achieve the goal of healthy and sustainable development.

REFERENCES

Chenglong Jiang. 2020. Research on the Development Status and Innovation Model of Supply Chain Finance [J]. *China Logistics & Purchasing.*

Jiangbo Qin. 2021. The Development Status and Countermeasures of Supply Chain Finance in China[J]. *Academic Exchange.*

Mohamed Abdel-Basset, Rehab Mohamed, Karam Sallam, Mohamed Elhoseny. 2020. A Novel Decision-Making Model for Sustainable Supply Chain Finance Under Uncertainty Environment[J]. *Journal of Cleaner Production.*

Mehdi Fathollah. 2019. Development of Financial Supply Chain Management and Supply Chain Finance Model[J]. *Research Journal of Finance and Accounting.*

Rijanto Arief. 2021. Blockchain Technology Adoption in Supply Chain Finance[J]. *Journal of Theoretical and Applied Electronic Commerce Research.*

Xiaolong Liang. 2018. The Development Status and Risk Prevention of Supply Chain Finance[J]. *V Marketing China.*

Yanming Feng and Da Zhang. 2022. Research on Optimization of Supply Chain Finance Mode Based on Blockchain Technology[J]. *Rural Finance Research.*

Zunli Zhang*, Xinyi Li. 2019. Innovation of Supply Chain Finance Model Based on Blockchain Technology [J]. *International Journal of Computational and Engineering.*

Economic and Business Management – Lent & Zhang (Eds)
© 2023 the Author(s), ISBN 978-1-032-24482-2

The impact of online pork product attribute combinations on consumer preferences

Hanyang Zhao

Affiliation School of Business and Tourism, Sichuan Agricultural University, Chengdu, People's Republic of China

ABSTRACT: In this paper, nine attribute combinations of online traceable pork products are selected by SPSS orthogonal analysis, and the data of consumer preferences are processed by conjoint in R language to calculate the utility of different attribute combinations. The results show that the utility value of the whole process level in the traceability information attribute and the fresh level in the appearance attribute is the highest, and consumers value these two attributes most. Product price attribute is not the key factor to determine consumers' product preference. Accordingly, this paper puts forward corresponding suggestions to help e-commerce enterprises accurately grasp the needs and utility of consumers and achieve the best combination of various attributes. At the same time, help e-commerce enterprises judge whether the attribute combination of existing products can obtain consumers' preferences, which products should be selectively abandoned and which products should be strengthened.

1 INTRODUCTION

Food safety problems at home and abroad have always existed [1]. Research shows that the traceability system can monitor food safety [2], and its implementation will help improve consumer confidence [3,4], thereby helping to improve food safety issues. But this will cause the product price to rise. Research shows that consumers are willing to pay a premium for traceable food [5]. How much can consumers accept the price increase? According to Lancaster demand theory, product attributes are the source for consumers to obtain utility in consumption [6]. Consumers' purchase behavior of agricultural products is actually a process of weighing and choosing attributes [7]. It can be inferred that other attributes of online traceable pork products will also affect demand. So, what kind of attribute combination is the best combination for consumers to buy traceable agricultural products online? This paper discusses this point.

At present, there have been studies on the preference of traceable pork for offline transactions at four levels: traceability information, certification of traceability information, appearance and price [8]. With the development of e-commerce, online trading of agricultural products has become a consumption trend. Online transactions have exacerbated consumers' concerns about food safety. Offline and online transactions are very different in all aspects, but there is no discussion from the perspective of "online".

Intention and preference can effectively predict behavior [9], and it is necessary to study preference. Scholars have proposed a multivariate statistical method to quantitatively analyze consumers' preferences through attribute decomposition, namely joint analysis [10], which is considered to be one of the best tools to study consumers' consumption preferences for different traceable foods [11]. In view of this, this paper uses conjoint in R language to analyze the utility of different attribute combinations from four attributes: traceability information, security authentication, appearance and price.

DOI: 10.1201/9781003278788-14

2 RESEARCH DESIGN

The innovation of this paper is that the orthogonal experiment method and R language are used for data processing when researching attributes. Another innovation is that the research object is no longer offline trading pork, but online pork products. Therefore, the selection of product attributes and possible attribute combinations refer to existing experiments.

2.1 Setting of attribute combination

(1) no traceable information, (2) traceable information includes breeding information, (3) traceable information includes breeding, slaughtering and processing, transportation and sales information (the whole process); Certification options for traceable information: (1) government certification, (2) domestic third-party organization certification, (3) international third-party organization certification; Appearance selection: (1) fresh, (2) relatively fresh, (3) general; Price options: (1) 12 yuan / 500 g, (2) 14 yuan / 500 g, (3) 16 yuan / 500 g.

2.2 Joint analysis in R language

In joint analysis, products or services are described as "profiles", which are composed of attributes that can describe the important characteristics of products or services and different horizontal combinations of each attribute [12]. The basic assumption of joint analysis is that consumers understand and make preference judgment according to multiple attributes constituting products or services. It adopts the decomposition method to calculate preference parameters by allowing consumers to assign values to a series of product contours. These parameters can be path worth, importance weights, ideal points and so on [13]. The utility of different profiles can be calculated by the following formula:

$$U(X) = \sum_{i=1}^{n} \sum_{j=1}^{m} VijXij \qquad (1)$$

Where, U is the preference score of the contour.I is the number of attributes, j is the number of levels, Xij is the attribute variable of the ith level of different attributes, that is, Xij = 1 (the jth level of the ith attribute) or Xij = 0 (others), and Vij is the utility estimate of the jth level of the ith attribute. First, we need to get the score of each attribute combination, and then calculate the utility of each attribute at different levels. Second, add up the utility of each level to get the overall utility of the attribute combination. Finally, compare the size according to the overall utility.

2.3 Orthogonal experimental design

This study adopts attribute combination scoring, so we should consider the possibility of all combinations between attributes. Based on the number of direct attribute combination is too large and the actual operation workload is large. In order to improve the research accuracy, this paper uses the contour number algorithm to calculate the total number of attribute layers. On the basis of ensuring the accuracy, this paper uses SPSS software for orthogonal design. By combining different product attributes and attribute levels, 9 groups of representative design combinations of simulated products are generated: (1) No information, government certification, fresh, 12 yuan. (2) No information, domestic third-party certification, relatively fresh, 14 yuan. (3) No information, international third-party certification, general, 16 yuan. (4) Breeding information, government certification, relatively fresh, 16 yuan. (5) Breeding information, domestic third-party certification, general, 12 yuan. (6) Breeding information, international third-party certification, fresh, 14 yuan. (7) The whole process, government certification, general, 14 yuan. (8) The whole process, domestic third-party certification, fresh, 16 yuan. (9) The whole process, international third-party certification, relatively fresh, 12 yuan. The specific content is shown in Table 1.

Table 1. Property combination table.

Number	Traceability information	Authentication mode	appearance	Price
1	No	Government certification	fresh	12
2	No	Domestic third party certification	Relatively fresh	14
3	No	International third party certification	commonly	16
4	Breed	Government certification	Relatively fresh	16
5	Breed	Domestic third party certification	commonly	12
6	Breed	International third party certification	fresh	14
7	Whole process	Government certification	commonly	14
8	Whole process	Domestic third party certification	fresh	16
9	Whole process	International third party certification	Relatively fresh	12

There is no exact same combination between each combination, and there is no similar situation with no traceability at the same time, domestic third-party certification, average appearance, and the highest price. This situation is extreme and the score can be seen at a glance.

3 RESEARCH DESIGN

In the form of online questionnaires randomly distributed in Sichuan Agricultural University, this study requires consumers to score 9 online traceable pork product attribute combinations in Table 1, ranging from 1 to 9 (from the most unlikely purchase to the most likely purchase). The questionnaire design refers to the existing consumer preference questionnaire for product attribute combinations. The subjects selected each age group as evenly as possible, with uniform gender distribution, and fully considered the factors that may affect the questionnaire results, such as the possible reading habits of consumers. 200 valid questionnaires were collected.

The R language was used to conduct joint analysis and processing on the collected data, and the data in Table 2 were obtained. Table 2 shows the utility scores of different levels of each attribute collected and sorted by the conjoint analysis method. The higher the score, the more preferred by consumers, and the negative level consumers do not like very much. According to the conjoint analysis in the R language, the results of each utility score are significant.

Table 2. Utility score of each attribute.

Attribute	Arrangement	Utility score	Attribute	Arrangement	Utility score
Traceability information	No	−0.6091	Authentication mode	Domestic third party certification	−0.2222
	Breed	0.0635		International third party certification	−0.1687
	Whole process	0.5456		Government certification	0.3909
Appearance	Commonly	−0.7341	Price	12	0.2421
	Relatively fresh	0.1409		14	−0.0496
	fresh	0.5933		16	−0.1925

For the first group of attribute combinations, using the calculation formula of contour utility, we can get that its utility is u = −0.6091 + 0.3909 + 0.5933 + 0.2421 = 0.6172, and the utility of all attribute combinations are 0.6172, −0.74, −1.7044, 0.4028, −0.6507, 0.4385, 0.1528, 0.7242 and 0.7599 respectively.

4 DISCUSSIONS

In the traceability information attribute, the utility of "whole process" level is the highest, and the utility of "no information" is negative. Among the authentication attributes, consumers prefer government authentication most, and other utilities are negative. Among appearance attributes, consumers have the highest utility of "fresh" and negative utility of "general" level. As prices rise, the utility of consumers decreases, which is in line with the demand theory.

Through the data of each group, it is found that the attribute combination utility of the eighth and ninth groups is high. Even if they do not have the highest level of utility in some attributes, it is mainly due to the high level of utility in the whole process and appearance attributes in the traceability information. Therefore, when selling traceable pork products online, businesses should focus on the traceability attribute and appearance attribute.

In addition, the utility of the fifth attribute combination is negative. Consumers do not choose products only because of price. In other words, price is not the key factor to determine consumers' product preference. Thirdly, the third attribute combination has the lowest utility. Businesses can consider giving up the products with such attribute combination and focus on developing other online traceable pork products with higher utility.

The limitation of this study is that the selection of attributes is not comprehensive, and there is no quantitative analysis of the importance of a single attribute. Future research can consider more possible attributes.

REFERENCES

[1] Sarig Y. 2003. Traceability of Food Products. *Agricultural Engineering International: The CIGR e-journal* 4(12).

[2] Islam S., Cullen J. M. 2021. Food Traceability: A Generic Theoretical Framework. *Food Control* 123: 107848.

[3] Matzembacher D. E., Stangherlin I. C., Slongo L. A. 2018. An Integration of Traceability Elements and Their Impact in Consumer's Trust. *Food Control* 92: 420–429.

[4] Qian J., Shi C., Wang S., Song Y., Fan B., Wu X. 2018. Cloud-based System for Rational Use of Pesticide to Guarantee the Source Safety of Traceable Vegetables. *Food Control* 87: 192–202.

[5] Loureiro M. L., Umberger W. J. 2007. A Choice Experiment Model for Beef: What US Consumer Responses Tell us About Relative Preferences for Food Safety, Country-of-origin Labeling and Traceability. *Food Policy* 32(4): 496–514.

[6] Lancaster, Kelvin J. 1966. A New Approach to Consumer Theory. *Journal of Political Economy* 74(2): 132–157.

[7] Green, Paul, E., et al. 2001. Thirty Years of Conjoint Analysis: Reflections and Prospects. *Interfaces* 31(3): 56–73.

[8] David L. Ortega, H. Holly Wang, Laping Wu, Nicole J. Olynk. 2010. Modeling Heterogeneity in Consumer Preferences for Select Food Safety Attributes in China. *Food Policy* 36(2): 318–324.

[9] HaoThi Nguyen H., Nguyen C., Kabango A., et al. 2019. Vietnamese Consumers' Willingness to Pay for Safe Pork in Hanoi. *Journal of International Food & Agribusiness Marketing* 31(4): 1–22.

[10] Luce R. Duncan, Tukey John W. 1964. Simultaneous Conjoint Measurement: A New Type of Fundamental Measurement. *Journal of Mathematical Psychology* 1(1): 1–27.

[11] Font i Furnols M., C. Realini, F. Montossi, C. Sañudo, M. M. Campo, M. A. Oliver, G. R. Nute, L. Guerrero. 2011. Consumer's Purchasing Intention for Lamb Meat Affected by Country of Origin, Feeding System and Meat Price: A Conjoint Study in Spain, France and United Kingdom. *Food Quality and Preference* 22(5): 443–451.

[12] Louviere J. J., DA Hensher, Swait J. D., *et al.* 2000. Stated Choice Methods: Analysis and Applications. *General Information* 89(8): 227–251.

[13] J. R. Hauser, V. R. Rao. 2002. Conjoint Analysis, Related Modeling, and Applications. *Springer US* 161(5): 9–23.

Economic and Business Management – Lent & Zhang (Eds)
© *2023 the Author(s), ISBN 978-1-032-24482-2*

How will people adopt digital inclusive finance? – Evidence from China

Erqian Zhu, Xiaoling Song, Zijiao Zeng, Rui Wang & Siyi Wu
Department of Finance, Beijing Language and Culture University, Beijing, China

ABSTRACT: In order to explore ways to enhance financial inclusion in the context of digital economy, this study uses extended UTAUT model, and constructs a structural equation model (SEM) of the factors impacting users' adoption behavior of digital inclusive finance. We collected data through an online questionnaire distributed across villages and towns in remote areas in 18 provinces of China and used Amos26.0 for path analysis and moderating effect. The results show that performance expectations, effort expectations, social influence, and facility conditions have a positive impact on behavioral intention. Perceived risk negatively affects behavioral intention. Financial education and supervision can significantly reduce perceived risk and positively affect behavioral intentions. Based on the individual characteristics of users, age and individual innovation played a moderating role between effort expectation and use intention, financial education and supervision, and perceived risk. Therefore, the key to promoting the development of digital inclusive finance in China lies in increasing investment in capital resources, improving digital infrastructure, and strengthening financial education for inclusive groups.

1 INTRODUCTION

Digital inclusive finance is an initiative to promote financial inclusion using digital financial services. Due to the "digital gap," it is still difficult for certain users, such as those in remote rural areas in China, to enter the purview of digital inclusive finance. This study emphasizes the core meaning, evaluation system, and impact mechanism of digital inclusive finance and focuses on individuals such as rural residents, urban and rural low-income groups, and individual businesses from a micro perspective to explore the internal mechanism of users' adoption of digital inclusive financial products or services.

2 RESEARCH FRAMEWORK AND ACADEMIC BASIS

Existing research mainly discusses the impact on digital inclusive finance from macro (Anand & Chhikara 2013) and micro (Dupas & Robinson 2013; Karlan & Zinman 2010) aspects. However, the existing Chinese literature on the relationship between digital inclusive finance and financial investment behavior is less, and more focused on the macro level, mainly discussing its relationship with economic development and regional inequality (Li et al. 2016; Zhu & Wang 2017), and the economic benefits of digital inclusive finance (Liu & Liu 2020; Liang & Liu 2019; Song 2017; Zhang et al. 2019; Zhou 2009). At the meantime, research on user adoption behavior has focused on specific products or services (Jiang et al. 2020; Xu et al. 2014; Zhao & Cheng 2016). Research on how to improve the inclusiveness of digital inclusive finance for micro-user groups is limited and lacks a holistic perspective.

DOI: 10.1201/9781003278788-15

Therefore, from a micro perspective, this study focuses on the micro-inclusive groups in 18 provinces across China and studies the factors influencing the adoption of digitally inclusive financial products or services from the user end (UTAUT and extended, Venkatesh & Davis 2003). With the introduction of the theory of perceived risk, individual innovation, financial education, and regulatory factors, this study builds a structural equation model of the factors affecting the adoption of digital inclusive finance. Through empirical analysis and testing, it classifies, summarizes, and organically integrates digital inclusive finance, helping improve the inclusiveness of digital inclusive finance in China.

3 MODEL CONSTRUCTION AND RESEARCH DESIGN

3.1 *Development of hypotheses*

Based on the UTAUT model (as stated in Venkatesh & Davis 2003), this study retained four basic explanatory variables: performance expectation (PE), effort expectation (EE), social impact (SI), and convenience (FC). Supported by relevant theoretical research and according to the specific characteristics of digital inclusive finance, we further introduced perceived risk (PR), financial education and supervision (FES), and studied the factors influencing users' adoption of digital inclusive finance. Each explanatory variable influences the user's use behavior (UB) by influencing the use intention (BI) of the intermediary variable, considering the moderating effect of gender, age, and individual innovation. An extended UTAUT model was constructed based on the research hypotheses (H1-H10b, Table 1).

Table 1. Research hypotheses.

Hypothesis
H1: Performance expectations (PE) positively affect users' willingness (i.e., behavior intention, BI) to use digital inclusive finance
H2: Effect expectation (EE) positively affects users' willingness to use digital inclusive finance
H3: Social impact (SI) positively affects users' willingness to use digital inclusive finance
H4: Convenience (FC) conditions positively affect users' willingness to use digital inclusive finance
H5: Perceived risk (PR) negatively affects users' willingness to use digital inclusive finance
H6: Financial education and supervision (FES) negatively affect users' perceived risk of digital inclusive finance, thereby enhancing their willingness to use it
H7: The users' willingness (BI) positively affects the user's use behavior (UB)of digital inclusive finance
H8a: The positive impact of performance expectation on willingness to use is moderated by gender, which is greater for male users
H8b: The positive impact of effort expectation on use intention is regulated by gender, and the impact is greater for male users
H8c: The positive impact of social impact on the willingness to use is regulated by gender, which is less significant for male users
H9a: The positive impact of effort expectation on the willingness to use is adjusted by age, which is greater for middle-aged users
H9b: The negative impact of financial education and supervision on perceived risk is adjusted by age, and the impact on middle-aged users is greater
H9c: The negative impact of perceived risk on willingness to use is adjusted by age, and the impact is greater for middle-aged users
H10a: The positive impact of social impact on willingness to use is regulated by individual innovation (PI) which is greater for users with strong individual innovation
H10b: The negative impact of financial education and supervision on perceived risk is regulated by individual innovation, which is greater for users with strong individual innovation

3.2 Data collection

Based on the relevant information required in the expanded UTAUT model, we selected towns or remote villages in 18 provinces in China as the research area. The specific research objects were farmers, urban low-income groups, and other micro-inclusive groups in the region. The study period was from December 2021 to March 2022. The questionnaire was divided into two parts. The first part includes the user's basic information, such as gender, age, and other regulatory variables. In the second part, the Likert five-point scale was used to quantify the observation variables needed for the study to facilitate data analysis. The questionnaire was revised after the pre-test and then distributed online to ensure that it met the requirements of the survey analysis steps.

4 ANALYSIS OF SURVEY RESULT

A total of 652 questionnaires were collected, of which, 385 valid questionnaires (hereinafter referred to as "sample") were finally obtained based on the screening criteria of using digital financial products and filling the questionnaire carefully and completely, with a response rate of 59%.

4.1 Preliminary analysis

4.1.1 Reliability and validity analysis of the scale

Cronbach's alpha (α) was used to analyze the reliability of the model. The social impact α coefficient was 0.689, close to 0.7, and for other factors, the α coefficients, were all above 0.8, indicating that the data of each dimension is consistent. Therefore, the model passed the reliability tests.

Before the factor analysis, we examined the KMO and Bartlett's sphere test values. The results showed that the overall KMO and Bartlett's sphere test values were 0.925 and 0.001, respectively. Therefore, the factor analysis is appropriate. The factor load matrix rotated using the maximum variance method was also investigated. Six factors were extracted that were consistent with the questionnaire. The factor load corresponding to each index was greater than 0.5, most of them were greater than 0.7, indicating good validity.

4.1.2 Descriptive statistics

Through the descriptive statistical analysis of the samples, we found that the data conforms to the real laws and covers the financial inclusive groups well, thereby meeting the requirements of this survey. It is of practical significance to study user adoption behavior of digital inclusive finance.

4.2 Structural equation model analysis

4.2.1 Model identification and fitting

The hypothesis of each path in the structural equation model was verified using AMOS tools. After deleting some factors with low factor loads, the structural equation model shown in Figure 1 was obtained. The overall fitting coefficients are presented in Table 2. In general, the goodness-of-fit of the simulation was acceptable.

The path coefficients are presented in Table 3. Since all p-values are significant, Hypotheses H1–H7 are established.

4.2.2 Influence of moderator variables

This study introduced gender, age, and individual innovation as moderating variables to jointly analyze the moderating effect. Gender and age are significant variables, while individual innovation is a potential variable. Multi-group analysis was conducted using AMOS (see Wen et al. in 2004 and 2005). As for the potential variable of individual innovation,

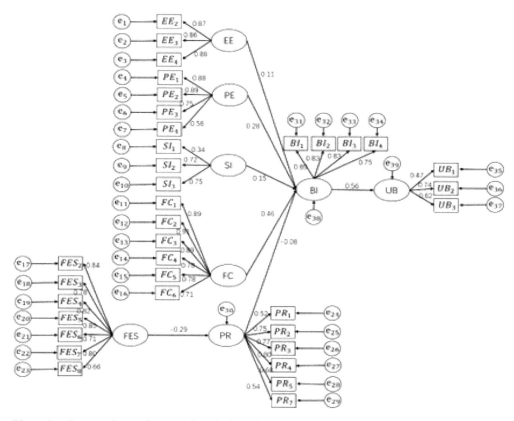

Figure 1. Structural equation model analysis of the sample variables.

Table 2. Overall fitting coefficient of sample variables.

Goodness of fit		PSMIN/DF	RMSEA	GFI	AGFI	NFI	IFI	TLI	CFI
Actual Value		2.543	0.063	0.816	0.783	0.853	0.906	0.894	0.905
Standard	Good	<3	<0.08				>0.9		
	Acceptable	<5	<0.1				>0.7		

Table 3. Path coefficients for sample variables in the structural equation model.

Path	Non-standard coefficient	Standard coefficient	Standard errors	Critical ratio	P-value	Hypothesis YES/NO
PE→BI	0.264	0.282	0.055	4.771	***	H1 YES
EE→BI	0.093	0.115	0.040	2.322	0.020	H2 YES
SI→FC	0.285	0.148	0.105	2.728	0.006	H3 YES
FC→BI	0.495	0.465	0.055	9.014	***	H4 YES
PR→BI	−0.106	−0.081	0.046	−2.323	0.020	H5 YES
FES→PR	−0.161	−0.287	0.035	−4.661	***	H6 YES
WU→UB	0.350	0.558	0.055	6.382	***	H7 YES

Note: ***indicates that the p-value is less than 0.001.

Mplus first used LMS (latent modified structural equations) to verify the existence of the regulatory effect. If the parameter estimation of the interaction term is significant, further multi-group analysis is conducted. Table 3 shows the chi-square difference of each group's verification regulation effect as well as the path coefficients and significance under multi-group analysis.

Based on gender, the samples were divided into separate men (N = 152) and women (N = 233) groups. The results show that the moderating effect of sex on the relationship between performance expectation, effort expectation, social impact, perceived risk, convenience, and willingness to adopt digital inclusive finance (H8: Δx^2 = 13.424, p = 0.063) was not significant at the 5% level; thus, H8 is not supported.

For the moderating effect test between age, expectation of effort → willingness to use (H9a: Δx^2 = 6.618, p = 0.013), financial education and supervision → perceived risk (H9b: Δx^2 = 7.030, p = 0.008), and perceived risk → willingness to use (H9c: Δx^2 = 0.041, p = 0.840), were divided into two groups: young (under 30 years old) and middle-aged (30–50 years old). The sample sizes for each group were 152 and 156, respectively. The results shown in Table 4 indicate that except for H9c, H9a and H9b are supported.

With regard to the moderating effect of the latent variable of individual innovation, the estimated values of the interaction parameters of social impact and individual innovation were not significant (p = 0.985); thus, H10a is not supported. The interaction coefficient of financial education, supervision, and individual innovation is significant (H10b: β = −0.172, p = 0.016); therefore, H10b is supported (Table 5).

Table 4. Results from moderating effect.

Moderator Variables Gender	Model	x^2(d.f.)	Δx^2(p-value)	Men (N = 152)	Women (N = 233)
				Standardized coefficients	
	Model 1	2195.631 (1134)		–	–
	Model 2	2209.055 (1141)	13.424 (0.062)		
Age				**Youth (N = 152)**	**Mid-aged (N = 156)**
	Model 1	3235.013 (1800)			
	Model 3	3241.181 (1801)	6.168 (0.013)	0.016	0.241***
	Model 4	3242.043 (1801)	7.030 (0.008)	−0.070*	−0.256***
	Model 5	3235.054 (1801)	0.041 (0.840)	0.262	0.213
Individual Innovation				**High (N = 201)**	**Low (N = 184)**
	Model 1	2163.470 (1134)			
	Model 6	2171.199 (1135)	7.728 (0.005)	−0.052	−0.256***

Note: *p<0.05, **p<0.01, ***p<0.001. Model 1 is unrestricted model, Model 2 restricted path: EE→BI, PE→BI, SI→BI, FC→BI, FES→PR, PR→BI, Model 3 restricted path: PE→BI, Model 4 restricted path: FES→PR, Model 5 restricted path: SI→BI, Model 6 restricted path: FES→PR.

Table 5. Verification of the moderating effect of individual innovation.

Path	Moderating Effect	Estimate	P-Value
EE→UI	EExPI	−.004	.94
FC→UI	FCxPI	.027	.803
SI→UI	SIxPI	−.002	.985
PE→UI	PExPI	.041	.466
PR→UI	PRxPI	−.055	.511
FES→PR	ESxPI	−.172**	.016
UI→UB	UIxPI	−.065	.361
FES→PR→UB	PRxPI	.009	.868

5 CONCLUSION AND SUGGESTIONS

5.1 *Conclusion*

The findings are as follows: (1) Performance expectation, effort expectation, social impact, and convenience conditions all have a significant positive impact on the willingness to use digital inclusive financial products, whereas perceived risk has a significant negative impact on the willingness to use digital inclusive finance products. From the perspective of the path coefficient, inclusive users will be strongly affected by convenience conditions before they are willing to adopt digital financial technology and then make decisions based on the expected benefits, ease of use, and the use of the surrounding people. (2) Willingness to use mediates the relationship between the above variables and usage behavior. Simultaneously, the strengthening of financial education and supervision plays a role in improving willingness to use by reducing perceived risks. (3) Based on the individual characteristics of users, age played a moderating role between effort expectation and use intention, financial education and supervision, and perceived risk. Individual innovation also regulates the relationships between financial education, supervision, and perceived risk. Middle-aged people pay more attention to the ease of using digital inclusive financial technology than young people do. At the same time, the marginal utility of education and supervision in reducing risk perception is greater in middle-aged people and those with low individual innovation.

5.2 *Suggestions on promoting the development of digital inclusive finance*

The above research conclusions provide some reference for promoting digital inclusive finance in China. This study provides three suggestions as follows:

First, increase investment in capital resources and improve digital infrastructure. The positive effect of convenience should be enhanced by accelerating the spread of relevant infrastructure. All urban and rural areas should strengthen the construction of new infrastructure, improve the speed of development of information infrastructure and innovation infrastructure, and carry out upgrading of traditional infrastructure in terms of intelligent, network and digital transformation. This is the way to consolidate the underlying foundation for the development of digital inclusive finance.

Second, pay attention to the innovation of inclusive financial products and improvement of risk governance systems. We need to gradually build a digital risk governance system. Strengthen the capacity building of regulatory authorities and financial institutions' risk control capacity. Financial institutions should simultaneously optimize the risk control system, investigate, and sort out the potential risks of digital inclusive finance, improve the risk prevention and control level, and protect the interests of users.

Third, strengthen the publicity of digital finance knowledge and improve the financial literacy of inclusive groups. By combining online and offline promotion channels, we will build a three-dimensional publicity platform to improve the financial literacy of rural residents and lay a good foundation for the development of rural digital inclusive finance.

ACKNOWLEDGEMENT

This work is supported by grant of the National Social Science Fund titled "A Multidimensional Study on the Comparative Evaluation and Enhancement Mechanism of Inclusive Finance under Digital Empowerment" (No: 21BJL087), thank you very much for anonymous reviewers suggestions.

REFERENCES

Anand S.K. and K.S. Chhikara. 2013. A Theoretical and Quantitative Analysis of Financial Inclusion and Economic Growth, *Management and Labour Studies* 38(1–2): 103–133.

Dupas, P. and J. Robinson. 2013. Why Don't the Poor Save More? Evidence from Health Savings Experiments, *American Economic Review* 103(4): 1138–1171.

Jiang Ruiqing, Xie Fei, Ke Chuqiu, Chen Yucong. 2020. Research on Influencing Factors of Willingness to Use Based on TPB/UTAUT and Trust – Taking Ant Flower as an Example, *Journal of Nanchang University (Humanities and Social Sciences Edition)* 51(06): 70–78.

Karlan, D. and J. Zinman. 2010. Expanding Credit Access: Using Randomized Supply Decisions to Estimate the Impacts, *Review of Financial Studies* 23(01): 433–464.

Li Tao, Xu Xiang, and Sun Shuo. 2016. Inclusive Finance and Economic Growth, *Journal of Financial Research* (04): 1–16.

Liang Shuanglu, Liu Peipei. 2019. Digital Inclusive Finance and Urban-rural income gap, *Journal of Capital University of Economics and Business* 21(01): 33–41.

Liu Jinyi, Liu Chunyang. 2020. The Rural Poverty Reduction Effect of Digital Inclusive Finance: Effect and Mechanism, *Economic and Financial Essay* (01): 43–53.

Song Xiaoling. 2017. Empirical Test of Digital Inclusive Finance to Narrow the Income Gap between Urban and Rural Areas, *Financial Science* (06): 14–25.

Venkatesh V., Morris M.G., Davis G.B., et al. 2003. User Acceptance of Information Technology: Toward a Unified View, *MIS Quarterly* 27(3): 425–478.

Wen Zhonglin, Hou Jietai, Zhang Lei. 2005. Comparison and Application of Regulatory Effect and Mediation Effect, *Journal of Psychology* (02): 268–274.

Wen Zhonglin, Zhang Lei, Hou Jietai, Liu Hongyun. 2004. Mediation Effect Test Procedure and its Application, *Journal of Psychology* (05): 614–620.

Xu Lei, Wang Jianqiong, Zha Jianping. 2014. Research on E-commerce Adoption Behavior of Micro enterprises Based on UTAUT, *Journal of Central University of Finance and Economics* (07): 107–112.

Zhang Xun, Wan Guanghua, Zhang Jiajia, He Zongyue. 2019. Digital Economy, Inclusive Finance and Inclusive Growth. *Economic Research* 54(08): 71–86.

Zhao Baoguo, Cheng Yinghui. 2016. Research on Factors Affecting the Acceptance Behavior of Online Investment and Financing Individual Users, *Research on Financial Issues* (08): 50–55.

Zhou Tao, Lu Yaobin, Zhang Jinlong. 2009. Research on Mobile Banking User Adoption Behavior From the Perspective of Integrating TTF and UTAUT, *Management Science* 22(03): 75–82.

Zhu Yiming and Wang Wei. 2017. How Does Inclusive Finance Achieve Targeted Poverty Alleviation?, *Journal of Finance and Economics* (10): 43–54.

Economic and Business Management – Lent & Zhang (Eds)

Exhibition: A systematic literature review (1997–2022) and research agenda

Qianhong Chen & Songhong Chen

Faculty of Hospitality and Tourism Management, Macau University of Science and Technology, Taipa, Macau, China

ABSTRACT: With recognizing the importance of exhibition in destination's local economy, the academic interest in the exhibition is increasing. The purpose of this paper is to categorize the main research themes of exhibition research, identify the research gaps and provide future research directions. By using HistCite tool, a systematic literature review was conducted. The results of 153 publications in exhibition of hospitality and tourism field from WoS show 7 existing research themes: exhibition visiting motivation, destination attractiveness, relationship management, economic impact, value co-creation, evaluation of experience, exhibition workforce. The results of this study contribute to understanding the trends of exhibition research in hospitality and tourism field, as well as providing instructions for industry practitioners.

1 INTRODUCTION

Exhibition has been regarded as one of features in regional economy and represents a destination's prosperity (Chen & Mo 2012). Especially in many Asian countries, exhibition industry has growing rapidly and becomes the mainstream of improving local economy. Exhibition organizer provides service, venue, advertising for exhibitors, and exhibitors partner with exhibition organizers to serve visitors (Wong & Lai 2018). Exhibition provides the opportunities for visitors to form the brand image, reinforce the relationship and promote the products (Lee et al. 2018).

Despite the recognized importance of exhibition, the exhibition related research is still under-explored. Starting from 1997, scholars investigated the role of exhibition in the hospitality and tourism field. In the recent decades, researchers have investigated the exhibition related studies in various topics, such as service quality (Jung 2005), exhibition visiting motivation (Yi et al. 2018), relationship quality (Lai & Wong 2021). As an increasing number of topics is emerging from exhibition context, it is necessary to understand the research trend from an overview of exhibition research, which can provide the future research directions.

To achieve this purpose, this study conducts a systematic literature review by the content analysis, along with research tool of HistCite that helps to generate the highly cited articles. In the following sections, the methodology will be present first. Then, the results section provides the overview of descriptive analysis, citation analysis and research themes, following by conclusion and discussion.

2 METHODOLOGY

This study employs the systematic quantitative approach that provides a more comprehensive coverage of a focused area. As Pickering and Byrne (2014) discussed, this method is the most appropriate for identifying research gaps. Following Yang et al. (2017)'s process of systematic literature review, this study firstly identified the term "exhibition" and selected Web of Science (WoS) as database. Choosing Web of Science as the database for this study because it is one of world leading citation database of scholars and has high reliabilities (Lopez et al. 2020). Until July 17th of 2022, a total of 153 exhibition publications under the category of Leisure, Hospitality and Tourism field in WoS were identified for further content analysis. The 153 publications were imported to HistCite tool and it generated the citation analysis of most 30 trending articles. The citation analysis and research themes will be discussed in the following sections.

3 RESULTS

3.1 *Descriptive analysis of exhibition research*

The results reveal that the period of exhibition research is between 1997 and 2022. Despite a significant growth of publications since 2008 to 2018, there is a decreasing number of related publications since 2019. Only 3 articles were recorded in 2022. 25 articles were mostly published in exhibition related journals (Journal of Convention and Event Tourism), Visitor Studies (10), Tourism Management (9), International Journal of Hospitality Management (8). Overall, Weber Karin is the most influential author in this field, followed by Jin Xin (Cathy) and Bauer Thomas. The institution which has the most publications is Hong Kong Polytechnic University, followed by Griffith University and California State Polytechnic University Pomona. The most influential country is China, followed by USA and Australia (shown in Table 1).

Table 1. Top 10 Journals, influential authors, institutions and countries (1997–2022).

Journals	No.	Authors	No.
Journal of Convention & Event Tourism	25	Weber Karin	11
Visitor Studies	10	Jin Xin (Cathy)	8
Tourism Management	9	Bauer Thomas	5
International Journal of Hospitality Management	8	Lai Ivan Ka Wa	4
Asia Pacific Journal of Tourism Research	7	Lee Myong Jae	4
Event Management	7	Ladkin Adele	3
International Journal of Contemporary Hospitality Management	4	Wong Jose Wong Chou	3
Journal of Hospitality and Tourism Management	4	Fu Xiaoxiao	2
Journal of Travel & Tourism Marketing	4	Huang Bin	2
Journal of China Tourism Research	3	Jin Wenmin	2

Institutions		Countries	
The Hong Kong Polytechnic University	17	Peoples R China	53
Griffith University	7	USA	25
California State Polytechnic University Pomona	5	Australia	18
University of Macau	5	UK	16
City University of Macau	4	Unknown	12
Tianjin University of Finance and Economics	4	South Korea	10
Unknown	4	Taiwan	8
Bournemouth University	3	New Zealand	6
Jinan University	3	Spain	4
Macau University of Science and Technology	3	Egypt	3

3.2 Citation analysis and research themes

By using HistCite that generates the citation overview, Figure 1 shows the relationships among top 30 highly cited articles. The articles with bigger circle indicate to the frequency of being cited. The mostly cited article is "Determinants of Exhibition Service Quality as Perceived by Attendees" from Jung (2005), which is identified as the most important article in exhibition research. The second mostly cited article is "Which exhibition attributes create repeat visitation?" from Whitfield and Webber (2011). It can be identified that these 30 top cited articles focus on period between 2005 and 2018 and in two major area. The first hot area focuses on the role of visitors, which scholars attempted to understand visitors' motivation (Rittichainuwat & Mair 2012), and destination attractiveness (Jin et al. 2012a) prior to visiting the exhibition. The second hot area focuses on the role of relationship between exhibition organizers and exhibitors, which discussed the way of improving their relationship quality (Jin et al. 2012b) and create value co-creation activities. Furthermore, the most cited articles are mainly from perspectives of either visitor-exhibitor or exhibitor-exhibition organizers.

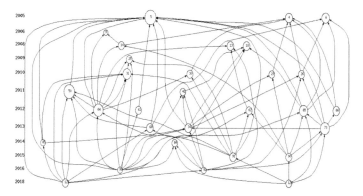

Figure 1.   HistCite citation analysis.

By the content analysis, the related exhibition research is classified into 7 different themes: (1) exhibition visiting motivation; (2) destination attractiveness; (3) relationship management; (4) economic impact; (5) value co-creation; (6) evaluation of experience; (7) exhibition workforce. More specifically, under the research theme "motivation", most articles are empirical studies and aim to understand what factors motivate attendants' engagement in an exhibition. For example, Yi et al. (2018) and Whitfield and Webber (2011) identified multiple motivators (e.g. contact with the vendor, knows the competitors, understand the products, reputation of exhibition, networking opportunities). Under destination attractiveness, most authors generally focused on exhibition site selection (Jin et al. 2013) (e.g. host city leadership) and attractiveness from visitors (Jin & Weber 2016) (e.g. leisure environment, accessibility). Within relationship management, past studies explored the factors that influence exhibitors' relationship with organizers, such as service quality and relationship quality, trust and affective commitment, relationship on social media marketing (Jin et al. 2012b). Under "economic impact", past studies indicated that the role of exhibition industry in regional economy (Kim & Chon 2009) by estimating the expenditures of different stakeholders. Under value co-creation, few studies (Wong & Lai 2019) examined the effects of value co-creation activities between different stakeholders. Concerning that experience is an important antecedent of behavioral intention, many scholars mainly focused on exhibition visitors' satisfaction, loyalty, emotion (Wu et al. 2016) with the purpose of providing strategies for further visitation, thus these are classified under "evaluation of experience". Last, leading by McCabe (2012), the "exhibition workforce" research theme is emerging, which involves employee recruitment, retention, development strategy and management practices.

4 DISCUSSIONS AND CONLCUSIONS

This paper presents the findings of a systematic literature review in exhibition context between 1997 and 2022 and identifies 7 research themes. This study contributes to understanding an overview of the research hotspots and themes of exhibition. The results show that the exhibition research in recent years has shown a decreasing trend from 2019. One of the possible reasons is that COVID-19 may greatly influence the development of exhibition industry (Rwigema & Celestin 2020). As more and more exhibition organizers currently adopt the online exhibition format, it can be expected that the future trend of exhibition will adopt both virtual and physical exhibition. Therefore, future studies may benefit from the inclusion of publications in online or hybrid format to provide additional insights for exhibition development in post-COVID-19.

Second, the research themes emerging from this study show the most recent topic in exhibition research involves value co-creation and relationship management. The results provide directions that there are still potentials on discussing value co-creation and relationship management in exhibition context. Third, this study shows that exhibition research faces the lack of awareness from perspective of exhibition organizers. As previous exhibition studies mainly focused on visitor-exhibitors and exhibitors-exhibition organizers, it is necessary to understand the relationship between visitor-exhibition organizers. Future studies may also need to analyze how to effectively improve the performance of exhibition market and how to enhance the cooperation with exhibition organizers to promote the exhibition development.

Despite above contribution of this study, there are several limitations. First, the data of this study were exported from WoS database. As the single database may not fully cover the exhibition research, the future studies can consider multiple databases, such as EBSCOHost, Scopus. Second, the content analysis of this study was conduct on the published articles until 17th July 2022. The number of publications may have limitation since there may some research on the peer-review and in production process. When conducting the systematic literature review in the future studies, it is necessary to include more recent articles.

REFERENCES

Chen, Y.-F., & Mo, H.-E. 2012. Attendees' Perspectives on the Service Quality of An Exhibition Organizer: A Case Study of a Tourism Exhibition. *Tourism Management Perspectives* 1: 28–33.

Jin, X., & Weber, K. 2016. Exhibition Destination Attractiveness–organizers' and Visitors' Perspectives. *International Journal of Contemporary Hospitality Management*.

Jin, X., Weber, K., & Bauer, T. 2012a. Impact of Clusters on Exhibition Destination Attractiveness: Evidence from Mainland China. *Tourism Management* 33(6): 1429–1439.

Jin, X., Weber, K., & Bauer, T. 2012b. Relationship Quality Between Exhibitors and Organizers: A Perspective from Mainland China's Exhibition Industry. *International Journal of Hospitality Management* 31(4): 1222–1234.

Jin, X., Weber, K., & Bauer, T. 2013. Dimensions and Perceptional Differences of Exhibition Destination Attractiveness: The Case of China. *Journal of Hospitality & Tourism Research* 37(4): 447–469.

Jung, M. 2005. Determinants of Exhibition Service Quality as Perceived by Attendees. *Paper Presented at the Journal of Convention & Event Tourism*.

Kim, S. S., & Chon, K. 2009. An Economic Impact Analysis of the Korean Exhibition Industry. *International Journal of Tourism Research* 11(3): 311–318.

Lai, I. K. W., & Wong, J. W. C. 2021. From Exhibitor Engagement Readiness to Perceived Exhibition Performance Via Relationship Quality. *Journal of Hospitality and Tourism Management* 46: 144–152.

Lee, T. H., Fu, C.-J., & Tsai, L.-F. 2018. Why Does a Firm Participate in a Travel Exhibition? A Case Study of the Taipei International Travel Fair. *Asia Pacific Journal of Tourism Research* 23(7): 677–690.

McCabe, V. S. 2012. Developing and Sustaining a Quality Workforce: Lessons from the Convention and Exhibition Industry. *Paper Presented at the Journal of Convention & Event Tourism.*

Pickering, C., & Byrne, J. 2014. The Benefits of Publishing Systematic Quantitative Literature Reviews for PhD Candidates and Other Early-career Researchers. *Higher Education Research & Development* 33(3): 534–548.

Rittichainuwat, B., & Mair, J. 2012. Visitor Attendance Motivations at Consumer Travel Exhibitions. *Tourism Management* 33(5): 1236–1244.

Rodríguez-López, M. E., Alcántara-Pilar, J. M., Del Barrio-García, S., & Muñoz-Leiva, F. 2020. A Review of Restaurant Research in the Last Two Decades: A Bibliometric Analysis. *International Journal of Hospitality Management* 87: 102387.

Rwigema, P. C., & Celestin, R. P. 2020. Impact of Covid-19 Pandemic to Meetings, Incentives, Conferences and Exhibitions (Mice) Tourism in Rwanda. *The Strategic Journal of Business and Change Management* 7(3): 395–409.

Whitfield, J., & Webber, D. J. 2011. Which Exhibition Attributes Create Repeat Visitation? *International Journal of Hospitality Management* 30(2): 439–447.

Wong, J. W. C., & Lai, I. K. W. 2018. Evaluating Value Co-creation Activities in Exhibitions: An Impact-asymmetry Analysis. *International Journal of Hospitality Management* 72: 118–131.

Wong, J. W. C., & Lai, I. K. W. 2019. The Effects of Value Co-creation Activities on the Perceived Performance of Exhibitions: A Service Science Perspective. *Journal of Hospitality and Tourism Management* 39: 97–109.

Wu, H.-C., Cheng, C.-C., & Ai, C.-H. 2016. A Study of Exhibition Service Quality, Perceived Value, Emotion, Satisfaction, and Behavioral Intentions. *Event Management* 20(4): 565–591.

Yang, E. C. L., Khoo-Lattimore, C., & Arcodia, C. 2017. A systematic literature Review of Risk and Gender Research in Tourism. *Tourism Management* 58: 89–100.

Yi, X., Fu, X., Jin, W., & Okumus, F. 2018. Constructing a Model of Exhibition Attachment: Motivation, Attachment, and Loyalty. *Tourism Management* 65: 224–236.

Economic and Business Management – Lent & Zhang (Eds)
© 2023 the Author(s), ISBN 978-1-032-24482-2

The present situation, problems and countermeasures of social financing of digital cultural industry in China

Yang Liu & Xuliao Zhu

Canvard College, Beijing Technology and Business University, China

ABSTRACT: With the development of economy and digital technology, digital cultural industry has become a key area of cultural industry development and an important part of digital economy. Financial support is an important driving force to promote digital cultural industry to have high-quality development. Under the influence of COVID-19 and international economic situation, the total amount of social financing of digital cultural industry has decreased, and the main channel of financing is bond financing, which is mainly distributed in Beijing, Shanghai and Guangzhou regions. Based on the analysis of the current situation and problems of social financing of digital cultural industry in China, this paper puts forward some countermeasures. and suggestions for its further development.

1 INTRODUCTION

Digital cultural industry is the deep integration of the digital technology and the cultural industry, which takes cultural and creative content as the core and relies on digital technology to create, produce, spread and serve. It covers digital games, interactive entertainment, film and television animation, digital video and audio, digital education, digital publishing, digital collection, digital performance, network services, content software, smart tourism and so on. Digital cultural industry is an intelligence-intensive and high-value-added emerging industry. It presents the characteristics of rapid technological change, digital production, network communication, and personalized consumption. It will help to foster new supply and promote new consumption [2]. Digital cultural industry has gradually become a key area of cultural industry development and an important part of the digital economy. The development of digital cultural industry cannot be separated from financial support, which is an important driving force to promote digital cultural industry to have high-quality development.

The academic researches on digital cultural industry started late, which mainly focused on the basic concept of it, the current situation of the industry, and international experience. There are many studies on the financing of the cultural industry, but there are almost no studies on the social financing of the digital cultural industry. Yang Xiuyun, Li Min, Li Yangzi (2021) insisted that the investment and financing support mechanism of cultural enterprises should be improved [3]. Zhang Xiaohuan (2021) noted that we should not only attach great importance to the development of the digital cultural industry itself, but also provide support in policies such as funds, cultivate the digital cultural consumer market, and expand digital cultural enterprises [5]. Bao Guoqiang, Chen Tiancheng and Huang Cheng (2021) pointed out that the reform and opening up should be used as guidance to reduce the restrictions on foreign investment, actively develop a mixed-ownership economy, and support digital cultural enterprises to list in the international capital market [1]. The existing

DOI: 10.1201/9781003278788-17

research is only involved in the analysis of the development status and problems of China's digital cultural industry, no detailed and targeted research on financing. It is particularly important to clarify the current situation of social financing of China's digital cultural industry, analyze the existing problems, and find the future path to promote its long-term and healthy development. Based on the analysis of the current situation and problems of social financing of China's digital cultural industry, this paper puts forward some counter-measures and suggestions for its further development.

2   CURRENT SITUATION OF SOCIAL FINANCING

2.1   Total scale of financing

In 2020, China's cultural industry achieved 1778 social financing events through private equity financing, new third board financing, listing financing, bond financing, trust financing, crowd funding and other channels (excluding bank loans), and the scale of social financing reached 271.762 billion Yuan. Due to the combined effects of the COVID-19, the complex international political situations, and the intensified trade frictions, the scale of social financing in China's digital cultural industry declined significantly in 2020. The number of cases was 292, a year-on-year decrease of 23.56%. The financing scale was 123.490 billion Yuan, a year-on-year decrease of 11.97%, accounting for 45.44% of the total scale of social financing of the national cultural industry [4].

2.2   The scale of financing through various channels

In 2020, in addition to bank loans, the financing channels of China's digital cultural industry mainly include bonds, IPO financing, private equity financing, IPO refinancing, new third board financing, crowd funding, etc. The specific financing scale is shown in Figure 1 below. Among them, bonds were the main source of funds, and the financing scale was as high as 66.364 billion Yuan, accounting for 53.74% of the total social financing scale in various channels of digital cultural industry. Followed by the IPO financing, the financing amount was 33.167 billion Yuan, accounting for 26.86%. The third was private equity financing, with a financing amount of 15.386 billion Yuan, accounting for 12.46%. The scale of IPO refinancing reached 8.373 billion Yuan, accounting for 6.78% [4]. New third board financing, crowd funding and other channels raised 199 million Yuan, accounting for 0.16%.

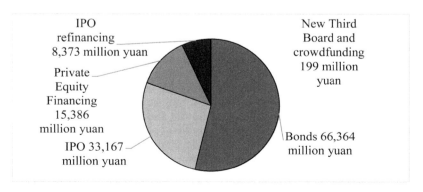

Figure 1.   Sub-channel financing scale of China's digital cultural industry in 2020 [4].

2.3 *The scale of financing by region*

In 2020, China's digital cultural industry mainly raised funds in Beijing, Shanghai and Guangdong, of which Guangdong ranked first with a total amount of 51.899 billion Yuan. The second was Beijing with a total amount of 37.587 billion Yuan. The third was Shanghai with a total amount of 23.410 billion Yuan. The above three regions accounted for 91.42% of the total scale of social financing in the digital cultural industry. Besides, Zhejiang, Guangxi, Shaanxi, Jiangsu, Hubei, Sichuan and Hunan ranked fourth to tenth, with financing amounts of 5.279 billion Yuan, 2.267 billion Yuan, 1.051 billion Yuan, 956 million Yuan, 802 million Yuan, 117 million Yuan and 60 million Yuan respectively. The total financing from other regions amounted to 62 million Yuan [4]. The size of the financing is shown in Figure 2 below.

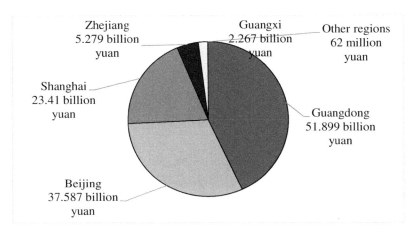

Figure 2.   Financing scale of China's digital cultural industry by region in 2020 [4].

3   EXISTING PROBLEMS

3.1 *Aggregate problems*

Although the total amount of social financing of digital cultural industry still accounts for half of the total scale of social financing of the national cultural industry, judging from the comparative data over the years, it is undeniable that the scale of social financing and the number of cases of the digital cultural industry in 2020 have shown a downward trend. From the view of the macro-economic situation, the epidemic situation of COVID-19 will be the most critical variable in economic, cultural and social development for a long time. The changing trend of global economic and political pattern will influence the development of macro-economy and also transmit to the field of culture and finance.

The digital cultural industry is an important focus of cultural construction. It should not only become the dissemination channel of social mainstream values, but also become the guidance of the era culture, and the source of culture and value innovation. With the widespread popularity of the Internet and digital technology, animation games, online literature, online music, live broadcasts, micro-films have developed rapidly, becoming the main products of mass cultural consumption. Compared with the developed countries' development of digital cultural industry, we still need continuous improvement in technological innovation and application. Rich cultural resources and civilization accumulation are the advantages of developing digital cultural industry, but they have not been transformed into

112

product and service advantages, and the development capacity of cultural industry needs to be broken through. In addition, the digital cultural industry's development urgently needs to explore diversified business models, so as to make it sustainable. Different from the short-term returns of the capital's profit-pursuing nature, the cultural industry's development requires long-term accumulation, and presents an obvious characteristic of 'asset-light'. It needs sufficient financial support, and social financing is an important source of funds.

3.2 *Structural problems*

Regional absorption of funds is unbalanced. Beijing, Shanghai and Guangdong absorb more than 90% of the funds, while other regions absorb less. Among the three regions, Guangdong attracted the most funds with 51.899 billion Yuan, accounting for 42% of the total social financing of the digital cultural industry. Due to the effect of locations, market choices and industrial policies, the industrial development of a country or region is unbalanced at any time. And the digital cultural industry in the mid-west area lags behind the eastern region as a whole. Because of insufficient social financing, it is difficult for the digital cultural industry to form a large scale in some mid-west provinces, such as Jilin, Gansu, Anhui and Shaanxi, and even some eastern provinces. However, the differences between regions are difficult to change over a long period of time. To some extent, the unbalanced regional development affects that the proportion of the added value of cultural industry to GDP in the western provinces is lower than the national average.

There are obvious differences in the financing scale of different financing channels. Bond financing is the main financing channel. From the data in 2020, it can be seen that 53.74% of funds were absorbed by the bond channel. The bond market performed well, Guangdong ranked first, and Shanghai increased, but the scale of financing in other regions was relatively low. The initial public offering financing and private equity financing also reached more than 10 billion Yuan, 33.167 billion Yuan and 15.386 billion Yuan respectively; the initial public offering refinancing reached 8.373 billion Yuan; the new third board financing was close to 200 million Yuan. The financing market of the digital cultural enterprises on the new third board was sluggish, and the type of financing was directional stock issuance financing. The amount of financing from other channels such as crowdfunding was small. Guangdong and Zhejiang performed better, while crowdfunding in other regions attracted less funds.

The financing ability of enterprises at different stages is obviously different. Digital cultural enterprises in the mature stage have better ability to absorb social financing, while those new and growing digital cultural enterprises are more difficult to obtain financing. The scale of initial public offering financing and refinancing scale of listed digital cultural enterprises have increased, but the financing is mainly distributed in Beijing, Guangdong, Shanghai and Guangxi.

4 COUNTERMEASURES AND SUGGESTIONS

4.1 *Total amount of financing*

The healthy and rational development of digital cultural industry needs the support of government, market and social forces. It's necessary to establish and improve the National Cultural Operation System, perform the government's supervision and guidance responsibilities, give full play to the market function, and make up for the supporting force of social weaknesses.

The healthy and rational development of digital cultural industry needs to consolidate the multi-level financing system of digital cultural industry, especially developing stock investment market. The Financial Supervision Department vigorously encourages the innovative development of the direct financing market. Under the principle of controllable risks, the policies should be adjusted and more detailed incentive measures should be introduced to put into practice the principled requirements of encouraging and supporting policies. The cultural sector should create a better cultural policy environment to prevent investors from taking advantage of policy arbitrage, while creating a safer investment environment for long-term investors.

4.2 Financing structure

We will effectively increase support for the digital cultural industry's development in the mid-west area, particularly financial support. Each region will formulate policies and measures to support financial backing for it in light of their own conditions. Improve the information infrastructure in urban areas and lay the foundation for the development of digital cultural industry. Cultivate the potential market of digital cultural industry and accelerate the industrialization and marketization of digital cultural services and products. Relying on the regional traditional cultural resources to develop characteristic digital cultural industry.

The digital cultural industry is limited by its own operating characteristics. There are many problems in the issuance of bonds, so it needs to further strengthen policy support. We will continue to promote the development of special bonds for the cultural industry and boost product innovation of the digital cultural industry bond market by making full use of the close ties between the government, industry organizations and enterprises, and giving full play to the role of platforms such as cultural financial service centers. In addition, the financing support and guidance for the IPO financing, private equity financing, listing refinancing, and new third board financing of the digital cultural industry will be increased from the perspectives of policy support and guidance.

Under the guidance of the national financial support policy for the cultural industry, local governments pay more attention to the development of the cultural industry, actively promote cooperation with cultural enterprises and financial institutions, and strengthen financial support for culture. The shift of resources from concentrating on large enterprises to taking into account small and medium-sized cultural enterprises will change the financial constraints of the small and medium-sized enterprises and improve the financing situation.

REFERENCES

[1] Bao Guoqiang, Chen Tiancheng, Huang Cheng. The Connotation Construction and Path Selection of High-quality Development of Digital Cultural Industry, *Publication*, 2021(3), pages 36–38.

[2] The Guiding Opinions on Promoting the Innovative Development of Digital Cultural Industry, *Issued by the Ministry of Culture*, 2017.

[3] Yang Xiuyun, Li Min, Li Yangzi. Research on Ecosystem Optimization of Digital Cultural Industry, *Journal of Xi'an Jiaotong University (Social Sciences)*, 2021(9), pages 127–135.

[4] Yang Tao and Jin Wei. Report on the Development of Chinese Culture and Finance (2021), *Social Sciences Academic Press* 2021,1 September.

[5] Zhang Xiaohuan. Development Trend, Problems and Countermeasures of digital Culture Industry, *Journal of Chongqing University of Technology (Social Sciences)* 2021(2), pages 1–7.

Economic and Business Management – Lent & Zhang (Eds)
© 2023 the Author(s), ISBN 978-1-032-24482-2

Impact of Covid-19 epidemic on the development of smart accounting in China

Ran Liu & Lantian Jiang

College of Economic Management, Dalian University, Dalian, China

ABSTRACT: In the present paper, the impact of the Covid-19 epidemic on the annual/monthly accounting reports of listed and non-listed companies, accounting work office mode, and key links of the accounting workflow in the era of artificial intelligence was explored and analyzed based on the questionnaire of the Covid-19 epidemic on accounting work. The Covid-19 outbreak has greatly affected accounting profession. In the era of artificial intelligence, accounting reform and development from the aspects of government, enterprises, and accounting personnel should be achieved in the future. The accounting personnel should develop intelligent finance, and explore remote intelligent accounting work to promote the construction and development of intelligent financial accounting.

1 INTRODUCTION

In recent years, with the widespread applications of internet technology and the rise of artificial intelligence and big data technology, artificial intelligence has been widely applied in social and economic activities. In this regard, accounting has also gradually transformed from computerized accounting to intelligent or smart accounting (He 2022; Lee & Tajudeen 2020; Mancini et al. 2021; Virtanen 2021; Zhang et al. 2020). Artificial intelligence can fundamentally replace a large number of accounting-based financial management tasks, thereby greatly reducing the number of middle and low-level financial personnel (Arroyo Esteban et al. 2022). However, high-end accounting personnel should play an active role in intelligent or smart accounting, for instance, observing professional ethics, establishing correct strategic thinking, using professional judgment and information technology to strengthen communication with business, etc., though artificial intelligence is playing an important role in the development of intelligent or smart accounting (Stancheva-Todorova 2018). Yoon (2021) documented changes in accounting areas due to the adoption of IT technologies in the era of technology and information, defined the required accounting professions in this era, and presented efficient educational methodologies for training such accounting experts. Traditional financial management has the basic characteristics of being separate from business, only being responsible for the preparation of monthly, quarterly, and annual reports, post-processing of accounting, static digital management of financial management, relatively closed accounting department, and strong professionalism of the accounting department. In the era of internet technology and big data, accounting business and accounting information increasingly present new features such as massive data processing and real-time cloud computing (Askary et al. 2018; Greenman & Management 2017; Saukkonen et al. 2018; Zhang et al. 2020). It is necessary to possess fundamental characteristics of financial and business digitalization, performing pre- and in-process accounting, static financial management, and dynamic digital management. This necessitates a comprehensive opening of the department through accounting, as well as accounting used as a decision-making service.

A sudden Covid-19 epidemic widely swept the globe in early 2020, it is difficult to accurately predict when it will end and how much it will impact and change the world economy. However, the impact of the pandemic on the world economy has been complicated by the risks accumulated over the years, If the pandemic continues, the world economy may be caught up in a prolonged downturn. It still has had a serious and widespread impact on global social and economic activities so far (Parichehr & Ahmad 2022; Xu 2020). Under the epidemic, many companies cut down salaries and downsized employment to reduce costs. A large number of small and medium-sized companies are facing a crisis of bankruptcy caused by the exhaustion of liquidity due to their weak anti-risk capabilities. But there are also opportunities hidden in the crisis. The home-office approach has brought new growth points to online businesses relying on internet technology. Emerging industries such as cloud conferences, cloud education, and cloud tourism have sprung up during the epidemic, and big data accounting generated by internet technology has also been promoted accordingly. The Covid-19 epidemic has also had a huge impact on the economy and people's livelihood in China, changing the lifestyle and working methods of people, as well as changing accounting work. During the epidemic, the Beijing National Accounting Institute conducted a questionnaire mainly for business organizations to fully understand and grasp the research purpose of the impact of the epidemic on accounting work and accounting personnel (Institute 2020; Zhang 2020). The scope of this questionnaire survey is mainly limited to enterprises. The questionnaire was carried out online from March 9, 2020. As of March 11, a total of 10,970 questionnaires have been received from 34 provinces, municipalities, autonomous regions, and municipalities (except Hong Kong, Macao, & Taiwan), of which 10,341 are valid questionnaires. Among the respondents of this questionnaire survey, there were 3,484 males and 6,857 females, of which 4,063 were from listed companies, accounting for 39.29%, and 6,278 were from unlisted companies, accounting for 60.71%. Based on the results of the questionnaire survey, this paper further analyzes the impact of the epidemic on accounting work in the era of artificial intelligence and the enlightenment of the epidemic on the future development of intelligent and smart accounting, and explores the future development direction of intelligent and smart accounting in order to enrich the intelligent and smart accounting theory in China.

2 IMPACT OF COVID-19 EPIDEMIC ON ACCOUNTING

2.1 Impact on annual or monthly reports completed among different industries

In terms of enterprises surveyed, state-owned enterprises account for 82.95%, private enterprises account for 15.29%, foreign-funded enterprises account for 0.49%, and Sino-foreign joint ventures account for 1.27%. Furthermore, in terms of enterprise scale, large enterprises accounted for 62.3%, medium-sized enterprises accounted for 22.36%, small enterprises accounted for 12.03%, and micro enterprises accounted for 3.32%. The survey shows that most companies can complete the annual report or monthly report according to the scheduled time, and the completion rate is as high as 94.19%. Only 2.91% of the companies cannot complete the annual or monthly reports, 29.74% of the companies completed the annual or monthly reports within 10 days, and 59.58% of the companies completed the annual or monthly reports within 30 days. Figure 1 shows the comparison of annual or monthly reports completed among cross-industries. As shown in Figure 1, most industries can complete their annual or monthly reports on time. Among the industries that cannot be completed, the industries that account for a relatively high proportion include IT, FFLF (farming, forestry, livestock, and fishing), medical insurance, media, and entertainment, accounting for 11.11%, 10.71%, 10%, and 9.68%, respectively.

116

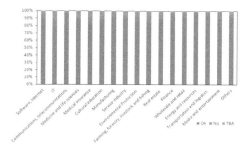

Figure 1. Comparison of annual or monthly reports completed among cross-industries.

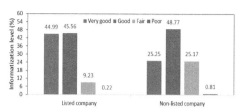

Figure 2. Comparison of informatization level of listed companies and non-listed companies.

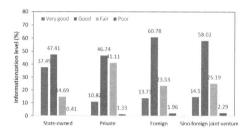

Figure 3. Comparison of informatization level of different types of enterprises.

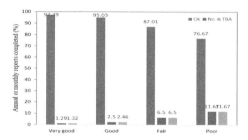

Figure 4. Comparison between informatization levels and the annual or monthly reports completed.

Is the completion of the annual or monthly reports necessarily related to the informatization level of enterprise? Figures 2 and 3 show the comparison of the informatization level of listed companies and non-listed companies, and the informatization level of different types of enterprises, respectively. As shown in Figures 2 and 3, the respondents reported that the informatization level of enterprises is generally good, and the informatization level of listed companies (good or better accounted for 90.55%) is better than that of non-listed companies (good or better accounted for 74.02%). State-owned enterprises (84.9% of them are good and above) are better than other enterprises. As shown in Figure 4, the results show that the informatization level has a certain impact on the completion of the annual report or monthly report, but the impact is insignificant.

In addition, the construction of the financial shared service center helps complete annual or monthly financial reports during the epidemic. According to the respondents, 26.51% of the companies have completed the construction of the financial shared service center, 49.53% of the companies are under construction, and 3.76% of companies are considering construction after the epidemic. The results show that 97.08% of the companies have constructed a financial sharing service center that can complete the annual or monthly reports according to the scheduled time.

2.2 Impact on accounting work mode

According to the questionnaire survey, 55.91% of the companies before the epidemic follow dominantly on-site (offline) accounting, 34.75% of companies consist the combination of on-site and remote (online) accounting, and only 9.34% of companies are based on remote accounting. It's one of the reasons for the decline in the efficiency of working from home during the epidemic. After the resumption of work, the understanding of accountants has changed. The proportion of combination of on-site and remote accounting has sharply increased to 71.58%, an increase of 36.83% from before the epidemic. In addition, interviewees believe that the proportion of 100% on-site office work is only 8.27% with the improvement of informatization in the future (Figure 5), but online work (remote accounting) cannot completely replace on-site (offline) accounting work.

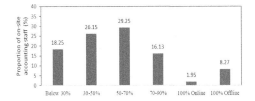 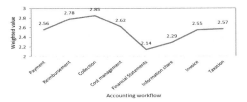

Figure 5. The proportion of on-site accounting staff with the increase of informatization level.

Figure 6. Work links in the current accounting workflow affected by the epidemic.

Respondents believe that only 1.95% of the companies completely adopt online remote accounting work. This further validates that the combination of on-site (offline) and online remote accounting is the best accounting work mode for the companies in the future, and the proportion of on-site accounting workers should currently be around 50% of the total workers. The possible reasons for negative viewpoints on online remote accounting are: 1) the data security and effectiveness in the remote or cloud server are not guaranteed. There are a series of risks in the accounting data of enterprises under the cloud accounting model and Covid-19 conditions. 2) Remote online accounting is very dependent on service suppliers. Since remote online accounting is inseparable from service providers in software development, hardware construction, and even subsequent business processing, this may lead to increasing pressure on both companies and service providers.

2.3 *Impact on work links in the current accounting workflow*

Figure 6 shows work links in the current accounting workflow affected by the epidemic. As shown in Figure 6, although the survey found that the report generation process was the least affected, the respondents still believed that the five major work links, i.e., collection (2.85), reimbursement (2.78), cost management (2.62), tax (2.57), and payment (2.56) are greatly affected by the epidemic. Companies of different types variously affected by the epidemic have differences in the aspects of accounting workflow. Table 1 lists the comparison of the

Table 1. Comparison of the differences in the accounting work of the greatly affected industries.

	X\Y	The most affected accounting links	The least affected accounting links
Great loss	Medical Insurance	Cost management	Taxation
	Wholesale and retail	Collection	Financial statements
	Transportation and logistics	Reimbursement	Financial statements
Great benefit	Software, internet	Collection	Financial statements
	Communication, telecommunications	Collection	Financial statements
	Medicine and life sciences	Collection	Payment

differences in the accounting work of the greatly affected industries. As listed in Table 1, except that the transportation and logistics industry with a great loss focuses on reimbursement, and the medical insurance industry focuses on cost management, other industries that are greatly affected believe that the collection process is the most affected in the accounting process.

3 DISCUSSIONS

Based on the above results, it can be seen that although the overall informatization level of the company is relatively good through the previous survey, the specific implementation of the daily accounting workflow in the contact link is generally relatively large. This should also be considered as a key link for enterprises to consider and optimize the process of accounting informatization in the future after the epidemic. That means how to further help enterprises create smooth communication and efficiency improvement, as well as how to effectively solve these key problems. After the epidemic, the information technology issues that need to be resolved in the future include: (1) VPN remote secure tax filing and mobile login; (2) remote secure electronic tax filing; (3) approval of digital signatures, electronic tax filing invoices, and mobile informatization. Among them, the VPN remote security tax filing mobile login system is a key technology to further solve the remote tax filing users' inability to access sensitive data such as corporate information. The remote tax filing technology can break the time and space constraints of taxpayers' tax filing, reduce the tax management cost of enterprises, and improve the work efficiency of enterprises. Digitally signed invoices, as one of the important means to ensure the security of corporate network information, can effectively solve the problems of forgery, denial, impersonation, and tampering. The purpose of digitally signed invoices is to completely replace the traditional taxpayers' hand-printed signatures and electronic seals in the network environment. Remote secure electronic tax declaration and invoice mobile approval system can be combined with the internal ERP, CRM, SCS, and other electronic invoice systems of the enterprise. The invoice information is fully electronic and processed in a centralized manner, which is helpful for the enterprise's own accounting processing and can provide timely financial decision-making support to business operators and employees.

The diversity and gradual popularity of artificial intelligence technologies not only provide richer and more reliable accounting information for accounting but also improve and shorten the time required for accounting, ensure its quality, and reduce the cost. When accounting work is subject to smaller time and space constraints, the accounting will also become more scientific and effective.

4 CONCLUSIONS

The impact of the Covid-19 epidemic on the annual/monthly accounting reports of listed and non-listed companies, accounting work office mode and key links of the accounting workflow in the era of artificial intelligence were explored and analyzed based on the questionnaire of the Covid-19 epidemic on accounting work. The Covid-19 outbreak has greatly affected the accounting profession. The epidemic has completely changed the work and daily lifestyle of people. The accounting industry should further develop its business and services online to create a "zero-contact" business model. Exploring the remote online office mode and strengthening the construction of information-sharing platform will become the key content of accounting work. The government should strengthen the construction of information-sharing platforms and improve financial standardization processes, and the accounting personnel should develop intelligent finance, and explore remote intelligent accounting work to promote the construction and development of intelligent financial accounting. Accounting reform and development from the aspects of government and accounting personnel should be achieved in the future in the era of artificial intelligence.

REFERENCES

Arroyo Esteban, S., Urquía Grande, E., Martínez De Silva, A. & Pérez Estébanez, R. 2022. Big Data, Accounting and International Development: *Trends and Challenges*.

Askary, S., Abu-Ghazaleh, N. & Tahat, Y. A. Artificial Intelligence and Reliability of Accounting Information. *Conference on e-Business, e-Services and e-Society*, 2018. Springer, 315–324.

Greenman, C. & Management 2017. Exploring the Impact of Artificial Intelligence on the Accounting Profession. *Journal of Research in Business, Economics*, 8, 1451.

He, B. 2022. The Impact of Intelligent Accounting Information Management on Corporate Governance Information Transparency. *J Security Communication Networks*, 2022.

Institute, B. N. A. 2020. *The Impact of COVID-19 Epidemic on Corporate Accounting Work and Accounting Personnel*. Beijing: Beijing National Accounting Institute.

Lee, C. S. & Tajudeen, F. P. 2020. Impact of Artificial Intelligence on Accounting: Evidence From Malaysian Organizations. *Asian Journal of Business and Accounting*, 13.

Mancini, D., Lombardi, R. & Tavana, M. 2021. Four Research Pathways for Understanding the Role of Smart Technologies in Accounting. *J Meditari Accountancy Research*.

Parichehr, Z. F. & Ahmad, G. 2022. The effect of COVID-19 on Audit Quality During Social Distancing. *Journal of Industrial Engineering Management Studies*, 1–8.

Saukkonen, N., Laine, T. & Suomala, P. 2018. Utilizing Management Accounting Information for Decision-making. *Qualitative Research in Accounting & Management*, 15, 181–205.

Stancheva-Todorova, E. P. 2018. How Artificial Intelligence is Challenging Accounting Profession. *"Journal of International Scientific Publications" Economy & Business*, 12, 126–141.

Virtanen, V. 2021. Effects of Intelligent Process Automation Implementation on Used Time and Manual Work in Finnish Accounting Software.

Xu, X. 2020. The Impact of COVID-19 on World Economy and China's Role. *Belt and Road Initiative Tax Journal*, 1, 114–119.

Yoon, S. 2021. Accounting Education in the Era of Information and Technology: Suggestions for Adopting IT Related Curriculum. *Journal of Information Technology Services*, 20, 91–109.

Zhang, Q. 2020. The Impact of COVID-19 Epidemic on Corporate Accounting Work and Accounting Personnel. *Finance and Accounting*, 16–20.

Zhang, Y., Xiong, F., Xie, Y., Fan, X. & Gu, H. 2020. The Impact of Artificial Intelligence and Blockchain on the Accounting Profession. *IEEE Access*, 8, 110461–110477.

Economic and Business Management – Lent & Zhang (Eds)
© 2023 the Author(s), ISBN 978-1-032-24482-2

Death or rebirth? A framework for reviving vanished brands from the perspective of cognitive neuroscience

Yajun Lin
School of Business Administration, Chongqing Technology and Business University, Chongqing, Nan'an

ABSTRACT: The disappearance of classic brands and the idleness of Chinese time-honored brands have caused a huge waste of social resources. Whether such delisted brands can be reused and how to revive them effectively has become the focus of this theoretical research. Aiming at the bottleneck faced by consumers' subconscious dialysis under the traditional research background, this paper breaks through the single discipline perspective, and proposes to deconstruct the dormant value of disappeared brands from the perspective of cognitive neuroscience, and implant appropriate nostalgia feelings: Personal nostalgia, historical nostalgia, and inter-generational nostalgia. According to different memory levels of brand element information, that is, brand memory, brand familiarity, brand awareness, and brand Forgetting, the paper aimed to take brand activation path, brand regeneration path, brand fabrication path, or give up reviving.

1 INTRODUCTION

Many brands in the business circle temporarily or forever have withdrawn from the market due to poor management, market withdrawal, merger and reorganization, product (service) injury crisis, and other reasons. It resulted in brand dormancy and idling brand names, which caused huge waste of social resources. In practice, enterprises try to revive some brands such as Beetle (car), Huili (shoes), LvYe (beer), Tianfu (cola), Xinting (shampoo), Shuangmei (cosmetics), huoli28 (washing powder), etc. Only Beetle (car) and Huili (shoes) are successfully and effectively revived, whereas the market benefits of other products are not good. In the process of revival, there are many problems: Poor benefits after revival (such as Tianfu Cola), unreasonable use of familiarity clue potency (such as Xinting shampoo), and abuse of nostalgic marketing (such as green leaf beer). The question is are all the disappeared brands worth reviving? How to choose between death and rebirth? Can all the disappeared brands take advantage of nostalgic marketing? What's the difference between nostalgia and nostalgia? So, what is the relationship between the reviving strategy and the "dormancy time" of the disappeared brand? When does "dormancy value" come into being? What are the changes of these brands in the consumers' brains at different times after the disappearance of these brands? Is there any rule to follow in the "black box" of the brain? What is the effect of brand memory information on the revival of disappeared brands? How to achieve a successful and effective revival? Therefore, the in-depth exploration of these problems can better guide the practice of enterprises, and help enterprises achieve the successful and effective revival of disappeared brands with fewer mistakes and as little cost as possible, which can save hundreds of millions of market investment and generate economic benefits of tens of thousands and hundreds of millions of yuan.

DOI: 10.1201/9781003278788-19

2 ANALYSES OF PRACTICAL CASES

From the perspective of marketing practice, there are many successful cases of disappeared brand revival at home and abroad, which further guides the detailed theoretical research on the operation of the disappeared brand revival.

2.1 The classic cases of using nostalgic marketing to revive the disappeared brands

① Food brand reviving: Cadbury and General Mills, PepsiCo and other enterprises have repeatedly put in the old brands, or the old taste, or the old style, or the old name, etc., to wake up the nostalgia, revive the frontal cortex, and hippocampal gyrus of the brain region. It causes consumers to secrete the catalyst "dopamine," urge consumers to make purchase decisions, and bring considerable benefits to enterprises.

② Brand reviving of durable goods: In 1998, the American Volkswagen Corporation adopted the method of combining traditional appearance with high technology, and romantically turned it into a utopian ideal in brand promotion, and successfully launched the new "beetle" car in Detroit, USA. This "beetle" car was once popular in Europe and North America during the Third Reich of Germany for its durability, economy, user-friendly, and special shape design, as well as for the "the temperament of the common people."

2.2 The classic case of enterprise brand crisis management strategy

In 1996, the PPA event led to "Kangtaike Capsules" completely withdraw from the market, and the "Kangtaike" brand became a dormant brand. In September 2001, the brand of "Kangtaike" launched a new brand called "without PPA." It successfully revived the brand, reappeared its glory, and became the first brand of cold medicine sales.

2.3 A classic case of enterprise merger and reorganization

The advertising slogan "use Xinting, have a good mood" is well-known, but "Xinting" shampoo disappeared after its popularity. Five years later, Guangzhou Haodi company merged "Xinting" and successfully revived "Xinting" brand, achieving the target of 300 million yuan in sales, which is three times the previous glorious era.

2.4 Foreign enterprises specialized in idle brand revival

In the United States, a company named "West River" is engaged in the work of waking up the brands that have disappeared on the shelves by adopting the strategy of retro marketing, and has successfully awakened a large number of dormant brands, such as Taurus (auto-mobile), napkin (painkiller), eagle Snacks (food), salons electives (hair care), brim (coffee), etc., have created huge economic benefits.

2.5 The domestic industrial and commercial administrative departments implement the trademark "awakening project"

During the period from January to May, in 2012, the administrative departments of Pujiang County collect 175 idle registered trademarks and revitalize 25, Among them, 19 idle trademarks were transferred and 16 idle trademarks were licensed, which brought economic benefits of nearly 2 million yuan.

In the above practice cases, the reviving strategy of the disappeared brand first retains the brand name of the original brand, and on this basis, there are some differences: ① Implant consumers' nostalgic emotion, adopt the old taste or old style. ② the brand name is added with "new"; the function remains unchanged and the product is improved. ③ Make use of brand advertisement and familiarity of name, adopt function improvement and original product. ④ Using the familiarity of the brand name, extend the product variety or category, even recreate the product series and change the original product entity.

Therefore, what is the relationship between the reviving strategy and the "dormancy time" of the disappeared brand? When does "dormancy value" come into being? What are the changes of these brands in the consumers' brains at different times after the disappearance of these brands? Is there any rule to follow in the "black box" of the brain? What is the effect of brand memory information on the revival of disappeared brands? These problems need to be further studied.

3 LITERTURE REVIEW

In the research process of brand life cycle, the research system of brand introduction period, growth period, maturity period, and recession period is relatively mature. Some scholars also study brand activation after the brand recession period, including brand activation with temporary break of brand relationships and revival of brand carrier delisting for many years. Based on this, related or similar research can be divided into the following four categories.

3.1 *Research perspective based on the definition of disappeared brand*

There are many ways to define the name of the disappeared brand. Walker (2008) proposed death brand, baby brand, ghost brand, orphan brand, sleeping brand, etc., Kozinets and Sherry (2003) proposed nostalgic brand for nostalgic marketing; Yajun Lin et al. (2012) proposed and demonstrated that brand disappeared for more than 3 years, which would slow down the forgetting of brand relationship and become a "dormant brand." Delphine and Gerald (2018) call the revived lost brand "Sleeping Beauty" and believe that it contains brand heritage.

3.2 *Research perspective based on f brand relationship fracture and brand relationship continuation*

From the perspective of brand relationship fracture, the current research can be divided into two categories: One is that the carrier of a brand is not completely delisted or temporarily delisted. Foreign scholars proposed to restore marketing (Durocher 1994), brand customer conversion (Keaveney 1995), relationship fracture (Fajer & Schouten 1995), and brand relationship renewal (Aaker & Fournier 2001), Chinese scholars Jing Huang et al. (2009, 2011). Aiming at the wrong brand, this paper verifies the influence of three strategies (apology, tangible return and preferential treatment) on consumers' intention to renew the relationship, and also tests the moderating effect of brand relationship quality on consumers' intention to renew relationship. This paper also tests the effectiveness of two information communication strategies, diagnostic and argumentative, on the renewal intention of brand relationships. The other is that brand's carrier completely withdrew from the market or has a long-term withdrawal from the market, Yajun Lin et al. (2011–2015) makes an empirical study on the influencing factors of brand relationship renewal intention, customer gender difference strategy, dormant brand and enterprise brand integration mechanism, customer difference strategy, mechanism of dormant brand and enterprise brand integration, symbol value activation mechanism, and brand symbol triangle element matching model. Fei Li (2015) theoretically proposed that Chinese time-honored brands enter the dormant stage after the growth, maturity and aging stages, and corresponding revival strategies can be adopted which are based on the perspective of brand life cycle.

3.3 Research perspective based on the strategy of vanishing brand reviving

On this aspect, the research methods mainly adopt the social science research methods such as questionnaire survey, interviews, direct observation, and behavioral experiments to obtain the subjective judgment data of consumers. The typical ones are mentioned in the following sections.

3.3.1 Activate brand memory of disappeared brand

Thomas and Kohli (2009) theoretically analyzed the reason leading to brand recession and brand death and proposed that the feasibility of brand revival needs to be evaluated, and it is suggested to adopt multiple strategies to strengthen the brand. Arezoo, Pramod, and Francisco (2017) demonstrated the positive effects of the function utility, perceived brand advantage, social adjustment utility, and value expression utility of the disappeared brand on the brand revival movement through the questionnaire. Delphine and Gerald (2018) take Moynat Monet (leather luxury goods) as an example to activate brand equity of disappeared brands based on consumers' memory. Russell, Schau, and Bliese (2019) introduced the concept of transference from psychiatry to explore how consumers' continuing relationships with a defunct brand and they explored that transference of allegiance from the dead brand to competitor alternatives is possible under the right market conditions.

3.3.2 Implantation of nostalgic emotion derived from time factor

At present, the research is based on the awakening strategy of the existing brands and the disappeared brands which contains nostalgic elements. There is no distinguishing research on the above two types of brands with different attributes (in the market brand and the delisted brand). Brown, kozinets, and sherry (2003) analyzes the revival conditions of nostalgic brands from the consumers' perspectives but did not conduct empirical research.

To sum up, the following conclusions are drawn: ① According to the existing state of brands, there are declining brands (or aging brands) and disappearing brands: At present, the research mainly focuses on the declining brands, while the disappeared brands mainly focus on the brands whose brand relationship is temporarily broken and the products or services have not really delisted; ② According to the different stages of a brand life cycle, the research mainly focuses on the study of the duration of brand relationship. In the renewal of brand relationships, the research mainly focuses on the repair after the temporary break-up of the relationship, while research on the breaking of the long-term relationship and the delisting of products or services is still rare; ③ From the perspective of revival strategy, the research mainly focuses on the declining or aging brands and temporarily delisted brands in the existing brands, and the revival strategies are mainly based on brand equity and brand relationship From the perspective of brand equity remodeling, brand relationship repair, emotional marketing, and nostalgic marketing mainly focus on disappeared brands and time-honored brands, but there is no clear judgment on whether or not to implant nostalgia emotion and when to implant nostalgia emotion; ④ According to the research methods and perspectives, this studymainly focuses on social science research methods and research consumer awareness level.

Professor Zaltman (2002) of Harvard University believes that people often don't know what they know—95% of consumers' ideas come from the subconscious, while traditional research methods can't touch the subconscious. The bottleneck in dialysis the real needs of consumers is becoming more and more serious. With the development of cognitive science, neuroscience, artificial intelligence and other fields, and the breakthrough of brain measurement technology, cognitive neuroscience technology is applied more and more in the field of marketing. For example, Fox company uses eye trackers and EEG equipment to measure the advertising effect.

Based on the opportunity points that have not been proposed or demonstrated in the above research, through the perspective of neuromeric measurement of cognitive neuroscience and the deconstruction of the "black box" of the brain, we can establish a clear-cut strategy system for brand revival, which mainly solves "nostalgic emotion" reconstruction or fiction and brand memory information remodeling.

4 CONCEPTUAL FRAMEWOK

The research can follow the route from the brain reaction mechanism of disappeared brands to brand revival mechanism to brand revival path, which is divided into three parts. The relationship between the three can be states as follows. **The first part** theoretically deduces how the brain "black box" operate and brand elements information evolves in the process of market entry, brand experience, brand delisting, and brand dormancy. **The second part** uses the unprocessed original information of the disappeared brand to start memory, identify and deconstruct the type and strength of the element information, measure the "wake-up degree" of different elements information, and finally establish the relationship between brand element information and neural activity. The first part and the second part are the theoretical foundation of the third part. **The third part** is based on the degree and type of brand element information, making the choice of brand revival path, and taking effective revival strategy. It is based on memory information reconstruction and fictitious brand reconstruction to create the revival path of disappeared brands and realize the entity or carrier of disappeared brand to enter the market again.

4.1 *Theoretical framework on brain reaction mechanism of disappeared brands*

Based on the theory of cognitive neuroscience, different types of long-term memory involve different regions of brain. The brand elements information of the disappeared brands, such as brand name, brand advertisement words, brand trademark, brand slogan, product quality, brand advertisement song, brand spokesperson, brand emotion, brand story, brand packaging design, brand value, consumption habits, background music, and so on belong to long-term memory, which correspond to different types of memory such as declarative memory (semantic memory, situational memory) and non declarative memory (priming memory, skill memory and tendency memory). First of all, by recalling or recognizing the original brand elements information of the disappeared brand, and using the non-destructive brain injury measurement technology to determine whether the change intensity of different brain regions is significant, it can realize the identification and deconstruction of the brand elements information type and long-term memory trace intensity, and establish the relationship between the brand elements information of the disappeared brands and neural activities, to start brand elements. Second, according to the type and intensity of brand information traces, we can excavate the dormant value, reconstruct or make up nostalgic feelings, carry out brand reconstruction, entice consumers' purchase intention, and finally achieve the revival of the disappeared brand and realize the re-listing of the carrier (original carrier or new carrier) of the lost brand. The specific evolution process is shown below.

4.1.1 *The first stage: Market entry*
According to the theory of cognitive neuroscience, the information of different brand elements enters the different brain areas of consumers. In the marketing input stage, brand information mainly depends on the sensory input of vision, hearing, touch, and hearing/ smell, which is a bottom-up attention capture, involving the corresponding brain region changes such as occipital lobe/parietal lobe/temporal lobe, parietal lobe/temporal lobe, parietal lobe, and base of the temporal lobe.

4.1.2 *The second stage: Brand attention*
When brand elements information enters the attention stage, consumers can selectively pay attention in the brain through sensory filters and integrate information. Selective attention

can be arbitrary or unintentional, and the synergistic effect between them is controlled by the combined cortical network of the frontal and parietal cortex respectively.

4.1.3   *The third stage: Brand perception*
In the brand experience stage, consumers' consciousness begins to leave traces in memory, some are unconscious, and some are conscious perception (consumers experience and consume brand products or services), involving the activation of the frontal/parietal cortex.

4.1.4   *The fourth stage: Delisting/dormancy*
After the brand exits the market, the brand element information will continue to leave memory traces in consumers' brain memory, and the short-term memory information will continue to be transformed into long-term memory. This transformation process involves the activities of the hippocampal gyrus and medial temporal lobe. According to the German psychologist Hermann Ebbinghaus's memory forgetting curve, with the passage of time, the speed of forgetting the brand element information in consumers' brains in the initial stage is very fast, gradually slowing down and then entering a "dormant period" of memory.

4.1.5   *The fifth stage: Information activation*
By recalling or recognizing the original brand element information of the disappeared brand, the long-term memory trace of the consumer will be activated. At the same time, consumers will enter the short-term memory according to the existing brand knowledge. The combination of the two will produce new information about the disappeared brand, which will enter into the consumer's working memory for processing and sorting.

4.1.6   *The sixth stage: Brand revival*
By detecting the activation state of different brain regions, we can infer and deconstruct the types of brand elements information, the intensity of long-term memory traces, and the variation information after interaction with new short-term memory. According to the type and intensity of brand information traces, we should excavate dormant value, implant appropriate nostalgic emotion, carry out brand reconstruction, arouse consumers' purchase intention, and re-enter the market of the entity or carrier of disappeared brand. If it causes strong activity in the medial temporal lobe/neocortex/hippocampus region, it indicates that the brand has been successfully revived.

4.2   *Conceptual framework of the revival mechanism of disappeared brands*

Based on the theory of cognitive neuroscience, after the delisting of a brand, the information of brand elements will enter the "black box of information processing." The information processing process will experience attention selection, attention processing, information integration and information activation, and then purchase behavior will be made. However, most of these decision-making behaviors belong to the potential conscious behavior.

4.2.1   *Attention choice of information*
Consumers use the guided search model to pay limited attention to endogenous cues (determined by individual factors of consumers, such as involvement, familiarity, motivation, experience, etc.) and exogenous cues (determined by the perceptual significance of stimulus features, such as shape, color, size and other brand element information), and selectively pay attention to some information and reduce the number of information or perceived less evaluation risk, such as the familiarity of the product or service, emotion (nostalgic emotion, etc.) and the perceived intensity of brand element information.

4.2.2 Attention processing and information integration
Consumers selectively filter and integrate the activated part of the brand elements information of the disappeared brands and the information of the competitive brands. In this process, information attenuation and interference may occur, and different parts of the brand element information may have false memory, or even distorted.

4.2.3 Information activation
According to the reconstruction or fictitious content of the brand elements information of the disappeared brand, the "awakening degree" of different brand elements information is measured, and then the relationship between the brand element information of the disappeared brand and the neural activity is established.

Therefore, using non-destructive brain injury measurement technology to determine the change intensity of different brain regions, the research can realize the identification and deconstruction of the information type of brand elements and the intensity of long-term memory traces of disappeared brands, and measure the "arousal" of different brand element information according to the information changes caused by the length of disappearance time (i.e., whether there is neuron response in corresponding brain regions and how strong the response intensity is). It can establish the relationship between the brand element information of the disappeared brand and neural activities, and then establish the activation mechanism of the brand element information (see Figure 1).

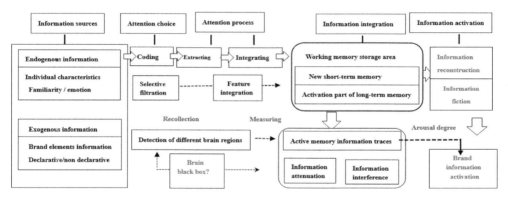

Figure 1.   Revival mechanism of vanished brands.

4.3 Conceptual framework on the revival path of disappeared brands (Figure 2)

Based on the theory of cognitive neuroscience and the revival mechanism of vanished brands, the intensity of long-term memory and the type of memory content (divided into semantic memory, situational memory, priming memory, skill memory, tendency memory, etc.) were measured according to the correlation between the memory traces of "brand element information" and various brain regions, and corresponding brand element information. When the brand disappears, there will be distortion and rearrangement of memory traces: In the degree of brand element information memory, there are four states, that is, brand remembering, brand familiar, brand knowing, and brand forgetting. At the same time, there may be different types of nostalgia (personal nostalgia, historical nostalgia, and intergenerational nostalgia). Therefore, different and targeted strategies to revive the disappeared brands will have a significant effect on the revival of the disappeared brands.

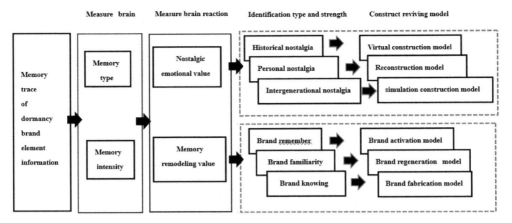

Figure 2.   Conceptual framework on the revival path of dormant brands.

4.3.1 *Research on the dormant value of lost brands*

The carrier of the disappeared brands will enter the "dormant state" after a period of delisting, which will have the "dormant value," including: ① Nostalgic emotional value. According to the research of memory time theory, it takes a period of time for a human to have nostalgic emotion for something and for someone. Only when the brand desisted for at least 3 years can the memory reverse, that is, nostalgia emotion; ② Memory remodeling value. The researcher has previously verified that consumers' memory of brand elements of the disappeared brands will enter the turning point of forgetting degrees and enter the "dormant period" of psychological energy for more than three years. If the old memory is activated again, the memory system will be highly plastic, consumers may forget the details of the brand, and the old memory and the new memory will be confused. This provides the opportunity and "dormant value" for the revival of the disappeared brands, especially the "familiar" type revival.

Through the research methods of neuroscience theory, we can explore and deconstruct the evolution of brand elements information and how the dormant value is generated, when it is generated, and what kind of memory remodeling occurs, so as to effectively use the dormant value of the disappeared brands.

4.3.2 *Research on the revival path of the vanished brands: Emotional implantation path*

In the process of revival, consumers will have nostalgic feelings because of the time factor. Nostalgia is not only an emotion but also an autobiographical memory. According to the relevant research, it can be divided into personal nostalgia (personal real-life experience in early years, which is the idealized reappearance of the past memory), historical nostalgia (nostalgia caused by social political, economic and cultural symbols, with distinct characteristics of the times and historical brand), and generation nostalgia (the memory of the past that is produced indirectly through contact and interaction with others). By detecting the different responses of brain nerves, we can distinguish the types of nostalgic emotion aroused by the brand element information traces of the disappeared brands, and then we can revive the disappeared brands by three "emotional implantation" methods, namely, reconstruction, virtual construction, and simulation construction.

4.3.3 *Research on the revival path of the vanished brands: Memory remodeling path*

By deconstructing the information intensity and type of brand elements of the disappeared brand, we can observe the "purchase response button" in the consumer's brain (the brain area that attracts consumers' attention, recognition, decision-making, and advanced cognition). According to different memory levels such as brand memory, brand familiarity, and brand knowing, we can make strategic choices on whether to revive the disappeared brands, brand activation model, brand regeneration model, and brand fabrication model.

5 CONLUSIONS

First, breaking through the traditional research methods and using the neural measurement of cognitive neuroscience, our research puts forward the dormant value of the disappeared brand for the first time and the neural measurement index of the brand element information of the disappeared brand. It improves the strategy system of the disappeared brand revival.

Second, our research suggests using the non-destructive brain injury measurement technology and dialyze consumers' subconscious, accurately implanting nostalgia emotion and remodeling memory information, and fundamentally solving the problem of revival of disappeared brands from the consumer's brain reaction mechanism.

6 FUTURE RESEARCH

The above research is only a theoretical exploration. In the next step of research, it needs to be further demonstrated from the following three aspects.

6.1 *To develop the neural measurement index of brand elements information of disappeared brand and establish the revival mechanism of disappeared brands*

The non-destructive brain injury measurement technology is used to determine whether the change intensity of different brain regions is significant, which can realize the recognition and deconstruction of brand element information type and long-term memory trace strength of the disappeared brand. According to the information change caused by the disappearance time, the "arousal" degree of information of different brand elements can be measured (i.e., what are the corresponding brain regions and what the reaction intensity is). We can establish the relationship between the brand elements information and neural activities of the disappeared brand, and then establish the activation mechanism of the brand elements information of the disappeared brand, so as to start the brand information memory.

6.2 *Research on precise implantation of "dormant value" in the process of brand revival*

After the disappearance of the brand carrier or entity for a period of time, the memory of the disappeared brands will be "dormant," and the appropriate "dormant period" will be the memory remodeling. Then, the information evolution of brand elements in different memory stages will become the focus of the next research, which is the key issue of whether the disappeared brands can be revived and revived successfully.

6.3 *The correct use of nostalgic marketing is particularly important for the revival of time-honored brands and classic brands*

Based on the perspective of cognitive neuroscience, we will deeply study the influence of time factor on the lost brand memory, and analyzes what kind of nostalgia emotion is produced by different age groups? Is it personal nostalgia or historical nostalgia? Or is it generational nostalgia? It is to establish the consumer nostalgic emotion mechanism from the perspective of cognitive neuroscience.

FUNDINGS

This study was supported by Key projects of Chongqing Technology and Business University (1952003) "Research on dormant brand activation from the perspective of cognitive neuroscience" and General program of Chongqing Natural Science Foundation (cstc2020jcyj-msxmX0052). "Research on dormant brand activation from the perspective of cognitive neuroscience."

REFERENCES

Aaker, J., Fournier, S. & Brsel, S. 2001. Charting the Development of Consumer-brand Relationships. *Research Paper Series, Graduate School of Business Stanford University* 11.

Arezoo, D., Pramod, I. & Francisco. 2017. Determinants of Brand Resurrection Movements Why Consumers Want Dead Brands Back? *European Journal of Marketing* (11): 1896–1916.

Brown, S., Kozinets, R. V. & Sherry, J.F. 2003. Teaching Old Brands New Tricks: Retro Branding and the Revival of Brand Meaning. *Journal of Marketing* (7): 19–33.

Delphine, D. 2018. Gerald Reviving Sleeping Beauty Brand by Rearticulating Brand Heritage. *Journal of Business Research* (4): 5894–5900.

Durocher, J. 1994. Recovery Marketing: What to do After a Natural Disaster. *The Cornell Hotel and Restaurant Administration Quarterly* (2): 66–71.

Fei, L. 2015. Research on the life cycle of Chinese Time-honored Brands. *Journal of Beijing Technology and Business University (Social Science Edition)* 30(4): 28–34.

Fajer, M.T. & Schouten J.W. 1995. Breakdown and Dissolution of Person-brand Relationships. *Advances in Consumer Research* 22: 663–667.

Jing, H. & Yifan, Z. 2011. Brand Relationship Renewal Communication Strategy Based on Ability and Integrity Fracture. *Scientific Decision Marketing* 60(5): 60–70.

Jing, H. & Wei X. 2009. The Impact of Wrong Brand Investment on Consumers' Willingness to Renew Relationships. *China Soft Science Magazine* 6: 119–127.

Keaveney, S.M. 1995. Customer Switching Behavior in Service Industry: An Exploratory Study. *Journal of Marking* 59: 753.

Russell. C. A., Schau H. J. & Bliese P. 2019. Brand afterlife: Transference to alternate brands following corporate failure. *Journal of Marking* 97: 257–267.

Thomas, S. & Kohli, C. 2009. A Brand is Forever! A Framework for Revitalizing Declining and Dead Brands. *Business Horizons* (52): 377–386.

Walker, R. 2008. Can a Dead Brand Live Again? *The New York Times Magazine* (3.18): 3.

Yajun, L. & Jiafeng, L. 2012. An Empirical Study on the Influencing Factors of Beverage Dormant Brand Resurrection. *Journal of Southwest University for Nationalities (Humanities and Social Sciences Edition)* 33(3): 119–125.

Yajun, L. 2011. Analysis on Influencing Factors of Brand Relationship Renewal Intention of Dormant Brands. *Statistics & Decision* (11): 102–104.

Yajun, L. 2011. Research on Brand Relationship Renewal and Brand Activation Strategy of Dormant Brands. *Economy and Management* (6): 40–44.

Yajun, L. & Min, Zh. 2012. Research on the Integration Mechanism of Dormant Brand and Enterprise Brand. *Theoretical Investigation* (3): 101–104.

Yajun, L. & Wubin,T. 2014. A Study on Consumers 'Difference about Reviving Strategies of Dormant Brands on Cue Theory. *Journal of Chongqing University (Social Science Edition)* 20(4): 86–92.

Yajun, L., Min, Z. & Wubin, T. 2014. Research on the Mechanism of Dormant Brand and Enterprise Brand Integration. *Business Review* (12): 56–67.

Yajun, L., Wubin, T. & Yongjian, L. 2015. Research on the Activation Mechanism of Dormant Brand Symbolic Value. *Enterprise Economy* 415(3): 26–30.

Zaltman, G. 2002. Hidden Minds, When It to Mining Consumers' views, We've Only Scratched the Surface. *Harvard Business Review* (6): 26–27.

Economic and Business Management – Lent & Zhang (Eds)
© 2023 the Author(s), ISBN 978-1-032-24482-2

A brief analysis of how e-commerce companies can adapt to the new revenue standard—Take bear electric appliance as an example

Haixia Ren

School of Accounting, Shandong Technology and Business University, Yantai, Shandong, China

ABSTRACT: With the increasing development of the market economy and the increasing complexity of transaction matters, revenue recognition and measurement in practice will face more and more problems. In order to further standardize revenue recognition, measurement and related information disclosure, the new revenue standard came into being. The new standard mainly adjusts in terms of confirmation basis, confirmation time point, and confirmation measurement. Bear Electric Appliance is an online sales-based "small household appliances + Internet" enterprises with a complex and diverse sales model. Taking the revenue recognition of Bear Electric Appliances as an example, analyzing the misunderstandings that enterprises may enter in the implementation of the new revenue standards, which can provide feasible suggestions for China's enterprises, especially e-commerce enterprises, to comply with the development trend of accounting standards and ensure the good operation of enterprises.

1   INTRODUCTION

Income is the basic element of financial accounting and an important embodiment of the operating results of enterprises; the recognition and measurement of revenue are directly related to the economic benefits of enterprises. With the rapid progress of the social economy, the business model of enterprises has also undergone tremendous changes, and the meaning, category, and scope of income have been greatly enriched, resulting in the old income standard becoming increasingly unsuitable for the financial environment. In July 2017, the Ministry of Finance promulgated Accounting Standard for Business Enterprises No. 14—Revenue, hereinafter referred to as the "New Revenue Standard" or "New Standard", which focuses on the basis for revenue recognition, the time node of revenue recognition and the main procedures for revenue recognition, etc., and stipulates that all enterprises should fully implement it from 1st January 2021. At present, most enterprises are still in the stage of adapting to the new revenue standard, and various problems have arisen due to insufficient understanding of the content of the standard, especially e-commerce companies that are significantly different from the offline real economy, and as the "dark horse" of e-commerce enterprises, the study of small bear electrical appliances is of representative significance. Therefore, this paper analyses the main changes in the new revenue standard, and takes the revenue recognition of Bear Electric Appliance as an example to give suggestions for e-commerce companies to adapt to the new revenue standard, as well as to promote the development of accounting practices in the field of e-commerce industry.

2 LITERATURE REVIEW

At present, the research on the new revenue standard mainly starts from four aspects: the basis of recognition, the time point of recognition, the measurement of recognition, and the disclosure of statements.

2.1 *Differences in revenue recognition basis*

Under the old revenue standard system, the type of transaction of revenue was the basis for revenue recognition, and different processes and standards were implemented depending on the categories of income such as the sale of goods, the provision of services, and the transfer of usage rights. Such a classification method can facilitate the supervision of personnel to quickly classify, control and check, which is more suitable for the market environment with relatively single economic activities. However, with the development of the new economy and the emergence of more and more business models, the drawbacks of the above standards have gradually become prominent [8]. Many of the provisions are not specific enough, and the documentary materials involved can also be provided by the enterprise at its discretion, which gives the enterprise excessive right of independent interpretation [11].

The new revenue standard limits all transactions to the framework of "contract" first, distinguishes different types of transactions based on the transaction contracts between buyers and sellers, and most of the relevant supporting materials required come from the contract itself, reducing the possibility of enterprises abusing the right of interpretation to whitewash the statement [3].

2.2 *Differences in the timing of revenue recognition*

Under the old standard system, the revenue from the sale of goods should meet five conditions before recognition, and the most important of which are: first, the enterprise has transferred the main risks and rewards of ownership of the goods to the buyer; second, the enterprise has neither retained the right of continued management, which is usually associated with ownership nor has it exercised effective control over the goods sold. The old standard stated that the point at which revenue recognition is recognized depends on whether the transfer of the risk and reward of the item has been completed.

Article 4 of the new revenue standard stipulates the time point at which revenue is recognized, that is, the enterprise should fulfill the performance obligation in the sales contract, that is, when the customer acquires control of the relevant commodity, the recognition of revenue and the acquisition of control of the relevant commodity refers to the ability to dominate the use of the commodity and obtain almost all the economic benefits from it [9]. In addition, the new revenue standard further distinguishes the performance obligation in the sales contract into an obligation performed at certain time nodes and an obligation performed at a certain time, and defines the issue of revenue recognition that requires the long-term performance of the contract [10].

2.3 *Differences in revenue recognition measures*

In the old revenue standard, the relevant provisions on the measurement of the amount of revenue from the sale of goods are relatively simple, and Article 5 stipulates that the amount of income is determined according to the agreed price, and Articles 6 to 8 stipulates the recognition method when discounts occur, which are essentially same as the new revenue standard. Article 9 of the old revenue standard provided that recognized revenue should be flushed back at the time of refund if a refund had occurred, but it did not provide that the proportion of the refund should be estimated and included in the cost in the current period. The old revenue guidelines did not have relevant provisions on warranty issues [1].

For sales contracts where there is a risk of being returned, the new standard requires that enterprises only recognize the revenue determined in the accounts, the proportion of which is estimated based on sales experience and market conditions; the amount expected to be returned is recognized as a liability to be liquidated at the balance sheet date [5]. In addition, for sales with quality assurance clauses, if the strength of the quality assurance exceeds the basic limit of the national "three guarantees" provisions, it should be determined that the enterprise provides an additional separate service to enhance the competitiveness of goods, which is an obligation to be fulfilled within a certain period of time, which is different from the provision of goods, and therefore treated as a single performance obligation [6].

Article 34 of the new standard also makes clear provisions on the choice of netting method and total amount method, the main responsible person should choose the total amount method, and the agent, should choose the net method, and recognize income according to the amount of commission or handling fee expected to be entitled to receive [2].

3 REVENUE RECOGNITION OF BEAR ELECTRIC APPLIANCE UNDER THE NEW STANDARD

3.1 *Case background*

Bear Electric Appliance was established in March 2006, and on August 23, 2019, Bear Electric (002959. SZ) ended the road to IPO for more than a year, officially listed on the Shenzhen stock exchange's small and medium-sized board, as the "first stock of creative small household appliances", Xiao bear electrical appliances rose by 44% on the first day, with a market value of about 5.9 billion yuan, becoming the most eye-catching dark horse in the creative small household appliances market. The main business is to develop small household appliances and complete their production and sales. Its sales model presents a diversified characteristic, composed of online channels and offline channels, online channels account for 90% of revenue, and online sales are mainly divided into online direct sales, online distribution, and e-commerce platform cooperation, and other ways.

3.2 *Changes in revenue recognition for bear appliances*

3.2.1 *Confirmation of changes in the basis*
Since the new standard uses "contract" as an important basis for revenue recognition, the balance sheet change of Xiao bear electric appliances is mainly due to the addition of two accounts, "contract assets" and "contract liabilities". By comparing the balance sheet data before and after the revision of the new revenue standard, it can be found that it is mainly related to the contract liabilities of the account changed, Bear Electric Appliance under the New Revenue Standard, the amount of its advance receipts changed to "contract liabilities" and "other current liabilities". Under the new revenue standard, the amount of "advance collection tax" of $5.5 million in the original advance receipts will be adjusted to other current liabilities, and the others will be adjusted to contract liabilities. It can be seen that after the implementation of the new revenue standard, through the readjustment of the amount, it better reflects the matching relationship between the income and cost of the enterprise.

3.2.2 *Confirmation of changes in time*
Under the old guidelines, the online distribution of Bear Electric Appliances is to recognize revenue after the goods are issued and confirmed by the online distributor or handed over to the customer's designated logistics company; offline distribution is the company's recognition of revenue after the goods are issued and confirmed by the customer's signature or delivered to the customer's designated logistics company. Bear electrical offline distribution in the delivery of logistics company to recognize revenue, the reason is that offline distribution returns are

very small and controllable, according to national regulations, only in the case of non-human quality problems to support 7 days return; however, online distribution has a 7-day no reason return period, delivery logistics is no longer suitable as a node to confirm revenue.

Under the new standard, both online direct sales and online distribution consignments recognize revenue 10 days after the company ships or when the consumer receives the goods or at which the system receives the goods by default or the company receives the payment. Recognizing revenue at that time nodes in accordance with the new revenue standard complies with the transfer of control requirement, as after the seven-day unjustified return ends, the buyer acquires ownership and controls the physical goods while deeming the buyer to accept the product, thus avoiding the tedious operation of reducing revenue in a frequent return environment.

Bear electrical appliance cooperates with many e-commerce platforms in the e-commerce platform warehousing mode, so the revenue recognition time of Bear electric appliance varies from platform to platform. JD.com, Suning Tesco, Ping An Good Doctor, and No. 1 Store respectively pay and settle after 7, 30, 30, and 45 days of receiving the invoice, and Bear Electric Appliance should immediately recognize revenue after receiving the invoice; VIP shop will pay and settle after receiving the invoice 5 days later, at this time, Bear Electric Appliance should continue to wait for seven days without reason to return the goods before confirming revenue, otherwise, it may inflate revenue.

3.2.3 *Confirm the difference in measurements*

In order to attract users and facilitate transactions, e-commerce companies often participate in platforms or carry out their own coupon-giving activities, and a large number of coupons given away are essentially equivalent to discounts, but because consumers use coupons are highly uncontrollable, it is difficult to accurately calculate the actual value of each coupon [7]. The old standards lacked specific provisions for such situations, and enterprises could account for coupons themselves. In addition, while the old standards provided for estimated return rates and recognized the expected non-return portion as revenue, there was no specific guidance on how return rates were calculated.

According to the new revenue standard, Bear Electric appliances will be divided into two categories: the first type is for customer acquisition directly to give the user coupons, not accounting treatment when issued, and when the user uses it as a discount sales, the relevant costs are included in the sales cost; the second type is the coupons given by the user after purchase, the purpose is to promote repurchase, such coupons can not only be used at the next consumption but also its existence objectively promotes the transaction, so it is partially recognized as a liability when it is given away, and then reduced after the expiration date, the confirmation ratio is determined according to the sales experience.

4 RECOMMENDATIONS FOR E-COMMERCE COMPANIES TO BETTER APPLY THE NEW STANDARDS

4.1 *Pay attention to the new subjects and grasp the basis for confirmation*

The core of the new revenue standard change is the "control transfer" model [4], the currently new revenue standard on the model is not detailed enough, in the actual application process, because of the complexity of the e-commerce sales process, Courier Station may sign on behalf of the customer, the customer has control of the goods at the time and the time of confirming the receipt of the goods is likely to be not the same time, so E-commerce enterprises should combine their own specific physical objects to formulate more detailed internal implementation standards and make more detailed landing plans for issues such as revenue timing to ensure the consistency of revenue recognition standards before and after. For example, collecting deposits is a promotion method often used by e-commerce companies every year, especially in the increasingly intensive promotion activities, the management of deposits is particularly prominent. After receiving the deposit, the performance obligation of the enterprise has not yet been formed, so the deposit should be included in the contract liability first, rather than the previously customary account of advance receipts.

4.2 *Upgrade internal standards and refine the confirmation time point*

The main reason why the time of revenue recognition of e-commerce enterprises is unclear is that it is difficult to predict in advance such behaviors as seven-day no-reason returns, platform payment time, user confirmation of receipt time, and even users taking the initiative to extend the receipt time, which interferes with the judgment of the transfer of control. Therefore, it is necessary to upgrade the internal implementation standards and conduct classification discussions. First, for the general cash-on-delivery business similar to offline sales, e-commerce companies can recognize revenue when consumers pay, because, in such consumption, consumers have formed a full recognition of the product; second, for users who buy online but actively confirm the receipt of goods, e-commerce companies can directly confirm revenue; third, for users who do not actively confirm the receipt of goods, regardless of whether they have extended the delivery time, e-commerce companies should recognize revenue after their return authority expires; finally, the return problem occurs outside the return time. E-commerce companies can separately account for and adjust their revenues.

4.3 *Clarify the account to which the key amount belongs*

Under the new revenue standard, the estimated value of coupons and the expected return rate need to be accounted for, and accounting estimates are a more important new content in the new revenue standard. For various uncertain amounts, uncertain revenues, and uncertain refunds that occur in the new sales methods, it is necessary to determine the proportion of recording through the enterprise's independent estimation. This aspect requires financial personnel to be more familiar with the business process of the enterprise, to better understand the company's products and business, and to strengthen their understanding of the new standards. For example, the judgment of the point of recognition in different cases is discussed in Section 4.2, and in addition, the return rate suitable for each situation should be calculated separately based on the sales experience in these cases, to measure revenue more accurately.

5 CONCLUSIONS

The new revenue standard mainly has an impact on the basis of revenue recognition, the time point of recognition, the measurement of recognition, etc. E-commerce enterprises should strengthen the training of financial personnel, familiarize themselves with the new provisions based on the contractual relationship as soon as possible, clarify the use of relevant subjects, pay special attention to the differences in the timing and amount of revenue recognition in different channels and categories, strengthen information disclosure, and standardize financial activities.

REFERENCES

[1] Feiyu Wu. 2019. Comparative Analysis of Revenue Recognition in New and Old Revenue Standards [J]. *Business Accounting* (21):59–62.
[2] Guifang Jiao, Xiufen Lu. 2018. Comparative Analysis of New and Old Revenue Standards[J]. *Friends of Accounting* (08):140–143.

[3]   Jinghe Xiang, Yiqiao Wang, Yu Chen, Yan Guo. 2018. The Impact of the New Revenue Standard on the Revenue Recognition of Internet Enterprises[J]. *Business Accounting* (09):25–28.

[4]   Peipei Huang. 2015. Research on the Recognition and Measurement of Income of Internet Enterprises [D]. *Master's Thesis of Institute of Fiscal Sciences, Ministry of Finance.*

[5]   Qiao Fu, Ying Ran. 2018. Fiscal and Tax Treatment of Sales Returns Under the New Revenue Standard[J]. *Friends of Accounting* (8):144–145.

[6]   Treasury. Accounting Standard for Business Enterprises No. 14 – Revenue (2017)[S], Cai Hui [2017] No. 22.

[7]   Veiguo Lu. 2019. Discussion on the Revenue Recognition Problem of O2O E-commerce Enterprises[J]. *Finance and Accounting Newsletter* (31):61–65.

[8]   Xinshi Liu, Weichen Sun. 2019. Theoretical Characteristics and Economic Consequences Analysis of the Evolution of Revenue Recognition Model[J]. *Friends of Accounting* (19):48–52.

[9]   Xin Xu. 2018. The Impact and Reflection of the New Revenue Standard on the Treatment of Enterprise Income Tax[J]. *Journal of Tax Research* (10):115–118.

[10] Xuejie Wang. 2020. Analysis on Revenue Recognition of E-commerce Enterprises Under the New Revenue Standard[J]. *Finance and Accounting* (13):44–46.

[11] Yongkui Du, Jing Wang. 2019. Analysis of Tax Difference and Risk Aversion Under the New Revenue Standard[J]. *Journal of Finance and Accounting* (21):47–52.

Economic and Business Management – Lent & Zhang (Eds)
© 2023 the Author(s), ISBN 978-1-032-24482-2

The impact of the integration of agriculture and tourism on the economic development of urban tourism in China

Tingjie Wang & Yanxiu Liu
Sichuan Agricultural University, Chengdu, Sichuan, China

ABSTRACT: Using panel data from 264 cities in China from 2010–2019, this paper empirically examines the impact of the integration of agriculture and tourism on urban tourism economies using leisure agriculture demonstration counties and modern agricultural industrial parks as examples, while conducting a heterogeneity analysis. The results of the study show that the integration of agriculture and tourism can contribute to an increase in urban tourism revenues and tourist arrivals. Further research found that this boosting effect was more pronounced in cities with a high level of agriculture and a high number of urban dwellers.

1 INTRODUCTION

Since the 1970s, thanks to advances in digital information technology, technological convergence, business convergence and market convergence occurring at the boundaries and intersections of various industries. The boundaries between industries are becoming increasingly blurred and industrial integration has become a common trend in modern industrial development. Tourism is a comprehensive industry, highly interconnected with other industries and has direct or indirect economic links with almost all sectors of the national economy. As China's economy and society continue to develop and income levels continue to rise, residents' demand for tourism consumption is gradually changing in the direction of differentiation and diversification. The dynamics of tourism consumer demand and the comprehensive nature of the tourism industry inevitably require that tourism is integrated with other industries in the process of development. At the same time, the industrial integration of other industries with tourism also gives the tourism economy a new dynamic and growth engine.

China has been an agricultural power since ancient times, and between 1949 and 2000, China mainly pursued the economic function of agriculture to secure the supply of agricultural products. In the 21st century, rapid urbanization and industrialization continue to penetrate into rural areas, and Chinese agriculture is facing many problems such as low labor productivity and poor economic efficiency. The upgrading of agricultural industrial structure is imminent, and diversified demands such as leisure tourism function and ecological protection function of agriculture are gradually coming to the fore (Chen 2015). Since the concept of "agricultural tourism" was introduced by the National Tourism Administration in 2001, China's Ministry of Agriculture and Rural Affairs has introduced various measures to develop resources such as natural ecological landscapes, folk culture and agricultural activities in rural areas into tourist attractions. These measures have met the multi-functional expansion of agriculture and also provided more opportunities for the development of urban tourism economy.

For a long time, academia has paid extensive attention to industrial integration. In the area of industrial integration, Geum (2016) analyzes the process of industrial integration from the perspective of input and output. Sick (2019) and Hacklin (2009) regard industry integration as a dynamic process, and discuss the stages of the industry integration process. Sick proposes three stages of industrial integration in the early, middle and late stages, while

DOI: 10.1201/9781003278788-21

Hacklin divides industrial integration into four stages: knowledge integration, technology integration, application integration and industry integration. On the integration of agriculture and tourism, some scholars have studied the connotation of integration of agriculture and tourism (Phillip 2010), the path of integration (Cao 2015) and the measurement of the level of integration (Liu 2016). On this basis, scholars have developed a more profound analysis of the efficacy of integrating agriculture and tourism. Yang (2020) empirically tested that the integration of agriculture and tourism plays an effective role in alleviating rural poverty using panel data of 30 provinces from 2005–2016; Zhong (2020) used data related to prefecture-level cities from 2010–2017 to verify that the integration of agriculture and tourism facilitates the optimization and upgrading of rural industrial structure.

Compared with the existing literature, the advancement of this paper is reflected in: First, most scholars pay attention to the impact of the integration of agriculture and tourism on agriculture. This paper empirically tests the impact of the integration of agriculture and tourism on the development of urban tourism economy, enriching the relevant research on the impact of the integration of tourism industry on tourism economy; Second, the findings of this paper also provide an important basis for government departments to formulate policies for the integrated development of agriculture and tourism.

2 THEORETICAL ANALYSIS AND RESEARCH HYPOTHESIS

The integration of agriculture and tourism is based on agriculture, and through the intersection and penetration of agriculture and tourism, capital and resources are allocated intensively between agriculture and tourism, and finally a new industrial mode is formed to achieve the best combination of supply and demand advantages (Zhong 2020).

From the supply point of view, first of all, the integration of agriculture and tourism expands the functions of agriculture and develops some activities that originally belong to the scope of agricultural production, such as farming work, flower cultivation and folk customs, into tourism resources; Secondly, tourism is a labor-intensive industry with low employment threshold and strong inclusiveness, which has demand for different levels of labor. The excavation of ecotourism and recreation functions of agriculture provides new recreational places for residents in urban centers, creating a large number of jobs in the tourism sector. At the same time, tourism allows rural residents to earn more additional income, which motivates idle rural labor to shift to employment in the tourism sector and contributes to the prosperity of the urban tourism economy; Third, the integration of agriculture and tourism enhances economic ties between rural and urban areas. By investing in the countryside, businesses improve the countryside's infrastructure, which effectively increases the countryside's tourism service capacity and reduces tourists' sense of rejection of rural life.

From the perspective of demand, on the one hand, the organic combination of the six elements of agricultural tourism, such as food, accommodation, travel, tourism, shopping and entertainment, so that agricultural tourism is no longer the traditional "horse and buggy" way to increase the tourist experience at the same time, but also to promote the growth of tourism consumption. On the other hand, the integration of agriculture and tourism has resulted in a variety of new industrial formats, such as leisure agriculture, rural tourism, and agro-industrial parks, which have contributed to the establishment of city tourism brand images. Each city greatly enhances the attractiveness of its tourist destination by building its own unique brand. Based on the above analysis, the following hypothesis is proposed in this paper:

Hypothesis I: There is a positive contribution of agricultural and tourism integration to urban tourism economic development, controlling for other factors.

Different levels of agricultural development have different agricultural infrastructure conditions. Agricultural base is the origin of the development of agricultural tourism, and a good agricultural base can provide rich agricultural resources and labor for the development of agricultural tourism.

Hypothesis II: The degree of agricultural development affects the effect of agricultural and tourism integration for tourism economic development, controlling for other factors.

The majority of tourism workers work in hotels, restaurants and scenic spots. The larger the population of urban citizens, the more hotels, restaurants and scenic spots they own, which provides a large number of jobs in the tourism industry.

Hypothesis III: Differences in the number of people living in urban areas lead to different effects of agriculture and tourism on tourism economic development, controlling for other factors.

3 STUDY DESIGN

3.1 Model design

Based on the above theoretical analysis and research hypotheses, the following econometric regression models were constructed:

$$TD_{i,t} = \partial_0 + \partial_1 IAT_{i,t} + \partial_j X_{i,t} + v_i + \theta_{i,t} \tag{1}$$

In equation (1), the subscripts i and t denote the i-th city and year t, respectively, and TD (Tourism Development) represents the level of urban tourism economic development.; IAT (Integration of Agriculture and Tourism) represents the level of integration of agriculture and tourism. $X_{i,t}$ represents the matrix of control variables consisting of eight characteristic variables that affect regional tourism development, including the level of economic development, infrastructure construction input, service industry development level, transportation convenience, ecological environment construction level, information technology level, higher education level, tourism resource level, etc.; ∂_0 represents the constant term, and the regression coefficient ∂_1 and its significance level measure the effect of urban agriculture and tourism integration on tourism economic development; ∂_j denotes the regression coefficient of the control variables, where $j = 2,3,...,9$; v_i denotes the fixed effect of the city, and $\theta_{i,t}$ denotes the random error term.

3.2 Variables and data

3.2.1 Explained variables

In this paper, the level of tourism economic development (TD, Tourism Development) of the city is selected as the explanatory variable, which is subdivided into total tourism earnings (TET, Total Earnings from Tourism) and total number of tourist visits (TNT, Total Number of Tourists) in the baseline regression. To eliminate the effect of price factors, the value-based variables are deflated by using the consumer price index (CPI) in this paper.

3.2.2 Core explanatory variables

The core explanatory variable of this paper is the level of integration of agriculture and tourism (IAT, Integration of Agriculture and Tourism). Leisure agriculture and modern agricultural industrial parks link the whole industry chain of production, processing, marketing and service, and promote a new type of agricultural industry form that deeply integrates rural industries of one, two and three industries around the ecological, leisure, entertainment and cultural values of agricultural industry. Leisure agriculture demonstration counties and modern agricultural industrial parks are models of agriculture and tourism integration, and can better represent the level of agriculture and tourism integration in cities. Because of the differences in size among cities, this paper uses the ratio of the total number of cities selected as national leisure agriculture and rural tourism demonstration counties and national modern agricultural industrial parks to the total number of all county-level administrative units under the jurisdiction of the city to quantify the level of integration of agriculture and tourism in cities.

3.2.3 *Control variables*

In order to control for other factors affecting the economic development of tourism in cities, eight variables, such as the level of economic development (PGDP), investment in infrastructure construction (GFE), the level of service industry development (Service-Sector), ease of transportation (Traffic), the level of ecological environment construction (Green), the level of information technology (Internet), the level of higher education (Education), and the level of tourism resources (Resource), were selected as control variables in this paper.

3.3 *Descriptive statistics*

This paper uses panel data consisting of 264 cities from 2010–2019 to verify the impact of agricultural and tourism integration on urban tourism economic development. To eliminate biased distributions as much as possible, all variables are taken as logarithms. The descriptive statistics of each variable are shown in Table 1. All data are from "The China City Statistical Yearbook".

Table 1. Descriptive statistics of variables and calculation methods.

Variable Name	Variable calculation method	Average value
lnTET	Total domestic and foreign tourism revenue (billion yuan)	3.347
lnTNT	Total number of domestic and foreign tourist arrivals (million)	2.249
lnIAT	Cumulative number of model counties and industrial parks (one) / Total number of county-level administrative districts (one)	0.0321
LnPGDP	Gross regional product per capita (yuan)	4.566
LnGFE	Government public finance budget expenditure (million yuan)	6.366
LnService-Sector	Share of tertiary sector in GDP (%)	1.600
LnTraffic	Number of actual rental cars (vehicles)	3.197
LnGreen	Greening coverage rate of urban built-up areas (%)	1.596
LnInternet	Number of Internet broadband access users (million)	1.776
lnEducation	Number of college students in school (persons)	4.568
lnResource	Number of 4A-class scenic spots*2.5 + Number of 5A-class scenic spots*5	1.204

4 RESULTS AND DISCUSSIONS

4.1 *Baseline return*

In this paper, we report the results of both OLS, random effects model (RE) and fixed effects model (FE) regressions in the baseline regression, and explore only the fixed effects model regression results in the heterogeneity process.

Table 2 shows the regression results of the level of integration of agriculture and tourism on the total number of tourist trips and total tourism income in the city. The results show that an increase in the level of integration of agriculture and tourism can significantly contribute to the economic development of urban tourism. Thus hypothesis 1 is verified. In depth, this paper suggests that the possible reasons are, firstly, the tourism industry has higher income and a large amount of labor from agriculture is increasingly flowing to the tourism industry in the process of deep integration of agriculture and tourism. Second, the integration of agriculture and tourism has stimulated the demand for rural tourism among the urban population, which has promoted tourism consumption.

Table 2. Baseline regression results.

Explanatory variables	Explained variables: lnTET			Explained variable: lnTNT		
	OLS	FE	RE	OLS	FE	RE
lnIAT	0.5369***	0.1941**	0.3033***	0.8967***	0.1721**	0.3005***
	(5.3832)	(2.1981)	(3.5977)	(9.0329)	(2.4308)	(4.3251)
Control variables	YES	YES	YES	YES	YES	YES
_cons	−3.8174***	6.0759***	−5.4335***	−0.0464	−4.0540***	−3.3874***
	(−19.4500)	(−28.4351)	(−28.5287)	(−0.2373)	(−23.6649)	(−21.1242)
R^2	0.7770	0.8080	0.7500	0.7000	0.8460	0.6470
N	2640	2640	2640	2640	2640	2640

Note: Values in parentheses are robust standard errors (t-values). ***, **, and * indicate significant at the 1%, 5%, and 10% levels, respectively. Same below.

4.2 *Heterogeneity analysis*

This paper divides the sample of prefecture-level cities into two subsamples based on the size of the primary industry as a share of GDP in 2019, and divides the sample into two subsamples based on whether the number of urban residents of the city exceeds 2 million in 2019. Table 3 reports the regression results for heterogeneity, and the results show that cities with a developed agriculture and a high number of citizens have a more significant effect of agricultural and tourism integration on the tourism economy. Looking deeper into the reasons, firstly, in cities with developed agriculture, agricultural production is no longer limited to providing agricultural products, and farmers have more opportunities to develop the ecotourism value of agriculture as a way to earn higher income. Second, the increasing population of urban citizens can lead to urban traffic congestion, environmental damage, and other problems, ultimately leading to a decline in the quality of life of residents in the city. Therefore, the residents of big cities are more eager for the leisurely lifestyle of the countryside and the beautiful natural environment of the countryside, which provides an opportunity for the development of rural tourism.

Table 3. Heterogeneity regression results.

Variables	Developed agriculture		Underdeveloped agriculture		More urban residents		Fewer urban residents	
	lnTET	LnTNT	lnTET	lnTNT	lnTET	lnTNT	lnTET	lnTNT
lnIAT	0.234*	0.47**	0.13	0.13	0.34*	0.38**	0.17*	0.14*
	(1.68)	(2.43)	(1.22)	(1.35)	(1.8800)	(2.03)	(1.65)	(1.85)
Control variables	YES	YES	YES	YES	YES	YES	YES	YES
_cons	−6.74***	−3.57***	−5.49**	−4.01**	−5.62**	−4.42**	−6.35**	4.06**
	(−19.77)	(−7.55)	(−19.70)	(−15.98)	(−11.66)	(9.021)	(−24.96)	(21.01)
R^2	0.80	0.60	0.82	0.82	0.84	0.81	0.80	0.86
N	1320	1320	1320	1320	580	580	2060	2060

5 CONCLUSIONS

This paper theoretically analyzes the role of agriculture and tourism integration in promoting urban tourism economic development, and empirically demonstrates the impact of agriculture and tourism integration on urban tourism economic development based on panel data of 264 cities nationwide from 2010–2019, while finding through heterogeneity analysis that the promotion effect is more significant in cities with developed agriculture and a large number of citizens. Based on the above findings, this paper draws the following insights:

First, local farmers and SMEs should be encouraged to participate in the process of integrating agriculture and tourism. For local farmers, they should be trained and guided to improve their tourism service capacity; for SMEs, they should be given funds through policies such as inclusive finance to encourage them to start their own businesses in the countryside.

Second, in cities with developed agriculture, attention needs to be paid to expanding the tourism function of agriculture so that agricultural production is no longer limited to providing only agricultural products. Enterprises can cooperate with universities to train a group of professional managers who understand agricultural production, business management and tourism services, and build a number of agricultural industrial parks that integrate agricultural production, sales and tourism. In cities with large populations, emphasis should be placed on improving the transportation infrastructure between urban and rural areas. This can meet the demand of urban residents to travel to the countryside while promoting local tourism consumption.

Third, attention should be paid to the value of agricultural culture in the integration of agriculture and tourism. Different historical backgrounds and geographical environments have bred different agricultural cultures, and the original traditional buildings, cultural sites and customs should be protected in the development of agricultural tourism. Enterprises should establish unique tourism brands through in-depth excavation of agricultural culture and form a model of integration of agriculture and tourism with local characteristics.

This study still has the following shortcomings: First, this paper discusses the effects of the integration of agriculture and tourism on urban tourism economy, but the development of urban tourism economy may also promote the integration of agriculture and tourism. Secondly, this paper uses leisure agriculture demonstration counties and modern agricultural industrial park as models to measure the degree of integration of urban agriculture and tourism, but does not discuss the impact of leisure agriculture demonstration counties and modern agricultural industrial park on urban tourism economy in detail.

REFERENCES

Chen, Xiwen. 2015. The Development Situation of Chinese Agriculture and the Challenges it Faces, *Rural Economy* (1): 3–7.

Cao Wen. 2015. The Road Strength of Integrating Rural Tourism and Agricultural Modernization, *Rural Economy* (05): 61–65.

Geum, Y., Kim, M., Lee. S. 2016. How Industrial Convergence Happens: A Taxonomical Approach Based on Empirical Evidences. *Technological Forecasting and Social Change* 107: 112–120.

Hacklin, F., Marxt, C., Fahrni, F. 2009. Coevolutionary Cycles of Convergence: an Extrapolation from the ICT industry, *Technological Forecasting and Social Change* 76(6): 723–736.

Liu Xia. 2016. Research on the Integrated Development of Agriculture and Tourism in Henan Based on Path Dependence, *China Agricultural Resources and Zoning* 37(03): 233–23.

Phillip, S., and C. Hunter. 2010. Blackstock K.A Typology for Defining Agritourism, *Tourism Management* 31(6): 754–758.

Sick, N., Preschitschek, N., Leker, J. Broring, S. 2019. A New Framework to Assess Industry Convergence in High Technology Environments, *Technovation* 84–85: 48–58.

Yang Geyao, Zhou Changchun, Yang Guangming. 2020. The Relationship Between Industrial Integration of Agriculture and Tourism and Rural Poverty Alleviation, *Statistics and Decision Making* 36(5): 81–86.

Zhong Yi-Ping, Tang Lin-Ren, Hu Ping-Bo. 2020. Mechanisms and Empirical Analysis of Agricultural Tourism Integration to Promote the Optimization and Upgrading of Rural Industrial Structure–Taking National Leisure Agriculture and Rural Tourism Demonstration Counties as an Example, *China Rural Economy* (07): 80–98.

Economic and Business Management – Lent & Zhang (Eds)
© 2023 the Author(s), ISBN 978-1-032-24482-2

Impact of IFDI on China's carbon emissions based on industry perspective

Zhibin Chen & Yongjian Zong
School of Economic & Management, Nanjing University of Science & Technology, Nanjing, China

ABSTRACT: Under the dual carbon target, it is still of great significance to study the impact of Inward Foreign Direct Investment (IFDI) on China's carbon emissions. A study of China's carbon emissions levels and IFDI from 2012 to 2019 found that growth in foreign direct investment increased China's carbon emissions. However, the impact of carbon emissions is different from that of industries, and the characteristics of industries determine the level of carbon emissions. Therefore, the government should improve the investment rules, optimize the investment structure, and gradually promote the industrial structure adjustment. They should also actively guide foreign investment flows to low-carbon industries, constantly improve environmental protection standards, supervision of enterprises to comply with the standards, accelerate the formulation of industrial carbon emission reduction standards.

1 INTRODUCTION

1.1 *Research background*

Through more than 40 years of reform and opening up, China's economy has developed rapidly and grown into the world's second-largest economy. However, China's development model has also led to high energy consumption, high pollution, and high emissions. In 2016, China formally joined the Paris Climate Change Agreement. According to the World Energy Statistics Yearbook 2019, China's carbon emissions accounted for 27.8% of the world in 2018, standing as one of the largest carbon emitters in the world. As a responsible country, the Chinese government promises to reverse the carbon emission peak around 2030 and achieve carbon neutrality in 2060. The proposal of dual carbon targets poses a profound challenge to the balance between China's economic development and CO_2 emission reduction. On the one hand, as one of the "three carriages" to promote national economic growth, China needs to continuously attract IFDI to promote economic development. According to the latest statistics released by the Ministry of Commerce of the People's Republic of China, the actual use of foreign capital in 2021 for the first time exceeded trillion, reaching 1.1 trillion yuan. On the other hand, the rapid introduction of foreign capital also has a negative impact on China's environment. In order to attract IFDI, local governments in China have reduced environmental standards, resulting in low levels of environmental regulation and environmental pollution. Therefore, IFDI presents an uncertain challenge to achieve China's dual-carbon goals.

1.2 *Significance*

With the growth of the total economy, the consumption of resources is also growing, which further leads to the continuous improvement of China's carbon emissions. In the case of no significant improvement in technical level and energy efficiency, relying solely on domestic production resources consumption to maintain economic growth is unsustainable. Therefore, expanding openness and constantly attracting high-quality IFDI remain necessary measures to promote economic development. An in-depth analysis of the environmental effect of IFDI on various industries in China and an understanding of the actual impact of IFDI on carbon emissions of various industries are of great practical significance for China to rationally use IFDI to promote the green and high-quality development of various industries and achieve the dual carbon goals.

1.3 *Content*

By reviewing the development status of carbon emissions and IFDI in various industries in China, as well as some existing problems, and taking this as the starting point for empirical analysis, we draw following conclusions: IFDI has a positive effect, increasing China's total carbon emissions. We also give some policy recommendations accordingly.

1.4 *Innovation*

There is still room for discussion in the existing research. At present, IFDI in different countries or regions has different impacts on the environment in different periods, and there is no conclusion regarding the impact of IFDI on China's environmental pollution and carbon emissions. The latest research is based on national, provincial, or regional analysis. Only a few scholars have analyzed China's industrial segmentation and made a lot of specific analyses of the impact of international direct investment and carbon emissions in China's sub-sectors or industries. Therefore, it is innovative and practical to study the relationship between international direct investment and China's carbon emissions by industry.

2 LITERATURE REVIEWED

While FDI is increasing year by year, China's carbon dioxide emission situation is also deteriorating. There are conflicting views on the impact of foreign direct investment on CO_2 emissions. One view is that most capital-poor economies attract investors by removing restrictions and loose environmental regulations. Therefore, IFDI can impose high costs on the environment (Shahbaz et al., 2015; Salahuddin et al., 2018; Sarkodie et al., 2020; Cao et al., 2020). Another view is that IFDI has a positive impact on the environmental performance of developing countries due to relevant eco-friendly technologies (Liu et al., 2014; Mert and BoluK, 2016). IFDI is considered a source of ecological innovation, promoting energy efficiency and shifting the industrial structure from nonrenewable energy to sustainable energy (Doytch and Narayan et al., 2015). Therefore, with the existence of high-tech innovation (TI) and rec, IFDI can reduce CO_2 emissions. However, Ansari et al. (2020) believe that IFDI has a weak binding force on the host country's environmental protection policies, resulting in an increase in CO_2 emissions from developing countries. Based on the above analysis, it is difficult to reach a consensus on the relationship between IFDI and carbon emissions.

In view of the controversy over China's macro research, we focus on the meso level, and the research and analysis based on different industries have more practical guiding significance to deal with the relationship between carbon emission reduction and FDI in China. Existing studies are mostly based on industrial sectors, and Yang and Ye (2017) believed that the difference in carbon dioxide emission reduction effect between foreign direct investment and technological progress is obvious. Li (2013) believes that China's environmental regulation has a negative effect on industrial enterprises to attract foreign investment, and this negative effect contains industry heterogeneity. The industry is still with strong heterogeneity. Differences between industries such as construction, manufacturing, and mining are more pronounced. Whether there are significant differences in the impact of IFDI on carbon emissions due to industry heterogeneity is more worthy of discussion.

3 CURRENT SITUATION OF CARBON EMISSION AND FOREIGN INVESTMENT IN CHINA

3.1 Current situation of foreign investment in China

Research shows that the IFDI infused in China increased from US $2 billion in 1985 to US $138 billion in 2019. In 2016, China became the third-largest IFDI country in the world after the United States and the United Kingdom. However, from the perspective of the sub-sectors of the trade and circulation industry, there are obvious differences in the amount of FDI used in different industries. The actual amount of FDI used in the transportation, warehousing, and postal industries increased significantly (46.9% in 10 years), while the actual amount of FDI used in the wholesale and retail industries and the actual amount of FDI used in the accommodation and catering industries increased relatively slowly. In the past 10 years, the growth rate was 13.52% and 11.97% respectively.

3.2 Current situation of carbon emission in China

China has the highest carbon emissions in the world. Research shows that in 2015, China's total carbon emissions accounted for 29% of the world's carbon emissions, and its per capita carbon emissions exceeded that of the EU, becoming the world's second-largest per capita carbon emitter. Figure 1 shows, from 1990 to 2015, China's total carbon emissions and per capita carbon emissions increased by 346% and 355%, respectively. China's CO_2 emissions per unit of GDP show a gradual decline year by year, from 2.03 in 1990 to 0.68 in 2019. From the development trend over the years, China's CO_2 emissions per unit of GDP have been declining for a long time. In 2019, China's CO_2 emissions per unit of GDP decreased by 4.1% compared with 2018, and in 2020, China's CO_2 emissions per unit of GDP decreased by 18.8%.

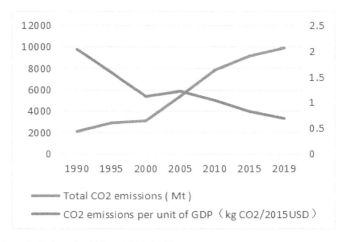

Figure 1.   Carbon Emissions in China, 1990–2019.
[Source: International Energy Agency (IEA).]

145

Table 1. China national CO_2 emission inventory, 2010–2019 (by IPCC Sectoral Emissions).

Industry	2010	2012	2014	2016	2018	2019
Total Consumption	7904.55	9080.55	9451.28	9256.25	9621.12	9794.76
Farming, Forestry, Animal Husbandry, Fishery and Water Conservancy	79.07	86.15	94.51	100.40	94.66	91.45
Mining	206.62	209.02	157.57	127.79	125.64	122.16
Manufacturing Industry	3399.88	3741.18	3909.28	3642.22	3431.73	3510.92
Production and Supply of Electric Power, Steam and Hot Water	3198.84	3857.12	3984.30	3962.14	4514.66	4646.59
Construction	37.01	38.73	44.67	46.35	45.01	44.09
Transportation, Storage, Post and Telecommunication Services	482.72	577.35	638.80	689.50	741.36	732.48
Wholesale, Retail Trade and Catering Services	66.94	80.15	83.83	86.64	71.30	67.60
Others	133.13	156.24	162.75	175.91	160.04	153.30
Urban	168.07	187.14	213.89	245.08	270.32	271.69
Rural	132.26	147.46	161.69	180.22	166.41	154.48

Source: Carbon Emission Accounts and Databases for emerging economies (CEADs).

As shown in Table 1, China's CO_2 emissions come mainly from these two industries such as the manufacturing industry, production and supply of electric power, steam, and hot water industry. In 2019, China's Manufacturing Industry industry emitted 3.51 billion tons of CO_2; the production and supply of electric power, steam and hot water CO2 emission is 4.65 billion tons. The CO_2 emissions from transportation, storage, and postal services cannot be ignored. In 2019, the CO2 emissions in this field were 732.48 million tons. The CO2 emissions generated by direct consumption of residents are not high by comparison. The emissions in 2018 were 350 million tons. However, in combination with the CO2 emissions generated by the indirect consumption of residents. In 2018, the proportion of CO2 emissions generated by direct and indirect consumption of residents was 27.92%. China's carbon emissions mainly come from the secondary industry, especially the six energy-intensive sectors. Power generation and heat supply emissions account for about half of the country's total emissions.

3.3 Reasons for conflicts between dual carbon goals and foreign investment

3.3.1 The impact of international investment on China's carbon emission level

On the one hand, the government needs to promote transnational investment by promoting the liberalization of transnational investment. On the other hand, policies should be implemented and investment regulation strengthened. With the changing views of the government on the rights and obligations of the state and investors, it has become a difficult task to seek a balance between liberalization and investment regulation.

Multinational corporations have dual identities, and they both are investors and carbon emitters. Therefore, while using low-carbon production processes to reduce greenhouse gas emissions, they are also very likely to avoid the rise in production costs caused by the strict carbon emission standards in their home countries, transfer the facilities that emit greenhouse gases to areas with relatively loose environmental supervision, and "export" CO_2 to the host countries along the value chain, which is the so-called "carbon leakage"

3.3.2 Crowding out effect of environmental regulation

Environmental regulation refers to the policy measures formulated by the government to ensure the coordinated development of economy and ecological environment, which are used to regulate the production and operation activities of manufacturers due to unsustainable energy consumption and the uneconomic external production and life. It is generally believed that strict environmental regulations will crowd out innovation funds and the investment of enterprises. This is because enterprises need to pay additional costs for emissions of pollutants, production costs will increase, which will also lead to reduced investment in innovative research and development. At the same time, strict environmental regulation will encourage enterprises to invest in places where environmental regulation is relatively weak. This crowding-out effect will lead to a decline in local GDP levels.

4 THEORETICAL ANALYSIS

Grossman and Kruger (1991) first put forward the view that economic activities affect the environment through three effects: scale effect, structure effect, and technology effect. Obviously, FDI is a kind of economic activity, and the impact of FDI on carbon emissions is naturally included in the impact on the overall environment. Therefore, these three effects are also applicable to the analysis of this paper.

Scale effect refers to the change in carbon emissions caused by the change of economic scale caused by the introduction of FDI. Generally speaking, the introduction of FDI will expand the scale of the original enterprises in the host country, which will increase the overall scale of enterprises in the host country. Due to the expansion of production scale and the increase of production factors, energy consumption also increases. When the technology level remains unchanged and the awareness of energy conservation and emission reduction is not built, the increase of FDI will inevitably exacerbate the deterioration of the environment, increasing carbon emissions. Therefore, from this perspective, the scale effect brought by FDI has an adverse impact on carbon emissions.

The structural effect refers to the change of the industrial structure of the host country caused by the entry of FDI, which increases or decreases the proportion of high-energy consumption industries, and thus has an impact on carbon emissions. If the speculative motive of IFDI is low threshold environmental protection standards, it will lead to the transfer of high-energy consumption industries or enterprises from countries with high threshold environmental protection standards to countries with low threshold environmental protection standards, thus forming an environmental refuge. If foreign-funded enterprises produce products in the host country and they export the products to foreign countries and leave the carbon emissions from the production process at home, it will obviously put an adverse impact on the host country.

The introduction of FDI has not only directly or indirectly brought advanced technology to the host country but also brought a higher awareness of the concept of green production and management. Advanced technology can improve energy efficiency, to achieve energy conservation and emission reduction. The green production, operation, and management concept will bring demonstration effect to local enterprises. To a certain extent, it can stimulate local enterprises' awareness of environmental protection. With the gradual strengthening of environmental protection awareness, enterprises will actively introduce foreign advanced technologies, or increase the research and development of energy-saving and emission reduction technologies, so as to achieve the goal of low energy consumption and low emissions.

It can be seen that the scale effect of IFDI on carbon emissions in various industries mainly increases the carbon emissions of various industries. This further leads to the fact that for the whole country, the structural effect is stronger than the technical effect, which makes IFDI increase China's overall carbon emissions.

5 CONCLUSIONS AND SUGGESTIONS

5.1 *Conclusion analysis*

In general, IFDI has a positive effect, increasing China's total carbon emissions. However, when looking at the industry, it is different. The industry characteristics determine its carbon emissions. Industry, such as a traditional high-emission industry, has higher emissions in the three major categories of mining, manufacturing, and the production and supply of electricity, gas, and water. Manufacturing has always been an important sector of energy consumption and pollution emissions, especially the heavily polluting enterprises in the manufacturing industry. It is generally believed that their carbon emissions are higher than those of other industries. However, from the analysis results of this paper, it can be seen that IFDI only has a significant positive correlation in the emissions of mining industry. For other traditional high-emission industries, there is no result that the increase of IFDI has significantly increased the emissions. However, in the three industries of construction, wholesale (wholesale, retail, accommodation, and catering), and mining, IFDI still has a scale effect. Due to the expansion of production scale and the increase of production factors, energy consumption also increases. The increase in IFDI has significantly led to an increase in carbon emissions. This will inevitably lead to further deterioration of the environment.

5.2 *Policy suggestions*

First, optimize the investment structure, and gradually promote industrial restructuring. For industrial industries with high emissions, in particular, in the mining industry the proportion of industries with high energy consumption and high pollution introduced by IFDI should be reduced. Some enterprises with low added value, low production capacity, and high consumption should be shut down. For manufacturing and wholesale industries (wholesale, retail, accommodation, and catering), technology-intensive IFDI should be actively introduced to promote the development of high-end manufacturing industries and low-carbon saving technologies, and fundamentally curb the introduction of resource-consuming production and consumption patterns. At the same time, the higher energy consumption in the tertiary industry, such as transportation and real estate industry, should pay attention to its energy conservation and environmental protection work. The real estate industry as a pillar industry in China, in the completion of rough development and industrial scale, has been close to saturation, the government should limit the inflow of IFDI, and promote the development of low-carbon green real estate industry. For farming, forestry, animal husbandry, fishery, and water conservancy industries, the government should actively introduce IFDI, guide farmers to use low-carbon and environmentally friendly production materials, increase investment in agricultural research, and promote low-carbon production technology, so as to transform extensive agricultural production methods to intensive production methods.

Second, the government should constantly improve environmental protection standards, supervise enterprises to comply with them, speed up the formulation of industrial carbon emission reduction implementation standards, and improve the domestic ecological environment. For traditional high-emission industries such as mining, strict carbon emission reduction and environmental management policies will be implemented to urge enterprises to improve production technology and optimize production processes to reduce carbon emissions, and gradually eliminate the extensive development model in the past.

Third, establish a diversified assessment system, continue to reduce the weight of GDP in the assessment, carbon emission reduction as an important assessment content into the promotion assessment mechanism of local governments, and actively change the concept of government governance. In local government assessment, to achieve real economic and ecological benefits of unity.

REFERENCES

Cao, W., Chen, S., Huang, Z., 2020. Does Foreign Direct Investment Impact Energy Intensity? Evidence from Developing Countries. *Math. Probl Eng.* 1–11.

Doytch, N., Narayan, S., et al. 2015. Does FDI Influence Renewable Energy Consumption? An Analysis of Sectoral FDI Impact on Renewable and Non-renewable Industrial Energy Consumption. *Energy Econ.* 54: 291–301.

Li, G.P., et al. 2013. Environmental regulation, FDI and Pollution haven effect - Empirical Analysis from the Perspective of Industrial Heterogeneity in China. *Science and Technology Management* 34(10): 122–129.

Liu, X., Yu, L., Qiu, Z., Ru, Z. 2014. FDI and Economic Development: Evidence from China's Regional Growth. *Emerg. Mark. Financ. Trade* 50 (sup6), 87–106.

Mert, M., Boluk, G. 2016. Do Foreign Direct Investment and Renewable Energy Consumption Affect the CO2 Emissions? New Evidence from a Panel ARDL Approach to Kyoto Annex Countries. *Environ. Sci. Pollut. Res.* 23: 21669–21681.

Salahuddin, M., et al. 2018. The Effects of Electricity Consumption,Economic Growth, Financial Development and Foreign Direct Investment on CO2 Emissions in Kuwait. *Renew. Sust. Energ. Rev.* 81, 2002–2010.

Sarkodie, S.A., Adams, S., Leirvik, T. 2020. Foreign Direct Investment and Renewable Energy in Climate Change Mitigation: Does Governance Matter? *J. Clean. Prod.* 263: 121262.

Shahbaz, M., Nasreen, S., Abbas, F., Anis, O. 2015. Does Foreign Direct Investment Impede Environmental Quality in High-, middle-, and low-income Countries? *Energy Econ.* 51: 275–287.

Economic and Business Management – Lent & Zhang (Eds)
© 2023 the Author(s), ISBN 978-1-032-24482-2

Main determinants of 'green' investment in environmental protection: World experience and Ukraine

Z.S. Varnalii, O.V. Cheberyako, N.S. Miedviedkova & O.A. Borysenko
Taras Shevchenko National University of Kyiv, Kyiv, Ukraine

D.V. Nikytenko & O.V. Kaletnyk
National University of Water and Environmental Engineering, Rivne, Ukraine

ABSTRACT: The article considers the main determinants of 'green' environmental investment. The financial instruments that stimulate green investment are highlighted as: 'green' credit lines, 'green' private lending, and 'green' bonds. In this study, an example is given of providing 'green' credit under the condition of transforming the technology of service provision of a logistics company. In addition to the financial determinants of 'green' investment, the institutional factor—regulatory and technical requirements for investment has been identified. The desire to increase foreign direct investment and environmental regulations and technical requirements is contradictory. The discussion defines the duration of the use of budgetary funding and its value for stimulating renewable electricity as a type of green investment project.

1 INTRODUCTION

The economic security of the state and the level of its provision have been and remain to be relevant from both a theoretical and a practical point of view, especially when the foundations of sustainable development are respected. Trends in such indicators as decarbonization of production, reduction of energy intensity of production, growth of real GDP, level of enterprises introducing innovative, and energy-saving technologies are evidence of the precarious state of economic security in Ukraine. The energy intensity of Ukraine's GDP is still more than 2–3 times higher than in the European Union (Table 1). This is due to the structure of the country's economy, where coal is the main source of heat generation, metallurgy, and chemical industry, as well as because of the urgent need for energy modernization of equipment and the introduction of advanced technologies. This situation leads to a weakening of economic potential, hinders the modernization of domestic production and the strengthening of the competitiveness of the national economy, and complicates the implementation of the social functions of the state.

One of the key factors for the improvement of the environment is the increase of 'green' investment, which is reflected in the growth of the qualitative component—the reduction of greenhouse gas (GHG) emissions, rational waste management, effective wastewater management and counteracting various environmental risks, supporting eco-stability by introducing energy efficiency measures, and developing renewable energy and environmentally friendly technologies. Such investments can have a positive impact on the energy security of the State, the energy efficiency of the economy, and the competitiveness of domestic products in world markets, as well as the solvency of the population, particularly for housing utilities. At the same time, for the current stage of the development of the Ukrainian economy, the reasons for the low level of 'green' investment are the mismatch of the actual

DOI: 10.1201/9781003278788-23

Table 1. Energy intensity of GDP at constant purchasing power parities (koe/$15p) (Energy intensity 2020).

Country	1990	1995	2000	2005	2010	2015	2020	2000–2020 (%/year)
World	**0,177**	**0,168**	**0,153**	**0,146**	**0,137**	**0,123**	**0,114**	**−1,4**
European Union	**0,127**	**0,119**	**0,106**	**0,103**	**0,095**	**0,083**	**0,075**	**−1,7**
France	0,121	0,121	0,112	0,110	0,102	0,093	0,081	−1,6
Germany	0,130	0,113	0,103	0,101	0,092	0,079	0,070	−1,9
Italy	0,077	0,079	0,076	0,079	0,075	0,068	0,064	−0,8
Netherlands	0,128	0,126	0,104	0,104	0,101	0,085	0,078	−1,4
Poland	0,248	0,215	0,149	0,133	0,115	0,094	0,083	−2,9
United Kingdom	0,125	0,120	0,105	0,091	0,081	0,066	0,058	−2,9
Norway	0,123	0,114	0,106	0,099	0,114	0,094	0,087	−1,0
Turkey	0,076	0,077	0,079	0,069	0,074	0,064	0,060	−1,4
Russia	0,291	0,339	0,305	0,238	0,211	0,196	0,204	−2,0
Ukraine	0,345	0,466	0,421	0,305	0,274	0,215	0,193	−3,8
Canada	0,255	0,260	0,238	0,216	0,183	0,178	0,173	−1,6
United States	0,195	0,185	0,165	0,148	0,136	0,120	0,107	−2,2
China	0,530	0,355	0,254	0,251	0,209	0,169	0,145	−2,7
Pacific	**0,166**	**0,158**	**0,151**	**0,134**	**0,130**	**0,115**	**0,108**	**−1,6**
Africa	**0,169**	**0,179**	**0,166**	**0,153**	**0,139**	**0,136**	**0,133**	**−1,1**
Middle-East	**0,111**	**0,133**	**0,128**	**0,136**	**0,144**	**0,152**	**0,164**	**1,3**

(current) conditions, necessary for the effective transformation of domestic and foreign investment potential into a real investment factor for both economic development and environmental improvement. Therefore, the realization of the necessity of the state policy of 'green' investment is becoming more relevant.

2 LITERATURE REVIEW

Many Ukrainian and foreign scientists are involved in solving environmental problems. Systematization of theoretical approaches to the essence of green investment is engaged by Chariri et al. (2021), Eyraud et al. (2011) Eyraud et al. (2013), Murovec et al. (2012), and Pimonenko (2018). The characteristics of various financial instruments for stimulating 'green' investments are dealt with by Dyma (2020) and the comparative characteristic of the 'green' economy, 'green' growth, and sustainable development are carried out by Kvach et al. (2020) and Doroshenko (2018). Green economy research in the system of strategic priorities for the safe development of Ukraine is reflected in the work of Potapenko (2012). Some researchers have found a positive and significant effect of green investment and CSR investment on financial performance and sustainable performance (Chariri et al. 2021). Eyraud et al. (2013) found that green investment is driven by economic growth and some green policy interventions. Yousaf et al. (2022) show that green investments are not luxury goods for investors, but have now developed into a necessity with the potential to provide significant investment benefits, even during periods of crises. Thi Thanh Tu Trana et al. (2020) demonstrate the factors affecting green investment and Baietti et al. (2012) in a World Bank study concluded the main challenges for green investment on the micro level of the national economy. Testa & Gusmerottia (2016) studies the factors that have an impact on the proactive environment strategy of small and micro firms. The research claimed that external pressures and entrepreneurs' attitudes are the most important factor influencing the proactive environment strategy at both micro and small company levels. Kvach et al. (2020) have shown that environmental taxes are used in EU countries as a means of influencing the behavior of economic entities. Dyma (2020) attracted attention to improving the legal and organizational mechanisms to stimulate investment attraction into promising, environmentally sound sectors of the economy.

3 PROBLEM STATEMENT

In contrast to the research mentioned above, our work will look at the determinants of 'green' investment from a macro-level perspective, those circumstances that create the preconditions for the activization of 'green' investment at the micro level. The main objectives of the article are to identify the main determinants of 'green' investment in environmental protection and to analyze World and Ukrainian experience in stimulating 'greening' the economy.

4 MATERIAL AND METHODS

In order to achieve the objectives of this paper, general scientific and special methods have been used, namely: theoretical generalization method for the study of the essence of 'green' investments in economic security; grouping method for characterizing financial instruments that promote 'green investment'; the systematic approach to identifying constitutive segments and relevant financial instruments in the Green Investment System. Moreover, a comparison method was used to differentiate the promotion of 'green' investments in Ukraine and other countries.

5 RESULTS

The classical interpretation lies in that it is an investment is made by economic agents for profit. The new development paradigm of modern society, integrating economic, social and environmental dimensions, calls for a redefinition of investment objectives (Mykytiuk et al. 2020). We maintain that in investment, economic benefits are the first objective and the social and environmental effects of such economic activities are derived objectives, which are achieved through the redistribution of economic benefits. As far as the 'green' investments are concerned, their interpretation is quite broad: 'clean', 'sustainable', 'responsible', 'ecological' or 'climate change investment'. According to the IMF, investment is considered to be 'green' with the ultimate result of reducing emissions of GHGs and pollutants into the atmosphere without significantly reducing the production and consumption of non-energy goods (Eyraud L. et al. 2011). The OECD interprets 'green' investments as investments in enterprises, projects and financial instruments, mainly in the renewable energy sector, which help to reduce carbon emissions, mitigate climate change and spread environmental technologies (Croce, R. D. et al. 2011). The same statement is shared by other scholars (Martinez-Oviedo & Medda 2018; Martin & Moser 2016). Despite the different approaches to the interpretation of this concept, what is common is that consider the non-financial aspects of investment. In our opinion, 'green' investments are investments whose conceptual purpose is to develop an ecosystem. In terms of economic impact, it may not be only market-based.

The determinants that directly affect the direction, volume, scale, and timing of 'green' investment, though similar to general investment activity, still had some special features. These determinants are macroeconomic, demographic, technological, monetary, and institutional.

Positive macroeconomic dynamics, as well as demographic factors, increase the demand for energy resources and, accordingly, affect the growth in pollution. However, only if society adheres to the principles of sustainable development, the hypothesis of the 'ecological curve' of S. Kuznets is valid. It means that higher levels of economic development, in turn, tend to influence structural changes in industrial production and services, international relocation, expansion of renewable energy, promotion of environmental awareness, and improvement in compliance with environmental norms and standards resulting in increased costs (hence, investments) for environmental purposes and gradual environmental improvements. Rising fossil fuel prices have also helped to attract 'green' investment, in particular, because of the relatively lower cost of electricity from renewable energy sources. This effect is also enhanced by carbon taxation (Markevych, K. 2019).

Technological progress and innovation (technological factors) also influence investment activity in areas related to environmental protection (e.g., the area of accumulation and storage from 'intermittent' energy sources).

High-interest rates (the monetary factor) tend to reduce the level of investment, particularly in risky ones such as the 'green'.

Among the many components of the institutional factor, there exist the climatic features of the state (number of sunny days, availability of wind) and adherence to the values of investment responsibility. The beginning of the third millennium was a period of renewed focus on the theme of sustainable development. The global investment community has begun to use environmental parameters intensively in the selection of subjects for investment.

Private businesses have become active in countering climate change by decomposing their investment preferences. Disinvestment is actively taking place, particularly in the coal and oil and gas industries. In 2021, Norway's trillion-dollar sovereign wealth fund sold the last of its portfolio of oil and gas companies in a major step giving up the country's reliance on its petroleum industry (Arvin J. 2021).

Moreover, there is a transformation of the corporations themselves. For example, Google and Apple have said that they will not only abandon any activity that generates pressure on the environment, and carbon emissions; however, they will also fully compensate for the negative impact on the environment, which these companies have posed throughout their existence. On Elon Musk's refusal to sell Tesla's cars on cryptocurrency, particularly Bitcoin, was caused by negative consequences for the environment as a result of the use of huge amounts of electricity at 'property'—creation of cryptocurrency. For example, a study by Cambridge University indicates that in 2019, 128.5 MW of electricity was spent on Bitcoin's 'property' more than Ukraine consumed 125 MW in that year.

Countries are gradually being implemented by 'greening' their economies, but the main problem for the vast majority of them, on the one hand, is the lack of public funding for high-risk research and, on the other hand, the lack of an adequate investment base. The state and local private investors are not always able to provide the necessary funding for green projects on their own, especially in developing countries and countries with economies in transition, particularly in Ukraine. One of the possibilities for mobilizing international investments is the use of various financial instruments.

'Green' investment is carried out by different financial instruments, the most common are credit 'green' lines, private 'green' lending, and 'green' bonds. However, their potential is still limited in the vast majority of countries of the world, they still do not form a single system of 'green' investment instruments, and the use of each depends more on the specific conditions of the sector or country, where 'green' project is realized. The German researcher Lindenberg N. (2014) divides the following instruments into three categories:

1. Shares, lines of credit, loans, and grants are instruments by which direct financing is provided.
2. Instruments that do not provide direct funding but can transfer knowledge or reduce risks (guarantees and technical assistance).
3. Instruments used to attract additional private funds that are transferred to 'green' projects through one of the above-mentioned instruments ('green' bonds and structured funds).

Although the global market for 'green' credits occupies a small niche in the debt capital market, it is growing rapidly: the total volume of issued loans almost reached $60 billion in 2018, which is 30% more than in 2017 (Mahmood Kh. 2019 & Tiftik E.). Among the markets where this instrument is most developed are the USA, the UK, Spain, India, and China. The average repayment period is 15 years. The Loan Market Association classifies 'green' credits into two main types: loans for environmental protection and emission reduction projects and services; credits for strategic industries (Loan Market Association 2018). A consortium of "green" banks has been established in the United States. A green bank uses public capital to mobilize more private investment into underserved green and resilient financing markets to fill market gaps. Green banks have the ultimate goal of enabling private capital partners to enter clean energy markets at scale without green bank assistance (American Green Bank Consortium 2021.) Today, there are many types of 'green' credit products offered by banks. In Ukraine, some state-owned banks that have received foreign 'green' investment are starting to deal with such a credit mechanism to encourage the public to exploit solar panels and wind turbines, biomass boilers, and business incentives to use the latest technologies. This type of lending may become a new form of financial regulation of environmental management at the local level in Ukraine. For example, in Ukraine, the logistics company 'Meest Express' was for the first time faced with the need to take into account the environmental factor when applying for a loan in the EBRD, which offered the best credit conditions when developing 'green' logistics. Cooperation with the EBRD has catalyzed changes in the management model of trunk transport logistics between cities and hubs in the form of: the introduction of software to optimize the load of large-tonnage transport; implementation of certain tools to eliminate expendable packaging; optimization of the warehouse. As a result of these measures, the company reduced costs by 3–5%, significantly reduced carbon dioxide emissions, and strengthened its competitive advantages. Large companies and banks that implement 'green' policies and, accordingly, are interested in 'green' logistics have begun to move to the company (CFA Society Ukraine. 2020).

As for the instruments that do not provide direct funding, then, for example, China actively uses bank guarantees on 'green' credits and technical assistance to market players, including utilities, equipment suppliers, and energy service companies, to order to promote energy efficiency projects. Additionally, South Korea and China are also providing technical assistance to reduce hydrocarbon emissions.

The 'green' bonds are a specific instrument, which by all indications is an ordinary bond, but the target is to use funds for the 'green' projects that will have a positive impact on the environment (Cheberyako O. et al. 2021). The largest (top five largest green bond issuers) issuers of 'green' bonds in 2020 were: Fannie Mae (USA) ($13 bn), Federal Republic of Germany ($12.8 bn), Société du Grand Paris ($12.2 bn) KfW ($ 9.4 bn), Republic of France ($ 6.9 bn), and other (Jones L. 2021). Thus, the United States (Hawaii) is actively using 'green' bonds, which provide income. Payments on such bonds are based on the proceeds from the project (Climate Bonds Initiative 2020). 'Green' investment funds are environmentally responsible, accumulate investment resources, and channel funds to finance green projects and companies. Nowadays in Europe, there are almost more than 200 different types of 'green' investment funds.

With huge global capital for 'green' projects in Ukraine, there is a shortage of both the resource and the corresponding infrastructure, which includes special trust funds carrying out 'green' investments (Lytvynenko, V. 2021). The presence of venture investors and business angels, having an entire portfolio of 'green' and climate innovations, is necessary; however, it is not a sufficient indicator of the level of infrastructure development. Currently, international financial institutions such as EBRD, EIB, IFC, and the World Bank are the main investors in the 'green' start-up and development of climate innovations and also catalysts of green business processes. On the other hand, there is a trend of personal business movement in 'green' business under the influence of requirements of consumers of production.

Currently, a number of investment incentives are applied to help solve the problems of energy conservation and construction of modern energy generating capacity, including renewable energy (Yakymchuk et al. 2017). Fiscal incentives in the form of tax credits are crucial elements in stimulating green investment in the United States and Canada. One of the fiscal tools to stimulate the development of renewable energy in Ukraine was the establishment of a 'green' tariff for electricity (feed-in tariff), produced from alternative sources.

In addition to the financial determinants of 'green' investment, attention should be paid to the institutional factor, such as regulatory and technical requirements for investment. Typically, the scarcity of domestic investment resources in most countries increases interest in attracting foreign capital (mainly FDI). On the one hand, the arrival of a foreign investor is a means of technological structural transformation in the recipient country. On the other hand, FDI can have negative effects, such as negative impacts on the environment, in particular through the relocation of environmentally 'dirty' industries from the base country to the recipient country, or if technology-based FDI is obsolete and unsuitable to use. Therefore, FDI can sometimes influence negative environmental impacts (footprints). They can occur in countries where, according to the theory of the pollution haven effect (Gray, K. R. 2002), there are no stringent environmental regulations and requirements. The decision of foreign investors to relocate their production lines abroad may be motivated by a desire to reduce the cost of environmental compliance in their country. Moreover, under the 'regulatory cooling' (Fortanier F. & Maher M. 2001) hypothesis, the countries themselves prefer not to adopt stringent environmental standards in order to maintain competitive advantages. As a result, the negative environmental impacts of FDI by enterprises in recipient countries are now concentrated in developing countries. The governments of these countries face a dilemma: economic development in brown economy or green economy in general, without significant signs of economic growth.

6 DISCUSSIONS

Among all areas of 'green' investment, the most popular in Ukraine are investments in the electric power industry. The economic factor was the introduction of a 'green' (feed-in) tariff on the generated electricity by alternative energy sources (solar, wind) and its guaranteed buy-back. The 'green' tariff in Ukraine is pegged to the euro exchange rate and is the highest in the world, the tariff is valid until January 1, 2030. At the same time, it created a contradictory and burdensome situation for the state budget, especially during the pandemic of 2020–2021, when overall electricity consumption declined. During this period, the state, as a guaranteed buyer, was obliged to buy back excess electricity generated by renewable energy sources, and suspend nuclear power generation in order to avoid imbalances in the interconnected power grid. This situation has raised the question of the feasibility of continuing the policy of stimulating 'green' investment in the electric power industry if there is no economic efficiency at the macro level. As of 2021, the debt to electricity suppliers had increased to $560 million which forced the Cabinet of Ministers to issue Eurobonds, which will have to be repaid at the expense of taxpayers. For developing countries, including Ukraine, economic incentives for "green" investment at the beginning of the 'greening' period, especially in the field of electricity generation, may become an economic upheaval (snag) without the prospects of resolving these issues for many years to come.

7 CONCLUSIONS

Compared to the world practice, in Ukraine, the direction of 'green' investment is developing slowly, but fairly promising. This issue remains relevant, as Ukraine's economy urgently needs a transition to a green basis for sustainable development. Investment in 'green' projects is one way to achieve this goal. Macroeconomic and monetary determinants negatively influence the development of 'green' investment both in Ukraine and in the World. The slowdown in economic growth and the expected restrictive monetary policy may have a negative impact on the rate of growth of 'green' investment. At the same time, rising hydrocarbon prices under the influence of geopolitical factors will further actualize the inevitability of the transition to a 'green' economy. In the case of Ukraine, the legal regulation of investment in green securities and the creation of a modern financial infrastructure remain relevant. Mechanisms for financing 'green' investments, which may be less budget-intensive, should also be developed. Revenue-backed bonds should be considered, particularly at the regional level. Given the limited financial resources and the high level of corruption in Ukraine, it is impossible to create a separate 'green' bank. Further research may be aimed at resolving the contradictions that arise between determinants of 'green' investment on macro and micro level.

ACKNOWLEDGEMENT

The article was prepared within the framework of the National Research Foundation of Ukraine project "New geostrategic threats to human social security in a hybrid war and ways to prevent them" № 2021.01/0239.

REFERENCES

American Green Bank Consortium. 2021. *American Green Bank Consortium's Annual Industry Report*. https://greenbankconsortium.org/annual-industry-report

Arvin J. 2021. Norway's Trillion-dollar Wealth Fund Sold the Last of Its Investments in Fossil Fuel Companies. *vox.com* https://www.vox.com/22256192/norway-oil-gas-investments-fossil-fuel.

Baietti, A., Shlyakhtenko, A., La Rocca, R. & Patel, U. D. 2012. *Green Infrastructure Finance: Leading Initiatives and Research*. The World Bank.

CFA Society Ukraine. 2020. *Environmental Investment: A Global Trend Already in Ukraine*. URL: https://ua.cfaukraine.org/ekologichni-investytsiyi-globalnyj-trend-yakyj-vzhe-v-ukrayini/

Chariri, A. & Indriastuti, M. 2021. The Role of Green Investment and Corporate Social Responsibility Investment on Sustainable Performance. *Cogent Business & Management* 8(1): 1–21.

Cheberyako, O., Varnalii, Z., Borysenko, O. & Miedviedkova, N. 2021. "Green" Finance as a Modern Tool for Social and Environmental Security *IOP Conf. Ser.: Earth Environ. Sci.* 915: 12–17.

Climate Bonds Initiative. 2020. Explaining Green Bonds. *Climatebonds.Net* https://www.climatebonds.net/market/explaining-green-bonds

Croce, R.D, Kaminker, Ch. & Stewart, F. 2011. The Role of Pension Funds in Financing Green Growth Initiatives. *OECD Working Papers on Finance, Insurance and Private Pensions* 10: 11.

Doroshenko, V. 2018 Modern Tools for Financing Energy Saving: "Green Finances". *Proc. Int. Conf. (Cherkasy)* 50: 49–54.

Dyma V. 2020. Financial Instruments to Stimulate the Development of "Green" Economy in Ukraine. *Investments: Practice and Experience* 5: 182–187.

Energy intensity. 2020. *Enerdata* www.enerdata.net; URL: https://yearbook.enerdata.net/total-energy/world-energy-intensity-gdp-data.html

Eyraud, L., Wane, A., Zhang, C. & Clements, B. 2011. Who's Going Green and Why? Trends and Determinants of Green Investment. *IMF Working Paper WP/11/296*.

Eyraud, L., Clements, B. & Wane, A. 2013. Green Investment Trends and Determinants. *Energy Policy* 60: 852–865.

Fortanier, F. & Maher, M. 2001. New Horizons and Policy Challenges for Foreign Direct Investment in the 21st Century. *Foreign Direct Investment and Sustainable Development, OECD Paper*. URL: https://www.oecd.org/daf/inv/investmentstatisticsandanalysis/2408079.pdf.

Gray, K.R. 2002. Foreign Direct Investment and Environmental Impacts. Is the Debate Over? *RECIEL.* 11 (3): 306–313. URL: http://www.worldtradelaw.net/articles/grayfdi.pdf.download.

Jones, L. 2021. Record $269.5bn Green Issuance for 2020: Late Surge Sees Pandemic Year Pip 2019 Total by $3bn *Climatebonds.Net* URL: https://www.climatebonds.net/2021/01/record-2695bn-green-issuance-2020-late-surge-sees-pandemic-year-pip-2019-total-3bn

Kvach, Ya., Piatka, N. & Koval, V. 2020. Management of Sustainable Entrepreneurship Adaptation to Tax Changes in Environmental Investment. *Baltic Journal of Economic Studies*. 6(5): pp. 96–105.

Lindenberg, N. 2014. Public Instruments to Leverage Private Capital for Green Investments in Developing Countries. German Development Institute. *Discussion Paper*, p. 50.

Loan Market Association. 2018. *Green Loan Principles*. URL: https://www.lma.eu.com/application/files/9115/4452/5458/741_LM_Green_Loan_Principles_Booklet_V8.pdf

Lytvynenko, V. et al. 2021. Dynamic Bayesian Networks Application for Evaluating the Investment Projects Effectiveness. In: Babichev S., Lytvynenko V., Wójcik W., Vyshemyrskaya S. (eds) *Lecture Notes in Computational Intelligence and Decision Making*. ISDMCI 2020. Advances in Intelligent Systems and Computing. 1246. https://doi.org/10.1007/978-3-030-54215-3_20

Markevych, K. 2019. *Green Investment in Sustainable Development: World Experience and the Ukrainian Context* 316 p. Kyiv: Razumkov centr.

Martin, P. R., & Moser, D. V. 2016. Managers' Green Investment Disclosures and Investors' Reaction. *Journal of Accounting and Economics*, 61(1): 239–254.

Martinez-Oviedo, R & Medda, F. 2018. Real Natural Assets: The Real Green Investment Alternative. *The Journal of Alternative Investments* 21(3): pp. 53–69.

Murovec, N., Erker, R., & Prodan, I. 2012. Determinants of Environmental Investment: Testing the Structural Model. *Journal of Cleaner Production* 17: 265–277.

Mykytiuk, O., Varnalii, Z., Nikytenko, D., Gędek, S. & Pashnyuk, L. 2020. Investment Determinants of Economic Growth: World Experience and Ukraine. *Intellectual Economics* 15(1): 106–123.

Pimonenko, T. 2018. Ukrainian Perspectives for Developing of Green Investment Market: EU Experience. *Economics and Region* 4(71): 5–15.

Potapenko, V. 2012. 'Green' Economics in the Strategicaly Priorities of Security Development of Ukraine. *Economic Annals-XXI* 3-4 URL: http://soskin.info/ea/2012/3-4/20125.html.

Testa, F., Gusmerottia, N., Corsini, F., Passetti, E., & Iraldo, F. 2016. Factors Affecting Environmental Management by Small and Micro Firms: The Importance of Entrepreneurs' Attitudes and Environmental Investment. *Corporate Social Responsibility and Environmental Management*. 23: pp. 373–385.

Thi Thanh Tu Trana, Hong Nhung Dob, Thi Ha Vub & Nguyen Nguyet Minh Doa. 2020. The Factors Affecting Green Investment for Sustainable Development *Decision Science Letters* 9(3): pp. 365–386.

Tiftik, E. & Mahmood, Kh. 2019. Sustainable Finance in Focus. Green Loans – Kickoff Time! Institute of International Finance, https://www.iif.com/Portals/0/Files/2_SF_green_loan_issuance%20vf.pdf

Yakymchuk, A., Mykytyn, T. & Valyukh A. 2017. Management of Protected Areas of Ukraine's Polissia: International Experience. *Problems and Perspectives in Management*. 15(1): 183–190.

Yousaf, I., Tahir, S. M. & Demirer, R., 2022. Green Investments: A Luxury Good or a Financial Necessity? *Energy Economics*, 105: 105745.

Economic and Business Management – Lent & Zhang (Eds)
© 2023 the Author(s), ISBN 978-1-032-24482-2

Research on night economy network information ecological chain from the perspective of brand communication

Ping Song*
School of Information and Business Management, Dalian Neusoft University of Information, Dalian, China

ABSTRACT: The purpose of this paper is to optimize brand communication chain of night economy by constructing the network information ecological chain model. First, it analyses the value of night economy network information ecological chain for brand communication optimization through literature review. Second, structure of night economy network information ecological chain of night economy is analysed. Third, a night economy network information ecological chain is built from the perspective of brand communication. Finally, it illustrates how night economy brands should take advantage of network information ecological chain to optimize the process of brand communication. This paper provides a reference for improving brand value of night economy and accelerating healthy development of night economy.

1 INTRODUCTION

In recent years, China's night economy has become an important driving force for the urban economy [14]. In 2020, night-time consumption exceeded 30 trillion yuan [11]. The demand for the night economy market continues to be strong [3]. Inspired by favorable policies and market demand, many cities have systematically developed the night economy and launched night markets, scenic spots, sightseeing, and catering cultural entertainment activities accordingly to promote consumption upgrading. Night economy brands with regional characteristics emerge one after another and become the important driving force of the city economy.

Internet technology is profoundly changing the way of brand expansion. The development of artificial intelligence, big data, and other technologies, the emergence of we-media social platforms, and the flexibility and convenience of third-party payment have overturned the previous ways of brand generation, communication, and experience. With the rise of the digital economy, more and more people realize that the night economy is not just "eating and drinking", and how digital technology and information technology light up the new business form of cultural travel has also attracted much attention [6]. This paper is targeted to build the city night economic network based on the theory of network information ecosystem and explore how to make use of information technology and development of business model optimization brand dissemination mechanism, so as to meet the demands of night economic consumption ecological brand and consumers.

The paper first reviews relevant research on brand communication and network information ecological chain, then analysis the structure of the night economy network information ecological chain with the framework of the network information ecological chain. Furthermore, this paper builds a night economy brand communication information network ecological chain by combining the process of brand communication and the framework of network information ecological chain together, logically. Finally, the pager puts forward specific strategies for night economy brand ecological development strategy from the perspective of brand generation, communication, and experience strategies.

---

*Corresponding Author: songping@neusoft.com

 DOI: 10.1201/9781003278788-24

2 LITERATURE REVIEW

2.1 *Literature review on brand communication*

Many scholars have conducted extensive research on intelligent and popular aspects of urban brand communication. Yang Xiaohong's team conducted an in-depth study on the role and significance of digital intelligent communication in brand communication [15]. Wang Jingqiang sorted out problems faced by urban brand construction and proposed promotion strategies [13]. Chen Hongbo put forward suggestions for regional tourism brand communication strategies [1]. Duan Chunlin introduced concepts related to the 5T model and pointed out that online word-of-mouth communication should strive for recognition and support of opinion leaders and create an exclusive "buzzer effect" [7]. Deng Liangliu proposed that urban brand communication should make use of fan economy and establish a long-term mechanism by creating IP value and UGC (User Generated Content) content [9]. These studies show that the mechanism of urban brand generation, communication, and experience has undergone fundamental changes due to changes in the marketing environment.

2.2 *Literature review on the ecological chain of network information*

The network information ecological chain is a chain-dependent relationship formed by the three main parts such as information producers, transmitters, and consumers [4]. Theories related to network information ecological chain have been widely studied and applied in economic and social development, such as business network information ecological chain [9], tourism network information ecological chain [16], government network information ecological chain [12], agricultural network information ecological chain [10], etc. These researches show ecological chain can achieve value creation and appreciation with technology empowerment and synergy mechanism [21]. This also provides an important research foundation for the dissemination and value creation of urban night economy brands in the network information ecological chain.

2.3 *Unexplored research area*

Many researchers studied the application of network information ecological chain theory in different areas as mentioned above, while there is little research on how information ecological chain theory can be applied in the brand commutation process, as well as the relationship between framework of information ecological chain and brand communication process. This article tries to find out the connection between those two factors and make suggestion on how night economy can take advantage of the Internet to reconstruct the information ecological chain and then enhance the efficiency of brand communication.

3 STRUCTURE OF NIGHT ECONOMY NETWORK INFORMATION ECOLOGICAL CHAIN

3.1 *Node*

Information subject refers to information users participating in network information activities of night economy such as information producers, organizers, transmitters, and consumers [17]. Night economy network information producers could be government staff, urban public service organizations, catering and entertainment operators, residents, tourists, e-commerce operators, and media personnel who create and produce night economy-related information. Information organizers and transmitters are linked to organize and forward night economy-related information, such as commercial websites, public service agency websites, search engine websites, applications, social media. Night economy network information consumers are in demand side of night economy information, such as city residents and tourists.

3.2 *Information*

Night economic network information refers to information related to night economics, including policy, activity, and promotional information released by government portal, traffic and weather information released by urban public service, catering, entertainment, culture information released by businesses, travel experience information released by tourists and city residents, and feedback information released by information subject. Information flow can be divided into forward information flow and reverse information flow. The information released by the government, public service, and businesses is transmitted to information consumers, which is a positive information flow. The feedback generated by information consumers after receiving night economy-related information is reverse information flow.

3.3 *Information environment*

The development of night economy network information ecological chain will be affected by political, economic, social, and technological factors. Under the action of the information environment, the information subject carries on the information transfer and interaction constantly, which constitutes the complete information ecological chain of the night economy network.

4 NIGHT ECONOMY BRAND COMMUNICATION INFORMATION NETWORK ECOLOGICAL CHAIN (NEBCINEC)

Night economic brand communication network information ecology chain (NEBCINEC) provides night economic policy information, business information, and a network of social interactions, including the process of information production, organization and dissemination, and information consumption. These three stages are highly compatible with the brand communication process of the night economy. Information generation corresponds to brand generation, information organization and dissemination corresponds to brand communication, and news consumption corresponds to brand experience and consumption. The generation, dissemination, and consumption of both information and brands constitute NEBCINEC, as shown in Figure 1.

4.1 *Information production and brand generation*

As shown in Figure 1, information producers in NEBCINEC are government, scenic spots, public management departments, catering, and entertainment businesses. As the Internet information ecological chain develops from a single linear chain to a decentralized network, a large number of Internet users and KOLs (key opinion leaders or Internet celebrities) are not only consumers of night economy network information, but also producers [2]. Information producers also generate brands such as city scenic spots, city service, commercial, and cultural brands, which belong to brand generation stage. At present, information generation and brand generation are changing from traditional "professional elite centered" brand communication mode to human-machine collaborative socialization and intelligent transformation of "professional operation + fan community + machine creation" [15].

4.2 *Information organization/transmission and brand communication*

Figure 1 shows that in NEBCINEC, in addition to traditional search, advertising, and content marketing, the rise of live broadcasts and short videos has given birth to scene marketing in the tourism industry. The popularity of we-media social networks, such as Weibo and TikTok, has given birth to marketing methods of night economy such as word-of-mouth marketing, KOLs marketing, and event marketing. In NEBCINEC, there is a complex communication structure relationship between the multiple communication subjects and brands information

160

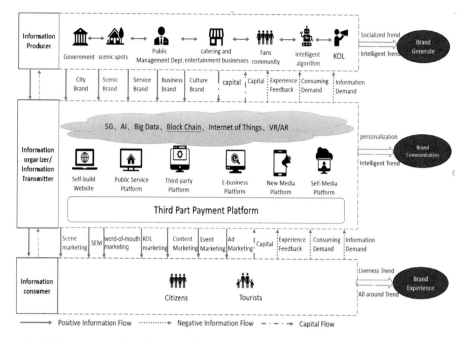

Figure 1. Night economy brand communication information network ecological chain.

disseminated, which caused a brand information overload, as well as the appearance of the trend of fragmentation of brand marketing[19].

4.3 *Information consumption/brand experience*

In NEBCINEC, after receiving brand information, information consumers form their cognition of relevant brands and transform their consumption online or offline to form capital flow. After consumption transformation, consumption feedback can be given in form of evaluation, such as collection, forwarding, or secondary creation and sharing, to generate reverse information flow of night economy. This reverse information is helpful for night economy brands to analyze the effect of brand communication in qualitative and quantitative ways, evaluate the quality of brand information, and then improve brand information quality, communication forms, and communication channels.

5 NIGHT ECONOMY BRAND NEW ECOLOGICAL DEVELOPMENT STRATEGY

5.1 *Brand generation strategy*

Internet information ecological chain has developed from a single linear chain to a decentralized network, in which network users have become an important node of information diffusion and an important source of brand generation. Therefore, information subjects should use information transmission platforms to provide users with a brand interactive interface, such as setting comments or discussion areas to guide network users to express views through texts and pictures. Moreover, improved humanized settings of information communication platforms, such as bullet screen function, words, and voice conversion should be used so as to facilitate communication between users and brands.

KOLs play a role of bridge linking brands and users [18]. Night economy brands should create communication scenes between brands and online fans based on KOLs and fan positioning, and use KOLs to generate high-quality night economy copywriting, pictures, short videos, and other diversified content to create differentiated night economy experience scenes. With the help of huge fan circle of super network IP, the rapid introduction of brand traffic can be realized to enhance the brand awareness. Due to the delivery capacity of KOLs, the sales volume of night economy-related products and services will be increased and the brand reputation will be enhanced.

In NEBCINEC, there is a variant of heterogeneous network chain, night economy brands should use social network analysis technology to dig huge amounts of consumer attributes, behaviors and motivation, and constructing user persona [20]. After understanding accurate consumer demand, artificial intelligence can be used to monitor brand text, graphics, animation, and other creative elements to optimize creative integration, so that brand creative production can directly generate brand stories in an intelligent and personalized way, precisely matching consumer needs.

5.2 *Brand communication strategy*

The government, scenic spots, and urban public service departments should break through traditional brand communication channels and create a three-dimensional media matrix of night economy brands. New media accounts and e-commerce platforms, as well as we media brand communication matrix, can also be constructed. Night economy brands can make use of intelligent information transmission to achieve brand precision and personalized communication. Artificial intelligence transforms positive or negative consumer information into massive labels to form user portraits, and consumers' cognition and attitude towards brands will be presented in three-dimensional form. Sensing technology of intelligent terminals and rich third-party payment programs provide real-time and whole-process consumption interface and guidance for brand information dissemination, forming "instant link" of brand communication. The information subject in NEBCINEC should embed the payment "instant link" as far as possible in three-dimensional matrix of brands, so as to form a seamless closed-loop communication and consumption process from brand generation to brand communication and then experience, finally to transaction.

5.3 *Brand experience strategy*

In NEBCINEC, information consumption process is also the brand experience process, which includes consumers' brand recognition, interaction, selection, and purchase. The brand experience of night economy includes online and offline parts. Online brand experience is more embodied in the sensory experience and emotional experience shaped by the dissemination of information, and a good online brand experience will directly promote consumers' demand for offline experience. The research shows that atmosphere of audio-visual co-occurrence can stimulate users' communication behavior more, and information experience is also developing toward the direction of all-round sensory, cross-screen experience, and diversified scene blending. The application of VR/AR and other technologies can help improve the appeal and expressiveness of brand information and attract consumers to watch it repeatedly [8]. On the other hand, short videos, live broadcasts, and other social media platforms are more likely to stimulate public sentiment and attract more users' attention [5], thus accelerating the speed of brand information dissemination.

6 CONCLUSIONS

The development and assistance of policies, economy, culture, and technology promote development of night economy in China to enter into a new stage, and brand communication plays an important role in the development of night economy. This paper constructs night economy network information ecological chain from the angle of brand communication. Due to the continuous development of network users, KOLs and machine intelligence in the main body of information, brand generation appears as the trend of intelligence and socialization. Among information organizers and transmitters, the emergence of "we media" makes network users become the core ecological niche in the network ecological chain of night economy. The development of technology makes brand communication appear intelligent and personalized. Information consumption is also the brand consumption link because of diversified and interactive forms of multimedia communication content; furthermore, brand consumption also tends to develop in all directions and the sense of presence. The brand side should constantly explore and try technology applications and mode innovation in the network information ecological chain of night economy, build a more efficient brand communication closed loop, so as to enhance brand equity, promote brand sales, and accelerate healthy development of night economy.

REFERENCES

[1] Chen Hongbo. Regional Tourism Brand Image Communication Strategy [J]. *News and Writing* 2015 (10): 101–104.

[2] Chinese Internet Data Network. The Alibaba Night Economic Report [EB/OL]. 2020-7-16, http://www.199it.com/archives/1088496.html

[3] China Tourism Academy. 2020. China Night [EB/OL] Economic Development Report. 2020-10-24, http://www.199it.com/archives/1142291.html

[4] Deng Liangliu. 2019. A New Approach to Ethnic Cultural Tourism Brand Marketing in Social Media Era: KOL Marketing [J]. *Guizhou Ethnic Studies* 40(01): 28–34.

[5] Du Xin. VR Technology Provides a New Perspective for Urban Brand Communication [J]. *Young Journalist* 2017(02): 110–111.

[6] Hornet's Nest Tourism. Tourism Nightlife Trend Insights "[EB/OL]. 2020-12-1, https://www.sohu.com/a/449579818_712171

[7] Intelligent Marketing and Communication Innovation [J]. *China Advertising* 2019(08): 107–108.

[8] Jiang Zhibin, Ma Xin. 2019. *Journal of Journalism and Communication Review* 72(03): 56–63.

[9] Luan Chunyu, Huo Mingkui, Lu Cai. 2014. *Information Science* 32(11): 30–35.

[10] Lu Xiaobin, Xu Chao. 2017. *Information Science* 35(11): 3–7.

[11] Moxa Media Industry Upgrading Research Center. The 2019-2022 China Night Economy Industry Development Trends and Consumer Behavior Research Report [EB/OL]. 2019-8-12, https://www.iimedia.cn/c400/65686.html

[12] Qin Zizhen, Lou Cequn. 2017. Construction and Analysis of Tourism Network Information Ecological Chain Structure Model [J]. *Information Theory & Practice* 40(07): 127–131.

[13] Wang Jingqiang. Problems and Promotion Strategies of Urban Brand Construction [J]. *Youth Reporter* 2018(35): 97–98.

[14] Xu Di. The Development of Urban Night Economy Under the New Development Pattern of Double Cycle [J]. *Beijing Cultural Creativity* 2021(01): 47–54.

[15] Yang Xiaohong, Tang Lixue. The Present and Future of Brand Communication: A Program Logic Empowered by ARTIFICIAL Intelligence [J]. *Modern Advertising* 2020(15):13–19.

[16] Zhang Haitao, Xu Hailing, Wang Dan, Tang Shiman. 2018. *Information Theory & Practice* 41(09): 12–17.

[17] Zhang Haitao, Xu Hailing, Wang Dan, Tang Shiman. 2018. *Information Theory & Practice* 41(09): 12–17. (In Chinese)

[18] Zang Lina. Brand Communication Scene Construction Based on "Scene New Five Forces" in 5G era [J]. *Contemporary Communication* 2020(06): 100–103.

[19] Zhou Xiang, Ding Minling. The Core Niche of Network users in China's External Communication From the Perspective of Information Ecology [J]. *International Communication* 2018(11): 48–51.

[20] Zhou Xiang, Zhong Jianqin. Computing Turn: Brand Concept Evolution and Communication Innovation in the Era of Intelligent Media [J]. *News Lover* 2020(11): 30–33.

[21] Zhang Xiuying. Research on the Construction and Development Path of Agriculture-related Network Information Ecological Chain [J]. *Business Economics Research* 2018(19): 111–114.

Economic and Business Management – Lent & Zhang (Eds)
© 2023 the Author(s), ISBN 978-1-032-24482-2

The trend of own-account workers in the V4 - two decades evidence

M. Knapková
Faculty of Economics, Matej Bel University, Banská Bystrica, Slovakia

A. Barwińska-Małajowicz
Institute of Economics and Finance, University of Rzeszów, Rzeszów, Poland

ABSTRACT: The aim of the paper is to analyze the development of the number of own-accounted workers in the V4 in the period Q1 2000 to Q4 2021. The results suggest that in Slovakia and the Czech Republic the group of own-accounted workers has an increasing trend (both in absolute terms and in relative terms as a share of own-accounted workers in the total number of self-employed persons). In contrast, in Hungary and Poland, the share of own-account workers in the total number of self-employed persons declines sharply over the period under review (until mid-2017) and then starts to increase again. In the period of the Covid-19 pandemic, the share of own-account workers in the total number of self-employed persons is increasing in the whole V4.

1   INTRODUCTION

A dependent own-account worker is a self-employed person whose economic activity borders on the line between employment (the activity of an employee carried out for an employer on the basis of an employment contract) and self-employment (the activity of an individual entrepreneur carried out in his/her own name and on his/her own responsibility pursuant to a commercial contract or a civil contract). This concept covers situations where a person de jure carries out an independent business activity but de facto is dependent on a single contractor (Knapková 2021).

In the European Union (further in text also EU), there are different approaches by Member States to the legal status and regulatory framework for dependent own-account workers. There are some countries in the EU that do not recognize dependent own-account workers at all (Slovakia, Hungary, Poland, Czech Republic). By contrast, countries such Denmark, France, Germany, Greece and Italy not only recognize the status of dependent own-account workers, but also extend social protection to specified categories of dependent own-account workers, even if they are not presumed to be employees (Tackling Dependent and Bogus Self-Employment 2016). As stated by Pedersini (2020), a dependent own-account worker is formally defined as a self-employed person who usually carries out his or her activity on the basis of a contract with a single principal upon whom he or she is then practically wholly or largely dependent for his or her income. Self-employment is an important part of every market-oriented economy. In the central Europe, self-employment (usually understood as a form of entrepreneurship) has only a short-lasting history (as part of socialistic block, self-employment and private entrepreneurship were not officially allowed until 1990). Within the self-employment, specific position belongs to own-accounted workers, it means those self-employed persons who does not have any employee. In the paper, we focus on the situation in Visegrad Countries (Slovakia, Czech Republic, Poland and Hungary; further in text also the V4). As stated by Dana (2013) the common features of the

DOI: 10.1201/9781003278788-25

V4 are previous centralized economy under the communist rule, transition into the marked oriented economy, liberalization of prices and privatization of state firms, and new re-establishment of the entrepreneurial activities in the 1990s. Since in the V4 the status of dependent self-employed person is not officially recognized and thus there is no official statistical reporting of data on this category of persons, we will focus in the following text and analysis on the closest officially statistically reported category of persons, i.e. own-accounted workers. The paper is divided into four parts: literature review (including litera-ture gap and paper's main research idea), methodology and data sources, results, and discussion, and conclusions.

2 LITERATURE REVIEW

The Organisation for Economic Cooperation and Development defines own-account worker as worker who, working on his/her own account or with one or more partners, hold the type of job defined as a self-employed job, and have not engaged on a continuous basis any employees to work for him/her (OECD: Glossary of statistical terms). Easier definition is provided by System of National Accounts (1993), according to which own-account worker is a self-employed person without paid employees.

There are various studies focusing on the specific status, regulations, social protection as well as feelings of own-accounted workers in the European environment. Millán et al. (2018) recognize true own-accounted workers (as real entrepreneurs with the full independency) and false own-account workers (employed with the same tasks by the same employer for whom they previously worked as employees). Schulze Buschoff and Schmidt (2006) pointed out that own-accounted workers in Europe are usually more flexible than other self-employed persons, however without adequate social protection and state insurance. Similar conclusion is evident from the study of Spasova et al. (2021). They classified dependent self-employed persons and false own-accounted workers as non-standard workers, to whom not enough social protection is guaranteed by state (which was significantly visible during the Covid-19 pandemic).

Within the V4 (Slovakia, Czech Republic, Poland, Hungary), research on own-account workers is not common. While there are several studies focusing on transition period and re-establishment of enterprises after the socialistic period (Dana 2013; Earle and Sakova 2000), insight into the new trends in entrepreneurship, including own-account workers is only in its early stage. Keese (2020) pointed to own-account workers in the connection to the labor trend and future of work in V4 countries. Two different reasons for undertaking self-employment (self-employment as the way of avoiding unemployment or entrepreneurial, risk-taking nature of self-employment) were analyzed by Cichocki (2012) in Poland. He pointed to entrepreneurial nature of own-account workers in Poland. Hašková and Dudová (2017) used an example of Czech Republic to point out a growing insecurity in precarious work (including own-accounted work) during the crisis periods.

Trends in own-account workers were recently analyzed also in connection with Covid-19 pandemic (Cereda et al. 2020; I.L.O. Monitor 2020; Maqueira and Torres 2021). However, focus on own-account workers during the Covid-19 pandemic in the V4 is almost missing. This paper attempts, at least partially, to fill the gap in the current research on own-account workers in the V4 area. The aim of this paper is to analyze the development of the number of own-account workers in the V4 between Q1 2000 and Q4 2021 (and to also highlight the changes in the development caused by the Covid-19 pandemic).

3 METHODOLOGY AND DATA SOURCES

The source of the data originated from Labor force survey (LFS), held quarterly in all member states of European Union. As defined by Eurostat, EU-LFS is a large household sample survey providing quarterly results on labor participation of people aged 15 and over as well as on people outside the labor force.

We used EU-LFS quarterly data on number of self-employed persons, and from them own-account persons for the V4, for the period of Q1 2000 to Q4 2021. In total, 88 values in time series were analyzed. Data on self-employed persons and own-accounted workers refer to 15 – 64 years old persons. The basic information about the research sample is summed up in Table 1.

Table 1. Descriptive statistics of the research sample (in thousands).

Country	Mean	Median	S. D.	Min	Max
Czech Republic	605.3	631.6	63.38	467.0	696.9
Hungary	263.3	253.3	40.26	206.2	355.1
Poland	2256	2225	113.9	2124	2584
Slovakia	244.6	281.4	65.41	108.5	310.6

We used the Gretl software package for data analysis. We used the four-month moving average to display the development of the number of own-account workers in the Q1 2000 – Q4 2021 period (Formula 1).

$$T_t = \frac{1}{2} \left(\frac{Y_{t-2} + Y_{t-1} + Y_t + Y_{t+1}}{4} + \frac{Y_{t-1} + Y_t + Y_{t+1} + Y_{t+2}}{4} \right) \qquad (1)$$

where T_t = centered moving average value in period t; Y_t = number of own-account workers in period t.

4 RESULTS AND DISCUSSIONS

First, we focus on the analysis of the evolution of the total number of own-account workers (four-month average) in the V4. Figure 1 shows the development of the total (absolute) number of own-account workers (four-month average) in Poland, Hungary, Slovakia, and the Czech Republic. Due to the significant differences in the absolute number of own-account workers across countries, we display the development of the number of own-account workers for each country in a separate graph.

As evidenced by Figure 1, number of own-account workers in Slovakia and Czech Republic has significantly increased in the analyzed period (from 109,400 in Q1 2000 to 310,600 in Q4 2021 in Slovakia, and from 467,000 in Q1 2000 to 649,500 in Q4 2021 in Czech Republic). On the other side, in Poland and Hungary, the number of own-account workers decreased firstly (from 2,258,200 in Q1 2000 to 2,123,700 in Q2 2014, and from 352,200 in Q1 2000 to 206,200 in Q3 2013 in Hungary). Consequently, from turning point in Q2 2017 (216,900 in Hungary) and in Q3 2017 (2,131,00 in Poland), there is a significant increase in the number of own-account workers in both countries. The period of the Covid-19 pandemic witnessed an increase in the number of own-account workers in Slovakia, Poland, and Hungary. One of the reasons behind this may be the increasing number of people who have been made redundant (losing their jobs due to the pandemic) and their efforts to enter the market as own-account workers. In the Czech Republic, although the number of own-account workers grew at the beginning of the pandemic, the number of this group of people declined between 2020 and 2021.

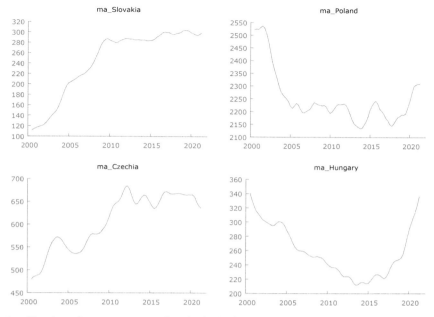

Figure 1.   Number of own-account workers in the V4 in Q1 2000 – Q4 2021, in thousands (four-month moving average).

In the next section, we focused on finding the share of own-account workers in the total number of self-employed persons. Figure 2 shows the development of this share for all 4 states.

In all four countries examined, the trend in the number of own-account workers follows the trend in the number of self-employed persons. In Slovakia, the share of own-account

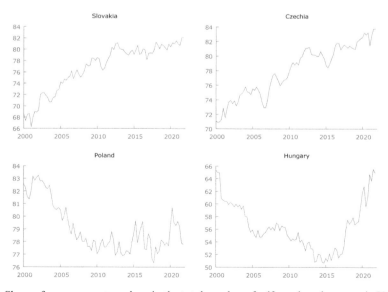

Figure 2.   Share of own-account workers in the total number of self-employed persons in V4 countries, in % (Q1 2000 – Q4 2021).

workers in the total number of self-employed persons ranged from 66.26% (minimum reached in Q1 2001) to 82.15% (in Q4 2021). In the Czech Republic, this share ranged from 70.89% (Q2 2000) to 83.78% (Q4 2021). In Slovakia and the Czech Republic, this share had an increasing trend, with a significant increase in the share of own-account workers in 2021 compared to 2000. In Poland and Hungary, the trend was different, with the share of own-accounted workers in total self-employed in Poland declining until Q3 2014, followed by a sharp increase in Q2 2015 (up to 79.65%), with a pronounced cyclical component in the following three years (always a decline in the share of own-accounted in total self-employed in the third quarters, followed by a rise in the share and its peak in the second quarters). This was followed by modest growth until Q2 2020 (80.7%) and since then the share of own-account workers has been declining. Thus, in the case of Poland, the evolution of the share of own-account workers in the total number of self-employed persons has a strongly fluctuating character, with changes in the trend in 2014, 2017 and 2020. In Hungary, the share of own-account workers in the total number of self-employed declined from Q1 2000 to Q3 2013 (from 65.37% in Q1 2000 to 50.83% in Q3 2013). This was followed by a period of relative stability (until Q4 2016), but with cyclical developments. From Q1 2017 onwards, the share of own-account workers in total self-employed has been rising, and by Q4 2021 reached a level of 64.93%.

5 CONCLUSIONS

One of the most important decisions individuals make is how they choose to earn their incomes. The main forms of income-generating activities in the V4 countries are employment and self-employment. In addition to the classic gainful activities (i.e. dependent work and self-employment), the V4 is also facing the new phenomenon of economically dependent self-employment. Although the legislation in these countries does not yet consistently regulate the issue of persons standing on the edge of dependent work and self-employment, its presence in the economy of the V4 is evident and requires its own research. As there is not de jure category of economically dependent entrepreneurs in the V4, there is also no statistical reporting of this category of persons. Thus, the closest to the category of dependent self-employed is the statistically officially reported category of own-accounted workers.

The results show that the absolute number of own-account workers has an increasing trend in two countries (Slovakia and the Czech Republic). In Poland and Hungary, the number of own-account workers, although initially significantly decreasing, has been on an increasing trend since 2017. The share of own-account workers in the total number of self-employed is increasing across the V4. We expect that in the future an increasing interest in self-employment in the form of own-account workers can be expected as well. In this respect, the group of self-employed persons requires deeper investigation, also considering that a large proportion of them are likely to work as dependent self-employed (given that this category is not separately reported in the whole V4, this is only an assumption that needs to be verified through primary research in the future). Future research should also focus on finding out what factors influence the trend in the number of own-account workers, and whether this is countercyclical or, conversely, entrepreneurial in nature (Cichocki, 2012).

ACKNOWLEDGMENT

This paper is an output of scientific project of Grant Agency VEGA no. No. 1/0366/21 "Dependent Entrepreneurship in Slovakia – Reflection, Measurement and Perspectives "at the Faculty of Economics, Matej Bel University in Slovakia."

REFERENCES

Cereda, F., Rubiao, R. M., & Sousa, L. D. 2020. *COVID-19, Labor Market Shocks, Poverty in Brazil: A Microsimulation Analysis*. Washington, DC: World Bank.

Cichocki, S. 2012. Self-employment and the Business Cycle: Evidence From Poland. *Post-Communist Economies* 24(2): 219–239.

Dana, L. P. 2013. *When Economies Change Hands: A Survey of Entrepreneurship in the Emerging Markets of Europe From the Balkans to the Baltic States*. Routledge.

Earle, J. S., & Sakova, Z. 2000. Business Start-ups or Disguised Unemployment? Evidence on the Character of Self-employment From Transition Economies. *Labour Economics* 7(5): 575–601.

Hašková, H., & Dudová, R. 2017. Precarious Work and Care Responsibilities in the Economic Crisis. *European Journal of Industrial Relations* 23(1): 47–63.

Keese, M. 2020. The Future of Work in the Visegrad Group of Countries. *Society and Economy* 42(2): 124–145.

Knapková, M. 2021. Dependent Self-employment – Italy as a Good Practice Example. *Ekonomika a Spoločnos'* 22(2): 33–50.

Maqueira, A., & Torres, A. 2021. Cuba in the time of COVID-19: Untangling Gendered Consequences. *Agenda* 35(4): 117–128.

Millán, A., Millán, J. M., & Román, C. 2018. Are False Own-account Workers Less Job Satisfied Than True Ones?. *Applied Economics Letters* 25(13): 945–950.

Monitor, I. L. O. 2020. *COVID-19 and the World of Work*. Updated Estimates and Analysis, 27.

OECD: *Glossary of Statistical terms*. https://stats.oecd.org/glossary/.

Pedersini, R. 2020. *Italy: Latest Developments in Working Life Q4 2019*. Eurofound. Ireland.

Schulze Buschoff, K., & Schmidt, C. 2006. *Own-account Workers in Europe: Flexible, Mobile, and Often Inadequately Insured*. Berlin: WZB.

Spasova, S., Ghailani, D., Sabato, S., Coster, S., Fronteddu, B., & Vanhercke, B. 2021. *Non-standard Workers and the Self-employed in the EU: Social Protection During the Covid-19 Pandemic*. ETUI Research Paper - Report 2021.02.

System of National Accounts. 1993. (SNA 93), European Commission, IMF, OECD, United Nations, World Bank.

Tackling Dependent and Bogus Self-Employment. 2016. *Discussion Note Prepared for Workshop 3, Improving Social Rights and Working Conditions for Atypical Workers*. Workshop, Ljubljana, Slovenia, 26 and 27 January 2016.

Economic and Business Management – Lent & Zhang (Eds)
© 2023 the Author(s), ISBN 978-1-032-24482-2

Proactive personality and work volition among Chinese undergraduates: The chain mediation model testing of career exploration and career decision self-efficacy

Li Huang & Kaiyuan Zhao
Yunnan University of Finance and Economics, Kunming, Yunnan, China

Jing Xiao*
Southwest Petroleum University, Chengdu, Sichuan, China

ABSTRACT: The Psychology of Working Theory was developed for complement existing vocational theories, and the work volition is a very important substance. Based on the theory of PWT, the present paper intends to construct a multi-mediation model between proactive personality, career exploration, career decision self-efficacy, and work volition with 866 samples from Chinese undergraduates at two-time nodes. The analysis results revealed that a proactive personality has lots of significantly good function on job exploration, career decision self-efficacy, and work volition. Accordingly, a proactive personality can indirectly influence work volition by career exploration and career decision self-efficacy. More importantly, a proactive personality can influence work volition by multi-mediation career exploration in tandem with career decision self-efficacy. Finally, we sum up the conclusions and the insufficient of this study, and discuss the viable research directions of the venture capital in the future.

1 INTRODUCTION

The work volition of all individuals could be explained by The Psychology of Working Theory. Within the PWT framework, volition is a central construct, as it represents a person's perception of choice in their future work about decision-making. Now, as time goes by, work volition is attracting increasing attention from researchers. However, the relevant research in China is almost blank.

For Chinese undergraduates, their career choices are both bound by traditional collectivist cultural values and influenced by their severe economic situations. First, with regard to being affected by a collectivist culture, Chinese college students will not only consider their actual situation but also their attachment to greatly important factors such as national needs and family conditions in their career choices. On the other hand, current Chinese economic development is facing many challenges such as slow growth and even a downward trend. The continuous expansion of university enrollment policies has led to a surge in the number of college graduates, and unemployment is becoming more common after graduation. Under this culturally impacted background and severe economic situation, it is especially important to explore the state of work volition among Chinese undergraduates.

Accordingly, it is necessary to verify the predictor of work volition, which includes that demographic, career difficulty, sense of control, and positive emotion (Duffy et al. 2016).

---

*Corresponding Author: xjndxj@163.com

DOI: 10.1201/9781003278788-26

Many empirical researches based on the PWT focused on the influence of marginalization and the constraints for economic growth on work volition such as lack of education, family pressures, and discrimination. This may limit an individual's ability to easily look for some particular careers (Blustein 2013). In these researches, although Blustein (2013) theoretically explained the positive impact of proactive personality on work volition according to the PWT, it is rarely tested in empirical research. Therefore, the internal influence mechanism between proactive personality and work volition has not been revealed. Recently, studies have found that a proactive personality plays an important part in people's future job development (Eric et al. 2013). Therefore, the internal influence mechanism between proactive personality and work volition among Chinese undergraduates will be revealed in this article.

2 THEORY AND HYPOTHESES

2.1 The Psychology of Working Theory (PWT)

The PWT is an important constituent of the vocational theories, and it involved so many subjects, such as intersectionality, vocational psychology, and multicultural psychology (Duffy et al. 2016). The theory said that if we want to know work volition and the important career decisions, sociocultural factors must be regarded as the most important ones. Work volition is the most important part of the PWT, which is considered to be partly influenced by environmental and personal work problems (Duffy et al. 2012). Individuals with greater work volition will feel less constraint and are more likely to choose the career that will be better matches their will. However, people who have the lower work volition will be aware of more constraints and a lack of resources (Kim et al. 2016).

2.2 Proactive personality and work volition

People who have proactive personalities will positively influence their surroundings. In addition, people who have a proactive personality has a higher willingness to use a positive attitude in face of their career (Major et al. 2012), as well as have the tendency to construct better social relationship with surrounding workmates (Crant et al. 2016). A lot of evidences indicate that individual who has career self-efficacy will be more active to look for their work. What's more, the chances could be easily found about their jobs (Tolentino et al. 2014). In others studies, we could also find lots of relationships between active characters and increased job search behaviors during the people when unemployed, having work engagement, and being in organizational citizenship behaviors (Bakker et al. 2012). According to a recent research among Chinese workers who live in the city, work volition will be affected by the proactive personality. Based on the above analysis, the following assumption is put forward:

Hypothesis 1: A proactive personality will have a significant positive impact on an individual's work volition.

2.3 The mediation of career exploration between proactive personality and work volition

The definition of career exploration resembles behavior with intentionality and perception. With this behavior, people would have a better will to find some new chances in their new job. (El-Hassan, & Ghalayini 2020). Individuals with highly proactive personalities are willing and able to actively participate in career exploration-related activities and they are more likely to identify and grasp the opportunity to enhance themselves (Jiang 2017). When individuals are able to conduct a sufficient and effective career exploration, they can better understand the relationship between self and career development prospects. By constantly seeking environmental feedback and career interest exploration to determine the direction of future career development, the flexibility and scope of individual career choices are increased, thus helping individuals to better match the actual careers they desire to pursue. Based on the above analysis, the following assumption is put forward:

Hypothesis 2: Career exploration will build a very good and useful mediating relationship between proactive personality and work volition.

2.4 *The mediation of career decision self-efficacy between proactive personality and work volition*

There had an early definition of career decisions and self-efficacy, and shows that a person who deeply believe that one could finish the essential tasks for their future career decisions. The existing research results show that proactive personality and career decision self-efficacy have an close connection (He et al. 2021). Research has shown that proactive personality and role breadth self-efficacy are positively correlated (Hua et al. 2020). Abdinoor & Ibrahim (2019) argue that career self-efficacy is mainly manifested about the degree to which people understand one's career-related needs, values, abilities, and interests. Moreover, it includes the degree of confidence in the responsibilities and tasks of a particular occupation at work; the degree of confidence in the ability to match personal attributes to job characteristics. This high level of self-confidence strongly convinces college students that they can decide for themselves to meet their inner needs. Based on the above analysis, the following assumption is put forward:

Hypothesis 3: Career decision self-efficacy will build a very good mediating relationship between proactive personality and work volition.

2.5 *The multi-mediation of career exploration and career decision self-efficacy between proactive personality and work volition*

During early career development, undergraduates with more proactive personality tendencies will try to link their career cognition with self-concept and have more career exploration behaviors. Moreover, some researchers also think that career exploration has a relationship with career decision self-efficacy, and a person will have a stronger career exploration willingness if he or she has a stronger career decision self-efficacy (Saks et al. 2015). As confidence in career decision-making increases, individuals will no longer be confused and overwhelmed when faced with career choices, and will have lower career decision-making troubles. On the whole, college students with more active character tendencies would like to perform career exploration, which in turn will improve one's career-making self-efficacy and ultimately increase their power to make their own future job decisions. In this regard, the following assumption is put forward:

Hypothesis 4: Career exploration and career decision self-efficacy has a sustain intermediary function in the connections between proactive personality and work volition.

3 METHODS

3.1 *Context*

Data were collected in Chinese universities in collaboration with the teachers. Based on the principle of cluster random sampling and convenient sampling, the school type (universities directly affiliated to the Ministry of Education vs. local universities), geographical distribution (central vs. west vs. east), and the feasibility of research (whether it is possible to obtain high-quality scales) were considered. Simultaneously, this study believes the undergraduate, juniors, and seniors involved in our study were the most concerned about future career development, so the survey sample focused on them.

3.2 Collection procedure and sample

Sample participants included 866 undergraduates who accepted the work volition survey by class teachers in universities. The samples were from 16 provinces and cities in China, with 44.7% (n = 387) males and 55.3% (n = 579) females, enrolled in universities. Of the survey sample, 37.2% (n = 322) come from universities directly under the Ministry of education; 62.8% (n = 544) come from local colleges and universities; 21.4% (n = 185) identified themselves as from China's central section; 40.8% (n = 353) come from China's western; and 37.8% (n = 328) come from China's eastern section. Juniors comprised 38.3% of the sample (n = 332) and 61.7% (n = 534) were seniors. The mean age of participants was 21.3 years. In order to test the intrinsic mechanism of proactive personality influence on work volition, questionnaires were conducted at two different time nodes (T1 and T2). Among them, demographic variables, proactive personality, career exploration, and career decision self-efficacy were reported at time T1. Demographic variables mainly include gender, student number, mobile phone number, school, grade, and family location. The work volition of college students was reported at time T2. The interval between the two tests was more than 3 months, and the questionnaires of the two period nodes were matched by the school, student number, and mobile phone number.

3.3 Measures

The scale of work volition about the undergraduate version (WVS-SV) with 16 items was compiled by Duffy, Diemer, and Jadidian (2012). Bateman and Crant's (1993) Proactive Personality Scale (PPS) was adopted in this research. Stumpf et al.'s (1983) Career exploration survey (CES) was adopted in this research. The original Career Decision-Making Self-Efficacy (CDMSE) made by Taylor and Betz (1983) contained 50 items.

4 RESULTS AND DISCUSSIONS

4.1 Results

The correlation of four variables has been examined by us. We could see in Table 1, proactive personality was found to moderately correlate with career exploration, moderately correlate with career decision self-efficacy, and moderately correlate with work volition. Career exploration and career-making self-efficacy were also thought a better relate to work volition, the above content meets the conditions for testing the mediation effect. Then, CFA was used to test the intrinsic structural validity of each scale. As shown in Table 2, we found the model is good.

Table 1. Descriptive statistics and correlations (N = 866).

	M	SD	1	2	3
proactive personality	3.521	0.517			
career exploration	3.260	0.745	0.444**		
career decision self-efficacy	3.951	0.636	0.401**	0.319**	
work volition	3.250	0.485	0.352**	0.458**	0.435**

Table 2. Validity test of related measuring tools (N = 866).

	χ^2/df	RMSEA	AGFI	GFI	IFI	CFI	NFI
proactive personality	2.486	0.075	0.933	0.971	0.978	0.978	0.964
career exploration	1.287	0.033	0.970	0.994	0.999	0.999	0.997
career decision self-efficacy	3.610	0.099	0.868	0.930	0.898	0.909	0.880

We examined the main effect and the mediation effect of what we said in the research (H1, H2, H3). Further, we used correlation variables to construct the three models (model 1, model 2, and model 3), as shown in Table 3. Since each value in Model 1 meets the requirement of structural validity, H1 was proved.

Next, we can also see the results in Table 3. Since each value in Models 2 and 3 meets the requirement of structural validity, we also tested the mediating effect by process V 3.1. The mediating effect of career exploration is 0.235, with a 95% confidence interval [0.132, 0.325], p=0.003, without 0. The mediating effect of career decision self-efficacy is 0.172, with a 95% confidence interval [0.123, 0.257], p=0.003, excluding 0, which proves H2 and H3.

Table 3. Each index of the model fit degree (N=866).

	χ^2/df	RMSEA	AGFI	GFI	IFI	NFI
Model 1	4.714	0.046	0.933	0.962	0.933	0.942
Model 2	3.116	0.066	0.970	0.997	0.994	0.991
Model 3	4.896	0.068	0.868	0.975	0.967	0.968

Finally, by combining the results of Table 4 and Figure 1, we can see that the upper and lower limits of each confidence interval of the three paths (PP→CE→WV, PP→CE→WV, PP→CE→CDS→WV) do not pass 0. Therefore, our hypothesis 4 is proved.

Table 4. Results of mediating effect test in multiple mediation models.

Intermediate path	Standardized indirect effect estimation	95% confidence interval Lower limit	Upper limit
PP→CE→WV	0.444×0.323 = 0.143	0.084	0.214
PP→CE→WV	0.324×0.296 = 0.096	0.045	0.138
PP→CE→CDS→WV	0.444×0.175×0.296 = 0.023	0.009	0.035

4.2 Discussions

This study points out that a proactive personality can enhance the autonomous perception of individuals in career management and career choice decisions. This aspect mainly relies on two paths: the action path and the cognitive path. First, from the learning theory of career choice and counseling, when compared with the less active personalities or individuals, the ones with highly proactive personalities tend to identify and grasp career promotion opportunities more easily in career orientation activities. Second, active exploration, active discovery, and active construction related to the profession have a good impact on the cognitive development of people. Accordingly, our study examined the above two impact paths among 866 Chinese undergraduates, which could significantly broaden the understanding of work volition.

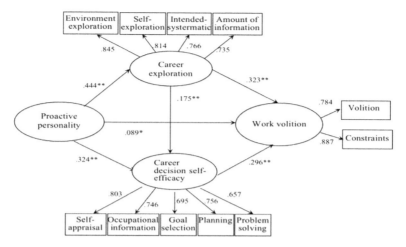

Figure 1. The standardized path coefficients in multiple mediation model test (N=866). (χ^2/df = 1.933; RMSEA = .050; AGFI = .955; GFI = .988; IFI = .991; CFI = .991; NFI = .982; NNFI=.976).

5 LIMITATIONS AND FUTURE RESEARCH

For future studies to proceed smoothly, we consider some limitations that should be thought. First, although the study collected data at two-time points, all the data were collected from college students and it subsequently failed to overcome the effect of common method variance. Therefore, future researchers may consider collecting data from different sources. Second, the all research subjects were college students. In the future, we can collect more samples from different universities, so that our research can be more generalized and enrich the study in this field.

6 PRACTICAL IMPLICATIONS

We suggest that professional career counseling centers should be established to assist college students with their preparation in the spirit of the well-known saying, "all roads lead to Rome." This will help the students understand their true selves as well as develop new professions by using interest, personality, ability, and value assessment tools. Encouraging college students to creatively and systematically think about the nature of the specific problems encountered in their career choices will reshape their lives. Vocational awareness education, the consistent dissemination of knowledge related to occupations, and the teaching of the dynamics of career development should be regularly carried out. Successful people from all industries should be invited to universities to present their work, professional characteristics, and interesting professional experiences to college students to deepen their understanding of careers and help them establish their career ideals as soon as possible.

FUNDINGS

This research was supported by the National Natural Science Foundation of China (No. 71802175); and the National Natural Science Foundation of China (No. 72262031).

REFERENCES

Abdinoor, N. M. & Ibrahim, M. B. 2019. Evaluating Self-Concept, Career Decision-Making Self-Efficacy and Parental Support As Predictors Career Maturity of Senior Secondary Students From Low Income Environment. *European Journal of Education Studies.*

Bakker, A. B., Tims, M., & Derks, D. 2012. Proactive Personality and Job Performance: The Role of Job Crafting and Work Engagement. *Human Relations*, 65(10): 1359–1378.

Blustein, D. 2013. *The Psychology of Working: A New Perspective for Career Development, Counseling, and Public Policy.* New York: Routledge.

Crant, J. M., Hu, J., & Jiang, K. 2016. Proactive Personality: A Twenty-year Review. *Proactivity at Work* 211–243.

Duffy, R. D., Blustein, D. L., Diemer, M. A., & Autin, K. L. 2016. The Psychology of Working Theory. *Journal of Counseling Psychology* 63: 127–148.

Duffy, R. D., Diemer, M. A., & Jadidian, A. 2012. The Development and Initial Validation of the Work Volition Scale–student Version. *The Counseling Psychologist* 40(2): 291–319.

Duffy, R. D., Diemer, M. A., Perry, J. C., Laurenzi, C., & Torrey, C. L. 2012. The Construction and Initial Validation of the Work Volition Scale. *Journal of Vocational Behavior* 80(2): 400–411.

Duffy, R. D., Douglass, R. P., Autin, K. L., & Allan, B. A. 2016. Examining Predictors of Work Volition Among Undergraduate Students. *Journal of Career Assessment* 24(3): 441–459.

El-Hassan, K., & Ghalayini, N. 2020. Parental Attachment Bonds, Dysfunctional Career Thoughts and Career Exploration as Predictors of Career Decision-making Self-efficacy of Grade 11 students. *British Journal of Guidance & Counselling* 48(5): 597–610.

Eric, W. L., Benjamin, D. M., & Muldoon, J. 2013. The Moderating Effect of Perceived Job Characteristics on the Proactive Personality-organizational Citizenship Behavior Relationship. *Leadership & Organization Development Journal* 34(8): 724–740.

He, Z., Zhou, Y., Li, F. et al. 2021. The Effect of Proactive Personality on College Students' Career Decision-Making Difficulties: Moderating and Mediating Effects. *J Adult Dev* 28: 116–125 (2021).

Hua, J., Zhang, G., Coco, C., Zhao, T., & Hou, N. 2020. Proactive Personality and Cross-cultural Adjustment: the Mediating Role of Adjustment Self-efficacy. *Journal of International Students* 10(4):817–835.

Jiang, Z. 2017. Proactive Personality and Career Adaptability: The Role of Thriving at Work. *Journal of Vocational Behavior* 98: 85–97.

Kim, N. R., Kim, H. J., & Lee, K. H. 2016. Social support and occupational engagement among Korean undergraduates: The moderating and mediating effect of work volition. *Journal of Career Development* 45(3): 285–298.

Major, D. A., Holland, J. M., & Oborn, K. L. 2012. The Influence of proactive personality and coping on commitment to STEM majors. *The Career Development Quarterly* 60(1): 16–24.

Saks, A. M., Zikic, J., & Koen, J. 2015. Job search self-efficacy: Reconceptualizing the construct and its measurement. *Journal of Vocational Behavior* 86: 104–114.

Taylor, K. M., & Betz, N. E. 1983. Applications of Self-efficacy Theory to the Understanding and Treatment of Career Indecision. *Journal of Vocational Behavior* 22(1): 63–81.

Economic and Business Management – Lent & Zhang (Eds)

Research on the relationship among leader-member exchange, psychological safety and organizational commitment

Yu Gao, Haiyan Liu* & Yuechi Sun
School of Economics and Management, China University of Geosciences (Beijing), China

ABSTRACT: At present, the relationship between leader-member exchange (LMX) and employee organizational commitment (OC), and the relationship between psychological safety (PS) and employee OC have not been unified, and similar studies have not been examined in scientific and technological enterprises. Few studies have examined the relationship among LMX, PS and employee OC at the same time. Based on social information processing model, this paper is to examine the relationship among LMX, PS and employee OC. Data came from 207 scientific and technological employees. Each employee completed the LMX scale, PS scale, and OC scale. The results show that both LMX and PS positively correlated with OC of employees. LMX positively correlated with PS. PS acted as a partial mediator between LMX and employee OC.

1 INTRODUCTION

The downward pressure of the global economy has increased in the context of increasingly fierce market competition and deepening organizational change. The rebound of the novel coronavirus pneumonia and the wide spread of mutant virus strains have also continued to make the global economic growth slowdown. Digital economy has increasingly become the engine of global economic recovery. As an important symbol of the development of digital economy, the development of scientific and technological enterprises (technology R&D as the main goal) has gradually become the backbone to promote global economic growth. However, patent monopolies and vicious competitions among scientific and technological enterprises have emerged one after another (Xu et al. 2021). The increasingly fierce involution of employees, mutual suspicion and distrust among employees have reduced employees' OC. Under lower OC, employees are unwilling to invest too much enthusiasm and energy (Liang et al. 2012), which will reduce employees' work performance (Wang et al. 2020). The reduction of employee work performance affects the overall performance of the enterprise, which is not conducive to the stable operation and healthy development of the enterprise (Gao et al. 2022). In this context, it is urgent to improve employee OC in scientific and technological enterprises.

OC is an employees' work attitude (Lambert et al. 2021), which refers to "feelings and/or beliefs concerning the employee's relationship with an organization". It includes three dimensions: affective commitment, continuance commitment and normative commitment (Meyer & Allen 1991). Looking at the existing literature, few studies have examined OC of employees in scientific and technological enterprises. In previous enterprise practices, managers often believe that employee OC can be improved through increasing salaries, increasing the benefits, providing equipment (Gao & Liu 2021), and focusing on employee personal development (Park et al. 2021), but the results were minimal. The reason may be that employees do not exist in isolation, while interact with other members in the organization, which affects their own attitude (OC) or behavior (reciprocal behavior) (Meng et al. 2019).

---

*Corresponding Author: liuhy@cugb.edu.cn

DOI: 10.1201/9781003278788-27

LMX represents the quality of the relationship between employees and their leaders (Meng et al. 2019). In the context of "relation-oriented" Chinese culture, the quality of the LMX relationship directly affects the career success of employees (Wei 2022). For example, employees with high-quality LMX relationships have sufficient resources (such as support and rewards), which can help employees relieve work stress (Meng et al. 2017), and can also stimulate employees' sense of responsibility, making employees feel that they are an important member of the organization (Gao et al. 2022), prompting employees to put more effort into their work, thereby bringing continuous benefits to themselves and the enterprise (Xia et al. 2020). However, employees with low-quality LMX relationships have less resources, which will inhibit employees' work autonomy, initiative and creativity, and is not conducive to the sustainable development of employees and enterprises (Deng et al. 2017). In addition, with the advent of the digital economy era, the traditional command or obedient leadership style has been unable to meet the needs of employees (Wei 2022). At this time, high-quality LMX are increasingly favored by employees. Therefore, this paper focuses on the impact of LMX on employees' OC.

Throughout the existing literature, the relationship between LMX and employee OC can be summarized as follows: (1) The relationship between LMX and employee OC has not been unified, and similar studies has not been explored in scientific and technological enterprises. For example, most studies have found that LMX is positively correlated with employee OC (Li et al. 2018, Yu et al. 2014). However, in a study conducted in an engineering and construction services company in China, Lee et al. (2019) found that high psychological entitlement employees do not have a strong sense of obligation to repay benefits given by leaders, then reducing their own level of OC. (2) In the research on the relationship between LMX and employee OC, previous studies have found that job satisfaction (Cheung & Wu 2012), organizational justice (Arshadi & Ghanenia 2012) and sales performance (Li et al. 2018) plays an important process mechanism in the relationship between the two. However, the important role of cognitive factors in the relationship between LMX and employee OC has been ignored. Cognitive factors are also known to be closely related to employee OC (Kim 2020). Existing studies have also begun to explore the important role of cognitive factors in the influence of different antecedents on employees' work attitudes (Gao et al. 2022; Xu & Gao 2019). PS refers to employees' cognition of the consequences of interpersonal risks in the workplace (Edmondson & Lei 2014), which stems from the mutual trust and respect among team members (Edmondson 1999). In enterprise management, the lack of PS will make employees feel pressure, make it difficult for employees to express themselves without fear (Edmondson 1999), and will regard other employees as competitors in the organization (Kim 2020), which will inevitably affect employees' positive attitudes and behaviors towards the organization. However, the role of PS in the relationship between LMX and employee OC remains unclear. (3) The relationship between PS and employee OC has not been unified, and similar studies has not been explored in scientific and technological enterprises. For example, most studies have argued that PS is positively correlated with employee OC (Frazier et al. 2017; Kim 2020). However, in a study comparing the relationship between PS and affective commitment of domestic (Germany) employees and immigrant (Turkish) employees, Ulusoy et al. (2016) found that the relationship between PS and affective commitment of domestic employees was lower than that of immigrant employees. In a study of Nigerian military personnel, Ahmed et al. (2019) found no significant correlation between PS and OC. According to this, the purpose of this paper is to examine the relationship among LMX, PS and employee OC in scientific and technological enterprises.

2 THEORETICAL BASIS AND RESEARCH HYPOTHESES

Based on social information processing model, LMX can be used as external information resources obtained by employees (Gao et al. 2022), and these external information resources can directly affect employees' attitudes and behaviors (Salancik & Pfeffer 1978). Hence, we speculate that employees with high-quality LMX will receive more trust and attention from their leaders, and obtain more job opportunities, work rights and work resources (Cicekli & Kabasakal 2017). At this time, employees will show attitude (being more loyal to the organization) and behavior (extra-role behavior) beneficial to the organization (Lee et al. 2019). Previous studies have also given some support to our speculation. For example, in a study of Chinese employees, Yu et al. (2014) found that LMX was positively correlated with employee OC. This finding was also verified in the survey of salespersons by Li et al. (2018). Therefore, the following hypothesis is put forward.

Hypothesis 1: LMX positively correlate with employees' OC.

Based on social information processing model, external information resources not only directly affect employees' attitudes and behaviors but also indirectly affect employees' attitudes and behaviors via affecting employees' cognition (Zalesny & Ford 1990). Therefore, we speculate that employees with high-quality LMX will improve their PS cognition. Specifically, employees with high-quality LMX will feel trust, respect, and support from leaders (Hu et al. 2018, Gao et al. 2022), obtain more job opportunities, work rights and work resources (Cicekli & Kabasakal 2017). These information resources can help employees eliminate worries and uncertainties in the work process, reduce the perceived risks in the work process (He et al. 2020), and then enhance PS of employees. Previous studies have also given some support to our speculation. For example, Gao et al. (2022) conducted a survey on employees in scientific and technological enterprises, service enterprises and manufacturing enterprises, and found that LMX was positively related to employee PS. This conclusion was also verified by Hu et al. (2018) in a survey of employees of a telecommunications industry. Therefore, the following hypothesis is put forward.

Hypothesis 2: LMX positively correlate with employees' PS.

Based on social information processing model, employees' cognition also affects their attitudes and behaviors (Zalesny & Ford 1990). Therefore, we speculate that employees who perceive PS will perceive care and respect from the organization (Kim 2020), and will feel that it is safe to express, make advices and challenge the current way of doing things (Walumbwa & Schaubroeck 2009), which is conducive to employees to form emotional attachment and identification with the organization (Chen et al. 2014), then strengthen their commitment to the organization (Frazier et al. 2017). Previous studies have also given some support to our speculation. For example, in a study of Chinese company (such as communication, information technology, electronic technology, and pharmaceutical and medical equipment), Li & Ling (2010) found that PS was positively related to employee OC. This finding was also verified in the survey of Korean company by Kim (2020). Therefore, the following hypothesis is put forward.

Hypothesis 3: PS positively correlate with employees' OC.

In addition, based on social information processing model, external information resources not only directly affect employees' attitudes and behaviors but also indirectly affect employees' attitudes and behaviors via affecting employees' cognition (Zalesny & Ford 1990). Therefore, combined with the above inferences, we further speculate that LMX also indirectly affects employee OC through PS. Although previous empirical studies have not found that PS can mediate the relationship between LMX and employee OC, previous empirical studies have found that PS plays a mediating role in the relationship between LMX and employee behaviors, which can be used as a supplementary theoretical basis for this paper. For example, in a study conducted in a telecommunications industry, Hu et al. (2018) found that high-quality LMX can improve employee PS and then affect employee voice behavior. Li et al. (2021) studied a semiconductor company in China and found that LMX can improve employees' PS and then promote employees' creative performance. Therefore, the following hypothesis is put forward.

Hypothesis 4: PS act as a mediator between LMX and employees' OC.

In summary, this paper proposes the following conceptual model (Figure 1):

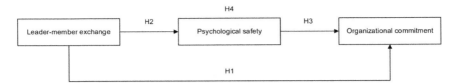

Figure 1. The conceptual model.

3 METHOD

3.1 *Sample and procedure*

The researcher and assistant posted information on the Internet (with the help of various APPs, such as WeChat, QQ and forums) to recruit employees of scientific and technological enterprises, and adopted snowball sampling. Recruited employees must meet the following criteria to be included in the questionnaire: (1) The chronological age is over 18 years old. (2) Work in scientific and technological enterprises. (3) No dyslexia. We contacted all employees who met the criteria to inform them about the purpose and requirements of this survey. All employees were also told that the survey was anonymous, and they have the right to withdraw from the survey at any time. Demographic information and questionnaires data were collected from "Wenjuanxing" platform. Fill in the survey questionnaire and submit it online was equivalent to obtaining the informed consent. Finally, a total of 30 enterprises were involved and 207 valid questionnaires were obtained. Among them, 45.9% were female, 54.1% were male. 34.8% were 25 years old and below, 65.2% were 26 years old and above. 75.4% were bachelor and below, 24.6% were master and above.

3.2 *Measures*

In this paper, questionnaire items were structured on 5-point Likert scales (1 = strongly disagree to 5 = strongly agree). LMX was assessed using the twelve-item scale by Liden & Maslyn (1998). A sample item includes "I like the person in charge very much". Alpha was 0.90. PS was measured using the seven-item scale by Edmondson (1999). A sample item includes "In this team, some risk-taking behaviors are allowed at work". Alpha was 0.60. The reliability is not very high, but 0.6 is also acceptable for the 5–9 item scale (Kennedy et al 2015). OC was assessed using the eighteen-item scale by Meyer & Allen (1991). An item includes "I feel that I am a member of this enterprise and feel at home". Alpha was 0.90. In addition, we utilized gender, age, and education level as a control variable as gender (Nazilah et al. 2018), age (Fu et al. 2011) and education level (Liu et al. 2021) have been shown to relate to OC.

3.3 *Analysis*

Mplus 8.3 was used for confirmatory factor analysis of all variables. SPSS 24.0 was used for descriptive statistics and pearson product-moment correlation analysis of all variables. SPSS PROCESS macro was used for hypothesis testing (Hayes & Rockwood 2017). First, the control variables entering the equation were virtualized (0,1). Second, model 4 was selected and bootstrapping method was used for repeated sampling 5000 times. Third, the direct effect and indirect effect were determined.

4 RESULTS

4.1 *Confirmatory factor analysis*

The results showed that the fitting effect of the initial three-factor model was poor (χ^2/df = 2.255, RMSEA = 0.078, CFI = 0.862, TLI = 0.847, SRMR = 0.092). Therefore, we modified the model using the modification indices (MI) reported by the software (Feng et al. 2014), and the modified data fit well (χ^2/df = 1.819, RMSEA = 0.063, CFI = 0.911, TLI = 0.900, SRMR = 0.089), and the three-factor model was significantly better than other models, indicating that the measurement scale has good discriminant validity.

4.2 Descriptive statistics and variable intercorrelations

Table 1 shows the means, standard deviations and correlations for the measures. It can be seen that LMX, PS and OC were all positively correlated.

Table 1. Means, standard deviations and correlations of variables.

	Mean	SD	1	2	3
1.LMX	3.93	0.69	—		
2.PS	3.55	0.52	0.51***	—	
3.OC	3.53	0.66	0.49***	0.39***	—

Note. ***$p < .001$.

4.3 Hypothesis testing

As shown in Table 2 and Table 3, LMX was positively associated with OC, hypothesis 1 was verified. LMX was positively correlated with PS, hypothesis 2 was supported. PS was positively correlated with OC, hypothesis 3 was supported. The impact of LMX on OC was weakened after adding PS. In addition, the bootstrap 95% confidence interval of indirect effect does not include 0, indicating that the mediating effect of PS was significant. However, the bootstrap 95% confidence interval of direct effect also does not include 0, indicating that PS played a partial mediating role in the influence of LMX on OC, hypothesis 4 was verified.

Table 2. Direct and indirect effects of LMX on OC.

Variable	OC		OC		PS	
	B	t	B	t	B	t
Gender	−0.14	−1.81	−0.14	−1.71	0.03	0.46
Age	0.11	1.29	0.15	1.72	0.17	2.51
Education level	−0.11	−1.17	−0.12	−1.24	−0.04	−0.49
LMX	0.36	5.41***	0.45	7.66***	0.39	8.42***
PS	0.22	2.47*				
R^2	0.29		0.27		0.29	
F	16.69***		18.85***		20.21***	

Note. *$p < 0.05$. ***$p < .001$.

Table 3. Decomposition results of direct effect, indirect effect and total effect.

	Effect	SE	Boot LLCI	Boot ULCI
Direct Effect	0.36	0.08	0.22	0.52
Indirect Effect	0.08	0.04	0.01	0.16
Total Effect	0.44	0.07	0.32	0.60

Note. LLCI = lower limit confidence interval. ULCI = upper limit confidence interval.

5 DISCUSSIONS

Based on social information processing model, our purpose in this paper was to examine the relationship among LMX, PS and OC in scientific and technological enterprises.

5.1 Theoretical implications

This paper found that LMX was positively correlated with employee OC in scientific and technological enterprises. This finding is consistent with previous research, which show that high quality LMX is more beneficial to employee work attitude (Usadolo & Usadolo 2019). This paper reinforces the importance of LMX in enterprise management. However, the result of this paper is different from those of Lee et al. (2019). The reason may be that the research focuses in our paper is different from Lee et al. (2019). This paper only explored the impact of LMX quality on employee OC, and did not explore the differential impact of relationship quality on different members. Because the differential relationship between leaders and different employees will trigger mutual comparison among members, that is, the employees' own LMX relationship will be compared with the colleagues' LMX relationship, and then affects employee work attitude (Ma & Zhu 2015). Therefore, future research can further explore the impact of LMX social comparison on employee OC in scientific and technological enterprises.

This paper found that PS was positively correlated with employee OC in scientific and technological enterprises. Our finding is consistent with previous research that employees with positive self-awareness will show a strong commitment to the organization (Kim 2020), but different from those of Ahmed et al. (2019). The reason may be that the research comes from different cultural contexts. In the cultural context of Western individualism, members are encouraged to pursue personal goals and achievements. Employees may express new ideas directly and participate, and are less concerned about the negative interpersonal consequences related to failures and mistakes (Deng et al. 2019). Therefore, they may not pay attention to PS to encourage them to take interpersonal risks. However, in the cultural context of Oriental collectivism, more emphasis on interpersonal harmony, and the positive role of PS may be more reflected in the culture of collectivism. This paper strengthens the importance of PS in enterprise management.

This paper also found that in scientific and technological enterprises, LMX was positively correlated with employee PS, and PS plays a mediating role in the relationship between LMX and employee OC. To our knowledge, no studies have examined the role of PS in the relationship between LMX and employee OC. However, the results of this paper are similar to the research of Xu & Gao (2019), that is, positive and effective leadership style (leadership integrity) will affect employees' affective commitment through influencing employees' psychological factors. At the same time, our finding is also in line with the view of social information processing model. LMX can be used as an important source of information for employees, which will affect employees' attitude (OC) and behaviors through affecting employees' cognitive assessment (PS) (Zalesny & Ford 1990). Therefore, by introducing PS, this paper provides important insights into the process mechanism of the relationship between LMX and employee OC. This paper also provides different theoretical paths for managers of scientific and technological enterprises to effectively enhance employees' OC and further promote the stable operation and healthy development of enterprises.

5.2 Practical implications

Based on the relationship among LMX, PS and employee OC found above, this paper provides the following inspirations for managers of scientific and technological enterprises to enhance employee OC and further promote the stable operation and healthy development of enterprises.

In scientific and technological enterprises, it is necessary to improve the relationship between leaders and employees. Because of the high-quality exchange relationship between leaders and members, employees will perceive recognition, respect and support from leaders. Employees will think that they are valuable to the organization, thereby enhancing their sense of belonging, sense of responsibility as well as improving their affective commitment and normative commitment. As time goes by, employees will strengthen their continuance commitment to the organization in order to avoid losses when they leave the organization. Therefore, leaders should not only give employees some material information (such as salary rewards, free development spaces, more decision-makings and authorizations) but also give employees appropriate communication and care (such as timely feedback, empathy and encouragement) so as to improve the relationship between leaders and employees.

In scientific and technological enterprises, it is necessary to cultivate PS of employees. When employees perceive PS, they have more trust in leaders and colleagues and dare to put forward unique opinions without fear of ridicule or exclusion (Edmondson 2004), which can reduce interpersonal uncertainty and risks in team interactions, thereby helping employees alleviate work pressure. In return, employees will show attitude (commitment) and positive behaviors that are beneficial to the organization. Therefore, leaders can enhance employees' self-confidence and make employees feel comfortable at work by giving them respect, support, trust, and emotional care. At this time, employees can communicate openly, discuss issues and share knowledges at work (Van Den Broeck et al. 2014) to enhance employees' familiarity and identity with the organization.

5.3 *Limitations and future research*

This paper also has some limitations, and provides research directions for future research. First, we use the questionnaire survey method to measure LMX, PS and OC, the measurement results may be affected by participant subjective tendency and social desirability. Future research can use other evaluations by leaders and colleagues to improve the reliability and external validity of research results. Second, due to the limitation of research time and cost, the participants of this study are employees of scientific and technological enterprises under the cultural context of Chinese collectivism. Whether the findings are applicable to scientific and technological enterprises under the cultural context of individualism remains to be verified. Future research can compare and analyze the OC of employees in scientific and technological enterprises under different cultural contexts. Third, this paper is a cross-sectional study, which fails to draw causal inferences. Future research can use longitudinal research to explore the causal relationship between LMX, PS and employee OC. Fourth, based on social information processing model, this paper explores the process mechanism of PS in the influence of LMX on OC of employees. However, the process of social information processing is also affected by individual differences, such as employee abilities and personality. Future research can incorporate individual difference factors, explore its boundary role in the relationship between LMX and employee OC, and further deepen the understanding of the relationship among variables.

6 CONCLUSIONS

This paper found that LMX can directly affect employees' PS, both LMX and PS can directly affect employees' OC, and LMX can also indirectly affect employees' OC through PS. Therefore, to strengthen employees' OC in scientific and technological enterprises should pay attention to the improvement of the relationship between leaders and employees and the cultivation of employees' PS.

REFERENCES

Ahmed, B. K., Ujoatuonu, I. V. N., Ogba, K. T. U. & Kanu, G. C. 2019. Political Influence on Military Wimpy in Organizational commitment: Roles of Team Psychological Safety and Spirit at Work. *Nigerian Journal of Social Psychology* 2(1): 166–184.

Arshadi, N. & Ghanenia, M. 2012. Leader-member Exchange and Subordinates' Job Satisfaction and Organizational Commitment: Mediating role of Organizational Justice. *International Journal of Psychology* 47: 487–488.

Chen, C., Liao, J. & Wen, P. 2014. Why Does Formal Mentoring Matter? The Mediating Role of Psychological Safety and the Moderating Role of Power Distance Orientation in the Chinese Context. *International Journal of Human Resource Management* 25(8): 1112–1130.

Cheung, M. F. Y. & Wu, W. 2012. Leader-member Exchange and Employee Work Outcomes in Chinese Firms: The Mediating Role of Job Satisfaction. *Asia Pacific Business Review* 18(1): 65–81.

Cicekli, E. & Kabasakal, H. 2017. The Opportunity Model of Organizational Commitment: Evidence from White-collar Employees in Turkey. *International Journal of Manpower* 38(2): 259–273.

Deng, C. J., Liu, Z. Q. & Qiu, H. H. 2017. Middle-level Formal Status and Employee Job Performance: The Moderated Effect of Leader-member Exchange. *Chinese Journal of Management* 14(10): 1456–1464.

Deng, H., Leung, K., Lam, C. K. & Huang, X. 2019. Slacking off in comfort: A Dual-pathway Model for Psychological Safety Climate. *Journal of Management* 45(3): 1114–1144.

Edmondson, A. 1999. Psychological Safety and Learning Behavior in Work Teams. *Administrative Science Quarterly* 44(2): 350–383.

Edmondson, A. C. 2004. Psychological Safety, Trust, and Learning in Organizations: A Group-level Lens. *Trust and Distrust in Organizations: Dilemmas and Approaches* (12): 239–282.

Edmondson, A. C. & Lei, Z. 2014. Psychological safety: The History, Renaissance, and Future of an Interpersonal Construct. *Annual Review of Organizational Psychology and Organizational Behavior* 1(1): 23–43.

Feng, D., Ji, L. & Yin, Z. 2014. Personality, Perceived Occupational Stressor, and Health-related Quality of Life Among Chinese Judges. *Applied Research in Quality of Life* 9(4): 911–921.

Frazier, M. L., Fainshmidt, S., Klinger, R. L., Pezeshkan, A. & Vracheva, V. 2017. Psychological Safety: A Meta-analytic Review and extension. *Personnel Psychology* 70(1): 113–165.

Fu, W., Deshpande, S. P. & Zhao, X. 2011. The Impact of Ethical Behavior and Facets of Job Satisfaction on Organizational Commitment of Chinese Employees. *Journal of Business Ethics* 104(4): 537–543.

Gao, Y. & Liu, H. Y. 2021. How Supervisor-subordinate Guanxi Influence Employee Innovative Behavior: A Moderated Mediation Model. *Psychology Research and Behavior Management* 14: 2001–2014.

Gao, Y., Liu, H. Y. & Sun, Y. C. 2022. Understanding the Link Between Work-related and Non-work-Related Supervisor–subordinate Relationships and Affective Commitment: The Mediating and Moderating Roles of Psychological Safety. *Psychology Research and Behavior Management* 15: 1649–1663.

Hayes, A. F. & Rockwood, N. J. 2017. Regression-based Statistical Mediation and Moderation Analysis in Clinical Research: Observations, Recommendations, and Implementation. *Behaviour Research and Therapy* 98: 39–57.

He, P., Sun, R., Zhao, H., Zheng, L. & Shen, C. 2020. Linking Work-related and Non-work-related Supervisor–subordinate Relationships to Knowledge Hiding: A Psychological Safety Lens. *Asian Business & Management* 1–22.

Hu, Y., Zhu, L., Zhou, M., Li, J., Maguire, P., Sun, H. & Wang, D. 2018. Exploring the Influence of Ethical Leadership on Voice Behavior: How Leader-member Exchange, Psychological Safety and Psychological Empowerment Influence Employees' Willingness to Speak Out. *Frontiers in Psychology* 9: 1718.

Kennedy, P., Rooney, R. M., Kane, R. T., Hassan, S. & Nesa, M. 2015. The Enhanced Aussie Optimism Positive Thinking Skills Program: The Relationship Between Internalizing Symptoms and Family Functioning in Children Aged 9-11 Years Old. *Frontiers in Psychology* 6: 504.

Kim, B. J. 2020. Unstable jobs harm performance: The Importance of Psychological Safety and Organizational Commitment in Employees. *SAGE Open* 10(2): 1–10.

Lambert, E. G., Pasupuleti, S., Cluse-Tolar, T., Srinivasa, S. R. & Jiang, S. 2021. Research note: The Effects of Organizational Trust on the Work Attitudes of U.S. Social Workers. *Journal of Social Service Research* 1–14.

Lee, A., Gerbasi, A., Schwarz, G. & Newman, A. 2019. Leader–member Exchange Social Comparisons and Follower Outcomes: The Roles of Felt Obligation and Psychological Entitlement. *Journal of Occupational and Organizational Psychology* 92(3): 593–617.

Li, R. & Ling, W. S. 2010. The Impact of Perceived Supervisor Support on Employees' Work-related Attitudes and Silence Behavior. *Journal of Business Economics* (5): 31–39.

Li, C., Wu, C. H., Brown, M. E. & Dong, Y. 2021. How a Grateful Leader Trait Can Cultivate Creative Employees: A Dual-level Leadership Process Model. *Journal of Positive Psychology* 1–11.

Li, L., Zhu, Y. & Park, C. 2018. Leader–member Exchange, Sales Performance, Job Satisfaction, and Organizational Commitment Affect Turnover Intention. *Social Behavior and Personality: An International Journal* 46(11): 1909–1922.

Liang, J., Farh, C. I. C. & Farh, J. L. 2012. Psychological Antecedents of Promotive and Prohibitive Voice: A Two-wave Examination. *Academy of Management Journal* 55(1): 71–92.

Liden, R. C. & Maslyn, J. M. 1998. Multidimensionality of Leader-member Exchange: An Empirical Assessment Through Scale Development. *Journal of Management* 24(1): 43–72.

Liu, T., Gao, J., Zhu, M. & Jin, S. 2021. Women's Work-life Balance in Hospitality: Examining its Impact on Organizational Commitment. *Frontiers in Psychology* 12, 625550.

Ma, L. & Zhu, S. 2015. The Influence of Relative Leader-member Exchange on Employees' Work Attitudes. *Science & Technology Progress and Policy* 32(24): 149–153.

Meng, H., Luo, Y., Huang, L., Wen, J., Ma, J. & Xi, J. 2019. On the Relationships of Resilience with Organizational Commitment and Burnout: A Social Exchange Perspective. *International Journal of Human Resource Management* 30(15): 2231–2250.

Meyer, J. P. & Allen, N. J. 1991. A Three-complement Conceptualization of Organizational Commitment. *Human Resource Management Review* 1(1): 61–89.

Nazilah, A., Rozmi, I., Fauziah, I. & Nadia, N. 2018. The Influence of Gender on Organizational Commitment Among College Student Volunteers. *Advanced Science Letters* 24(4): 2554–2556.

Park, C. J., Kim, S. Y. & Nguyen, M. V. 2021. Fuzzy Topsis Application to Rank Determinants of Employee Retention in Construction Companies: South Korean case. *Sustainability* 13(11): 5787.

Salancik, G. R. & Pfeffer, J. 1978. A Social Information Processing Approach to Job Attitudes and Task Design. *Administrative Science Quarterly* 23(2): 224–253.

Ulusoy, N., Mölders, C., Fischer, S., Bayur, H., Deveci, S., Demiral, Y. & Rössler, W. 2016. A Matter of Psychological Safety: Commitment and Mental Health in Turkish Immigrant Employees in Germany. *Journal of Cross-Cultural Psychology* 47(4): 626–645.

Usadolo, S. E. & Usadolo, Q. E. 2019. The Impact of Lower Level Management on Volunteers' Workplace Outcomes in South African Non-profit Organisations: The Mediating Role of Supportive Supervisor Communication. *Voluntas* 30: 244–258.

Van Den Broeck, A., Sulea, C., Elst, T. Vander, Fischmann, G., Iliescu, D. & De Witte, H. 2014. The Mediating Role of Psychological Needs in the Relation Between Qualitative Job Insecurity and Counterproductive Work Behavior. *Career Development International* 19(5): 526–547.

Walumbwa, F. O. & Schaubroeck, J. 2009. Leader Personality Traits and Employee Voice Behavior: Mediating Roles of Ethical Leadership and Work Group Psychological Safety. *Journal of Applied Psychology* 94: 1275–1286.

Wang, Q.. Weng, Q. & Jiang, Y. 2020. When Does Affective Organizational Commitment Lead to Job Performance? Integration of Resource Perspective. *Journal of Career Development* 47(4): 380–393.

Wei, S. L. 2022. The Influence of Servant Leadership On Employees' Career Success: The Mediating Role of Leader-Member Exchange and the Moderating Role of Perceived Organizational Support. *Academic Exploration* (5): 106–115.

Xia, Y. H., Zhang, M. Y. & Li, S. 2020. Voice Endorsement and Work Engagement: The role of Leader-member Exchange and Perceived Power Distance. *Journal of Shandong University (Philosophy and Social Sciences)* (6): 113–121.

Xu, X. F. & Gao, R. G. 2019. The Influence of Leader Integrity on Employees' Affective Commitment: A Moderated-mediation model. *Forecasting* 38(3): 1–8.

Xu, Z. R., Liu, J. & Sun, Y. X. 2021. Monopoly Characteristics and Governance of Internet Platform Enterprises. *Fujian Tribune (The Humanities & Social Sciences Monthly)* 352(9): 67–75.

Yu, J. J., Zhao, S. M. & Jiang, S. F. 2014. An Empirical Study on the Relationship of Abusive Supervision Between Employee Affective Commitment and Workplace Deviance Behaviors: The Mediating Role of Leader-member Exchange. *Research on Economics and Management* (3): 120–128.

Zalesny, M. D. & Ford, J. K. 1990. Extending the Social Information Processing Perspective: New Links to Attitudes, Behaviors, and Perceptions. *Organizational Behavior and Human Decision Processes* 47(2): 205–246.

Economic and Business Management – Lent & Zhang (Eds)
© 2023 the Author(s), ISBN 978-1-032-24482-2

The impact of HRM practices and job satisfaction on employee retention in an organization: A case of Cambodia's context

Marilen Hong, Socheata Ngeth & Phichhang Ou
Royal University of Phnom Penh, Phnom Penh, Cambodia

ABSTRACT: Changes in technology, global economics, trade agreements, and working culture create barriers in employee and employer relationships. Until recently, loyalty was the cornerstone of those relationships. The loss of talented employees could also be very detrimental to the company's future success. However, the retention of skilled employees is a critical concern for human resource managers due to the unprecedently high rate of employee turnover. In addition, there were limited studies of employee retention in Cambodia's context, and it required more research. Therefore, this study aims to investigate the effects of HRM practices (recruitment and selection, compensation and rewards, performance appraisal, work environment, training and development) and job satisfaction on employee retention. The research was conducted on 225 employees working in both the public and private sectors of Phnom Penh as the target sample. The results of structural equation modeling (SEM) reveal that HRM practices and job satisfaction have a positive effect on employee retention. Job satisfaction is positively predicted by HRM practices.

1 INTRODUCTION

In today's business environment, human capital is recognized as the key player in the company's productivity and success. Based on Cook (2008), human capital is a source of competitive advantage in any case over technology and finance. Human capital can be a person, a labor force, or an employee in a company. Drucker (1999) believed that employees were the most valuable assets in an organization. Indeed, an organization can achieve nothing without resourceful and competent employees. Organizations rely on the expertise of their employees to compete in today's business environment and gain a competitive advantage in the market.

Besides, employment has become different due to globalization, changing marketplaces, high competition, growth of consumer power, technological advancement, market pressure, and demands, thus presenting employees with more choices in career selection (Cook 2008). Simultaneously, increasing employee turnover can cause serious consequences for the organization's growth (Ahmed et al. 2016). Hence, organizations all over the world are paying attention to this issue as high employee turnover not only reduces organizational performance and productivity but also inflates the expenses related to recruitment and new employee training (Chen et al. 2011). However, the retention of skilled employees is a critical concern for human resource managers due to the unprecedently high rate of employee turnover. Recent studies have shown that employee retention has become a difficult task for managers as they are being attracted by numerous organizations at a time with various kinds of incentives (Samuel & Chipunza 2009).

Malik et al. (2020) introduced human resource management (HRM) as an extremely important component in an organization because it facilitates managers in implementing strategies that keep their employees satisfied and retained. Therefore, organizations should

 DOI: 10.1201/9781003278788-28

apply effective HRM practices to meet emerging trends and enhance organizational performance. Indeed, the task of human resource management in an organization is done flawlessly if it places the right person in the right job at the right place at the right time, but retention is more critical than hiring. Biason (2019) stated that talented employees will never lack opportunities as they have numerous options to choose from different organizations to be with. Besides, satisfied employees are more dedicated to the organization's growth and will stay with the organization. Contrastingly, they may shift to different careers without job satisfaction. Thus, job satisfaction is a key element of employee retention, which influences an organization's success (Biason 2019).

As a developing country, Cambodia has been relying on labor-intensive manufacturing and low-skilled service sectors to support its growth. As the country develops toward an emerging market economy, more sophisticated production processes and a highly skilled labor force are required to sustain its rapid growth and compete in global markets. Thus, many companies are willing to provide favorable working conditions, fair remuneration, and professional career development to acquire potential human capital. This stated that Cambodian employees are frequently poached to different companies in a short period to seek higher remuneration (B2B CAMBODiA 2021). Further, some companies failed to retain their skilled employees, which led to low productivity and organizational performance. Hence, solutions to employee retention have become essential in every organization in Cambodia. However, there were limited studies of employee retention in Cambodia's context and it required more research. In this study, we aimed to investigate the effect of HRM practices and job satisfaction on employee retention.

To achieve the aim of this study, three research questions were formulated as follows: (1) Do HRM practices influence employee retention? (2) What is the relationship between HRM practices and job satisfaction? (3) Is job satisfaction related to employee retention?

2 LITERATURE REVIEW AND HYPOTHESES DEVELOPMENT

2.1 HRM practices and job satisfaction

It is an indispensable role for human resource managers to hire suitable candidates with the required capabilities and competencies to fill the advertised positions (Marques 2007). Recruitment and selection processes are the most crucial practices of human resources management that affect the success of the organization (Bakhashwain & Javed 2021). Indeed, proper recruitment practices will make employees feel that they have come to the right place and be satisfied with their jobs. Recruitment and selection play a vital role in job satisfaction and obtaining high-quality talents into the organization (Gopinath & Shibu 2014). Based on Anwar and Shukur (2015a), effective recruitment and selection will assist managers in increasing job satisfaction among employees in an organization.

H1a: Recruitment and selection are positively related to job satisfaction.

Swanepoel et al. (2014) defined compensation as financial and non-financial rewards provided by an employer to employees for their precious time and efforts in fulfilling organizational goals. This factor refers to how attractive the compensation employees receive is compared to the earnings received by the other members of the organization. Compensation can help strengthen the organization's key values and facilitate organizational achievement. Employees who are compensated will be content with their work and will do their jobs better (Mabaso & Dlamini 2017). Besides, a former study also confirmed that compensation can increase employees' satisfaction in their job (Saman 2020).

H1b: Compensation and reward are positively related to job satisfaction.

Performance appraisal increases employee satisfaction by allowing them to improve their weak areas and develop themselves accordingly in the organization (Khan et al. 2020). Employee feedback shows that an effective performance appraisal system is considered one of the major factors that affect employee satisfaction (Saleem & Shah 2015). Organizations must focus on developing an effective appraisal system to enhance employee satisfaction (Kampkötter 2017). There's a positive association between performance appraisals and job satisfaction when there is an increase in employee productivity (Kaur & Kiran 2020).

H1c: Performance appraisal is positively related to job satisfaction.

A supportive and positive working environment motivates the employees to remain in their professions and encourages them to work effectively. To increase efficiency, effectiveness, productivity, and job commitment, a business must satisfy the needs of its employees by providing good working conditions. Bad working conditions restrict employees' ability to devote their full capabilities, so businesses must realize the importance of a good working environment (Raziq & Maulabakhsh 2015). By offering the most facilities with a motivating working environment, the goal of an organization can be easily accomplished. In a profit-oriented organization, creating an enabling environment for satisfied employees may lead to long-term prosperous bottom lines (Agbozo et al. 2017), and Taheri et al. (2020) confirmed that job satisfaction depends on the working environment.

H1d: Work environment is positively related to job satisfaction.

Training and development are very important functions of the human resource department because employees need to be trained to be familiar with their job, and they most often have a desire to acquire new skills and attain self-development. By providing effective training and development programs to their employees, companies may achieve high employee satisfaction and low employee turnover (Wagner 2000). Anwar and Shukur (2015b) disclosed that training and development increase organizational performance as well as the level of satisfaction among employees. Better training and development opportunities positively influence job satisfaction (Chaudhary & Bhaskar 2016; Paposa & Kumar 2019).

H1e: Training and development are positively related to job satisfaction.

2.2 *HRM practices and employee retention*

The process of recruitment and selection refers to the delivery of job opportunities to potential candidates, assessments, and a fair selection of each employee to fill the right position with a comprehensible job description (Miheso et al. 2019). Also, recruitment and selection practices have a fairly high association with employee retention and are found to have the greatest forecasting ability for employee retention (Janjua & Gulzar 2014). Sutanto and Kurniawan (2017) found that recruitment processes have a significant impact on the employee retention of a company. This means that employee retention depends on the recruitment and selection process.

H2a: Recruitment and selection are positively related to employee retention.

A compensation system is essential for any organization to withstand competition in today's global market with numerous competitors, and it entails cutting-edge policies and innovative practices to retain employees and attract talent from competitors. When employees receive fair compensation from the organization, they are committed to repaying the organization and staying in the organization (Moncarz et al. 2009). Hence, compensation has become a profound element in reducing turnover and increasing retention (Liao 2011). If the compensation provided by the organization is no longer balanced with the contributions of the organizational members, the employee will quit the organization. Previous studies have intimated a positive connection between compensation and employee retention (Bibi et al. 2018).

H2b: Compensation and rewards are positively related to employee retention.

Performance appraisal refers to the evaluation of employees' performance periodically to enhance the application of human resources strategy within the organization (Raihan 2012). Appraisals can also justify many personnel actions such as promotions, pay raises, or terminations, so managers must be honest and objective in their appraisals of performance and ensure that employees understand the process's intention (Mathis et al. 2016). Jehad and

Farzana (2011) argued that performance appraisals increase employees' perceptions of being valued by the organization and thus encourage them to remain in the organization. A prior study also pointed out a significant positive relationship between performance appraisal and employee retention (Bibi et al. 2018).

H2c: Performance appraisal is positively related to employee retention.

The perception entirety of non-monetary elements that provide the surroundings for an employee's job is defined as the working environment (Chao 2008). The work environment positively or negatively affects certain job outcomes like involvement, commitment, and the intention to remain in a corporation (Gunaseelan & Ollukkaran 2012). The work environment is one of the factors that affect employees' decisions to stay with the organization. Kundu and Lata (2017) also argued that a satisfactory working environment encourages employees to complete their work effectively and is expected to have an impact on employee retention and commitment.

H2d: The work environment is positively related to employee retention.

Training has been defined as a planned activity aimed at ameliorating employees' performance by helping them realize an obligatory level of understanding or skill through the impartation of data (Forgacs 2009). Training and development help increase the commitment of employees to remain for an extended period with the organization. Simply put, it decreases turnover and enhances retention (Samuel and Chipunza 2009). When an organization provides sufficient training and development opportunities, employees are more motivated to stay with the organization (Ahmad et al. 2017). An earlier study also found a significant positive relationship between training and development and employee retention (Bibi et al. 2018).

H2e: Training and development are positively related to employee retention.

2.3 *Job satisfaction and employee retention*

Future personal goal realization, personal satisfaction, and personal sense of accomplishment are the factors that reinforce employee retention (McCrensky 1964). Job satisfaction is a key element of employee retention as it comforts the employees physically and psychologically (Biason 2019). Greater workplace satisfaction typically results in higher retention of workers, while greater dissatisfaction among employees results in greater employee turnover (Ramapriya & Sudhamathi 2020). So, organizations have to work on various job-related factors like work design, work conditions, ergonomics, pay packages, job enrichment, work-life balance practices, worker participation, security, authority, and responsibility to increase job satisfaction and retain talented and outstanding employees (Desai 2018).

H3: Job satisfaction is positively related to employee retention.

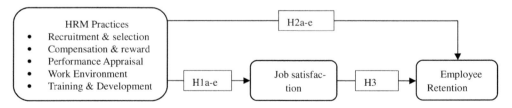

Figure 1. Summarized all of hypothesized variables.

3 METHODOLOGY

The study was conducted on 225 respondents, who are employees in the public and private sectors who reside and work in Phnom Penh, the capital of Cambodia. A convenience and snowball sampling technique were used to collect the primary data. The respondents were asked to rate each item on a five-point Likert scale, ranging from strongly disagree to strongly agree. The data were analyzed using the Statistical Package for the Social Sciences (SPSS) version 25 and Analysis of Moment Structures (AMOS) version 23. The measurement items of all research constructs were adapted from earlier studies as follows: five items of recruitment and selection (Fahim 2018), seven items of compensation and reward and four items of performance appraisal (Fong et al. 2011), three items of the work environment (Kaur et al. 2020), five items of training and development (Fong et al. 2011; Schmidt 2007), four items of job satisfaction (Kaur et al. 2020), and four items of employee retention (Fahim 2018).

4 ANALYSIS AND RESULT

4.1 Respondents' information

Of 225 responses, 47.11 percent were private sector employees, followed by students (36 percent), public sector employees (15.11 percent), and other sectors (11.78 percent). Related to gender, about 54 percent were female, and about 38 percent were male, followed by others who preferred not to mention their gender (8 percent). In terms of age, 72 percent were between the ages of 21 and 25, with 10 percent being under the age of 20, 7 percent being between the ages of 26 and 30, and about 2 percent being between the ages of 31 and 35. Employees who pursued undergraduate degrees accounted for approximately 81.78 percent, followed by master's degrees (8.44 percent), below high school (4.89 percent), and high school (4.44 percent). Respondents earning less than $300 had the highest frequency (51.11 percent), followed by those earning 301–500 dollars (33.33 percent), 501–700 dollars (9.33 percent), and more than 700 dollars (5.22 percent).

4.2 Confirmatory Factor Analysis (CFA)

The initial result of the confirmatory factor analysis showed a poor model fit, so we eliminated some redundant items to meet the requirements of the fitness index. The model fit assessment results are presented as follows: $\chi 2/df$ = 1.710, GFI = 0.939, AGFI = 0.906, CFI = 0.974, NFI = 0.939, and RMSEA = 0.056. Based on Hair et al. (2019), the model is a good fit. As shown in Table 1, all factor loading scores are greater than 0.70, and average variance extracted (AVE) values are greater than 0.50, while composite reliability (CR) values exceed 0.7. Based on the criteria suggested by Fornell and Larcker (1981), construct reliability and validity were achieved.

Table 1. The result of confirmatory factor analysis (n=225).

Construct	Item	Loading	t-value	AVE	CR	S.E.
Recruitment and selection	RS1	0.801[***]	A	0.589	0.741	0.358
	RS4	0.732[***]	7.709			0.464
Compensation and reward	CR3	0.706[***]	9.562	0.560	0.792	0.502
	CR6	0.77[***]	10.193			0.407
	CR7	0.768[***]	A			0.410
Performance appraisal	PA1	0.824[***]	A	0.609	0.824	0.321
	PA2	0.783[***]	12.594			0.387
	PA3	0.732[***]	11.595			0.464
Work environment	WE1	0.764[***]	10.298	0.591	0.743	0.416

(continued)

Table 1. Continued.

Construct	Item	Loading	t-value	AVE	CR	S.E.
	WE3	0.774***	A			0.401
Training and development	DT1	0.798***	12.794	0.603	0.883	0.363
	DT2	0.826***	13.344			0.318
	DT3	0.687***	10.672			0.528
	DT4	0.785***	A			0.384
	DT5	0.78***	12.436			0.392
Job satisfaction	JS1	0.874***	A	0.614	0.863	0.236
	JS2	0.781***	13.968			0.390
	JS3	0.755***	13.283			0.430
	JS4	0.717***	12.311			0.486
Employee retention	ER2	0.652***	9.071	0.542	0.778	0.575
	ER3	0.782***	A			0.388
	ER4	0.767***	10.474			0.412

Note: S.E = Standard Erro, A = parameter regression weight was fixed at 1.000., Significant level of p-value < 0.05, ***$p < 0.001$, **$p < 0.01$, *$p < 0.05$.

4.3 Structured Equation Modeling (SEM)

Structured equation modeling (SEM) was adopted to test the conceptual model and proposed hypotheses using AMOS version 23. For testing a hypothesis, Hair et al. (2019) recommended the rules of thumb as follows: p-value < 0.05 and t-value $> |1.96|$. Figure 2 presents the results of the model fit assessment as follows: $\chi^2/df = 1.363$, GFI = 0.953, AGFI = 0.927, NFI = 0.953, CFI = 0.987, and RMSEA = 0.040. Following the rule of thumb

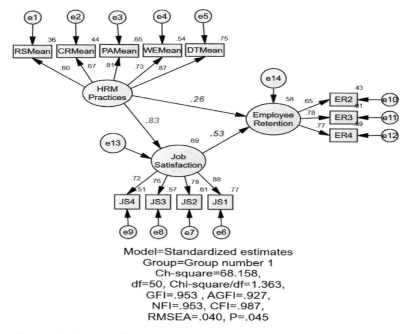

Model=Standardized estimates
Group=Group number 1
Ch-square=68.158,
df=50, Chi-square/df=1.363,
GFI=.953 , AGFI=.927,
NFI=.953, CFI=.987,
RMSEA=.040, P=.045

Figure 2. The result of structural equations modeling (n = 225).

Table 2. The result of hypothesis testing (n = 225).

Path Relationship	Path Coefficient	t-value	p-value	Hypothesis Testing
H1a-e: HRM → JS	0.83	12.743	***	(+) Supported
H2a-e: HRM → ER	0.26	1.908	0.056	(+) Partially Supported
H3: JS → ER	0.53	3.784	***	(+) Supported

Note: *, **, ***, indicate statistically at *p < 0.05, **p < 0.01, ***p < 0.001.

suggested by Hair et al. (2019), the model is confirmed to be good fit. According to Table 2, the results revealed that HRM practices have a positive impact on job satisfaction ($\beta = 0.83$, $t = 12.743$, $p < 0.001$), fully supporting H1-a-e. Moreover, HRM practices is positively associated with employee retention ($\beta = 0.26$, $t = 1.908$, $p = 0.056$), partially accepting H2-a-e. Finally, the results confirmed that job satisfaction has a positive influence on employee retention ($\beta = 0.53$, $t = 3.784$, and $p < 0.001$, supporting H3.

5 DISCUSSIONS, IMPLICATIONS, LIMITATIONS AND CONCLUSIONS

5.1 *Discussions and conclusions*

According to the results, HRM practices positively predict job satisfaction. Effective recruitment and a fair selection of potential candidates to fill vacant positions in organizations may result in later job satisfaction of employees, supporting the aforementioned studies (Anwar & Shukur 2015a; Gopinath & Shibu 2014). If an organization fails to implement a proper recruitment and selection strategy, employees are dissatisfied with their jobs and generate lower performance. Furthermore, employees feel satisfied when they receive reasonable remuneration and benefits, validating Saman (2020). Meanwhile, fair performance appraisal may lead to employees' positive attitudes and job satisfaction, according to earlier studies (Kampkötter 2017; Kaur & Kiran 2020; Saleem & Shah 2015). Consistent with Taheri et al. (2020), collaborative teamwork, a relaxing workplace atmosphere, and supportive relationship from managers indeed enhance job satisfaction among employees. As employees are motivated by the work environment, job satisfaction, and productivity increase. Moreover, developmental training programs may help employees advance their qualifications and skills and enhance job satisfaction, which confirms earlier findings (Anwar & Shukur 2015b; Chaudhary & Bhaskar 2016; Paposa & Kumar 2019).

Furthermore, the results verified that HRM practices are a critical predictor of employee retention. Effective recruitment and careful selection of employees may result in low employee turnover and strengthen employee retention. This outcome is in line with Janjua and Gulzar (2014) and Sutanto and Kurniawan (2017). Contrastingly, failure to implement a proper recruitment and selection process will increase the chance of turnover. Moreover, employees will stay with the organization if employees are properly compensated with better remunerations for their contributions. This finding is in accordance with early research (Bibi et al. 2018; Liao 2011; Moncarz et al. 2009). In concordance with Bibi et al. (2018) and Jehad and Farzana (2011), if employees feel that their performance is fairly evaluated, they will be motivated and stay longer in the organization. Besides, employees decide to remain in the organization due to good team relationships, friendly colleagues, and a motivating workplace, validating preceding studies (Kundu & Lata 2017; Ollukkaran & Gunaseelan 2012). In contrast, an unpleasant environment and employee relationships will increase employee turnover rates. Compatible with preceding findings (Ahmad et al. 2017; Bibi et al. 2018; Samuel & Chipunza 2009), employees can be retained if the organization provides excellent training opportunities for developing professional skills.

Simultaneously, job satisfaction also has a positive impact on employee retention, verifying preceding studies (Biason 2019; Desai 2018; Ramapriya & Sudhamathi 2020). This means that satisfied employees are likely to remain in the organization and devote all their efforts to achieving organizational goals and attaining high productivity. On the other hand, less job satisfaction may lead to low job performance and high turnover rates, which would contribute to an organization's talent and resources being lost. Therefore, human resource managers must develop effective strategies and HRM practices to satisfy and retain employees.

In conclusion, his research aimed to study the effect of HRM practices and job satisfaction on employee retention within an organization. The study was conducted on 225 respondents who work in the public and private sectors in Phnom Penh, the capital of Cambodia. Based on the results, we confirmed that HRM practices positively affect job satisfaction and employee retention. Employees in an organization will be satisfied with their jobs and choose to stay longer if the organization manages the HRM practices in an orderly manner (effective recruitment and selection, reasonable compensation and benefits, fair appraisal of an employee's performance, encouraging and positive working environment, opportunities for professional training and development). Meanwhile, employee retention is predicted by job satisfaction among employees. Indeed, job satisfaction is key as satisfied employees rarely switch over to different organizations.

5.2 *Theoretical and managerial implications*

In this research, we employed HRM practices (recruitment and selection, compensation and reward, performance appraisal, work environment, and training and development) and job satisfaction to investigate the effects of these two major factors on employee retention within an organization. As a result, the findings of this study can be used by future researchers who are interested in conducting studies on similar topics as fundamentals and backgrounds.

This research also provides several managerial contributions. First, the findings may be contributed to HR managers in recognizing the importance of employee retention and its antecedents such as HRM practices and job satisfaction so that they can enhance employee's performance and productivity as well as retain them in the company. In addition, this study is also extremely useful for future entrepreneurs who are dealing with employee turnover issues. This may assist them in understanding the HRM practices and formulating an effective HRM strategy that will facilitate skilled employees' work as well as enhance employee satisfaction and retention.

5.3 *Limitations and future research*

This study has some limitations, which provide opportunities for future researchers to conduct better studies. First of all, this study was only conducted in Phnom Penh, Cambodia, so future researchers can focus on different contexts and backgrounds to produce better insights from the study. Accordingly, the researcher used non-random samplings, which are convenient, and snowball samplings to distribute online questionnaires to respondents to collect data. Hence, the data collected might be biased and does not depict the whole population or generalize the findings. Thus, future studies are recommended to employ random sampling techniques to collect generalized data for the study. In addition, this study was only conducted on three main factors, such as HRM practices, job satisfaction, and employee retention, so insights in this study may be limited to these fundamental factors. Hence, future researchers are encouraged to broaden their knowledge by adding crucial factors such as supervisor support and organizational commitment.

REFERENCES

Agbozo G. K., Owusu I. S., Hoedoafia M. A. & Atakorah, Y. B. 2017. The Effect of Work Environment on Job Satisfaction: Evidence From the Banking Sector in Ghana. *Journal of Human Resource Management* 5 (1): 12–18.

Ahmad A., Bibi P. & Majid A. H. 2017. The Impact of Training & Development and Transformational Leadership Over Organizational Commitment Among Academic Staff in Public Tertiary Institutions: The Buffering Role of Coworker Support. *International Journal of Economic Perspectives* 11(1): 417–432.

Ahmed Z., Sabir S., Khosa M., Ahmad I. & Bilal M. A. 2016. Impact of Employee Turnover on Organisational Effectiveness in Tele Communication Sector of Pakistan. *IOSR Journal of Business and Management* 18(11): 88–96.

Anwar, G. & Shukur, I. 2015a. The Impact of Recruitment and Selection on Job satisfaction: Evidence from Private School in Erbil. *International Journal of Social Sciences & Educational Studies* 1(3): 4–13.

Anwar, G. & Shukur, I. 2015b. The Impact of Training and Development on Job Satisfaction: a Case Study of Private Banks in Erbil. *International Journal of Social Sciences & Educational Studies* 2(1): 65.

B2B CAMBODiA. 2021. People & Skills in Cambodia. https://www.b2b-cambodia.com/industry-overviews/people-skills/#1464436394041-5837cd01-a131. *Accessed Mar* 25, 2022.

Bakhashwain, S. A. & Javed, U. 2021. The Impact of Recruitment and Selection Practices on Employee Performance. *PalArch's Journal of Archaeology of Egypt/Egyptology* 18(14): 251–260.

Biason, R. S. 2019. The Effect of Job Satisfaction to Employee Retention. *International Journal of Economics, Commerce and Management* 8(3): 405–413.

Bibi, P., Ahmad, A., & Majid, A. H. 2018. HRM Practices and Employee Retention: The Moderating Effect of Work Environment. *Applying Partial Least Squares In Tourism and Hospitality Research*: 129–152.

Chao K. L. 2008. Relationship Among Organizational Commitment, Job Characteristics, Job Satisfaction, and Turnover Intention Within Kindergartens: An Empirical Study in Malaysia. *Journal of Educational Research* 44(1): 179–204.

Chaudhary, N. S. & Bhaskar, P. 2016. Training and Development and Job Satisfaction in Education Sector. *Journal of Resources Development and Management* 16(1): 42–45.

Chen, M. F., Lin, C. P., & Lien, G. Y. 2011. Modelling job Stress as a Mediating Role in Predicting Turnover Intention. *The Service Industries Journal* 31(8): 1327–1345.

Cook, S. 2008. *The Essential Guide to Employee Engagement: Better Business Performance Through Staff Satisfaction*. London: Kogan Page Publishers.

Desai, D. 2018. A Study on Linkage Between Job Satisfaction and Employee Retention. *International Journal for Research in Applied Science & Engineering Technology (IJRASET)* 6(6): 588–593.

Drucker, P.F. 1999. *Management Challenges for the 21st Century*. Harper Collins.

Fahim, M. G. A. 2018. Strategic Human Resource Management and Public Employee Retention. *Review of Economics and Political Science* 3(2): 20–39.

Fong, C. Y., Ooi, K. B., Tan, B. I., Lee, V. H. & Chong, A. Y. L. 2011. *HRM Practices and Knowledge Sharing: an Empirical Study. International Journal of Manpower* 32(5/6): 704–723.

Forgacs, L. 2009. Recruitment and Retention Across Continents. *Journal of Training and Development* 63(6): 40–44.

Fornell, C. & Larcker, D. F. 1981. Evaluating Structural Equation Models With Unobservable Variable and Measurement Error. *Journal of Marketing Research* 18(1): 39–50.

Gopinath, R. & Shibu, N. S. 2014. Recruitment and Selection Influencing Job Satisfaction–A Study with Reference to BSNL, Madurai SSA. *International Journal of Human Resource Management and Development* 4(1): 61–69.

Gunaseelan, R. & Ollukkaran, B. A. 2012. A Study on the Impact of Work Environment on Employee Performance. *Namex International Journal of Management Research* 71: 1–16.

Hair, J. F., Black, W. C., Babin, B. J. & Anderson, R. E. 2019. *Multivariate Data Analysis* (Eighth ed.). Hampshire, UK: Cengage Learning EMEA

Janjua, B. H. & Gulzar, A. 2014. The Impact of Human Resource Practices on Employee Commitment and Employee Retention in Telecom Sector of Pakistan: Exploring the Mediating Role of Employee loyalty. *IOSR Journal of Business and Management* 16(1): 76–81.

Jehad, M. & Farzana, Q. 2011. Organizational Justice and Organizational Citizenship Behavior: Evidences International Conference on Accounting, Business and from Malaysia. *Paper Presented in the 1st Economics (ICABEC)*.

Kampkötter, P. 2017. Performance Appraisals and Job Satisfaction. *The International Journal of Human Resource Management* 28(5): 750–774.

Kaur, G. & Kiran, D. 2020. Measuring the Effect of Performance Appraisal on Job Satisfaction. *International Journal of Management* 11(12): 2911–2918.

Kaur, P., Malhotra, K. & Sharma, S. K. 2020. Moderation-mediation Framework Connecting Internal Branding, Affective Commitment, Employee Engagement and Job Satisfaction: an Empirical Study of BPO Employees in Indian Context. *Asia-Pacific Journal of Business Administration* 12(3/4): 327–348.

Khan, M. A., Hussain, A., Hussain, J., & Khan, M. H. 2020. Effect of Performance Appraisal on Employees' Satisfaction: A Case Study of University of Peshawar, Khyber Pakhtunkhwa, Pakistan. *Review of Applied Management and Social Sciences* 3(2): 131–140.

Kundu, S. C. & Lata, K. 2017. Effects of Supportive Work Environment on Employee Retention: Mediating Role of Organizational Engagement. *International Journal of Organizational Analysis* 25(4): 703–722.

Liao, P. 2011. Linking Work-family Conflict to Job Attitudes: The Mediating Role of Social Exchange Relationships. *The International Journal of Human Resource Management* 22(14): 2965–2980.

Mabaso, C. M. & Dlamini, B. I. 2017. Impact of Compensation and Benefits on Job Satisfaction. *Research Journal of Business Management* 11(2): 80–90.

Malik, E., Baig, S. A. & Manzoor, U. 2020. Effect of HR Practices on Employee Retention: The Role of Perceived Supervisor Support. *Journal of Public Value and Administrative Insight* 3(1): 1–7.

Marques, J. 2007. HR in all its Glory. *Human Resource Management International Digest* 15(5): 3–6.

Mathis, R. L., Jackson, J. H., Valentine, S. R. & Meglich, P. A. 2016. *Human Resource Management*, (15th ed.). Cengage Learning.

McCrensky, E. 1964. Improving Recruitment and Retention of Public Health Personnel. *American Journal of Public Health and the Nations Health* 54(4): 624–626.

Miheso, P., Manyasi, J. & Wanjere, D. 2019. Effect of Recruitment and Selection Practices on Employee Retention in SACCOS in Kakamega County. *The Strategic Journal of Business & Change Management* 6 (3): 356–360.

Moncarz, E., Zhao, J. & Kay, C. 2009. An Exploratory study of US Lodging Properties' Organizational Practices on Employee Turnover and Retention, *International Journal of Contemporary Hospitality Management* 21(4): 437–458.

Paposa, K. K. & Kumar, Y. M. 2019. Impact of Training and Development Practices on Job Satisfaction: A Study on Faculty Members of Technical Education Institutes. *Management and Labour Studies* 44(3): 248–262.

Raihan, J. M. H. 2012. Mediating Effects of Organizational Commitment and Perceived Organizational Support on HRM Practices and Turnover Intention: A Study of Private Universities in Bangladesh. Doctoral Dissertation, Universiti Utara Malaysia.

Ramapriya, M. & Sudhamathi S. 2020. Impact of job Satisfaction on Employee Retention in Garment industry. *International Journal of Multidisciplinary Educational Research* 9(12): 68–72.

Raziq, A. & Maulabakhsh, R. 2015. Impact of Working Environment on Job Satisfaction. *Procedia Economics and Finance* 23: 717–725.

Saleem, H. & Shah, F. M. 2015. Impact of Performance Appraisal on Job Satisfaction in Banking Sector of Pakistan. *International Journal of Management Sciences and Business Research* 4(11): 74–82.

Saman, A. 2020. Effect of Compensation on Employee Satisfaction and Employee Performance. *International Journal of Economics, Business and Accounting Research (IJEBAR)* 4(1): 185–190.

Samuel, M. O. & Chipunza, C. 2009. Employee Retention and Turnover: Using Motivational Variables as a panacea. *African Journal of Business Management* 3(9): 410–415.

Schmidt, S. W. 2007. *The Relationship Between Satisfaction with Workplace Training and Overall Job Satisfaction. Human Resource Development Quarterly* 18(4): 481–498.

Sutanto, E. M. & Kurniawan, M. 2017. The Impact of Recruitment, Employee Retention, and Labor Relations to Employee Performance on Batik Industry in Solo City, Indonesia. *International Journal of Business and Society* 17(2): 375–390.

Swanepoel, B. J., Erasmus, B. J., Schenk, H. W. & Tshilongamulenzhe, M. C. 2014. *South African Human Resource Management: Theory and Practice* (4th Ed.). Cape Town: Juta.

Taheri, R. H., Miah, M. S. & Kamaruzzaman, M. 2020. Impact of Working Environment on Job Satisfaction. *European Journal of Business and Management Research* 5(6).

Wagner, S. 2000. Retention: Finders, keepers. *Training & Development* 54(8): 64.

Economic and Business Management – Lent & Zhang (Eds)
© 2023 the Author(s), ISBN 978-1-032-24482-2

Research on the impact of servitization on manufacturing firm performance

Fangyuan Dong, Pengbin Gao & Congshu Liu
Harbin Institute of Technology (Weihai), Weihai, Shandong, China

ABSTRACT: At present, the service-oriented transformation has become an important choice for many manufacturing firms to obtain competitive advantages. Based on previous studies, this paper discusses the influence of servitization on financial performance and market performance from the theoretical level and proposes the research hypotheses. Based on the panel data of 420 samples from 84 firms over the span of 5 years, regression analysis is performed using Stata15.1 to test the theoretical model hypotheses. The research results show that servitization has a u-shaped relationship with financial performance and a positive linear relationship with market performance. According to the theoretical and empirical research results, this paper further puts forward some countermeasures and suggestions.

1 INSTRUCTION

The manufacturing industry is the pillar China's economy. The reform and opening-up policy and the trend of globalization enabled the Chinese manufacturing industry to expand beyond the country, entering the global market. With the arrival of the service economy, the trend of integration of servitization and manufacturing is gradually becoming more and more apparent. More and more manufacturing firms hope to obtain new competitive advantages through the way of servitization transformation (Wei Houkai 2019). Currently, China has entered the transition stage of "supply-side" reform, and the transformation and upgrading of the manufacturing industry have become an urgent issue. As one of the important pathways of transformation and upgrading, the government is placing great importance to servitization. Therefore, it is necessary to analyze the impact of servitization on firm performance on manufacturing firms.

2 LITERATURE REVIEW

Previous scholars have studied the impact of servitization on firm performance, which can be broadly classified into the following categories: (1) Positive relationship. Servitization is the process of firm value focus transformation (Zhang Ruijun 2020), and it has a positive impact on the financial performance of the firm. Research shows that customer-oriented business models and after-sales services are increasingly important in generating new revenue (Majava 2019). Based on a study of 184 manufacturing firms, the structural equation model and qualitative comparative analysis results confirm that all servitization strategies can improve performance (Ambroise 2017). (2) Service paradox. Although some studies show that servitization has a positive impact on firm performance, in the process of servitization, it will also increase firm costs, put firms at risk, and even bankrupt the company. Valtakoski shows that there is also a negative relationship between background service capability and firm performance (Benedettini 2019). (3) Complex relationship. With further research, more

DOI: 10.1201/9781003278788-29

complex nonlinear relationship between the effect of servitization on firm performance is obtained (Valtakoski 2018). According to the service content, service integration and profitability show a U-shaped relationship, that is, when service integration reaches a certain level, it has a positive impact on firm profitability. (4) No correlation. In addition, some scholars believe that there is no significant relationship between servitization and financial performance (Zhou D 2020). Et al. study servitization and the average profit of firms and found that servitization did not affect the size of the average profit.

To sum up, the existing researches mainly focus on financial performance in the performance part and lack of influence on the comprehensive performance of firms. Second, considering the influence of servitization on performance, most studies have focused on simple linear relationships, whereas few studies have focused on more complex curvilinear relationships.

3 RESEARCH HYPOTHESIS

3.1 *The relationship between servitization and firm financial performance*

In the low service level stage, manufacturing firms will pay more attention to the provision, distribution, and use of services, which will make them incur high costs. Therefore, manufacturing firms generally cannot get rich returns in a short time; on the contrary, there is a chance to produce a certain amount of loss. When manufacturing firms gradually improve the level of service, organizational structure and personnel allocation gradually adjust, the relationship between firms and their customers is getting closer and closer, and service businesses can bring higher profits to firms. When the level of servitization is improved to produce economies of scale, firm income will be improved, and the trend of positive correlation between servitization and firm financial performance begins to appear. Therefore, the following hypotheses are proposed:

H1: *There is a u-shaped relationship between servitization and financial performance*

3.2 *The relationship between servitization and firm market performance*

In the initial stage of servitization, the services provided by firms are mostly related to products, which can improve the availability and stability of products, and increase the sales volume of products. When the servitization reaches a certain degree, the firm will provide more customer services, thus improving customer satisfaction and loyalty. Both the initial product service and the customer service, after the service reaches a certain level, can have a positive effect on the market performance of the firm. Therefore, the hypothesis is proposed:

H2: *Servitization has a positive effect on market performance*

4 DATA SOURCES AND VARIABLE MEASUREMENTS

This paper selects listed manufacturing companies as the research object. More than 2700 manufacturing enterprises are selected by analyzing annual reports. Data for 84 enterprises from 2015 to 2019 are finally determined, with a sample observation value of 420.

Explanatory variable—service level of manufacturing industry. This paper adopts the proportion of service income from total income to measure and use other business income to approximately replace service income. Explained variable—corporate performance. It is divided into financial performance and market performance. Return on total assets measures financial performance, while operating income measures market performance. Control variables—the size and age of the enterprise. This paper guarantees that the analysis result is not affected by the size and age of the enterprise.

5 RESEARCH RESULTS

5.1 *Descriptive statistics and correlation statistical analysis*

In this paper, The Pearson correlation coefficient is used to measure the correlation among explanatory variables, explained variables, moderating variables, and control variables. In addition, descriptive statistics are made for each variable, and the results are shown in Table 1.

Table 1. Descriptive and correlation statistical analysis.

Variable	AGE	SIZE	Serv	BV	NBM	FP	MP
AGE	1.000						
SIZE	−0.057	1.000					
Serv	0.105**	0.104**	1.000				
BV	−0.152***	−0.506***	−0.078	1.000			
NBM	0.191***	0.062	0.110**	−0.044	1.000		
FP	0.146***	−0.014	0.593***	0.011	0.088*	1.000	
MP	0.046	0.105**	0.552***	−0.026	0.087*	0.598***	1.000
Mean	20.464	23.877	0.025	488.1605	0.159	0.065	0.107
S.E.	4.911	1.298	0.031	565.7406	0.21	0.064	0.247
Min	8	21.308	0.0001	34.86	0	−0.094	−0.597
Max	39	27.468	0.206	4296.52	0.989	0.323	2.068

Note: $*p < 0.1$, $**p < 0.05$, $***p < 0.01$.

From the correlation results, the correlation between servitization and financial performance is significant at 0.01 level, and correlation between servitization and market performance is also significant at 0.01 level. To sum up, the results of correlation analysis to a certain extent show that the idea of this study is feasible.

5.2 *Regression statistical analysis*

Panel data samples are used for regression analysis. In order to determine whether to select a fixed-effect model or a random-effect model, The Hausman test is first performed on each regression model. When the test result of the P-value is less than 0.1, the fixed effect model is used to conduct the test. When the test result of the P value is greater than 0.1, the random effect model is used. After the Hausman test, the P values of all models are less than 1, so fixed-effect models are used for testing. The regression results are shown in Table 2.

Only control variables—firm age and firm size—are input in Model 1. As shown in Table 2, the regression coefficient of firm size and financial performance in Model 1 is 0.00093, and the regression coefficient of firm age, and financial performance is 0.000221. It shows that there is no significant relationship between firm size, firm age, and financial performance.

According to the results shown in Table 2, it can be concluded that in Model 2, the value of $R^2 = 0.5279$ is more than the R^2 of Model 1. The regression coefficient between servitization and financial performance is 0.239, which is significant at the statistical level of $P < 0.05$. The regression coefficient between the square term of servitization and financial performance is 6.802, which is also significant at the statistical level of $P < 0.01$. In other words, there is a significant non-linear relationship between manufacturing firms' servitization and financial performance. As the coefficient before the quadratic term is positive, according to the graphic properties of the quadratic function, the regression curve shows a

Table 2. Regression results.

Variable	Financial performance		Market performance	
	Model 1	Model 2	Model 3	Model 4
AGE	0.000930	0.000602	−0.0140	−0.0175*
SIZE	−0.000221	−0.000275	0.161*	0.201***
Serv		0.0239**		5.643***
Serv2		6.802***		
cons	−0.138	−0.136	−3.397*	−4.292**
Obs.	420	420	420	420
R-squared	0.0213	0.5279	0.0070	0.1248

Note: $^*p < 0.1$, $^{**}p < 0.05$, $^{***}p < 0.01$.

trend of the first decline and then uplifted, in the shape of "U", supporting that the hypothesis H1, H1 is valid.

Only control variables—firm age and firm size—are input in Model 3. As can be seen in Model 3, the regression coefficient between firm size and market performance is −0.140, and the regression coefficient between firm age and market performance is 0.161, which is significant at the statistical level $P < 0.1$, that is, there is no significant relationship between firm size and market performance; however, firm age has a significant positive impact on firm market performance, that is, the older a firm is, the higher the market performance it will get.

According to the results shown in Table 2, it can be concluded that in Model 4, R^2 = 0.1248 over R^2 of Model 3 = 0.0070 increased significantly, indicating that the explanatory ability of Model 4 was strengthened. The regression coefficient between servitization and market performance was 5.643, which is significant at the statistical level of $P < 0.05$. Therefore, hypothesis H2 is supported and H2 is established.

6 CONCLUSIONS

This paper discusses the relationship between manufacturing service and corporate financial performance, and corporate market performance, the results show that the servitization and financial performance of firms have a "U" type of relationship, which shows a turning point between the relationship between the two. Before the turning point arrived, servitization has a negative impact on the financial performance of the firms. After passing the turning point, the servitization has a positive impact on the financial performance of the firms. After crossing the turning point, servitization has a positive impact on the financial performance of firms, that is, with the increase of servitization, financial performance will be improved. Therefore, the timing of the turning point is an important milestone in the process of servitization. This shows that although in the initial stage of servitization, the financial performance of firms will be reduced due to the lack of service industry experience and cost input. Whereas, in the long run, once the "inflection point" is crossed, servitization will have a positive impact on the financial performance of firms. Therefore, in the long run, it is beneficial for firms to carry out the servitization strategy. As for the market performance of firms, there is a positive linear relationship between servitization and the market performance of firms. The rise of servitization will also improve market performance. In other words, the servitization of firms can help firms gain a more favorable market position, and thus generate higher income.

Although this study has a certain value, there are still some limitations. First, the samples in this paper cover most manufacturing industries, but due to the difficulty in obtaining relevant variable indicators, the data of different industry segments are not enough to be restructured. Moreover, manufacturing firms of different industry types cannot be classified into servitization research. Second, the samples selected in this study are all Chinese firms, which are not universal. If more firm samples from more countries are selected for comparative analysis, it is believed that the results will become more widely representative. In addition, variables such as financial performance and market performance in the study can be measured in different ways to further test the results.

REFERENCES

Ambroise L., Prim-Allaz I., Teyssier C. 2017. Financial Performance of Servitized Manufacturing Firms: a Configuration Issue Between Servitization Strategies and Customer-oriented Organizational Design. *Industrial The Marketing Management States*: 54–68.

Benedettini O., Neely A. 2019. Service Providers and Firm Performance: Investigating the non-linear Effect of flotation. *Journal of Service Management* 30(6): 716–738.

Majava J., Isoherranen V. 2019. Business Model Evolution of Customer Care Services. *Journal of Industrial Engineering and Management* 12 (1): 1–12.

Valtakoski A., Witell L. 2018. Service Capabilities and Servitized Sme Performance: Contingency research on Firm Age. *International Journal of Operations & Production Management* 38(4): 1144–1164.

Wei Houkai, Wang Songji. 2019. Analysis and Theoretical Reflection on "Excessive Deindustrialization" in China. *China Industrial Economics* 1:5–22.

Zhang Ruijun, Chen Juhong, Wu Di. 2020. The Matching of Manufacturing Enterprises' Servitization Strategy and Operation and Maintenance Business Model Innovation – Based on Multi-case Study. *Management Review* 032(002): 308–326.

Zhou D., Yan T., Zhao L, *et al.* 2020. Performance Implications of Servitization: Does a Manufacturer's Service Supply Network Matter? *International Journal of Production Economics* 219: 31–42.

Economic and Business Management – Lent & Zhang (Eds)
© 2023 the Author(s), ISBN 978-1-032-24482-2

Indicators of the transformation strategies of technology companies

A.K. Yakovleva, E.A. Fedulova & O.S. Salkova
Kemerovo State University, Kemerovo, Russia

ABSTRACT: The article discusses the specifics of technology companies in the financial sector that implement a digital transformation strategy (transformational strategy) in order to manage their activities. The study revealed that the essence of the introduction of a transformational strategy is to modify it into each component of the strategy system at the corporate level. In turn, the analysis and evaluation of the results of the transformational strategies' implementation of financial and technological companies requires the choice and validity of the evaluation indicators' application. A rational and thorough selection of the strategic development's indicators of technology companies in the banking sector makes it possible to solve the problem of information deficit, reduce the probability of analytical contradictions in the analysis of the company's financial information, and also ensure the adoption of competent management decisions. Based on the IFRS reporting data of such technology companies with a banking license as Sber and Tinkoff Bank, the results of their transformation strategies' implementation were assessed and indicators were identified that characterize the effectiveness of the analyzed companies' digital transformation.

1 INTRODUCTION

The relevance of the study is conditioned by the rapid introduction of digital technologies into the activities of companies, including financial ones, which are radically changing the business model of their development. The success of such companies in many ways determines the application of methods and techniques for managing digital transformation processes, including the use of strategic development indicators that provide the most optimal solutions in these conditions.

The existing traditional methods for assessing the quality of strategic decisions at the level of technology companies mainly allow assessing the performance of many reasons that affect the sustainability of their development, including those not related to the implementation of digital technologies. However, it is not always possible to reveal and identify the actions of digital processes occurring in a company. Meanwhile, digital transformation strategies require appropriate analytical support.

The purpose of this study is to select and justify the indicators of the strategic development of technology companies (indicators of financial analytics), which make it possible to improve the accuracy of assessments of digital decisions.

Determination of the most informative indicators of financial analytics will allow:

- predict the state of control objects as a result of the realization (implementation) of transformational strategies;
- make timely decisions to eliminate (or mitigate) the effects of negative causes hindering the achievement of the transformation strategies' goals.

DOI: 10.1201/9781003278788-30

2 THE SPECIFICS OF TECHNOLOGY COMPANIES

2.1 *Typology of technology companies*

Technology companies develop and market information technology products or services. The activities of such a company are always associated with digital products and software development[1].

Technology companies include manufacturers or technology developers themselves, as well as companies that actively use modern solutions in their work or help in their distribution and implementation in other organizations.

Classification of technology companies.

1. Giant corporations are innovative companies that provide the main products, services and services used by millions of other companies. Corporations are guided by the analysis of huge amounts of data and knowledge about users. And on the basis of this data, ecosystem services and products are created that are used by a huge number of customers.
2. IT companies – companies and start-ups that focus on the development and production of technological products or services. These are digital and electronic means – software, Internet services, automated services, e-commerce, mobile applications, etc.

    Such companies are trying to form joint technology centers. The most famous example is Silicon Valley. However, there is a similar concentration of top technology companies around the world. In Russia, a similar innovation center is Skolkovo.
3. Modern technology companies are the main market leaders, whose services people use regularly and which satisfy most of the needs of the population. For example, in Russia these are Yandex, Sber, Tinkoff, Mail.Ru Group, Wildberries[2].

All types of technology companies have similar characteristics, as presented below.

2.2 *Key features of technology companies*

A key indicator of technology companies is the preparedness to invest in technology. This includes investments in the development of our own services and products, as well as in the implementation of already developed ready-made technologies. This is due to the fact that the main task of technology companies is to provide users with an optimal service by building a customer-centric business model.

Technology companies influence the country's economy and set trends in industries. Commitment to progressive technologies, their rigorous applications in various fields contribute to an increase in the growth of capitalization of such companies, help to attract large investors. However, the introduction of relevant technologies into the company's work processes (automated systems, "cloud" services, data protection, etc.) does not yet make the company technological. A real technology company is a company that comes from how to improve the quality of services. The main goal for her is to make available the product that the consumer needs.

The considered characteristics determine the spheres of technology companies' functioning. Let's reveal their essence.

---

[1]How to start a technology company: a detailed guide. URL: https://www.purrweb.com/ru/blog/kak-otkryt-tekhnologicheskuyu-kompaniyu/.

[2]Which companies can be considered technological companies? URL: https://probusiness.io/tech/8066-nanyat-programmista-eto-eshche-ne-vse-proverte-mozhno-li-vash-biznes-nazvat-tekhnologichnym.html.

Which industries have the most tech companies? Technological companies that are engaged in the sphere of leisure and comfort of life (life-style services) are always relevant. Due to the lack of time in the modern world, there is a need for high-quality and fast service.

The financial and banking sector is no exception. Users need the widest possible range of options in this area, which will be ahead of their requests. They want to see customized offers and packages, loyalty programs tailored to individual needs. This requires analytics services and various applications for simplicity of use.

A technology company should have a modern approach to management, corporate culture, and communications. Everything should be aimed at improving the efficiency of the employee and customer satisfaction. To improve the performance of such a company, it is important to motivate its employees to move to a higher level of expertise, to create conditions conducive to their psychological stability.

As mentioned earlier, among companies that claim to be high-tech, the most important role belongs to those that not only follow the path of digital transformation themselves, but also help others develop in this direction.

Modern technologies and services based on them are the key to successful adaptation to challenges and effective work in changing conditions. The main thing that technologies give businesses is flexibility and speed of reaction to any changes, uninterrupted and secures all important processes, the ability to solve the necessary tasks without being tied to a specific place or device.

Thus, the ability to grow and develop together with its customers and their requests is the main indicator of a company that claims to be a technology company.

Undoubtedly, a technology company is constantly in the process of digital transformation. It regularly takes actions to introduce and implement a transformational strategy, improve its own business processes, sales system, products and services, as well as to optimize costs. The successful development of a technology company requires a strategy at its core.

Let's reveal its content.

2.4 *The mission of technology companies*

The mission statement is the first practical document of the strategy, created as a result of analysis and forecasts of the external and internal environment, the starting stage in the development of the strategy itself and the main guideline for all subsequent stages of strategizing. In several sentences of the mission, it should be formulated in which area the object operates, in which region, the reasons for the creation, as well as the validity of the existence of the object, that is, why this strategizing object is unique and valuable to the consumer (Kvint 2014).

The mission of technology companies determines the meaning and content of activities, emphasizing their crucial role in the Russian economy. Customers, their needs, dreams and goals are the basis of all activities of such companies. At the same time, the mission and activities of technology companies in the financial and banking sector are to revolutionize the financial landscape of Russia through the quality of products and customer centricity[3,4].

The digital transformation strategy of technology companies in the financial and banking sector as a whole involves the formation of interaction models with each client based on the principles of customer centricity and better understanding and anticipation of consumer behavior patterns. The basis of digital transformation in this area is the constancy of

---

[3]Mission and values of Sber Bank. URL: https://www.sber-bank.by/page/mission-values.
[4]Tinkoff Strategy 2023. URL: https://www.youtube.com/watch?v=SVWDgdrszXc.

interaction with the client, the offer's personalization, the transfer of services to online format, and a client-oriented approach.

By itself, a company's digital transformation strategy can't exist in isolation. It is built into the strategy of any level and becomes a necessary part of it. The next section of the study is devoted to the interaction of the transformational strategy with other types of strategies and determining its place in the hierarchy of goals for managing the activities of technology companies.

3 THE PLACE OF TRANSFORMATIONAL STRATEGY IN THE HIERARCHY OF GOALS FOR MANAGING THE ACTIVITIES OF TECHNOLOGY COMPANIES

3.1 *The content and features of the transformation strategy at different management levels of technology companies*

Changes in the economy and politics, the growth of consumer unrest can create problems for the viability of companies. In such cases, companies adopt and execute transformational strategies in order to secure their competitive advantage and position themselves for long-term profitability.

A transformational strategy is about making radical and significant changes within a company to change the course of its short and long term viability. The need for such a change in direction usually arises as a result of some external factor, such as a downturn in the economy or an increase in competitor activity that forces executives and managers to rethink their business model. Thus, the transformation strategy pursues the goals of increasing the company's revenue and market share, increasing customer satisfaction and retention, as well as reducing and optimizing costs for the reallocation of resources, taking into account the efficiency of their use[5].

Engaging key people in a company is essential to a transformation strategy. Board members, stakeholders, managers, as well as partners and key customers must be involved in the transformation process. Engaging stakeholders in the transformation strategy also helps broaden and deepen the resources and tools available to the company, which helps transform business models in a timely and effective manner.

An important part of the transformational strategy is the setting of goals and objectives. The first step is to recognize the need for change and then agree with stakeholders on the steps needed to implement those changes. It is important to note that the change strategy must be supported by management. Leadership and managers need to regularly review the transformation vision to ensure that it meets the stated goals.

The implementation of radical change involves the use of targeted tools to ensure the appropriateness and effectiveness of the transformation strategy. These tools correlate with elements of the corporate level strategy system.

At the corporate level, the system of strategies can be defined as a set of hierarchical levels of various kinds of strategies, depending on the goals of management. In this case, a hierarchy of strategies is presented based on the goals of managing the activities of technology companies (Figure 1).

The tools mentioned above just include an analysis of the company's environment, existing forecasts of future conditions for its development based on strategic thinking and accumulated experience (corporate strategy) (Kvint 2012), the study and analysis of financial data (financial strategy), the performance of employees and management (HR strategy), a thorough review of technologies and service programs, as well as the optimization of project management plans (investment strategy).

---

[5]Transformational Strategy. URL: https://smallbusiness.chron.com/transformational-strategy-61887. html.

Figure 1. The place of transformational strategy in the hierarchy of goals for managing the activities of technology companies.
Source: compiled by the authors based on the methodology of V.L. Kvint (2012).

Integration of the hierarchical levels of the strategy system and the use of tools for the effective implementation of the transformation strategy allow you to create an ideal corporate strategy. In this regard, the meaning of implementing a transformational strategy is that it should be embedded and implemented in every component of the strategy system at the corporate level: in financial, investment, marketing, HR-strategy.

For technology companies any investment decision is accompanied by the introduction of digital technologies. Therefore, the investment strategy of a technology company is characterized by the use of digital methods for implementing investment decisions that determine the nature and volume of its investments, which allows us to consider the transformation strategy as part of the company's investment strategy.

3.2 Transformation strategy as part of investment decisions of companies

The investment strategy of the company requires that the selection of investment areas, the selection of projects in the investment program, as well as the development of the capital investment budget, are consistent with the overall (corporate) and financial development strategies of the company, and also its functional strategies (marketing, logistics, HR-strategy, etc.). A distinctive feature in the development of an investment strategy is the consideration of a large number of investment alternatives, taking into account the influence of external factors on the investment, operating and financial activities of the company.

A strategic approach to investment decisions is the only way to harmonize the interests of different interested groups (stakeholders). It is expressed in the need to adapt to a changing world (flexibility becomes a competitive advantage). In addition, the investment strategy should take into account the potential to independently change the world (create new needs in the market) and create sustainable competitive advantages for a technology company.

All of the above circumstances are the reason for the emergence of different models of digital transformation.

4 DIGITAL TRANSFORMATION MODELS

4.1 Types of digital transformation models

Technology companies can be divided into subgroups:

1) Large companies (or innovators) develop and implement new technologies (from clothing production to fintech and telecom).

2) Medium companies develop and implement individual services and products for the convenience of users.

3) Small companies (or startups) – develop or refine individual products and services in the field of technology[6].

Based on the above classification of technology companies, one can single out their digital transformation models and approaches based on them to the development of transformation strategies for technology companies. The content of these approaches is reflected in the concept of digital transformation models.

4.2   *Concepts of digital transformation models*

The first model is based on the introduction of digital technologies as a separate project that does not imply a full-scale digital transformation. In this case, digital transformations are being introduced gradually, based on long-term planning and implementation of pilot projects.

This model reflects the concept of the improvement strategy (according to V.L. Kvint), which is based mainly on a system analysis of the strategizing object's subsystems, its elements and functions, as well as their interaction with each other, and which is focused on optimizing existing subsystems and technologies.

The second model of digital transformation is implemented through the creation of a subsidiary, which was initially built taking into account the needs of the digital economy. The advantages of the model are a clear focus on customer needs in the long term, the creation of teams within the organization, including specialists in various areas (information technology, software, analytics, marketing), due to which a high flexibility of the organizational structure is achieved, and it also becomes possible to test new areas of activity without prejudice to existing ones.

This model is associated with the implementation of the combination strategy approach, which assumes that, in parallel with the introduction and development of revolutionary innovative ideas and technologies, current efficiency and profitability are achieved through long-standing production and technological systems.

The third model of digital transformation is based on the recognition of digital technologies as the main value of a technology company. It implies a more complete implementation of the digital transformation strategy through the transformation of all internal and external processes of a financial technology company.

This model reflects the strategy of new horizons (according to the methodology of V.L. Kvint), which requires prospective long-term thinking far beyond the existing agenda of the strategic analysis' object. As part of this strategy, it is necessary to recognize and analyze innovative radical asymmetric and exponential paths to success, even if they fundamentally change the current activity of the object (Kvint 2020).

Thus, at present, digital transformation is seen as an integral element in maintaining the competitiveness of technology companies. The digital transformation process and its models should be based on a digital transformation strategy and approaches to its implementation, designed with the characteristics and needs of a particular company and its client audience.

The main content of the analysis' quality of the chosen digital transformation model is the analysis and evaluation of the results of transformation strategies' implementation. Conducting such an analysis, it is important to choose and justify the use of assessment indicators that take into account the characteristics of the analyzed phenomena.

---

[6]Which companies can be considered technological companies? URL: https://probusiness.io/tech/8066-nanyat-programmista-eto-eshche-ne-vse-proverte-mozhno-li-vash-biznes-nazvat-tekhnologichnym.html.

5 THE NEED TO USE INDICATORS TO EVALUATE THE RESULTS OF THE IMPLEMENTATION OF TRANSFORMATION STRATEGIES

5.1 *Purpose of transformational strategies' indicators of technology companies*

Modern financial analytics provides an opportunity to evaluate the results of the implementation of the company digital transformation to justify the financial aspects of the decisions made on the formation of a portfolio of the company's activities. Science and practice have developed certain groups of analytical indicators, the main purpose of which is to reflect the dynamics and contradictions of ongoing processes and phenomena at the organization level. At the same time, it is important to represent any of the analytical indicators (regardless of the interests of which capital providers it is in) as a micromodel of an economic phenomenon that adequately reflects such characteristics of a company's activities as versatility, dynamism, interconnectedness of its various parties, interdependence strategic goals and objectives of development.

Currently, about 80% of the company's financial performance is universal (Teplova 2019). Of course, for each industry and company, taking into account the characteristics of the chosen strategy, non-financial indicators will be different. The usefulness of a financial indicator will be determined by the presence of the ability to approach (not move away due to exposure to changes and fluctuations) to its main purpose – measuring and evaluating the essence of an economic phenomenon (Sheremet 2000). And since economic phenomena "absorb" the results of the transformational strategy's implementation, it is important to know the nature of each economic indicator, whether it is about the efficiency of the company or the projects it is implementing, or some other characteristic, to understand the essence of financial information, to clearly understand the boundaries of its analysis, take into account the "polymorphism of accounting interpretations" (Sokolova 2018), due to the presence of analytical procedures' variety. Otherwise, there is a high probability of obtaining superficial conclusions that are not adequate to the real state of the analyzed phenomena.

Among various systems and sets of economic indicators, indicators of market value, profitability, turnover, and financial stability attract attention. This group of indicators is the most applicable, as it is most often reflected in the economic literature. This group of indicators also includes well-known models of EVA, the economic profit of such large consulting companies as PWC, Accenture, Stern, Stewart & Co, McKinsey (Teplova 2019). For example, the McKinsey model is based on the invested (allocated, involved) capital and efficiency spread (Teplova 2019). The value of the latter indicator is used to judge the quality of the capital use, the efficiency of the company.

In Western economic thought there are a large number of scientific works devoted to the issues of capital management and the search for its optimal structure, as well as the development of financial management tools. These works have a fairly large area of practical application, as they form a theoretical basis for making managerial decisions and make it possible to increase the competitiveness of a company and manage its financial stability. An important contribution to the development of these problems was made by the works of J. Brigham (2001), L. Gapensky (2001), Van Horn (2011), A. Damodoran (2006), R. Brailey (2001, 2004), S. Ross (2001), and others.

5.2 *Company stakeholder groups*

The existence of objective reasons that affect the variability of decisions made (among them are the variability in the formation of financial statements and the variability of the methodology for analyzing financial statements) does not reduce the need of interested users to obtain the most informative indicators that give an objective and accurate picture of the results of the transformational strategies' implementation.

Potential investors, business partners, creditors are called upon to evaluate information about the financial and economic activities of the company. But first of all, the adoption of decisions of a strategic nature obliges the owners of the company to receive information that meets the criteria of "usefulness" and "sufficiency". A reasonable choice of indicators for the strategic development of technology companies will solve the problem of information sufficiency in the context of the implementation of digital solutions, reduce or completely eliminate analytical contradictions in the analysis of financial information, and ensure the adoption of competent management decisions.

The choice and justification of the indicators of transformational strategies can be carried out empirically based on the analysis of the company's IFRS reporting data.

6 EVALUATION OF THE RESULTS OF TRANSFORMATIONAL STRATEGIES BASED ON IFRS REPORTING DATA

6.1 *Financial reporting as a source of information for digital decision making*

A comprehensive business management information platform for any company includes four of its constituent elements: accounting – economic analysis – control – reporting (Kamordzhanova 2015). The listed elements are designed to solve current and strategic business problems. Also, the solution of strategic tasks requires special information support based on the integration of financial and non-financial reporting. Some companies in Russia already have some experience in generating such reports, which have been called "integrated reporting" in the world practice. However, the use of such a reporting format is not mandatory in Russia, and the preparation of an integrated report is possible only after the preparation of financial statements. This means that financial statements continue to serve as an information base for analyzing the performance of most companies. Its purpose is to provide information about the financial position, financial results and changes in the financial position of the company.

In Russia, financial statements are prepared in accordance with the Federal Accounting Standards (RAS) and International Financial Reporting Standards (IFRS). There are important differences between the listed standards: IFRS reporting procedures are based on principles, and not on rigidly prescribed rules inherent in national standards. There are no reporting forms in IFRS, there are only requirements for the minimum content of its articles. Profit and loss statement under IFRS can be formed in two ways: by function and nature of expenses. In RAS only the option by function is used. RAS reporting is aimed at regulatory authorities (including tax authorities). The primary user of the information presented in IFRS statements is the investor.

6.2 *Results of the assessment of technology companies' «Sber» and «Tinkoff Bank» financial statements under IFRS*

The authors of this article analyzed the IFRS reporting data of two companies: Sber and Tinkoff. Both companies are modern technology companies on the path of digital transformation to maintain their competitiveness.

The IFRS reporting data of Sber and Tinkoff were subjected to analytical processing, as a result, groups of indicator indicators were obtained that reflect the results of the implementation of the companies' transformation strategies (Table 1 and Table 2).

The choice of indicators is dictated by the need to disclose information about the activities of companies from different angles. The data on liquidity as an indicator of the financial stability of companies in the study are presented by current liquidity and urgent liquidity ratios. Indicators of financial stability are represented by autonomy and sustainable financing ratios. Indicators of asset turnover and non-current assets act as indicators of the

Table 1. Indicators of strategic development of Sber for 2016–2021.

Indicators	2016	2017	2018	2019	2020	2021
Liquidity indicators						
Current liquidity ratio, once	2,21	1,81	1,61	2,00	1,96	1,9
Quick liquidity ratio, once	2,13	1,75	1,54	1,92	1,85	1,76
Indicators of financial stability						
Autonomy coefficient, once	0,11	0,13	0,12	0,15	0,14	0,14
Sustainable financing ratio, once	0,57	0,48	0,47	0,54	0,53	0,52
Business activity indicators						
Asset turnover, once a year	0,09	0,09	0,08	0,08	0,07	0,07
Turnover of non-current assets, once a year	2,15	1,84	0,75	0,72	0,95	0,89
Efficiency and performance indicators						
Return on total capital (ROA), % per year	2,4	3,2	3,3	3,3	2,8	3,9
Return on invested capital (ROIC), % per year	3,8	5,5	6,1	5,5	4,3	6,2
Return on equity (ROE), % per year	19,2	23,9	22,8	20,3	16,0	23,3
Profitability of all activities, %	22,6	32,1	38,0	35,3	31,7	45,6
Risk indicators						
Effect of financial leverage, %	16,8	19,3	19,8	15,2	13,6	19,7
Operating leverage effect, once	5,7	3,9	3,4	3,7	6,7	3,5

Source: compiled by the authors based on[7].

Table 2. Indicators of strategic development of Tinkoff Bank for 2016–2020.

Indicators	2016	2017	2018	2019	2020
Liquidity indicators					
Current liquidity ratio, once	1,78	1,66	1,45	1,48	1,46
Quick liquidity ratio, once	1,69	1,57	1,38	1,41	1,39
Indicators of financial stability					
Autonomy coefficient, once	0,16	0,18	0,16	0,15	0,13
Sustainable financing ratio, once	0,47	0,42	0,34	0,34	0,34
Business activity indicators					
Asset turnover, once a year	0,27	0,27	0,23	0,23	0,18
Turnover of non-current assets, once a year	5,07	6,57	6,58	6,71	5,69
Efficiency and performance indicators					
Return on total capi-tal (ROA), % per year	7,9	10,4	10,5	9,2	7,1
Return on invested capital (ROIC), % per year	13,6	19,3	21,6	18,9	14,2
Return on equity (ROE), % per year	39,1	48,4	46,9	41,0	34,2
Profitability of all activities, %	23,4	31,7	34,9	28,4	27,1
Risk indicators					
Effect of financial leverage, %	31,2	36,1	38,4	32,7	29,2
Operating leverage effect, once	3,4	2,8	3,9	5,3	9,3

Source: compiled by the authors based on[8].

company's business activity. To assess the efficiency and effectiveness of activities allow indicators of profitability of total capital (ROA), return on invested capital (ROIC), return on equity (ROE), as well as the profitability of all activities. Risk indicators that give its

---

[7]IFRS financial statements. URL: https://www.sber-bank.by/page/financial-statements-IFRS.
[8]Financial statements. URL: https://www.tinkoff.ru/about/investors/11/.

quantitative characteristics are reflected in the effect of financial leverage (financial risk), the effect of operational leverage (production risk).

The values of the current liquidity ratio of Sber for the analyzed period are more than 1,5, which means that current assets are quite enough to pay off short-term accounts payable. Also, during the study period, the quick liquidity ratio is greater than 1,5, therefore, the exclusion of inventories from the current assets does not reduce the company's ability to repay current liabilities. However, liquidity ratios for 2016–2021 tend to decrease, which means a decrease in the share of working capital attributable to one ruble of short-term accounts payable. The dynamics of these ratios are already showing signs of the company's digital transformation.

The values of the financial stability ratios reflect an important characteristic of the company – its work on attracted capital, which, of course, is typical for a banking credit institution. But already from the dynamics of the coefficients of autonomy and sustainable financing, it can be seen that the company is increasing the share of its own capital in the structure of funding sources. The value of the share of funding sources that the company can use in its activities for a long time exceeds 50% over the past three years, therefore, all attention is focused on stable sources of capital and their ratio, which is required for the successful implementation of the transformation strategy.

The turnover of all assets, as well as non-current assets of Sber has been declining over the analyzed period. This situation is determined by the factors of increasing non-circulating capital, which is a necessary condition for the introduction of digital technologies. The decrease in business activity is offset by an increase in the profitability of all activities, which ensures an increase in the profitability of the company's entire capital raised. There is also a positive trend for the analyzed period of return on invested capital and return on equity. Funds invested in the company generate income, thus reflecting the success of the strategy chosen by the company's management.

The effect of financial leverage has a positive value throughout the analyzed period, while its fluctuations are noted, which is due to the unstable dynamics of the financial leverage ratio. In general, it is profitable for the company to work on borrowed capital.

There are jumps in the dynamics of the effect of operational leverage (decrease – increase – decrease). The average value is at the level of 4,5. The use of digital technologies leads to a high level of fixed costs associated with the operation of fixed assets, which means a higher value of operating leverage. The effect of operating leverage is very valuable information. Its growth means the use of new capital-intensive technologies, respectively their use is aimed at obtaining benefits with a possible increase in sales.

The values of the current liquidity ratio of Tinkoff Bank for the analyzed period are more than 1.4, which means that current assets are quite sufficient to cover current liabilities. The value of the quick liquidity ratio for the study period is more than 1,3, that is the exclusion of inventories from the composition of current assets does not fundamentally affect the ability of the remaining part of current assets to repay short-term accounts payable. Nevertheless, the liquidity ratios of Tinkoff Bank for 2016–2020 tend to decrease, which means that the dynamics of these coefficients (by analogy with Sber) reflects signs of the company's digital transformation, which is characterized by an increase in the share of capital allocation in non-current assets.

Based on the dynamics of financial stability ratios, we can conclude that Tinkoff Bank operates on borrowed capital, and throughout the analyzed period, the structure of funding sources does not fundamentally change. At the end of the study period, there is a slight increase in the share of borrowed capital, as evidenced by the dynamics of the coefficients of autonomy and sustainable financing.

The turnover of the company's assets tends to decrease over the analyzed period, while the turnover of non-current assets is stable and only in 2020 is slightly reduced. It can be argued that Tinkoff Bank is distinguished by the rational use of non-current assets, since such a bank operates through a high-tech platform (it does not have branches (offices), bank customers are served remotely). The active use of digital products by the bank (and its clients) is the main factor determining the high turnover of non-current assets (average turnover per year is 5,1).

The business activity of the company, measured by the turnover of funds, is an effective means of maintaining the profitability of capital, invested capital and equity, compensating for a slight decrease in the profitability of all activities, which allows us to state the high efficiency of the strategy implemented by the company's management.

The effect of financial leverage is positive throughout the entire analyzed period, which means that it is profitable for the company to work on borrowed capital.

There is an upward trend in the dynamics of the operating leverage's effect. The average value is at the level of 4,9. The use of digital technologies leads to a high level of fixed costs, which means a higher value of operating leverage.

In this way, the results of the analysis of the IFRS reporting data allow us to state the effectiveness of the transformation strategies' implementation of the analyzed companies. A distinctive feature of the strategies' formation is the use of methods to ensure and maintain efficiency: Sberbank maintains the profitability of operations mainly by increasing the profitability of sales, Tinkoff Bank – by striving to accelerate the turnover of the company's fixed capital.

Further, based on the results of evaluations of the activities of technology companies Sber and Tinkoff Bank, we will justify the choice of indicators that most accurately reflect the results of their strategic development in the digital decision-making process.

7 SUBSTANTIATION OF THE CHOICE OF INDICATORS OF STRATEGIC DEVELOPMENT OF TECHNOLOGY COMPANIES AT DIFFERENT STAGES OF TRANSFORMATION

Indicators used in assessing the strategic development of technology companies include the results of reasons' variety, embracing those not related to the company digital transformation. The most sensitive to changes in the company's activities are liquidity ratios. Among them, the current liquidity ratio stands out. The nature of this indicator attracts attention not only because it is the most accurate indicator of assessing the company's financial stability, but also because the dynamics of this coefficient can be used to trace how the nature of the company's capital investment changes at different stages of its transformation. The study showed that at the stage of active introduction of digital technologies, liquidity ratios, including current liquidity, tend to decrease, which is associated with a decrease in the share of working capital per one ruble of short-term accounts payable. A decrease in the source of covering current liabilities (current asset) may be a consequence of the redistribution of the company's capital for the creation and purchase of non-current assets (digital products).

Also, the turnover ratio of non-current assets is sensitive to ongoing changes in the activities of companies. Moreover, the growth stages of digital transformation will be distinguished by acceleration in the turnover of non-current assets. A decrease in the speed of their turnover is typical for the stage of the digital technologies' introduction in the company.

The effect of operating leverage is very valuable information. Its growth means the use of new capital-intensive technologies, causing a high level of fixed costs associated with the operation of the company's fixed assets.

The scientific and practical tools of modern financial analytics also make it possible to measure the effectiveness of the implementation of a company's transformational strategy in relation to either the amount of advanced resources or the amount of their consumption. In practice there are several criteria for evaluating efficiency. At the same time, the task of finding a universal criterion for evaluating efficiency, reflecting the effectiveness of the implementation of a company's digital product, can be solved by applying the efficiency ratio. This indicator can be defined as the ratio of the turnover's share of the company's base (or new) product in total sales to the calculated share of the company's technological resources spent on the production of the base (or new) product in the company's total costs. The value of the efficiency coefficient equal to one means its full achievement, more than one – high efficiency, less than one – incomplete efficiency (here you can determine the share of the effectiveness of the implementation of a digital product). At the same time, it is important to note that the proposed indicator can also be a controlled model for predicting the company's activities when its technological characteristics change.

8 CONCLUSIONS

Thus, the study showed that among the variety of financial indicators for evaluating the performance of companies, a group of financial analytics indicators stands out, qualitatively reflecting the processes of their digital transformation. Among them the authors of this study identified and substantiated:

- current liquidity ratio;
- turnover of non-current assets;
- the effect of operating leverage;
- an indicator of the effectiveness of activities, and as such, the authors proposed the use of an efficiency ratio and a criterion for its evaluation to reflect the achievement of the goals of implementing transformational strategies.

Such coefficients have the most pronounced properties of revealing the characteristics of technology companies.

In addition, the study will allow the management of technology companies, as well as its key stakeholders to make more informed decisions aimed at high-quality strategic development.

ACKNOWLEDGEMENT

The research was conducted on the equipment of the Research Equipment Sharing Center of Kemerovo State University, agreement No. 075-15-2021-694 dated August 5, 2021, between the Ministry of Science and Higher Education of the Russian Federation (Minobrnauka) and Kemerovo State University (KemSU) (contract identifier RF——2296.61321X0032).

REFERENCES

Brigham, Y., Gapensky, L. 2001. St. Petersburg: School of Economics. *Financial Management. Complete course in 2 volumes* 1166.

Brealey, R., Myers, S. 2004. M.: Olimp-Business. *Principles of Corporate Finance* 1008.

Damodaran, A. 2006. M.: Alpina Business Books. *Investment Valuation: Tools and Methods for Valuation of any Assets* 1341.

Kvint, V.L. 2014. St. Petersburg: North-Western Institute of Management – branch of the RANEPA. *Strategizing in the modern world* 52.

Kvint, V.L. 2012. M.: Business Atlas. *Strategic Management and Economics in a Global Emerging Market* 627.

Kvint, V.L. 2020. Kemerovo: Kemerovo State University. *Concept of Strategizing: Monograph* 170.

Kamordzhanova, N.A. 2015. M.: Prospect. *Development of an Integrated Accounting and Reporting System: Methodology and practice* 35.

Ross, S. 2001. M.: Basic knowledge laboratory. *Fundamentals of Corporate Finance* 720.

Sheremet, A. D., Saifulin, R. S., Negashev, E. V. 2000. M.: INFRA-M. *Methodology of Financial Analysis* 98.

Sokolova, Y.V. 2018. M.: INFRA-M. *Accounting (Financial) Reporting* 431.

Teplova, T.V. 2019. M.: Urayt Publishing House. *Effective CFO* 507.

Teplova, T.V. 2019. M.: Urayt Publishing House. *Corporate Finance* 390.

Van Horn, D., Vakhovich, D. 2011. M.: Williams. *Fundamentals of Financial Management* 1232.

Economic and Business Management – Lent & Zhang (Eds)

Employees conduct vs private interests: Prosecution vs values

B. Lent
University of Science and Technology, Bydgoszcz, Poland
Bern University of Applied Sciences, Bern, Switzerland

ABSTRACT: The aim of this paper is to present an analysis and findings related to the pursue of the covert private benefits extortion, based on the secondary data evaluation. Discursion has been paired with intuition. Whereas there is certain negative relation between the ranking in the corruption perception index and wealth, an individual behavior is rather conditioned by the cultural value systems and human brain operation. The last results in rather emotion than ratio based decisions. This hypothesis has been discursively elaborated. Paper concludes that the deliberate development of the moral standards and social group values, may be considered to be the only efficient and sustainable solution to the problem.

1 INTRODUCTION

Most of employees get hired to satisfy their basic need: shelter and nutrition. In return for their loyal work to the benefit of the company, they are remunerated along the mutually agreed contract.

Yet in many cases the remunerations are one-sided, often to the loss of the employer, "improved" by the employee himself.

Societies and organizations recognized the highly devastating social and economic impact of the pathologies in procurements and corruptive unauthorized use of social groups resource (e.g. Ivanyna et al. 2021; Jain A.K. 2012; Lagarde Chr. 2016). Public and private sector created numerous variations of the Code of Conduct which regulates the behavior atop the law, usually being part of the agreed contract. Violation of any term of the contract or Code of Conduct is variously treated: From mitigation of the risk up to the prosecution, in some cases even lethal penalty (Transparency International 2022). Yet this global problem exists ever since we developed first social groups, some 200'000–300'000 years ago (Singh M & Glowacki L 2022). The costs of mitigation are substantial and yet it cannot cover all possible risks – the criminal creativity knows no limits (Van Prooijen JW & Van Lange PAM 2016). Prosecution is effective, if socially actively supported by the witnesses. The main problem remains as long, as an employee values his personal and family benefits higher than the obligations towards his/her employer and agreed regulations. We are proud of truly few examples of altruists, who reverse those values and act accordingly; vast majority of the societies and individuals put personal and family interests first. The sensitivity on both sides is demanded: The regulations set up by the society, extending the legal base on one side, defining to the excess, which cases are not allowed, and personal perception development: is my handling crossing any limits? The necessity of improved sensitivity and awareness of any wrongdoing stretches from unqualified employee up to the highest echelons in both, private and public sector (resignation of the Austrian Chancellor in December 2021 amid corruptive use of public funds). The mitigation and prosecution measures proved to be ineffective. In this paper the source of the malicious behavior is identified and the sustainable measures with a potential improvement are proposed.

DOI: 10.1201/9781003278788-31

2   RESEARCH METHODOLOGY

The research question originated from the authors encounters and observations in different cultures. Even the death penalty in several countries does not improve the ranking in the corruption perception index CPI over the years. Same time the countries with the highest ranking in the CPI expose relatively low punitive measures (Transparency International 2022). Jong-sung and Khagram (2004) concluded that the income inequality increases corruption: The richer are more corruptive. So the research question is: What are the determinants of the private benefits extortion? The answer has been sought through the discursive research design. The starting point was the intuitive assumption, that there has to be a determinant of the human behavior, which is not directly related to the incomes and general society wealth. The secondary data analysis has been conducted, following the two criteria: relation of the corruption to the wealth and to the culture. The last has been further analyzed with respect to the individual value systems and its impact on behavior. The synthesis of the secondary data analyses led to the verification of the hypothesis that the covert private benefits extortion has a cultural background and is genetically conditioned across all cultures. The covert nature of the corruptive behavior excluded the experimental methods in this research.

3   CULTURAL AND GENETIC BACKGROUND OF PUTTING PRIVATE INTERESTS FIRST

When the first social groups, which consisted of the members of multiple families, went on hunting, they had to agree, best before the hunting, how the prey shall be divided among the hunters. These were the origins of value systems, which form the first moral norms and thus led to the development of the culture. Da Deppo (2015) defines culture as system of general principles adopted by a social group to regulate the way of meeting its basic needs. Basic needs consist of instinctive-needs (self-survival and reproduction) and cultural needs. Both provided by the group. Thus, culture is an attribute of a group, comprises shared and articulated values, philosophies, laws, religions, traditions, further standards as well as unsaid mental models, decision patterns and linguistic paradigms (Schein 2010). Individuals, who share this common culture, internalize the group values as personal values.

The individual behaves morally, if he acts along his ethics. This means that there is a causal heuristic relationship between the one's own values and his or her attitude and handling.

The end of the XX century brought substantial crisis in the values in western societies. Helgadottir (2008) experimentally verified four ethical models in six project groups. Two models based on the Ethics of Achievement: The Value Ethics (moral perfectionism), originating from Plato, Aristoteles and Sokrates and the Utilitarian Ethic of Success, identified by Humes, Bentham and Mill. The other two models referred to the so-called Procedural Ethics: The Ethics of Duty, prominently exposed by Kant, and the Contractual Ethics of natural laws (human rights) of Hobbs. All six groups aligned their ethical preferences along the Aristoteles Value Ethics of Achievement, rather than defended the Kant Ethics of Duty, which corresponded with the social group oriented interaction within those groups. "Preach what you pray" was and is not vastly practiced. Szutta (2007) confirms, in a fact sad, discrepancy between the "Business" handling of managers in their professional environment (Ethics of Achievement) and private behaviors, where the same individual pursues the Kant Ethics of Duty towards his or her children. One's ethic has to have only one system of values. So, one of the behaviors: Business, or private, is immoral. However, most of humans are unaware about the dichotomy in their values and their behavior, and consider themselves perfectly fine with this despairing attitude.

In emerging economies, and to higher extend in the ailing economies, the Da Deppo definition of the culture and of an individual, who strive to satisfy both his instinctive and cultural needs, wins even in significance. There is certain relation between the wealth of the society and corruption perception index. Denmark, GDP 67803 US$ per capita in 2021 (Trading Economics 2022), has repeatedly the highest score in corruption perception index (means perceived as the least corruptive nation, Transparency International 2022). South Sudan with GDP just 700 US$ per capita (Trading Economics 2022) has the lowest score, Somalia, second lowest (Ministry of Justice and Judical Affairs: Federal Government of Somalia, 2022) in the same classification reached GDP of 446 US$ per capita in 2021. The consumer goods are more or less within the same range in both countries. So the temptation to cross the values and laws increases with the decrease of the GDP value almost linearly. Ivanyna (Ivanyna et al. 2021) sees corruption as the failure of government, who ignore the public welfare in favor of narrow private interest.

Often, the Utilitarian Ethics of Success of large social groups and societies might be a source of conflict for an individual, which might even attempt the same Utilitarian Ethics of Success, however, much narrowly pursued for the personal and family benefits. The hierarchy of values is here in question: Is the success of my group more important than my individual or family success, or opposite? Often, an individual, even conscious of the group values, laws and norms, does not recognize, that his behavior contradicts the group value system, while subconsciously pursuing the values of private success and benefit.

The preference for the family benefits amid moral dilemma is, at least partially conditioned, by our neural brain operation. The cognitive part of cortex (where the values are evaluated) vote with amygdale cells (where emotions are placed) on any decision making (Beck 2017). As amygdale cells are usually stronger and better developed, our decisions are in most cases determined by our emotions, even if we claim to act deliberately. So it is understandable, that in weighting the values: What is good and what is bad?, the emotional bonds takes upper hand and we rather stretch our understanding of honesty and correctness towards our employer in favor of some benefits for those, emotionally close to us, than scarify family interest to the benefit of the group.

4 INEFFICIENCY OF LEGAL ANTI-CORRUPTION MEASURES

Negative impact of the illegal covert private benefits extortion on the economy and society is vastly recognized and documented (e.g. Ivanyna et al. 2021, Jain A.K. 2012; Lagarde Chr. 2016).

The governments, amid international transparency of economy and perceived corruption, attempt more (developed economies) or less (emerging and ailing economies) to counterpart the pathology and occurrence of corruptive behaviors.

Whereas in Denmark (Highest Corruption Perception Index, rank 1) the highest penalty for corruption violation is 6 years imprisonment (Schmith P. 2019), South Sudan, governed since 1998 by Sharia law (Constitution 1998) foresee the capital penalty for corruption (only recently limited to 7 years under the international pressure the maximum imprisonment (Dut 2019).

The national bodies, listed in Table 1, publish number of prosecuted cases. The statistics does not change significantly over the years, indicating that the source of malicious behavior has not been rooted out by the purgative means.

Prosecution in case of any violation might be devastating for one. Yet, the overall mitigation of the violation of contracts, and the control mechanisms in the developed economies are significantly reduced, as compared to the countries still on the way to their prosperity. And last not least: even the most rigorous legal systems serve their purpose as long as those, put in charge of their implementation, duly fulfill their task. This is aversely related to the rigidity of the law and the rank of the country in the corruption perception index (see

Table 1. The relation between the authority to prosecute of national control institutions and corruption perception in the selected countries (compiled from various sources: a.o. Denmark Folketinget Rigsrevisionen, 2021, Swiss Federal Audit Office, 2021).

Country	2020 Corruption Perception		Control institution	Number of detected law violations 2020	Number per 1 Mio. Inhabitants	Authority to prosecute
	Index	Rank				
Denmark	88	1	Folketinget Rigsrevisionen	0	0	no
Switzerland	85	3	Eidgenössiche Finanzkontrolle	0	0	no
Finnland	85	3	Valtiontalouden tarkastusvirasto	0	0	no
China	42	78	National Supervisory Commission	101	0.1	yes
Czech Republic	54	49	Najvyssi kontrolni urad	4	0.37	no
New Zeal-and	88	1	Serious Fraud Office	3*)	1.8	yes
Poland	56	45	Najwyzsza Izba Kontroli	102	2.7	no**)
France	69	23	Cour des comptes	220	3.4	yes
Somalia	12	179	National Anti-Corruption Commis.	88***)	5.9	yes
Italy	53	52	Corte dei Conti	869	14.7	yes
South Sudan	11	180	South Sudan Anti-Corruption Com.	n.a.	n.a.	yes

*) Arbitrary allocation of the six cases 2019 and 2020 acc. to the report of the SFO 15.07.2020. Two for party donations, the others against private organisations (New Zealand Serious Fraud Office 2021).
**) In proces of acquiring.
***) Data from WorldData (2022), no report from Somalia agency recorded.

Somalia & Ronan 2017). However, as the corruption may be adversely related to the general society wealth, Jong-sung and Khagram (2017) prove that it is rather the inequality within the social group leading to private benefits extortion primarily by rich, who has more opportunities. Therefore, developing the ethical values seems to be a more efficient and more sustainable way, rather than the mitigation of misbehaviors and extended controlling.

5 SOCIAL VALUE SYSTEMS DEVELOPMENT AS A SUSTAINABLE SOLUTION

Sustainable solution, in view of the author, may be achieved solely by the development of social value systems. The value systems lay down the foundations of the group ethics, which in turn belongs to the society culture, putting the values of a group over the family values. This process is difficult and may take generations; Over thousands of years, we cultivate the family as the basic and for the society most relevant social group. Certainly, the general society wealth and living conditions of an individuals impact this process. Yet the societies, which managed to align the group and individual values, getting the individuals to behave along those values, expose in general the higher corruption perception index (less corruption perceived). The lesser corruption leads to higher economy development levels, what proves that this may work. Best example is, dominated by the Chinese, family oriented, ethnic group (74.3 %) Singapore, which achieved 2021 the Corruption Perception Index 85, Rank 4 (Transparency International 2021), and the GNP per capita of US $ 106.969 (World Economics 2022).

Africa is the continent with the majority of the ailing economies. Liberated vastly in 1950 and 1960-ties, was encouraged to enter the western path of economic principles (Mankiw 2020). After more than five decades of the efforts, one has to recognize, that purely neo-liberal economy guidelines do not work. S. Ntibagirirwa (2009) advocate to include and develop the economic policies on the historical-cultural background of African context. Ntibagirirwa calls the relevance of the cultural values in economic growth, the "Ubuntu economy": State, markets and people are all agent and not the subjects of the economic growth.

Cultural value system changes are a tedious process, which demands certain continuity and persistence (Sifakis, 2022). Yet, in view of the author, it is the only way to combat sustainably the corruption.

6 CONCLUSIONS

The fight with the corruption is the duty of government. Even the most sophisticated and draconic anti-corruption laws do not prevent efficiently the corruption. To various extend the humans charged with the duty of preventing the corruption jeopardize the law enforcement.

Although there is a negative relation between the wealth and corruption perception index, the rich individuals in the wealthy economies are more prone to private benefits extortions, than those with lower incomes. It is rather the social disparity between rich and poor that impacts the corruption: the bigger disparity, the private extortion is likely to occur.

The preference of one's own and his closest relatives' gains over general society benefits origins from our genetically inherited, emotionally conditioned, universal decision-making.

Only personal value system, derived from the group values, which put the society common values over immediate personal gains, can curb sustainably the corruptive behaviors. This, however, requires the understanding that the personal gains may be reached through the overall general society gains. The process, which will take generations.

Author is conscious the postulate nature of this paper. Exposing the relationship between the economic growth and corruption, modelling the society value systems are important and invaluable tasks for both, the science and social groups.

The gratitude is expressed to the Conference Organizers and Reviewers for granting the author with the opportunity to enhance the paper and present the above research.

REFERENCES

Beck, H., 2017, *Irren ist nützlich: Warum die Schwächen des Gehirns unsere Stärken sind*, Munich: Carl Hanser Verlag, Constitution of the Republic of Sudan, 1998, https://ihl-databases.icrc.org/applic/ihl/ihl-nat.nsf/0/d728f18be88d9482c1256dc600507f33/$FILE/Constitution%20Sudan%20-%20EN.pdf accessed September 17, 2022.

Da Deppo S., 2015. *Reaching Intercultural Capability – a Team Achievement*, Prezi, Brussels.

Denmark Folketinget Rigsrevisionen, 2021, *Annual Report and Accounts 2020*, https://uk.rigsrevisionen.dk/Media/637571085389659367/Annual-report-2020.pdf accessed September 18, 2022.

Dut A.M.D. 2019. *Criminal Justice Response to Corruption in South Sudan*, https://www.unafei.or.jp/publications/pdf/RS_No98/No98_IP_South_Sudan.pdf accessed September 17, 2022.

Helgadottir, H., 2008. The Ethical Dimension of Project Management, *International Journal of Project Management* v 26 (2008) Elsevier, pp. 743–748.

Ivanyna, M., Mourmouras, A, Rangazas, P. 2021. *The Macroeconomics of Corruption: Governance and Growth*. Cham: Springer Nature Switzerland.

Jain, A.K., 2012. *Economics of Corruption*, Berlin/Heidelberg: Springer Science+Business Media, LLC

Jong-sung Y, Khagram S, 2004. *A Comparative Study of Inequality and Corruption*, Harvard University, J.F. Kennedy School of Government.

Lagarde, Chr., 2016. *Addressing Corruption Openly*, Washington: IMF.

Mankiw N.G., 2020. *Essentials of Economics*, Boston: Cengage Learning Inc.

Ministry of Justice and Judical Affairs: Federal Government of Somalia, 2022. *Anti-Corruption and Post-Conflict Environment: Lessons of Somalia*, https://www.unodc.org/documents/treaties/UNCAC/COSP/session9/special-events/15_Making_progress_in_the_integrity.pdf accessed September 17, 2022.

New Zealand Serious Fraud Office, 2021. https://sfo.govt.nz/assets/Uploads/Annual-Report-2020-web.pdf accessed September 18, 2022.

Ntibagirirwa S., 2009, Cultural Values, Economic Growth and Development, in *Journal of Business Ethics* 84:297–311, Cham: Springer Nature

Ronan, K., 2017. *Somalia: Overview of Corruption and Anti-Corruption*, Oslo: CMI Norway, https://www.alnap.org/system/files/content/resource/files/main/somalia-overview-corruption-and-anticorruption.pdf accessed September 17, 2022.

Schein E.H., 2010. *Organizational Culture and Leadership*, Wiley, San Francisco.

Schmith, P. 2019. *Anti-corruption and Bribery Penalties in Denmark*, Anti-corruption and bribery penalties in Denmark – Lexology Accessed September 17, 2022.

Sifakis J. 2022. Value Systems and Society in Understanding and Changing the World. *From Information to Knowledge and Intelligence*. Springer.

Singh M., Glowacki, L. 2022. *Human Social Organization During the Late Pleistocene: Beyond the nomadic-egalitarian model*, Evolution and Human Behavior Vol.43, No 5, Elsevier, pp.418–431.

Swiss Federal Audit Office, 2021, *Jahresbericht 2020*, https://www.efk.admin.ch/images/stories/efk_dokumente/publikationen/jahresberichte/2020/CDF_RA_2020_DE_web.pdf accessed September 18, 2022.

Szutta, N., 2007. *Współczesna etyka cnót, Gdansk*: Wydawnictwo: Uniwersytetu Gdańskiego.

The State Council The People's Republic of China, 2021. *Implementation Rules for China's Supervision Law Take Effect*, http://english.www.gov.cn/news/topnews/202109/21/content_WS614915f6c6d0df57f98e09c6.html accessed September 18, 2022.

Trading Economics, 2022. https://tradingeconomics.com/ accessed September 4, 2022.

Transparency International, 2022. *Corruption Perception Index*, 2021 Corruption Perceptions Index – Explore the … – Transparency.org , accessed September 4, 2022.

Van Prooijen JW, van Lange PAM, 2016. *Cheating, Corruption and Concealment, The roots of Dishonesty*, Cambridge: Cambridge University Press.

WorldData, 2022, *Corruption in Somalia*, https://www.worlddata.info/africa/somalia/corruption.php accessed September 17, 2022.

World Economics, 2022. *Singapore's GDP PPP per Capita*, https://www.worldeconomics.com/Wealth/Singapore.aspx#:~:text=The%20population%20of%20Singapore%20is%20estimated%20to%20be,options%20to%20allow%20easy%20comparison%20with%20other%20countries accessed September 17, 2022.

Economic and Business Management – Lent & Zhang (Eds)
© 2023 the Author(s), ISBN 978-1-032-24482-2

Affiliation research on enterprise credit risk evaluation and influencing factors with data mining

Jun Ren

Wenzhou Business College, Wenzhou, China

ABSTRACT: The importance of enterprise credit risk assessment is growing, and with the advent of digital economy, the explosion of social information has also spawned many credit data. Therefore, this paper evaluates the credit risk of enterprises based on the integrity behaviour and credit ability data of 292 enterprises. Based on the idea of data-driven, this paper evaluates the overall enterprise credit environment score from the macro and micro perspectives for the credit environment data. Choose an adaptive weighting method to evaluate the integrity behaviour of enterprises, and combined with improved support vector machine, data envelopment analysis and other methods to explore the fac-tors that affect the credit ability of enterprises. The k-nearest neighbor support vector machine model has high stability and prediction ability for enterprise credit ability; Enterprises can be divided into four categories according to their integrity behaviour and credit ability.

1   INTRODUCTION

The market transaction becomes more and more complex as the market economy develops, and the knowledge asymmetry between the two parties becomes more and more problematic (Tong et al. 2022). The analysis and research of enterprise credit can help to find the potential business risks and financial risks in the operation and management activities of enterprises and can effectively and quickly understand the basic credit of enterprises in the bidding link (Wang et al. 2019). In the specific bidding link, it is difficult for the tendered to understand the bidder's information. A thorough assessment of an enterprise's capacity and creditworthiness to fulfil a range of obligations is also helpful for the improvement of the enterprise's own credit management capabilities and the efficient growth of the latter. This study integrates the evaluation of the external credit environment with that of the internal enterprise credit ability and integrity behaviour to carry out a multi-dimensional evaluation of bidding enterprise credit. It also enhances the research framework of enterprise evaluation.

The following are this paper's primary innovations: First, this work uses bidding enterprises as the research object, in contrast to the previous literature on credit risk evaluation, which primarily uses the traditional financial industry as its research object. Credit ratings can help the bidder accurately and completely understand the enterprise's strength and financial situation, which can be used as a benchmark for bid evaluation and selection and lower potential risks associated with cooperative relationships. The project management capability of the bidding enterprise and the quality data of the personnel at all levels of the enterprise are also added considering the enterprise credit ability monitoring index system, in addition to the enterprise debt paying ability, enterprise profitability, and enterprise capital strength. A maximum number of indicators are chosen from each dimension to increase the breadth and depth of the bidding enterprise's credit ability monitoring. Third, the identification of enterprise credit risk does not select a single model that fits the data; rather, it combines LASSO-logistic model (Man et al. 2018), forwards and backwards logistic model comparison, and support vector machine prediction to provide the best prediction fitting model. Data from each aspect of the enterprise were filtered and fitted before DEA model analysis to remove the interference of multicollinearity. Following the clustering of enterprises, a detailed study of the data for each type of business is conducted to examine the influencing factors and potential areas for improvement in their credit ability.

The study is divided into three sections: the first section examines the bidding credit environment, constructs the method for evaluating the macro external credit environment and the micro credit topic environment, and computes the bidding enterprise credit environment index; In the second section, the enterprises taking part in the bidding and bidding are ranked following the assessment of the integrity behaviour, and the price of the evaluation of the integrity behaviour of micro enterprises eliminates the enterprises whose integrity behaviour is below the standard; The third section looks into the constancy of credit ability and honest business practices of enterprises that act honestly.

2 CREDIT ENVIRONMENT ASSESSMENT

2.1 *Construction of credit environment index system*

This study examines the assessment index system considering the definition of the credit environment and the actual evolution of the bidding environment (Luo & Tan 2017; Zhang 2019; Liu et al. 2019). The establishment of an index system for the following is based on the availability and efficacy of the data while also considering the social environment, government regulation of the macro external credit environment, enterprise bidding credit environment, and social acceptance of the micro credit body environment.

2.2 *Credit environment index calculation*

The primary techniques for evaluating the credit environment that are frequently employed are the fuzzy comprehensive assessment approach, the analytic hierarchy process, and others (Guo et al. 2019; Yu & Li 2019). The objective weighting method is adopted since the subjective weighting method is too time-consuming and subjective to weigh environmental factors. As a result, the norm grey relation approach is used to calculate the index's weight. Prior to determining the weight and score of the index layer, the data for each index are handled evenly and without regard to dimensions. The weight and score of the criterion layer are determined in the same manner. The weighted summary is created to calculate the index for the bidding credit environment. The calculation for the bidding credit environment index from 2016 to 2018 is provided in Table 1 based on the stages.

Table 1. Credit environment index of bidding.

	2016	2017	2018
Score	88.99	84.87	94.51

That the better the credit environment, the more enterprises into the bidding process. Taking 292 bidding enterprises as an example, the bidding credit environment index in 2018 was 94.51, which was significantly higher than the credit environment in the previous two years, and it was considered that the credit environment in 2018 was better.

3 ENTERPRISE INTEGRITY BEHAVIOUR EVALUATION

3.1 *Determination of index weight based on global sensitivity*

Based on the integrity of 292 bidding enterprises to determine whether enterprises can enter the bidding link. Sensitivity analysis, which can be further separated into local sensitivity and global sensitivity, focuses on the extent to which input random variables in the model influence the quantity of the output response. The uncertainty of the input variables' effects on the output response variables can be fully reflected by global sensitivity. Weight assignment makes use of global sensitivity analysis, which takes the index weight as an input, determines the index weight's global sensitivity based on the variance of each index weight of the evaluation.

3.2 *Analysis of enterprise integrity behaviour*

3.2.1 *Scores and rankings of enterprise integrity behaviour*
Use the formula: credit behaviour score = evaluation value *100. The comprehensive evaluation value of credit behaviour of 292 enterprises was calculated.

There is a significant discrepancy between the scores of the enterprises based on the credit behaviour score data. Screening out the 292 enterprises with bad credit behaviour is important to assess the remaining enterprises before conducting a more thorough investigation of the bidders' credit capabilities.

3.2.2 *Business integrity score division*
The clustering approach can get rid of the underqualified enterprises. The hard clustering algorithm, which maximizes the objective function, may clearly separate items into several categories, but it does not permit ambiguous outcomes. However, after evaluating several clustering algorithms, the soft clustering approach based on mixed Gaussian model is chosen since the credit score of enterprises in the credit division exhibits complexity and diversity.

The results of clustering the 292 enterprises are displayed in Table 2.

Table 2. Clustering results of Gaussian mixture model.

category	1	2	3	4	5	6	7	8	9
The number	21	23	32	13	80	15	70	31	7

The enterprise with the poorest integrity behaviour also has the lowest integrity score, according to the approach of identifying unqualified enterprises by integrating the clustering outcomes of the Gaussian mixture model with the score of enterprise integrity behaviour. As a result, the last group of enterprises designated as having integrity falls short of what would be considered appropriate. The remaining 285 enterprises were determined to be enterprises with good faith after the 7 enterprises were eliminated.

Additionally, it identifies the seventh and eighth types of enterprises—those with low integrity behaviour—as the two types that require severe supervision. The seventh group contains 70 enterprises altogether. The categorization findings are totally consistent with the integrity scores of 39 enterprises, or 55.71% of the enterprise clustering results are consistent with the integrity behaviour score ranking, according to the enterprise integrity score. The remaining 31 enterprises are divided into 14 that go under category 6, 15 that fall under category 5, and 1 that falls under category 4. Clustering outcomes in the eighth category, there are 31 enterprises, 27 of which are consistent with the integrity behaviour score.

4 ENTERPRISE CREDIT ABILITY EVALUATION

4.1 *Enterprise credit ability assessment*

Further study is required to determine whether there is a consistent association between the credit ability index system of enterprises and the credit behaviour score because the credit behaviour of enterprises is assessed in the research mentioned above (Zhang & Chen, 2018).

Some academics may believe that there is little difference between honest behaviour and credit ability when the concept is extended, however this cognitive error frequently lowers the reliability and accuracy of pertinent research findings. In its traditional sense, good faith behaviour emphasizes self-cultivation, but as the market economy system has developed, good faith has come to emphasize the social norm of "truthfulness without deception, compliance with the agreement, practice the promise, and pay attention to the credit," with the spirit of the contract serving as the fundamental component of credit. Credit is based on integrity, which is a type of willingness and a type of competence. Theoretically, a contract's good faith performance is consistent with its ability to pay; that is, the better the performance, the better the ability to pay, and vice versa.

The monitoring index system used to gauge a bidder's creditworthiness uses the enterprise's overall creditworthiness as its primary aim, with the enterprise credit value and enterprise credit evaluation serving as its sub-targets. The final index used to evaluate enterprise integrity is the score of behaviour. The first-level indicators are among the sub-objectives of enterprise credit value, enterprise quality, project management, guarantee ability, and operation ability. On this foundation, the secondary index and the final index were listed, further describing the system. However, the index system was later changed taking data availability into account, and the enterprise credit ability evaluation index system was finally displayed in Table 3.

4.1.1 *Model introduction*

1. Support vector machine
   To meet the goal of getting appropriate statistical rules even when the statistical sample size is small, Support Vector Machine (SVM) seeks to minimize structural risk, realizes the minimizing of empirical risk, and realizes the minimization of confidence range (Zhao & Bo 2022).
2. Dual membership fuzzy support vector machine
   In the dual membership support vector machine, the sample set form is

$$z = \left\{ z_i^A = (x_i, y_i, \mu_i^A), z_i^B = (x_i, y_i, \mu_i^B), \mu_i^A + \mu_i^B = 1, i = 1, \cdots, l \right\}$$

   The basic model of dual membership fuzzy support vector machine is

$$\min_{\omega, b} = \frac{1}{2} ||\omega||^2 + C \sum_{i=1}^{l} (\mu_i^A \xi_i + \mu_i^B \eta_i)$$

$$\omega^T \varnothing(x_i) + b \geq 1 - \xi_i$$
$$s.t. \quad \omega^T \varnothing(x_i) + b \leq \eta_{i-1}$$
$$\mu_i^A + \mu_i^B = 1$$

$$\mu_i^A \geq 0, \mu_i^B \geq 0, \xi_i \geq 0, \eta_i \geq 0, i = 1, 2, \cdots, l$$

3. KSVM algorithm
   An enhanced SVM-KNN approach called KSVM has been put out to address the SVM's uncertainty in the classification of unbalanced data near a hyperplane. Support vectors

Table 3. Credit ability index system of bidding enterprises.

Subgoals	Target layer	Rule layer	Index layer	
Enterprise integrity assessment	Enterprise integrity monitoring	Corporate integrity behavior	Enterprise integrity behavior score	X1
Enterprise credit value	Enterprise quality	Quality of management personnel	Legal person/project leader with the highest degree	D1
			Legal person/project leader highest technical title	D2
		Quality of employees	Number of Class I Registered Builders as a percentage of registered personnel	X2
			Number of Class II Registered builders as a percentage of registered persons	X3
		Enterprise qualification	Set up the year	X4
			Main item qualification and additional item qualification	D3
			The main qualification level	D4
	The project management	Project management quality	Engineering award	X5
			Enterprise honor	X6
	Support capability	Personnel security	The number of registered	X7
			Contributors in	X8
			Original value of fixed assets	X9
			Where the original value of mechanical equipment	X10
		Technical support	Qualification qualification	D5
			Number of Qualification Certificates	X11
			Intellectual property rights	X12
	Ability to operate	Capital strength	The registered capital	X13
			Contributed capital	X14
		collateral	Chattel mortgage	X15
			Equity pledge	X16
			Property rights pledge	X17

can be used by SVM in place of training sample sets to learn classification, which can shorten training times while maintaining classification accuracy. The fundamental tenet of KSVM is that SVM only uses one representative point for each class of support vectors, and that representative point may not always accurately represent that class. It is used with KNN in this instance to use all the support vectors for each class as representative points, increasing the classification accuracy of the classifier.

4.1.2 Model application

1. Build test set and training set
   Information from 285 enterprises is distributed in a 3:1 ratio between the training set and the test set to properly examine and understand the results of model fitting. The comparative test compares the discrimination accuracy of the KSVM model, the double membership degree SVM model, and the traditional SVM model.
2. Model parameter selection
   The two most important variables in the support vector machine model are C and gamma. C stands for the penalty coefficient, or error tolerance. The error is more

intolerant the greater the value. The 22 indicators of enterprise credit value are taken as independent variables, and the honest behaviour of enterprises in the previous part is taken as the dependent variable, represented by the dummy variable Y, Y = 1, indicating that the honest behaviour of enterprises is very excellent, and Y = −1, indicating that the honest behaviour of enterprises is still insufficient. When determining the best combination of parameters, the search range of C is {5,10,15,20,25}, and the search range of gamma is {10-3, 10-2, 10-1}, see Table 4.

Table 4.   Selection table of model optimization parameter combination.

gamma C	5	10	15	20	25
10-3	0.625	0.653	0.653	0.639	0.611
10-2	0.653	0.694	0.681	0.653	0.667
10-1	0.639	0.611	0.611	0.639	0.625

Finally, the radial basis kernel function with C = 2 and gamma = 0.1 as parameters was selected as the kernel function of dual-membership fuzzy support vector machine. The radial basis kernel function with C = 10 and gamma = 0.01 was used as the kernel function of traditional support vector machine.

3. Analysis of model results

Classification accuracy, or the percentage of properly identified samples in all samples, is typically employed as the evaluation metric in conventional classification learning techniques. It is not fair to gauge the effectiveness of classifiers using classification accuracy for data sets that are unbalanced. There are new evaluation standards for the imbalance problem, including F-value, G-mean, and other techniques, see Table 5.

Table 5.   Confusion matrix of the two types of problems.

Classification	The actual positive class	The actual negative class
Divided into positive class	TP	FP
Divided into negative class	FN	TN

$F - value$ is a classification evaluation index that comprehensively considers recall and precision. $G - mean$ represents the geometric mean of the classification accuracy of minority class and majority class:

The discrimination accuracy of the model test set is determined using the parameters chosen for the three models, and the results are displayed in the following Tables 6–9.

The classification accuracy of classic SVM is the weakest and the misjudgment rate is the highest, as shown by the findings in Table 10, with an overall accurate rate of only 70.04%. The upgraded dual-membership fuzzy support vector machine has a comparatively greater

Table 6.   Comparison of classification accuracy of models.

	Traditional SVM	Dual membership fuzzy SVM	KSVM
Overall error rate	29.96%	27.02%	18.95%
Overall accuracy rate	70.04%	72.98%	81.05%

Table 7. Confusion matrix of two types of traditional SVM problems.

Classification	The actual positive class	The actual negative class	total
Divided into positive class	82	23	105
Divided into negative class	51	129	180
total	133	152	285

Table 8. Confusion matrix of two types of problems of dual membership fuzzy SVM.

Classification	The actual positive class	The actual negative class	total
Divided into positive class	85	29	114
Divided into negative class	48	123	171
total	133	152	285

Table 9. Confusion matrix of two types of KSVM problems.

Classification	The actual positive class	The actual negative class	total
Divided into positive class	99	20	119
Divided into negative class	34	132	166
total	133	152	285

Table 10. Enterprise input and output index data.

Enterprise	Output	Input			
	Enterprise honesty Y1	Operation ability Z1	Enterprise quality Z2	Assurance ability Z3	Project management Z4
** Construction Co. LTD	0.915	0.346	1.044	0.272	0.1
** Landscape Group Co. LTD	0.923	3.056	1.621	1.586	0.203
** Engineering Co. LTD	0.851	2.416	1.594	1.664	0.1
… …	… …	… …		… …	… …

accuracy and misjudgment rate; its accurate rate is 2.94 percentage points higher than that of the conventional SVM, at 72.98%. The upgraded KSVM model has the highest overall accuracy (81.05%), 11.01 percentage points greater than the accuracy of the conventional SVM and 8.07% higher than the accuracy of the dual-membership fuzzy SVM. The best result from the right rate of classification comes from KSVM, which also supports the fact that the sample data of organizations does really have the issue of unbalanced data. The KSVM model can increase the proper recognition rate of enterprise integrity behaviour and credit ability consistency discrimination and lessen the misjudgment brought on by harsh discrimination.

The overall classification accuracy rate can nearly verify the overall classification situation, so further considering from $F-value$ and $G-mean$, the traditional SVM, dual membership fuzzy SVM and KSVM .. are 68.91%, 68.83% and 78.57%, respectively, and the

G-mean is 72.34%, 71.91% and 80.40%, respectively. KSVM outperforms traditional SVM and dual membership fuzzy SVM in terms of minority classification performance and overall classification performance. It can be considered that the KSVM is more suitable for enterprise sample data.

4.2 Enterprise credit efficiency

The credit ability evaluation of the tendering enterprises is further empirically investigated in this paper using the data envelopment analysis (DEA) method, and the evaluation results are clustered and the credit rating status of the tendering enterprises is determined using the K-means clustering algorithm.

Based on referring to relevant literature and combining the credit characteristics of bidding enterprises, this paper constructs DEA input and output indicators from the perspective of input-output.

4.2.1 Selection of input and output indicators

The enterprise credit system is made up of enterprise credit, enterprise quality, project management, guarantee ability, and operation ability because enterprise credit ability is based on enterprise credit behaviour, and the two are consistent. Enterprise integrity is selected by the output index. The elements of enterprise quality, project management, guarantee ability, and operation ability should be reflected in the input index of enterprise credit. To determine the efficiency of the enterprise, choose the important index variables. enterprises can be successfully categorized using the DEA model by grading their comprehensive efficiency.

4.2.2 Sample selection and data sources

The discrepancy of amount units across different indicators would result in unsatisfactory data analysis outcomes during the analysis process because of the vast number of input indicators in this article. Additionally, as the DEA technique is more sensitive to the choice of indicators utilizing units, there should be as little variation in data from different indicators as possible. To determine the value of each input index, it is then thought to build the weight of each variable under the same input index using principal component analysis.

4.3 Enterprise classification

4.3.1 Comprehensive efficiency analysis

Comprehensive efficiency is a crucial metric for assessing the production unit's scale rationality, allocation capacity, and utilization efficiency. If the efficiency number is 1, it means that the production unit can operate at the best size and with the most efficient use of resources. If the comprehensive efficiency rating is less than 1, it means that further optimization is necessary to address issues with resource duplication, insufficient output, and excessive operation scale in the production unit. The efficiency of all 285 bidders is examined in the section that follows. Enterprises are categorized based on their overall effectiveness, and the resulting Table 11 is as follows:

1. As can be seen from the above Table 11, there are 5 enterprises with comprehensive efficiency of 1, accounting for 2% of the total; There are 48 enterprises with comprehensive efficiency above 0.8, accounting for 17% of the total. The comprehensive efficiency of more than 80% of the enterprises is lower than 0.8.
2. Comprehensive efficiency and effective business under the current conditions of operation capability, business quality, guarantee capability, and project management, the efficiency output of the business's honest behaviour reaches the optimum level. These 5 enterprises

Table 11. Comprehensive efficiency of enterprises.

The comprehensive efficiency	1	0.8–1	0.5–0.8	0.2–0.5	0–0.2
The number	5	43	132	93	12
Proportion	0.02	0.15	0.46	0.33	0.04

also scored within the top 30 in terms of integrity behaviour. These 5 enterprises are thought to have strong credit behaviour and credit capacity.

4.3.2 Pure technical efficiency analysis

The link between scale efficiency, pure technical efficiency and comprehensive efficiency is that scale efficiency and pure technical efficiency lead to comprehensive efficiency. Pure technical efficiency, which indicates the amount of resource utilization of the evaluation unit, is exempt from the scale efficiency factor. If the production unit's operation capability and project management technology level are high and the pure technical efficiency is 1. If the evaluated unit's internal operating model and level of project management need to be improved to decrease redundancy, the pure technical efficiency must be greater than 1, see Table 12.

Table 12. Pure technical efficiency of enterprises.

Pure technical efficiency	1	0.8–1	0.5–0.8	0.2–0.5	0–0.2
The number	248	26	11	0	0
Proportion	0.87	0.09	0.04	0	0

1. The overall situation of pure technical efficiency is much better than the comprehensive efficiency, more than 80% of enterprises have reached the pure technical efficiency. Only 13 per cent of companies are pure technical inefficiency. Managers should consider how to improve the operation level, reduce the redundancy of resource utilization, and optimize the operation scale to achieve a matching state.
2. Among the 248 enterprises with pure technical efficiency of 1, only 5 enterprises reach the optimal state of comprehensive efficiency, indicating that the remaining 243 enterprises have a good level of operation management, but the scale efficiency is less than 1, and there are problems in the scale planning of operation. Optimizing the operation scale to match the current operation management level can effectively improve the credit ability of enterprises, to achieve DEA effectiveness.

4.3.3 Scale efficiency analysis

Scale efficiency refers to when an enterprise's operating capacity, quality, guarantee ability, and project management of these resources are equally ratio increases, the increase of honesty, and the added value of relative growth. It reflects when production unit operation scale expansion, the same proportion of resource inputs can buy equal proportion of output. The following Table 13 can be constructed based on the scale effectiveness of each enterprise:

1. In the enterprise scale efficiency, only more than 60% of enterprises scale efficiency is greater than 0.5, the overall level is not very good.
2. Among the six enterprises with scale efficiency and effectiveness, only one enterprise fails to achieve comprehensive efficiency and effectiveness due to pure technical efficiency, which indicates the need to improve the management level and technical ability of enterprises.
3. It can be understood that businesses clearly have a high bidding advantage, such as investment in many intellectual property rights or capital, but the increase of this part of

227

Table 13. Enterprise scale efficiency table.

The scale efficiency	1	0.8–1	0.5–0.8	0.2–0.5	0–0.2
The number	6	51	124	92	12
Proportion	0.02	0.18	0.44	0.32	0.04

the scale control performance is poor. Although there is a significant amount of investment at various levels, this part of the investment is ineffective resources to improve the efficiency of enterprise integrity is very low.

4.3.4 Enterprise credit classification

The paper makes a cluster study on the credit ability efficiency of enterprises according to the comprehensive efficiency (Zhou 2018). Considering the number of clusters and the number of samples, the K-means algorithm is adopted to set the number of clusters as 9, the maximum iteration as 30, and the convergence criterion as 0.1. After four iterations, the clustering result is achieved, and the cluster analysis is finished. The final cluster center is obtained, see Table 14.

Table 14. Clustering table of DEA model results.

	The final cluster center								
	1	2	3	4	5	6	7	8	9
The comprehensive efficiency	0.215	0.359	0.458	0.557	0.648	0.650	0.741	0.850	0.948
Pure technical efficiency	0.986	0.974	1.000	0.991	0.744	0.995	0.981	0.997	0.977
The scale efficiency	0.218	0.370	0.458	0.562	0.877	0.653	0.756	0.853	0.971
The number of	32	37	37	40	7	41	41	24	26

According to the above clustering results, the overall resource allocation level of enterprises is classified into 9 categories based on the standard of comprehensive efficiency. The following conclusions are obtained:

1. The ninth category of enterprises with the highest comprehensive efficiency can reach a better level in terms of resource allocation ability and use efficiency in terms of enterprise quality and other inputs, having high enterprise quality, strong enterprise operation ability, project management ability and guarantee ability.
2. Except for the fifth type of enterprises, in general, the comprehensive efficiency of other types of enterprises cannot reach the effective mainly because of the low scale efficiency. The scale efficiency of the first type of enterprises is very poor, which leads to low comprehensive efficiency. The credit score of the first type of enterprises is also the lowest.
3. For the fifth category, which has relatively low comprehensive efficiency, 7 enterprises have good credit behaviour scores. The pure technical efficiency and scale efficiency of the enterprises have not reached the optimal state. The comparison shows that the low comprehensive efficiency of these enterprises has a greater relationship with the low pure technical efficiency. The pure technical efficiency of 6 enterprises is lower than 0.8, which is the reciprocal position among 285 enterprises.

5 DISCUSSIONS AND IMPLICATIONS

5.1 Discussions

This paper classifies enterprises based on quantifying their integrity, which can reflect the possibility of subjective trust-breaking and default of enterprises more accurately.

Regulatory authorities can apply the classification results in market access, early warning, classification and classification supervision.

The evaluation of enterprise credit ability reflects the ability and strength of the enterprise to perform the contract in the bidding business, which can provide a basis for the selection of the tendered. At the same time in the classification of enterprise credit ability, enterprises according to the credit ability and integrity of the matching situation, further improve the internal credit management level of enterprise.

Based on the analysis results of the consistency of enterprise integrity and credit ability, it is considered that the index system of integrity and credit ability is reliable and can be applied in practice.

5.2 Implications

This paper makes a systematic study of enterprise integrity behaviour and enterprise credit ability considering the combination of the two. However, there are still many aspects worthy of further study:

Explore the order of Gaussian mixture model in the classification of enterprise integrity behaviour. In other words, that is the determination of the number of clustering categories. In practice, the model order has a great impact on the results.

Dichotomous division in the consistency study of honest behaviour and credit ability. The criterion of division has great influence on the result of fitting.

The data of enterprise credit ability indicators are partially missing, which brings some deviations to the analysis. The filling of appropriate missing values and the determination of alternative indicators will have a great impact on the results.

The credit environment index, as an external index, analyzes the relationship between credit environment index and enterprise integrity behaviour and credit ability.

REFERENCES

Guo, Y. C., Yang, Y. Q., Liang, Y. C. and Niu, B. 2019. Research on the Construction of Chinese Food Enterprise Credit Evaluation System. *China Dairy* (10): 21–29.

Luo, X. and Tan, L. 2017. Study on the Application of Analytic Hierarchy Process in the Evaluation Standard of Enterprise Quality Credit Rating. *China Standards Review* (6): 66–74.

Liu, J. Y., Wang, Y. J. and Wang, J. S. 2019. The Construction of SMEs Credit Risk Evaluation System under the Mode of Supply Chain Finance. *Journal of Financial Development Research* (11): 63–67.

Man, X. Y., Zhang, T. Y., Wang, C. and Ma, R. 2018. Credit Risk Factors Identification and Risk Measurement of Micro, Small and Medium Enterprises in China. *Journal of Central University of Finance & Economics* (9): 46–58.

Tong, S. K., Zhang, T. and Zhang, Z. G. 2022. Credit Risk Early Warning of Small and Medium-Sized Enterprises based on Blockchain Trusted Data. *Journal of Information and Knowledge Management*.

Wang, S. Y., Lan, X. R. and Liu, L. Y. 2019. Credit Risk Assessment of Small and Medium-sized Technological Enterprises with Non-convex Penalty. *Mathematics in Practice and Theory* 49(3): 307–312.

Yu, D. S. and Li, X. 2019. Credit Risk Assessment of smes Under Supply Chain Finance Model: A Case Study of Electronic Manufacturing industry. *Credit Reference* 37(10): 72–77.

Zhou, Z. C. 2018. Research on Credit Rating of Industrial Small Enterprises Based on K-means Clustering. *China Management Informationization* 21(13): 26–27.

Zhao, J. F. and Bo, L. 2022. Credit Risk Assessment of Small and Medium-sized Enterprises in Supply Chain Finance Based on SVM and BP Neural Network. *Neural Computing and Applications* 34(15): 12467–12478.

Zhang, Y. C. and Chen. 2018. Research on Credit Risk Evaluation and Application of Small and Medium-sized Enterprises Under the Background of Big Data. *E-Business Journal* (12): 34–35, 59.

Zhang, M. 2019. Construction of Business Enterprise Credit Evaluation Model Based on Analytic Hierarchy Process. *China Business & Trade* (14): 232–233.

Economic and Business Management – Lent & Zhang (Eds)
© 2023 the Author(s), ISBN 978-1-032-24482-2

Analyzing the impact of knowledge management on the performance in the Yemeni banking sector

Khalil M.A. Almuayad & Youzhen Chen*
School of Economics and Management, Southwest Jiaotong University, Chengdu, Sichuan, China

Amro A.S. Alammari
Department of Commerce, Mangalore University, Mangalore, India

ABSTRACT: Effective knowledge management (KM) can be a critical source of long-term competitive advantages sustained for business organizations. This paper examines the effect of KM on performance in the Yemeni banking sector. The sample of paper included 150 workers from the Yemeni banking sector. The survey method is used to collect data, and we used descriptive statistical analysis and regression analysis to examine the data (SPSS). The results found that KM positively and significantly influences performance of banking sector. The researchers recommended that the banking sector embrace the notion of KM by engaging in activities associated with it. According to the study, it is vital to offer training sessions for bank workers in Yemen to familiarize them with KM, its principles, and its significance to better comprehend their role in all KM-related operations.

1 INTRODUCTION

Knowledge management (KM) helps financial businesses store and organize knowledge more effectively. Bank managers and workers may cooperate better while maintaining alignment on immediate and long-term strategies. In addition, by incorporating customer information management into the process, banks get more insights into their clients and their preferences, making it simpler to create and market new goods and services. The use of technology in banks indicates a knowledge-based sector suitable for research. Banks have understood the importance of KM in attaining a competitive advantage. Disruptive innovation can enable the banking industry to confront new difficulties (Jawed & Siddiqui 2021).

The banking sector creates massive amounts of data regularly, from regular data and information such as the history of transactions and customer information to unstructured data such as client website activity (Vives 2017). To improve banking sector performance, banks must be aware of KM methods' value. They could also consider inspiring and educating their managers and staff to drive innovation by establishing a culture of practicing KM techniques (Al-Dmour et al. 2020). Banks must keep up with new developments in business, invest and use resources efficiently, and learn from the scientific experiences of other banks in the same field that have advanced over time to create and entrench a culture based on the dissemination of knowledge among employees and to encourage them to contribute work-related ideas. They must enhance competitiveness, entrepreneurialism, and innovation. As a consequence of these shifts, information has become the most important strategic resource for banks to gain a competitive edge and the most potent, influential, and

---

*Corresponding Author:

DOI: 10.1201/9781003278788-33

deciding reason for their success or failure (Zabiegalski & Marquardt 2022). Therefore, this paper aims to analyze the impact of KM on the performance of the Yemeni banking sector.

2 LITERATURE REVIEW

The term "knowledge management" first appeared in the early 1990s, when developed countries began to focus on and enhance commercial enterprises with medium and high levels of knowledge, which were characterized by the pursuit, use, and application of information at the proper time (Shawaqfeh et al. 2019). Business organizations are shifting toward KM, which emphasizes the importance of paying more attention to worker skills, allowing workers to behave freely in the face of problems while simultaneously providing them with the essential capabilities to ensure peak performance (Sjöblom 2020).

2.1 *Definition of KM*

KM is a contemporary management concept that is gaining traction among corporate executives. Furthermore, there is no single, broad definition of KM; there are several discrepancies in defining a single concept for this common term. KM comprises identifying and assessing existing and required knowledge assets, processes connected to these assets, and business planning for asset and process advancement to fulfill the organization's objectives (Asbari et al. 2019). Moreover, in addition to the methods of knowledge conservation and protection, use sharing, and development, it manages the processes that result in the creation of these assets. It also contains knowledge of innovations and goods as well as the marketplaces, and organizations that have or require them, which contributes to the advancement of the organization's functioning, resulting in value creation through efficient decision-making and increased profits through solving problems, and long-term planning. Taking everything into consideration, we find that the primary goal of KM is to coordinate, organize, and lead knowledge-based activities to accomplish strategic goals. KM is vital for firms that want to embrace digital commerce effectively. Business organizations face rising competition daily under the shadow of globalization (Abualoush et al. 2018). Many modern cultures are experiencing a complete, significant, and diversified transition toward knowledge-based companies. This trend affects the economics of whole nations and other aspects of daily life in many of these societies.

2.2 *Knowledge economy theory and KM*

The goal of the knowledge economic theory is to explain the most important economic problems that society is now facing, which, according to Hayek (Hayek 1945), is how to make the most effective use of the knowledge already available. Knowledge hierarchies are often utilized to learn and convey the same information to multiple actors. These hierarchies offer more time to agents with less experience in executing and solving common issues while giving less time to competent agents. Agents are expected to solve problems according to their degree of expertise, leaving the most capable of handling problems at a higher level.

KM is now mainly an administrative task that aids corporate organizations in designing, developing, and refining a solid innovation strategy (Al-Dmour et al. 2020). KM has been identified as a critical component for assisting corporate organizations in identifying knowledge gaps and delivering solutions to address these gaps to support organizational innovation (Mehrez et al. 2020). Organize and conduct a systematic evaluation of KM and company performance, two critical concepts in any organization.

Discovers a positive association between KM methods and organizational performance. Furthermore, the elements of business intelligence had a favorable influence on the organization's overall performance (Abusweilem & Abualoush 2019). Examine the literature on digital innovation in KM systems to better understand the role of digital innovation in corporate governance. Using digital innovation processes to analyze the KM subject, this research contributes to the current literature by emphasizing the need to implement new knowledge production and sharing strategies that encourage global and inclusive development, thus expanding the knowledge body. Banks cannot afford to be complacent in their operations (Di Vaio et al. 2021).

2.3 *KM on the banking sector*

KM in the banking industry is not different from KM in other industries; the main difference resides in the implementation of KM. The KM is still a relatively new idea in developing countries, especially Yemen, particularly in the banking sector, where it has only seen minimal implementation. Some industries, such as the telecom sector, information technology, the automotive sector, are experiencing growth and expansion in KM processes. On the other hand, some industries, such as banks, are currently introducing KM systems as part of the automation and computerization process, which is part of the financial sector reforms. In most circles, KM is understood to refer to a method by which organizations get value from their intellectual assets (Bukowitz and Williams 2000). The abundance of data companies produce as a natural by-product of their day-to-day operations presents a hurdle (Chandra & Khanijo 2011). Globalization has also compelled financial institutions to become knowledge-based and to improve the efficiency with which they manage the information associated with their banking activities. The banking industry was transformed into a robust financial sector by changes in the financial sector in the 1990s.

As a result of the massive changes that globalization has brought about in highly competitive information technology (IT) financial institutions, they must review their competitive advantages and strategies. According to the authors, the significance of relationship banking, which stimulates direct communication with bank clients, is emphasized in the research. Incentives are simplified, and bank clients' long-term needs are met when they engage in relationship banking with a long-term emphasis. Banks may be tempted to enter transaction banking in the future because of IT-driven economies of scale and competition from FinTech start-ups and IT businesses. In this context, the essay examines the effects of distance, AI, and behavioral biases on decision-making (Jakšič & Marinč 2019). Traditional banks have successfully implemented KM strategies based on various models to enhance their business performance. Meanwhile, only a limited amount of research has been suggested on how Islamic banks manage various knowledge bases to support their business processes. We investigated the KM process in two cases of Islamic banks in Indonesia using the KM lifecycle theory (Nurdin & Yusuf 2020).

2.4 *Performance of the banking sector*

Performance inside a company has become the most critical concern for any organization, regardless of whether they are for-profit (Abu-Jarad et al. 2010). Nevertheless, discussions over defining, conceptualizing, and quantifying performance have not been simple. According to (Lebas & Euske 2006), performance is defined as a collection of financial and non-financial metrics that provides information on the extent to which goals and outcomes have been achieved. The three main aspects of company outcomes that make up organizational performance are as follows: (1) financial performance (profits, return on assets, return on investment); (2) market performance (sales, market share); (3) shareholder return (Richard et al. 2009). The actions performed regularly to create organizational objectives, assess progress toward those goals, and make modifications to attain those goals more effectively and efficiently are included in the definition of organizational performance (Richard et al. 2009). The fact that different academics have different perspectives on the effect that information has on organizational performance may be the source of the notion that KM is necessary for knowledge accumulation to enhance organizational performance (Vera & Crossan 2003). It is anticipated that a particular category of information that is priceless, unique, unrepeatable, and impossible to replace would result in improved performance (Barney 1991). The writers who believe that there is no direct connection between knowledge and performance may be found on the opposite side of the debate. It is always possible for organizations to acquire information that may not result in intelligent behavior (Singh et al. 2006).

3 RESEARCH MODEL AND HYPOTHESES

KM and performance are necessary for a business to be successful. Writing reveals that KM has a decisive impact on productivity. Most firms guarantee that the sufficiency and efficacy of KM methods contribute to organizational success. KM is considered the originator of organizational performance (Darroch 2005). To a large extent, comparable to any other resource, effective organizational KM must include developing additional skills to contribute to the essential elements of organizational performance (Bovey & Hede 2001). As a result of improvements in its information management capabilities, the organization is now in a stronger position to fulfill the requirements of its customers by providing improved services (Hunt & Morgan 1995). This paper aims to investigate the influence of KM on the performance of the banking sector in Yemen:

H1: KM has a positive and significant impact on the performance of the Yemeni banking sector.

4 RESEARCH METHODOLOGY

Due to the nature of the study and the information needed to complete the questionnaire to achieve its objectives, the current study is a descriptive research in terms of data collection and analysis. It is a descriptive survey that depicts the state of variables and their relationships and evaluates and interprets concurrent association between variables using statistical analytical methods. The study's target population was the staff in the banking sector in Yemen.

4.1 *Sampling*

This research uses convenience sampling because it is effectively reachable, less time-consuming, less costly, and easy to decide on critical respondents. In this research, we focused on employees employed in the banking sector in Yemen. For a few examinations, banking sector employees are picked as the target population; although official-level representatives are seen as necessary, every employee inside the organization is essential. Consequently, each worker employed in the financial sector is essential. There is a lot of organization behind the drive to go into the banking industry, and there is open rivalry amongst banks in terms of the services they provide. The banking industry is experiencing a significant amount of data overload, and institutions are turning to innovation in order to manage their data.

When deciding the sample size, the ratio of observations to constructs used to establish the independent variables should not be lower than five. In the event that we are unable to meet these requirements, there is a possibility that the results will be unique to the example and will not be able to be summed up for the general population (Hair et al. 2019). This research has a sample size of 150, which satisfies all prerequisite requirements.

4.2 Data collection

The study relied on primary forms of data collection. The data were subjected to statistical and methodical analysis using data analysis tools (SPSS). The total number of questionnaires received is 150 out of 200. The questionnaire was developed following (Gold et al. 2001) and (Liao et al. 2010). This study focuses on the general method of gathering information on the effect of KM on performance in the Yemeni banking sector.

5 RESULTS AND DISCUSSIONS

5.1 Stability test

Cronbach Alpha is the most often cited measure of "reliability" when assessing an organization's capacity to maintain internal consistency. It was developed by Lee Cronbach in 1951 (Cronbach 1951) as a method for determining the degree to which an inquiry or scale is consistent within itself; it is expressed as a numeral that falls midway between 0 and 1. The concept of inner consistency describes the degree to which all of the test components compute the same notion and develops it in a manner that is associated with the between-relatedness of the components of the test itself. Before a test may be utilized for examination or examination purposes to confirm its legitimacy, the issue of its internal dependability has to be overcome. Alpha may have a value anywhere between 0.7 and 0.95 (Bland & Altman 1997); (Nunnally & Bernstein 1994). In order to increase the size of Alpha, more relevant objects that test the same notion need to be added to the test (Streiner 2003). if the broad recommendations that are included with this: Alpha that is equivalent to or more prominent than nine is considered to be superb. In contrast, Alpha that is equivalent to or more noteworthy than eight is considered to be Good, while Alpha that is equivalent to or more prominent than seven is considered to be satisfactory. Alpha that is equivalent to or more noteworthy than six is considered to be Questionable, while Alpha that is equivalent to or more prominent than five is considered to be Poor, and Alpha that is equivalent to or more noteworthy than five is considered to be Unaccepted.

Table 1 shows the reliability coefficient Alpha for all two variables .715, indicating that the scale utilized in this study is quite reliable and consistent. The reliability coefficient Alpha for all seven KM constructs is .711. The Alpha reliability coefficient for banking performance three constructs is .709, indicating that the KM and banking performance scales employed in this study are reasonably reliable and consistent (George 2011). As a result, the components employed in this study adequately explain the overall requirement to measure, and the results will be more trustworthy, consistent, and reproducible.

Table 1. Reliability Statistics.

Scale	Cronbach's Alpha
Total Scale	0.715
knowledge management	0.711
Banking performance	0.709

Source: (SPSS)

5.2 Demographic analysis

The study aimed to learn more about the respondents' demographics, including their job title, gender, age, educational background, number of years in the industry, and bank category. The demographic background of the respondents is explained in Table 2.

Table 2. Demographic profile of the respondents.

Demographic Profile of the Respondents		N = 150 Percentage
Gender	Male	61.3
	Female	38.7
Age	24–30 years	23.3
	31–40 years	38.7
	41–50 years	33.3
	Above 50 years	4.7
Educational Qualification	Diploma	36.7
	Graduate	44.0
	Post – Graduate	19.3
Bank Category	Local public	54.0
	Local private	46.0
Job position	Bank officer	23.3
	Branch manager	20.7
	Assistant Manager	26.7
	Others	29.3
Years of experience	Less than 5 years	24.7
	5–10 years	39.3
	11–15 years	25.3
	Above 15 years	10.7

Source: (author)

As shown in Table 2, majorities of the respondents were obtained from the male (61.3%) followed by the respondents from the female (38.7%). As depicted in the table, 38.7% of the respondents were between 31 and 40 years, while 33.3% were between 41 and 50 years old. About 23.3% of the respondents were aged between 24 and 30 years, and 4.7% of the respondents were aged above 50 years. From the table, 44% of the respondents are graduates, 36.7% of respondents have a diploma, and 19.3% have a post-graduate degree. Of the total, 54% of the respondents were from the local public bank while 46% were from the local private bank. Here, 26.7% of the respondents were Assistant managers, 23.3% were bank officers, 20.7% were branch managers, and the other respondents were 29.3%. As per the table, 39.3% of the respondents had served for 5–10 years in the bank, while 25.3% of the respondents had served for 11–15 years, and 24.7% had served for less than 5 years. Above 15 years, 10.7% of the respondents had served.

5.3 Regression analysis

Using regression analysis, the impact of the link between the independent variables (KM) and the dependent variable determined the banking sector's performance in Yemen. The Model Summary, ANOVA, and Regression Coefficients are provided below.

H1: KM has a positive and significant impact on the performance of the Yemeni banking sector.

5.3.1 Model summary

Table 3 shows that the coefficient correlation R between KM and banking performance is 0.784, which shows a strong positive relationship between KM and banking performance (Somekh et al, 2005). The results showed that the adjusted R Square was 0.634, which translates to 63.4 %, indicating that the following independent Variable, KM, impacts the banking sector performance. However, the new R Squared interpretation accurately

Table 3. Model summary.

			Model summary	
Model	R	R Square	Adjusted R Square	Std. Error of the estimate
1	.784[a]	.634	.614	.947
Predictors: (Constant), KM.				

Source: (SPSS)

Table 4. ANOVA test.

			ANOVA a			
	Model	Sum of squares	Df	Mean square	F	Sig.
1	Regression	140.446	5	140.446	255.709	.000
	Residual	127.294	142	.896		
	Total	131.740	149			
	Predictors: (Constant), Knowledge Management.					
	D. Dependent Variable: banking performance					

Source: (SPSS)

reflected the facts. In Yemen, the performance of the banking sector is greatly influenced by the model summary for KM.

5.3.2 ANOVA test

An ANOVA was carried out at a high significance level. If the p-value is less than .001, then the changes in the performance of the banking sector can be jointly influenced by KM, and at least one of the slope coefficients is none zero. The findings are shown in Table 5.

Table 5. Coefficients.

		Coefficients				
		Unstandardized coefficients		Standardized coefficients		
	Model	B	Std. Error	Beta	t	Sig.
1	(Constant)	0.273	.141		1.283	.000
	knowledge management	.843	.065	.761	14.022	.000
	Dependent Variable: banking performance					

Source: (SPSS)

The examination of the variance ratio is broken down into its component parts and shown in Table 4. It is a measurement of the degree to which the model has improved its ability to forecast the result in comparison to the amount of error that the model had previously shown (Field 2013). The table has an F ratio of 255.709, which is significant at p less than or equal to .001. In this case, the significance threshold is .000, which is much lower than .001. Therefore, the model works rather well.

5.3.3 Regression coefficients

The following coefficients were created to assess the relative importance of the various dependent variables in determining the overall performance of the banking sector. Table 5 shows the results.

Table 5 shows the results investigated using regression analysis to establish the significance of the link between KM and performance in the Yemeni banking sector. The table shows that the value of the constant term is 0.273, which will not be affected by any variable, while the coefficient of the regression line is .843, which shows that one unit change in KM will cause a .843 positive unit change in banking performance. So, hypothesis H-1 is proved, and it is true. This implies that KM has a favorable influence on the performance of Yemen's banking sector.

The study hypothesized that KM positively and significantly impacts the Yemeni banking sector's performance. The hypothesis is proved by our study results which are supported by previous studies (Holsapple & Wu 2011); (Liao and Wu 2009). This study's results show a positive impact of KM on performance in the Yemeni banking sector, which is necessary for an organization's survival. Without KM efforts, firms with significant staff turnover would suffer, especially in the case of the banking industry, where deliverables are inseparable, and a personalized response is required to an inquiry. Without KM, a company may lose track of a loyal client whose background information is already on file but is not being maintained appropriately. The organization's personnel will employ knowledge to accomplish regular duties. Knowledge acquired by employees and employed in everyday company activities results in the innovation of products and services. Product or service innovation drives client satisfaction inside a firm.

KM also reduces product or service costs by enhancing the operational flow and reducing wasteful activities. Banking sector can gain an advantage through high-quality products and services by implementing KM activities. By managing knowledge, firms can also respond quickly to environmental changes. Banking sector can retain existing and new customers by frequently providing innovative products and services, resulting in loyal customers and more financial gains. Therefore, the banking sector that lacks implementation of KM systems can improve its performance by implementing KM practices adopted by other successful organizations, s. There is also a need to identify other factors affecting KM. Some organizations implemented KM systems without considering their importance but failed to achieve desired objectives. The results of this study are in conformation with already studies (Vaccaro et al. 2010).

6 CONCLUSIONS

This paper has one main contribution to the literature: it is the study to analyze the impact of KM on performance in the Yemeni banking sector. This paper aims The empirical results to provide supportive data about the link between KM and the performance of the banking sector, which is in line with the KM literature that is already available (Khafajy et al. 2016) (Shawaqfeh et al. 2019). KM has a beneficial effect on the overall functioning of the Yemeni banking industry. However, further study is required to establish a direct relationship between KM and the success of the banking industry. Therefore, one of the most important contributions of this study is to give unambiguous proof of the so-called relationship between KM and the performance of the banking industry based on empirical data. This is one of the primary achievements of this research. The study discovered that the success of the Yemeni banking sector is often dependent on the abilities and expertise of its employees. It was also discovered that the Yemeni banking sector had a strong interest in the practice of

KM. The banking sector formerly depended on the interaction of employees to solve problems and generate new concepts. The study found KM had a positive, significant influence on the performance of the banking sector.

Additionally, the banking sector may benefit from this research to better understand. Even though this research achieved its goals, the report's authors admit that it has some flaws. For example, the study's conclusions only apply to Yemen's banking sector. The researchers recommended that the banking sector embrace the notion of KM by engaging in activities associated with it. According to the study, it is vital to offer training sessions for bank workers in Yemen to better familiarize them with knowledge management, its principles, and its significance to comprehend their role in all knowledge management-related operations.

REFERENCES

Abu-Jarad, I. Y., Yusof, N. A. & Nikbin, D. 2010. A Review Paper on Organizational Culture and Organizational Performance. *International Journal of Business and Social Science*, 1.

Abualoush, S. H., Obeidat, A. M., Tarhini, A. & Al-badi, A. 2018. The Role of Employees' Empowerment as an Intermediary Variable Between Knowledge Management and Information Systems on Employees' Performance. *VINE Journal of Information and Knowledge Management Systems*.

Abusweilem, M. & Abualoush, S. 2019. The Impact of Knowledge Management Process and Business Intelligence on Organizational Performance. *Management Science Letters*, 9, 2143–2156.

Al-dmour, A., Al-dmour, R. & Rababeh, N. 2020. The Impact of Knowledge Management practice on digital financial innovation: the role of bank managers. *VINE Journal of Information and Knowledge Management Systems*.

Asbari, M., Wijayanti, L. M., Hyun, C. C., Purwanto, A. & Santoso, P. B. 2019. Effect of Tacit and Explicit Knowledge Sharing on Teacher Innovation Capability. *Dinamika Pendidikan*, 14, 227–243.

Barney, J. 1991. Firm Resources and Sustained Competitive Advantage. *Journal of Management*, 17, 99–120.

Bland, J. M. & Altman, D. G. 1997. Statistics notes: Cronbach's alpha. *Bmj*, 314, 572.

Bovey, W. H. & Hede, A. 2001. Resistance to Organisational Change: the Role of Defence Mechanisms. *Journal of Managerial Psychology*.

Bukowitz, W. R. & Williams, R. L. 2000. *The Knowledge Management Fieldbook*, Financial Times/Prentice Hall.

Chandra, A. & Khanijo, M. 2011. *Knowledge Economy: The Indian Challenge*, SAGE Publications India.

Cronbach, L. J. 1951. Coefficient alpha and the internal structure of tests. *psychometrika*, 16, 297–334.

Darroch, J. 2005. Knowledge Management, Innovation and Firm Performance. *Journal of Knowledge Management*.

Di Vaio, A., Palladino, R., Pezzi, A. & Kalisz, D. E. 2021. The Role of Digital Innovation in Knowledge Management Systems: A Systematic Literature Review. *Journal of Business Research*, 123, 220–231.

Field, A. 2013. *Discovering Statistics Using IBM SPSS Statistics*, Sage.

George, D. 2011. *SPSS for Windows Step by Step: A Simple Study Guide and Reference, 17.0 Update, 10/e*, Pearson Education India.

Gold, A. H., Malhotra, A. & Segars, A. H. 2001. Knowledge Management: An Organizational Capabilities Perspective. *Journal of Management Information Systems*, 18, 185–214.

Hair, J. F., Page, M. & Brunsveld, N. 2019. *Essentials of Business Research Methods*, Routledge.

Hayek, F. A. 1945. The use of knowledge in society. *The American Economic Review*, 35, 519–530.

Holsapple, C. W. & WU, J. 2011. An Elusive Antecedent of Superior Firm Performance: The Knowledge Management Factor. *Decision Support Systems*, 52, 271–283.

Hunt, S. D. & Morgan, R. M. 1995. The Comparative Advantage Theory of Competition. *Journal of Marketing*, 59, 1–15.

Jakšič, M. & Marinč, M. 2019. Relationship Banking and Information Technology: The Role of Artificial Intelligence and FinTech. *Risk Management*, 21, 1–18.

Jawed, T. & Siddiqui, D. A. 2021. The Impact of Knowledge Management Practice on Digital Financial Innovation in Pakistan: The Role of Managers' Demographics and Leadership Styles. *Available at SSRN*.

Khafajy, N. A., Alzoubi, H. M. & Aljanabee, A. K. 2016. Analyzing the Effect of Knowledge Management Processes in The Services' Quality in Iraqi Commercial Banks. *International Review of Management and Business Research*, 5, 302.

Lebas, M. & Euske, K. 2006. A Conceptual and Operational Delineation of Performance, [in:] Business Performance Measurement. Theory and Practice, ed. A. Neely. Cambridge University Press, Cambridge.

Liao, C., Wang, H.-Y., Chuang, S.-H., Shih, M.-L. & LIU, C.-C. 2010. Enhancing Knowledge Management for RD Innovation and Firm Performance: An Integrative View. *African Journal of Business Management*, 4, 3026–3038.

Liao, S.-H. & Wu, C.-C. 2009. The Relationship Among Knowledge Management, Organizational Learning, and Organizational Performance. *International Journal of Business and Management*, 4, 64–76.

Mehrez, A. A. A., Alshurideh, M., Kurdi, B. A. & Salloum, S. A. Internal Factors Affect Knowledge Management and Firm Performance: A Systematic Review. International Conference on Advanced Intelligent Systems and Informatics, 2020. Springer, 632–643.

Nunnally, J. & Bernstein, I. 1994. Psychometric Theory 3rd edition (MacGraw-Hill, New York).

Nurdin, N. & Yusuf, K. 2020. Knowledge Management Lifecycle in Islamic bank: the Case of Syariah Banks in Indonesia. *International Journal of Knowledge Management Studies*, 11, 59–80.

Richard, P. J., Devinney, T. M., YIP, G. S. & Johnson, G. 2009. Measuring Organizational Performance: Towards Methodological Best Practice. *Journal of Management*, 35, 718–804.

Shawaqfeh, G., Alqaied, B. & Jaradat, M. 2019. The Impact of Knowledge Management on the Performance of Commercial Banks' Employees in Jordan (A Field Study on Commercial Banks' Employees in Irbid Governorate of Jordan). *European Journal of Accounting, Auditing and Finance Research*, 7, 1–16.

Singh, S., Chan, Y. E. & Mckeen, J. D. Knowledge Management Capability and Organizational Performance: A Theoretical Foundation. OLKC 2006 Conference at the University of Warwick, 2006. Citeseer, 1–54.

Sjöblom, K. 2020. Flourishing in 21st century workplaces: How to Support Knowledge Workers' Productivity and Well-being in Modern Environments. *Helsinki Studies in Education-Kasvatustieteellisiä tutkimuksia*.

Somekh, B., Burman, E., Delamont, S., Meyer, J., Payne, M. & Thorpe, R. 2005. Research Communities in the Social Sciences. *Research Methods in the Social Sciences*, 1–14.

Streiner, D. L. 2003. Starting at the Beginning: an Introduction to Coefficient Alpha and Internal Consistency. *Journal of Personality Assessment*, 80, 99–103.

Vaccaro, A., Parente, R. & Veloso, F. M. 2010. Knowledge Management Tools, Inter-Organizational Relationships, Innovation and Firm Performance. *Technological Forecasting and Social Change*, 77, 1076–1089.

Vera, D. & Crossan, M. 2003. Organizational Learning and Knowledge Management: Toward an Integrative Framework. *The Blackwell Handbook of Organizational Learning and Knowledge Management*, 122–142.

Vives, X. 2017. The Impact of FinTech on Banking. *European Economy*, 97–105.

Zabiegalski, E. & Marquardt, M. J. 2022. Action Learning and the Ambidextrous Organization. *Journal of Work-Applied Management*.

Model of service brand equity evaluation based on brand extension

Silei Feng
Sichuan Agricultural University, Sichuan Province, China

ABSTRACT: Based on the theory of consumers' brand equity, this research takes the service brand as the research object, and divides the brand extension path into: horizontal brand extension and vertical brand extension. Taking fit and extension distance as independent variables, the dimension of service brand equity as dependent variables, and customer value and customer satisfaction as moderator variables, a model of the influence of service brand extension on brand equity is constructed including moderator variables.

1 INTRODUCTION

With the continuous development of economic globalization, the competition among enterprises has become fiercer. The competition mode among enterprises has gradually shifted from competition between products to competition between brands. Brand competition has become an effective means of competition among enterprises and an integral part of businesses. It can help them obtain high benefits and maintain their competitive advantages. It can also help in improving their sales and gaining long-term stability.

When a company launches a new product, it will naturally take advantage of the brand's market influence, then brand extension is a natural choice. This strategy can save a lot of money and help extend the awareness of the brand to new products. It also helps avoid the costly and time-consuming launch of a new brand. But not all brand extension strategies are successful and therefore, it is necessary to analyze the factors that affect the success of brand extension strategies. By analyzing the service brand extension path, evaluate the brand extension assets, clarify the service brand extension strategy, and promote the appreciation of service brand assets.

2 LITERATURE REVIEW

2.1 *The concept of brand equity based on consumers*

Most scholars define brand equity as the value that a brand provides to consumers. Keller (1993) proposes the concept of Customer-based-Brand Equity and believes that the fundamental reason why brands are valuable to enterprises and distributors lies in the value of brands to customers. He affirms the important role that customers play in brand and brand extension but tends to focus on customer perception, and ignore market factors in the creation and management of brand equity.

The concept of brand equity is conceptualized from the cognitive perspective of the consumer. It is believed that the concept of brand equity is not derived from the consumers' one-way perception of the brand but from their two-way interactive relationship with it. With the rise of the brand relationship paradigm, consumer-based brand equity models have received more and more attention. Blackston (1993) first proposed that brand equity is created by the interaction between consumers' attitudes toward brands (objective brands) and brands'

DOI: 10.1201/9781003278788-34

attitudes toward consumers (subjective brands). Brand equity from the consumer perception perspective only focuses on objective brands, ignoring subjective brands, so this concept does not have high predictive ability. According to Fournier (1998), the quality of the relationship between consumers and the brands is the most important source of brand equity.

Keller's (1998) concept of consumer-based brand equity pertains to the way consumers respond to marketing activities based on their existing brand knowledge. Keller's definition of consumer-based brand equity is consumers' differentiated responses to brand marketing activities due to their existing brand knowledge in their minds. This definition includes three important concepts: "differentiated response", "brand knowledge", and "consumer response to marketing activities". Differentiated response refers to the response of consumers to the marketing mix of other imaginary or unnamed brands; brand knowledge includes brand awareness and brand image, and therefore generates specific brand associations. Consumer response to marketing activities refers to the impact of various marketing activities of the company on consumers' attitudes towards the brand (including cognition, emotion, and behavioral intentions) and the specific consumer behaviors that result from it, and many more.

According to Lassar et al. (1995), defining brand equity from a consumer's perspective requires consideration of the following four aspects: (1) Consumer-based perspective refers to how consumers understand and agree with the value of the brand, which is subjective. It is not an objective process of establishing a relationship between a brand and consumers; (2) Brand equity refers to the global value of the brand; (3) The brand must show unique advantages over competitors and differentiate from competitors; (4) A good relationship between a brand and consumers has a positive impact on the financial value of brand equity.

Based on their study, the concept of brand equity is the core of developing a good consumer-brand relationship. This process requires establishing a strong and familiar brand association with consumers. When consumers are familiar with a brand and have a favorite, strong and unique brand associations in memory, brand equity based on consumers is formed.

2.2 Influencing factors of brand extension

(1) At the parent brand level

According to Aaker (1991) and Keller's (1998) research, the perceived quality of the brand influences the evaluation of extended products, and the higher the perceived quality, the higher the evaluation. Sridhar Moorthy's (1997) research results show that brand extension depends on the foundation of the original brand rather than product quality signals. According to Broniarczyk & Alba (1994), the evaluation of a brand's extension is influenced by the association with the parent brand.

(2) The relationship between the extended product and the parent brand

Aaker and Keller took American consumers as the survey subjects and found that the perception of substitutability, complementarity, and transferability between the extension product and the parent brand directly affect consumers' perception of the fit between the extension product and the parent brand. Based on 276 brand extension examples, Tauber (1988) pointed out that the consistency between the extension product and the parent brand is related to the success of the brand extension. A study conducted by Bridges et al. (2000) states that the relevance of the parent brand and the extended brand is very important for most brands, particularly those with lowe physical attributes. The extension effect mainly works by introducing the extended attributes of the brand to customers.

(3) Internal environment level

The concept of internal factor theory has been used to study the link between personality traits and brand extension. Eric et al. (2010) studied the concept of personality traits as factors that influence brand extension. Smith and Park pointed out through research that publicity is very important for extending products.

(4) External environment level

Reddy et al. (1994) found that an analysis of the various factors that affect the extension of a brand's product introduction revealed that promotion and channel support are critical. The external environment and the parent brand level also affect the vertical and horizontal brand extension respectively. The price of the extended product can also be used as a main factor in the vertical brand extension. However, at the level of the extended product and the parent brand, it can be seen that the similarity and consistency of the extension is an important factors in the horizontal brand extension, and the price of the extended product is an aspect of the extension distance and can be used as the main factor of the vertical extension.

2.3 *The measurement based on consumer brand equity*

Aaker measured brand equity from five aspects: loyalty, perceived quality, brand association, brand awareness, and market behavior; and proposed 10 specific dimensions: brand premium, satisfaction/loyalty, perceived quality, leadership, perceived value, brand personality, organization association, brand awareness, market share, price, and distribution index. The evaluation factors of the Brand Equity Ten model are mainly about consumers, and the factors of market performance are also added. Moreover, all indicators are relatively sensitive, which can be used to predict changes in brand equity.

Brand awareness and brand image are two dimensions that measure the brand's equity. The former includes the brand's recall and brand recognition, while the latter refers to the perception of the brand; brand image is composed of three dimensions: (1) Brand characteristics (Attributes), including brand functional and symbolic characteristics; (2) Brand benefits (Benefits), including the functional and emotional benefits that consumers get after using the brand; (3) Brand Attitudes, which refers to the reputation of the brand.

Besides the above, brand equity can be measured from various dimensions, such as brand loyalty and brand relevance. For Shocher, these two dimensions can be compared, while Yoo focuses on perceived quality and brand awareness.

3 BRAND EXTENSION AND BRAND EQUITY

3.1 *Research on service brand*

O'cass & Grace (2004) pointed out that the service brand association includes the brand name, price, currency value, service environment, core value, employee service, emotion, and self-image consistency.

According to the research conducted by scholars, a service brand is a type of logo that can help customers identify their own brand characteristics. It can reflect the price of the service, the service environment, the core competitiveness, and the service of employees.

3.2 *The relationship between brand extension and brand equity*

3.2.1 *Brand equity is the basis and premise of brand extension*

Brand extension must have strong brand equity support because the purpose of brand extension is to quickly launch new products to the market with the help of existing brand reputation and influence, in order to quickly open the market. The brand's existing reputation and influence are not only reflective of its brand equity in the market, but also the role of rich brand knowledge (high brand awareness and a distinctive brand image, etc.) in creating a strong association with a brand in consumer memory as well as its uniqueness and affect.

Brand equity is the foundation, and also the beginning of brand extension. According to Katsanis & Pitta (1995), only strong brands have the necessary conditions to extend their brand. Aaker and Keller's study also showed that strong brands can better ensure the success of brand extension. Moreover, not all brands are eligible for an extension. When a brand is not strong, its radiation effect on the extension product is very limited, so the possibility of success is unlikely.

3.2.2 *Brand extension is a way to accumulate and expand brand equity*

Keller specifically points out that brand extension is a strategy that involves managing the value of the brand. It is also a means of maintaining and expanding the brand's marketability. Some scholars hold similar views, for instance, Pitta and Katsanis also pointed out in their paper that unsuccessful product extensions will seriously affect the original brand, and successful brand extensions will help companies change brand positioning and accumulate brand equity. According to Smith and Park, the value of brand extension is related to the cash flow generated by the new market during its introduction. This study shows that when new products are introduced with a brand extension strategy, they can gain a larger share of the market and reduce advertising costs. New products introduced into the market with a brand extension strategy can gain an average market share of over 8.3% more than new products introduced through independent brands. Expanding the market influence of the brand has a positive effect.

3.3 *Related theories about the relationship between brand extension and brand equity*

3.3.1 *Brand extension affects brand equity*

Brand extension is an integral part of brand equity management. It can maintain and expand the value that the brand has. In July 1993, Babara & Deborah's (1993) research on brand extension pointed out that Brand extension does not always damage brand equity. Tauber puts forward the concept of "competitive lever", which means a series of advantages that the brand passes to extended products in the new category. "If consumers know this brand, they will be able to perceive the new brand's competitive advantage over the same category of products."

3.3.2 *Brand equity is an important condition for brand extension*

Pitta and Katsanis believe that failure to extend a brand will have a serious impact on its original brand, and successful product extension will help companies improve brand positioning and brand equity.

Aaker and Keller found through experiments that not all brands can be extended. A weak brand's effect on an extended product is negligible. High-quality brands have a larger extension, that is, they can extend to product areas that are not too similar.

Smith and Park believe that an extended brand's ability to gain consumer recognition is easier to achieve than that of an independent brand.

4 THEORETICAL MODEL

4.1 *Service brand extension process model*

Brand extension can be utilized to enhance a brand's brand equity by attracting more customers and increasing market share. Conversely, if a failed out-of-date brand extension may cause customers to have a teetering effect on the brand, either too high or too low, this will not only fail to attract new customers, but may lose some of the original customers, and then affect brand equity. The direct feelings that customers get from the service and the attitude of service personnel and customers when they contact and communicate, all affect the customer's evaluation of the service brand. In this part, we will divide the service brand extension into horizontal and vertical extensions. The influencing factor of horizontal extension is fit, and the independent variable of vertical extension is brand extension distance, which plays an important role in service brand equity. The moderating factors of a service brand's extension and brand equity are customer value and satisfaction. For each variable, the model assumes that the degree of fit, extension distance, customer value, and customer satisfaction interact with the service brand equity. Finally, build an extended model with adjusted variables. As shown in Figure 1, the independent variables are fit and extended distance; the moderating variables are customer value and customer satisfaction; and the dependent variable is brand equity.

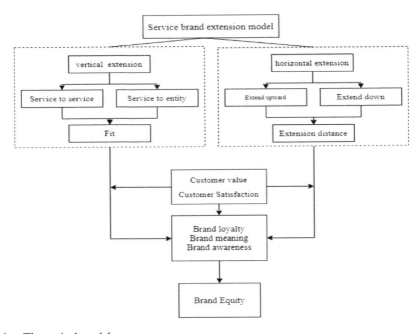

Figure 1.   Theoretical model.

In practice, various brand extension phenomena have complex and diverse effects, and their effects can vary widely. The degree of value transfer of each element of the brand equity to the target market of the new product during the extension process depends on the "degree of relevance" between the target market and the target market of the brand's original product. The greater the "degree of relevance", the higher the degree of brand equity value transfer. It can be seen from the model that "line extension" has a greater degree of brand equity transfer than "privilege extension".

4.2   *Analysis of brand equity changes in the process of service brand extension*

4.2.1   *Success and unsuccess of the extension result*

The importance of the brand's asset value and the target market's ability to support it will also affect the extension strategy's success rate. In addition, the influence of various external determinants also has a certain degree of influence on the final extension success rate. It is precisely because of the various differences between the above factors that have led to numerous extensions or successes or failures. When the brand equity status and the target market of the new product have been determined, whether to adopt the extension strategy will determine the amount of capital needed to improve the success rate of extension and improve various environmental factors and the amount of capital needed to invest in the independent brand to develop the market.

4.2.2 *The impact of the extension results on the original brand*

Brand equity will also change due to the success of extended products. This benefit will allow the brand to expand its market reach and improve its overall image. The successful extension will expand the reputation of the original brand and market resource conditions, and the adaptability of the brand will also increase. Consumers' overall evaluation of the brand image will also be improved to a certain extent, which will undoubtedly increase the original brand equity. If the brand extension doesn't work out, it will have a negative effect on the brand's image and adjust the brand's adaptability. The successful extension will increase its original brand equity, and the changes in brand equity will depend on the combined effects of the result of the above factors. In the long run, the failed extension will have a negative impact on the original brand equity, and the successful extension will increase the original brand equity. Brand extension is often an important strategy for companies to change brand positioning and accumulate brand equity.

5 CONCLUSIONS

On this basis, starting from the perspective of horizontal extension a theoretical model describing the transfer of asset value in the process of brand extension is established and analyzed the transfer of brand assets in the process of extension. The horizontal extension process is a closed-loop control process that relates to the control system, and each closed-loop control link has a forward transfer process and a feedback process. The goal of this process is to transfer the brand equity of the new product to the target market. The changing characteristics of each component of brand equity in this process are determined by the result of the extension.

REFERENCES

Aaker. David. 1991. *Managing Brand Equity. New York: FreePress* 3–7.
Aron O'Cass, Debra Grace. 2004. Exploring Consumer Experiences with a Service Brand[J]. *Journal of Product & Brand Management.*
Blackston. 1993. Beyond Brand personality: building brand relationships. *Brand Equity and Advertising: Advertising's Role in Building Strong Brands* 113–124.
Dennis A. Pitta, Lea Prevel Katsanis. 1995. Understanding Brand Equity for Successful Brand Extension[J]. *Journal of Consumer Marketing.*
Eric A.Y., Joseph C.N., Shashi M. 2010. The Malleable Brand: The Role of Implicit Theories in Evaluating Brand Extensions[J]. *Journal of Marketing* 74 (1): 80–93.
Keller K.L. 1993. Conceptualizing: Measuring and Managing Customer-based Brand Equity. *Journal of Marking* 57(1): 1–22.
Keller, K. 1998. *Strategie Brand Management. New Jersey: Prentiee Hall* 5–13.
Lassar, Banwari Mittal, Arun Sharma. 1995. Measuring Customer-based Brand Equity[J]. *Journal of Consumer Marketing.*
Sheri Bridges, Kevin L. Keller, Sanjay Sood. 2000. Communication Strategies for Brand Extensions: Enhancing Perceived Fit by Establishing Explanatory Links[J]. *Journal of Advertising* 29(4): 1–11.
Sridhar Moorthy, Brian T.R., Debarata T. 1997. Consumer Information Search Revisited: Theory and Empirical Analysis[J]. *Journal of Consumer Research* 23(4): 263–277.
Srinivas K. Reddy, Susan L. Holak, Subodh Bhat. 1994. To Extend or not to Extend: Success Determinants of Line Extensions[J]. *Journal of Marketing Research* 31 (2): 243–262.
Susan Fournier. 1998. Consumers and their Brands: Developing Relationship Theory in Consumer Research [J]. *Journal of Consumer Research* 24(4): 373.
Susan M. Broniarczyk, Joseph W. Alba. 1994. The Importance of the Brand in Brand Extension[J]. *Journal of Marketing Research* 31(2): 214–228.
Tauber, E.M. 1988. Brand Leverage: Strategy for Growth in a Cost-control World. *Journal of Advertising Research* (7): 26–33.

Economic and Business Management – Lent & Zhang (Eds)
© 2023 the Author(s), ISBN 978-1-032-24482-2

Mechanism of W_ICTs effects on work recovery

Xiaoxi Zhao
Shandong University, Jinan, Shandong, China

ABSTRACT: Online work practices have invariably increased employees' work-related use of information and communication technologies after hours (W_ICTs). Based on the Cognitive Affective Personality System (CAPS) theory and Regulatory theory, this study constructs a dual-mediated model of positive affect and cognitive input to explore the mechanism of the effect of W_ICTs on work recovery. The 316 questionnaires conducted in enterprises and institutions show that: W_ICTs has a negative effect on positive affect, and positive affect positively mediated the effect on work recovery. Meanwhile, W_ICTs has a positive effect on cognitive input, while cognitive input negatively mediated the effect on work recovery. Prevention focus positively moderated the relationship between W_ICTs and cognitive input.

1 INTRODUCTION

Affected by the increase in work volume, more and more individuals are actively or passively choosing to use electronic communication devices for work communication during non-working hours, giving rise to a new form of work-related use of information and communication technologies after hours (W_ICTs) (Derks et al. 2014). This new form of work breaks the temporal and spatial constraints of individual work, and companies will also increase the requirement for individuals to respond to work messages quickly (Ma et al. 2022). Work recovery ensures individuals have the energy to continue to meet work challenges and maintain physical and mental health (Demerouti et al. 2012; Tang et al. 2019). Therefore, how to help individuals to better recover from work after work, so as to balance the relationship between work demands and individual resources, is a question that managers and scholars given by the times need to think about and solve together.

Previous studies in the field of organizational behavior have focused on the negative relationship between non-work time electronic communication and work performance (Tian et al. 2020), or have considered individual role shifts from the "work-family boundary" domain (Derks et al. 2016). Psychologists have studied individual's perceptions of personal resource control or reconstruction in work recovery to better help individuals reduce stress, increase well-being (Sonnentag 2001), and stimulate individual creativity (Ma et al. 2022). In fact, work recovery is a process in which the individual interacts with the external environment and is influenced not only by the individual's subjective trait emotions, but also by other factors in the work context such as cognitive input. At the same time, although there is an interaction between emotion and cognition, they are mutually independent systems (Li Xingxing et al. 2021), and individuals often trigger the working mechanisms of both systems in electronic communication situations during non-working hours, which can affect both individual emotions and require cognitive input. This process can be explained by the CAPS theory proposed by Mischel and Shoda (1995), which is specifically described as a consistent pattern of behavior formed by an individual's mental representations during dynamic

DOI: 10.1201/9781003278788-35

interactions with a specific social environment. Considering both emotional and cognitive mechanisms is helpful to further clarify the relationship between W_ICTs and work recovery and enrich the research on the effects of W_ICTs on work recovery.

Although the CAPS model reveals two pathways for individuals during event processing, it does not focus on the mechanisms that generate individual personality processing dynamics (Kinnunen et al. 2011). In summary, this paper combines the CAPS model with regulatory focus theory to explore the effects of W_ICTs on individuals' work recovery through both emotional and cognitive mediators, and to explore its moderating effects on individuals' affect and cognition in the context of two regulatory focus systems arising from individual traits. The resulting model extends the study of the effects of W_ICTs on individuals, providing answers to the questions of "why" and "for whom" this new form of work is beneficial or harmful. It helps individuals to better regulate their work recovery in practice and provides ideas for managers to develop improvement programs.

2 LITERATURE REVIEW AND RESEARCH HYPOTHESIS

2.1 W_ICTs

W_ICTs can be seen as a popular way of working that has emerged with the development of technology, which changes the workplace and occurs outside of work hours (e.g., evenings, weekends, and holidays) (Xie et al. 2017). W_ICTs requires the use of tools such as smartphones and personal computers to handle work-related content (Butts et al. 2015; Ye Meng et al. 2018). Despite the growing body of research on W_ICTs, most scholars have only considered its negative effects on individuals' resources such as emotional exhaustion and energy dissipation (Bennett et al. 2018; Liao et al. 2022; Quick & Tetrick 2011), but have not examined the positive affect and cognitive input in this process. In recent years, some scholars have attempted to explain this in terms of a dual path mechanism of emotion and work (Ma et al. 2022), the outcome variables are mostly individual creativity or work performance. Obviously, the process of W_ICTs requires further resource input from individuals, which has usually been ignored. To sustain resource investment, individuals need to repair and rebuild depleted resources (Zijlstra & Sonnentag 2006), a process called "work recovery" (Meijman & Mulder 1998).

2.2 The mediating role of positive affect

Positive affect is a positive personality unit involving feelings and emotional reactions that can cause pleasurable feelings and motivate individuals to tend toward certain actions (Yu et al. 2003). Employees tend to view the work brought by W_ICTs as an additional task, which is detrimental to the generation of their positive affect (Matusik & Mickel 2011). What's more, this paper argues that positive affect generated by non-work time electronic communication has a positive effect on individuals' work recovery. Specifically, positive affect is a comfortable state of self-satisfaction (Despoina 2010), and the positive affect generated by individuals during non-working hours helps them to perform individual relaxation, which leads to a lower level of sympathetic nervous system activation (Sonnentag & Fritz 2007) and recovery from depleted resources. At the same time, the pleasure brought by positive affect causes individuals to overcome new challenges or learn new skills during the recovery process, thus increasing their level of mastery, increasing the speed of individual work recovery, and generating new individual resources through living self-satisfaction (Cavazotte et al. 2014). In summary, the following hypothesis is proposed.

H1a: W_ICTs after hours is negatively related to positive affect.
H1b: Positive affect has a positively influence on work recovery.
H1c: Positive affect mediates the relationship between W_ICTs and work recovery.

2.3 The mediating role of cognitive input

Cognitive input describes the degree of energy and contribution that individuals put into their work (William 1990), which is essentially a kind of resource-consuming (Li et al. 2021). Since the content of electronic communication during non-working hours is input from outside, which needs employees put in more cognitive resources (Park et al. 2011). As a result, the individual is a passive recipient of information, they cannot control the individual cognitive resources on their own. When people are continuously cognitively engaged, they cannot withdraw from the work and need to continuously think and solve the work content, which prevents them from psychological detachment. During this process, the individual's nervous system is at a high level of activation, and the continuous cognitive input of work causes personal work exhaustion (Derks et al. 2014), resulting in decreased sleep quality (Schieman & Young 2013), and thus inability to recover after work. In summary, the following hypothesis is proposed.

H2a: W_ICTs after hours is positively related to cognitive input.

H2b: Cognitive input has a negatively influence on work recovery.

H2c: Cognitive input mediates the relationship between W_ICTs and work recovery.

2.4 Moderating effect of prevention focus

In the CAPS model, individual responsiveness to situations and self-management plans influence the performance outcomes of personality systems (Mischel & Shoda 1995). According to regulatory focus theory, prevention focus is the most basic self-regulatory motivational system of human beings, which emphasizes the "ought self" and generates motivation by avoiding mistakes, non-losses (positive and expected) or losses (negative and undesired), minimizing the mismatch between the current state and the actual outcome (Qin Chia-Liang 2021). Prevention focus individuals aim to meet the most basic work requirements and seek work safety, stability, and security (Johnson Russell E. et al. 2015; Zhu et al. 2021). Thus individuals with a prevention focus will carefully complete the assigned work tasks (Higgins & Spiegel 2004), thus requiring them to invest more cognitive resources to prevent work errors and ensure completion of the work schedule. In summary, the following hypothesis is proposed.

H3: Prevention focus moderates the role of W_ICTs on cognitive input, compared to low-level prevention focus, individuals with a high level of prevention focus promote more cognitive input in the process of W_ICTs.

The above discussion shows that W_ICTs is a resource-consuming behavior that requires individuals to make cognitive input to ensure the completion of work, thus hindering their work recovery process. Individuals who have a lot of non-working time electronic communication tasks will be tied to the goal of "completing work" for a long time, and will continuously invest their cognitive resources to understand and complete their work tasks, thus hindering their personal work recovery process. Further, it can be noted that prevention focus personal goal pursuit has a greater impact on the above pathways. According to the self-regulatory system of prevention focus, individuals with prevention focus tend to perform basic work duties and ensure that there are no omissions and errors in the process of completing the work (Yuankun Cao & Hongdan Xu 2017), which requires their cognitive input for repeated checking and verification. Therefore, individuals with higher levels of prevention focus are more cautious in completing their work, spend more time and intensity on individual cognitive input, and are unable to complete mental detachment from their work (Park et al. 2011). Individuals with a lower level of prevention focus have less self-stress or pursue higher levels of personal fulfillment needs, thus feeling flexibility from the environment during non-work time electronic communication, investing a lower level of cognitive resources at work, and starting individual resource recovery earlier in the process of smoothly completing work tasks. In summary, the following hypotheses are proposed.

H4: Prevention focus positively moderates the mediating role of cognitive input between W_ICTs and work recovery, the mediating role of cognitive input between W_ICTs and work recovery is stronger in conditions with high-level prevention focus compared to low-level prevention focus.

3 STUDY DESIGN

3.1 *Study sample*

This paper collects data through a questionnaire survey, and the respondents are individuals working in various enterprises and institutions, involving transportation, science and technology, finance, media, and other industries. A total of 357 questionnaires were distributed through a combination of online platform and on-site distribution, and 316 valid questionnaires were excluded from the number of missing items and questionnaires, with a valid recovery rate of 88.51%, and the data came from 29 provinces except for Tibet, Qinghai, Hong Kong, Macao, and Taiwan.

The statistical results show that among the 316 valid sample subjects: 36.71% are male, 63.29% are female; 2.22% are 17 years old and below, 72.74% are 18–34 years old, 24.69% are 35–54 years old; 43.35% are general individuals, 31.96% are grassroots managers, middle-level and above managers 24.69%; 65.19% of individuals have a bachelor's degree; 34.49% are unmarried, 63.92% are married; 28.48% are state-owned enterprises, 55.70% are private enterprises, 10.44% are foreign-funded enterprises.

3.2 *Variable measurement*

This paper used a well-established scale, which is widely used in domestic and international studies, and adopted a "translation-back translation" method to finalize the measurement questions of the variables. Except for the control variables, all the variables involved in the study were evaluated using the Likert5 scale, with "1" representing "strongly disagree" and "5" representing "strongly agree". The scale names and contents are as follows.

W_ICTs: The scale developed by Ma Hongyu et al. (2016) was used to measure W_ICTs with three questions, such as "I use communication tools to be in close contact with other people because of work during the non-work time". The reliability coefficient of the scale, Cronbach's Alph coefficient 0.71.

Work recovery: Work recovery was measured by the Work Recovery Experience Scale developed by Sonnentag and Fritz (2007), which is divided into four sections: psychological detachment (Cronbach's Alph coefficient is 0.831), relaxation (Cronbach's Alph coefficient is 0.802), mastery Cronbach's Alph coefficient is 0.817), and control (Cronbach's Alph coefficient is 0.840), with four items in each section, for a total of 16 items. The reliability coefficient of the scale, Cronbach's Alph coefficient 0.922.

Positive affect: Positive affect is measured by the PANAS scale developed by Waston et al. (1988), which has 10 items divided into positive and negative dimensions. This paper uses 5 items as the measure of positive affect, such as "I feel excited by electronic work communication during non-working hours". Cronbach's Alph coefficient 0.853.

Cognitive input: Cognitive input is measured by a cognitive input Scale (May et al. 2004), with five questions, such as "I spend a lot of time thinking about my work". Cronbach's Alph coefficient is 0.826.

Prevention focus: Prevention focus was measured using the Regulatory Focus at Work Scale (Wallace et al. 2009). The original scale consists of 12 items, divided into 6 items each for promotion and prevention focus, and has been widely used in organizational management research. This paper used six of the prevention focus items and phrased them according to the measurement scenario, such as "I am concerned about completing my work tasks correctly during W_ICTs" and so on. Cronbach's Alph coefficient is 0.883.

Control variables: AS suggested in previous related articles, demographic variables such as gender, nature of business, education level, and position level can have different degrees of influence on the outcome variable work recovery, so they are treated as control variables.

4 RESEARCH RESULTS

4.1 Homogeneous variance test and multicollinearity test

To examine the discriminant validity between variables and to avoid the measurement results being affected by common method bias, this study used Harman's one-way method and validated factor analysis (CFA) to test for common method bias issues.

First, using the Harman one-way test, the variance explained by the first principal component was obtained as 29.941%, which is lower than 40%, indicating that there is no serious homogeneous variance problem in this study. In addition, the correlation model was tested for multicollinearity before regression analysis, and all variance inflation factors VIF were between 1.254 and 1.494 (less than 10) with a tolerance greater than 0.1, indicating that there is almost no multicollinearity problem among the variables. Therefore, further data analysis can be performed to test the relationship between the variables.

4.2 Validation factor analysis

In this paper, a validated factor analysis of the scale was conducted using Mplus 8.3. The study involved five variables, which were non-work time electronic communication, work recovery, positive affect, cognitive input, and prevention focus, and each of the five variables was composed to compare the fit of the nested models. Considering that the work recovery scale involves a large number of dimensions and question items, the item parceling method (item parceling) was used to reduce the error, and the four dimensions of work recovery were parceled into one package. By combining the variables, we examined the fit of the one-factor model, two-factor model, three-factor model, four-factor model, and five-factor model, as shown in Table 1. The results show that the five-factor model fits the data better (χ^2/df = 3.076, CFI = 0.858, TLI = 0.847, RMSEA = 0.065, SRMR = 0.058) and significantly better than the other models, indicating that the measurement has better discriminant validity.

Table 1. Validation factor analysis.

Models	Combination	χ^2 /df	RMSEA	CFI	TLI	SRMR
Five-factor model	W_ICTs;PA; CI; PF;WR	3.076	0.065	0.858	0.847	0.074
Four-factor model	W_ICTs;PA+CI; PF;WR	5.353	0.074	0.817	0.804	0.082
Three-factor model	W_ICTs+PF;PA+CI; WR	7.255	0.111	0.581	0.556	0.162
Two-factor model	W_ICTs+PF; PA+CI+WR	8.756	0.093	0.705	0.688	0.094
One-factor model	W_ICTs+PA+CI+PF+WR	11.474	0.120	0.506	0.478	0.136

Notes: W_ICTs indicates W_ICTs; PA indicates positive affect; CI indicates cognitive input; PF indicates prevention focus; and WR indicates work recovery.

4.3 Descriptive statistics and correlation analysis

Table 2 shows the means, standard deviations and correlations of the model variables. It can be seen that W_ICTs was negatively correlated with positive affect (r = −0.482, p < 0.01)

Table 2. Descriptive statistical analysis.

Variables	M	SD	1	2	3	4	5	6	7	8
1. Gender	–	0.483								
2. Nature of business	–	0.775	.123*							
3. Education level	–	0.700	−.029	−.059						
4. Position level	–	0.862	−.155	.068	.254					
5. W_ICTs	3.9283	.65637	−.050	−.154	.097	.036				
6. Positive affect	3.7386	.78955	−.081	−.047	.136	.168*	−.482**			
7. Cognitive input	2.4694	.94063	.157	−.005	−.108	−.106	.292**	−.441		
8. Prevention focus	3.8676	.76461	.066	.229	.071	−.053	.412**	.282	.063	
9. Work recovery	3.7654	.81011	−.041	.001	.080	.065	−.421*	.622**	−.489**	−186

Notes: n = 316; **. At 0.01 level (two-tailed), correlation is significant; *. At the 0.05 level (two-tailed), the correlation is significant.

and positively correlated with cognitive input (r = 0.292, p < 0.01), which provides initial support for H1a and H2a. Positive affect was positively correlated with work recovery (r = 0.622, p < 0.01) and cognitive input was negatively correlated with work recovery (r = −0.489, p < 0.01), which provided initial support for H1b and H2b.

4.4 Hypothesis testing

4.4.1 Mediating effect

In this paper, the hypotheses were tested using hierarchical regression methods, and the test results are shown in Tables 3 and 4. Using multiple regression analysis to test for mediating effects, individual positive affect were significantly and positively correlated with psychological disengagement (r = 0.280, p < 0.01), relaxation (r = 0.433, p < 0.01), mastery (r = 0.549, p < 0.01), and control (r = 0.387, p < 0.01), and cognitive input had only a significant negative correlation (r = −0.393, p < 0.01).

In order to investigate the specific factors influencing the parallel mediating effect and the relationship between the two mediating effects, a new interaction term was created and the significance of the coefficients was tested using the Bootstrapping Method with 5000

Table 3. Positive affect mediated regression model.

Variables		Positive affect		Work recovery		
		Model 1	Model 2	Model 3	Model 4	Model 5
Control variables	Gender	−.051	−.039	−.033	−.022	−.001
	Nature of business	−.044	.026	.006	.069	.055
	Education Level	.097	.059	.068	.034	.001
	Position Level	.138*	.128*	.042	.033	−.037
Independent variable	W_ICTs		.473**		.426	.166
Intermediate variables	positive affect					.550**
R^2		.043	.259	.010	.185	.410
$\triangle R^2$		.043	.217	.010	.176	.224
F		3.457**	21.701**	.753**	14.099**	35.718**

Notes: n = 316; **. At 0.01 level (two-tailed), correlation is significant; *. At the 0.05 level (two-tailed), the correlation is significant.

Table 4. Cognitive input mediated regression model.

Variables		Cognitive input				Work recovery		
		Model 1	Model 2	Model 3	Model 4	Model 5	Model 6	Model 7
Control variables	Gender	.148	.141*	.121*	.112	−.033	−.022	.034
	Nature of business	−.025	−.067	−.032	−.022	.006	.069	.042
	Education Level	−.090	−.067	−.075	−.065	.068	.034	.007
	Position Level	−.059	−.053	−.043	−.024	.042	.033	.012
Independent variable	W_ICTs		−.287**	−.365**	−.197**		.426	.311
Intermediate variables	Cognitive level							−.402**
Adjustment variables	Prevention focus			.201**	.295**			
Interaction items	Prevention focus × Awareness level				−.254**			
R^2		.039	.119	.151	.0166	.010	.185	.328
$\triangle R^2$		.039	.080	.032	.015	.010	.176	.142
F		3.192**	8.385**	9.163**	8.730**	.753	14.099**	25.081**

Notes: n = 316; **. At 0.01 level (two-tailed), correlation is significant; *. At the 0.05 level (two-tailed), the correlation is significant.

replicate samples. As shown in Table 5, the positive mediating effect of positive affect between non-working time e-communication and mastery perception was significant (r = 0.192, p < 0.05), with a confidence interval not including 0, and 62% of the combined mediating path. That is, non-work time electronic communication can enhance individuals' perceptions of personal mastery by increasing their positive affect, thus facilitating their work recovery, as confirmed by H2(c). The mediating role of cognitive input between non-work time electronic communication and psychological disengagement was significant (r = −0.252, p < 0.01) with a confidence interval excluding 0, and significantly accounted for 72% of the combined mediating path. That is, W_ICTs can reduce psychological disengagement by increasing individuals' perceived cognitive input, thereby adversely affecting their post-work recovery, as confirmed by H4(a).

Table 5. Mediation effect pathway relationships.

Variables	Psychological Detachment			Relaxation			Mastery			Control		
	B	SE	95% CI	B	SE	95% CI	B	SE	95% CI	B	SE	95% CI
Ind1	0.098	0.060	[0.018, 0.250]	0.151	0.080	[0.033, 0.336]	0.192*	0.083	[0.053, 0.372]	0.135	0.076	[0.026, 0.314]
Ind2	−0.252**	0.084	[0.109, 0.436]	−0.107	0.073	[−0.004, 0.283]	−0.118	0.068	[0.015, 0.283]	−0.089	0.073	[−0.025, 0.268]

Notes: Ind1 denotes positive affect-mediated pathway; Ind2 denotes perceived cognitive input-mediated pathway. n = 316; **. At the 0.01 level (two-tailed), the correlation is significant; *. At the 0.05 level (two-tailed), the correlation is significant.

4.4.2 Moderating effect

In this study, MPLUS 8.3 software was used to implement Preacher's mediated model test with moderation, and the interaction terms between W_ICTs, prevention focus, and W_ICTs and facilitation focus were introduced to construct the model and examine the significance of the interaction term regression coefficients, and the results are shown in Table 6. The results showed that the interaction term between W_ICTs and prevention focus had a significant positive effect on cognitive input (B = 0.156, SE = 0.158, p < 0.01), indicating a moderating effect, and hypothesis H3 was tested.

Table 6. Unstandardized regression coefficients.

Variables	Cognitive input	
	B	SE
Prevention focus	0.313	0.127
W_ICTs x prevention focus	0.156**	0.158

Notes: n = 316; **. At the 0.01 level (two-tailed), the correlation is significant

4.4.3 The mediating effect test of being regulated

In this study, the mean value of prevention focus plus or minus one standard deviation was taken and a Simple slope test (SST) was conducted to test whether the mediating effect was moderated, and the results are shown in Table 7. When the level of individual prevention focus was low (below one standard deviation), the indirect effect of non-work time electronic communication on work recovery through cognitive input was weak (r = 0.029, p < 0.01) with a confidence interval of [0.028,0.539]; when the level of individual prevention focus was high (above one standard deviation), the indirect effect of non-work time electronic communication on work recovery through cognitive input was strong (r = 0.029, p < 0.01). The indirect effect was stronger (r = 0.413, p < 0.01) with a confidence interval of [0.028,0.539] and did not contain 0. Thus, H4 was supported by data validation. The indirect effect of W_ICTs affecting work recovery through perceived cognitive input was moderated by prevention focus, which was enhanced when the level of prevention focus was higher.

Table 7. Moderated mediating effects.

Prevention focus	Effect Value	Standard error	95% confidence interval
Low level (−SD)	0.029**	0.097	[0.028,0.539]
High level (+SD)	0.413**	0.109	[0.028,0.539]
High-Low Difference	0.556	0.120	[−0.448,0.281]

Notes: n = 316; **. At the 0.01 level (two-tailed), the correlation is significant.

5 RESEARCH SUMMARY

5.1 Research findings

Based on the CAPS theory and regulatory focus theory, this paper examined the effects of W_ICTs on individual work recovery. As expected, W_ICTs affects workers' work recovery through two pathways (emotional mechanism and cognitive mechanism). From the

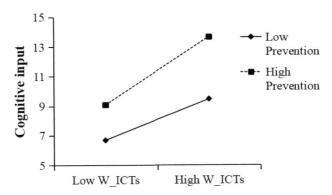

Figure 1. Moderating effect of prevention focus on the relationship between W_ICTs and cognitive input.

emotional mechanism, employees tend to view the work brought by W_ICTs as an additional task, which is detrimental to the generation of their positive affect (Matusik & Mickel 2011). What's more, positive affect generated by non-work time electronic communication is a comfortable state of self-satisfaction (Despoina 2010), which has a positive effect on individuals' work recovery. From the cognitive mechanism, since the content of electronic communication during non-working hours is input from outside, which needs employees to put in more cognitive resources (Park et al. 2011), so W_ICTs positively influences cognitive input. When people are continuously cognitively engaged, they cannot withdraw from the work and need to continuously think and solve the work content, which prevents them from recovering after work.

In addition, individuals with a prevention focus will carefully complete the assigned work tasks (Higgins & Spiegel 2004), thus requiring them to invest more cognitive resources to prevent work errors and ensure completion of the work schedule. So prevention focus positively moderates the effect between W_ICTs and cognitive input.

5.2 *Theoretical contributions*

Enriching the positive variables of W_ICTs. Previous research on out-of-hours work communication has often focused on its impact on individuals' home lives (Butts et al. 2015). However, W_ICTs is essentially an emerging work style within the work area, and its impact on individuals' perceptions of the day's work and the recovery of work resources has been largely overlooked. This paper expands the research related to non-work time electronic communication by extending the post-effect variables to work recovery.

A dual-path mechanism of positive affect and cognitive input is constructed, and the mechanism of the effect of non-work time electronic communication on work recovery is revealed from multiple perspectives. Based on the cognitive-affect personality system theory, this paper introduces two mediating variables, emotion and cognition, which unlock the black box of the driving mechanism of work recovery and facilitate an in-depth understanding of the influence process of non-work time work communication. In addition, the study finds a positive effect of positive affect on mastery factor and a negative effect of cognitive input on psychological detachment, further refining the study on the internal classification of work recovery and responding to previous scholars' call for "how" to access new resources (Tang, H. E., et al. 2019).

The boundary effects of prevention focus on work recovery were explored. This paper examines the moderating role of individual prevention focus goals in the relationship between electronic communication and cognitive input during non-work time, incorporating contextual factors into the study. On the one hand, this paper makes up for the lack of existing research on prevention focus at the safety level. On the other hand, it unveils the "why" of individual control over cognitive input, and integrates relatively stable cognitive variables with changing environmental factors, which can explain the influence of non-work time electronic communication on work recovery.

5.3 *Practice inspiration*

Electronic communication may in the future become a way of working that all employees of enterprises need to face. In order to better regulate personal life and work and help companies achieve employee management, employees and companies need to do the following.

Research results show that non-working time electronic communication is a potential risk factor that hinders work recovery, not only will consume the positive affect generated by individuals, but also increase the cognitive input pressure of individuals. Therefore, it is important to reduce the amount of non-working time electronic communication tasks and give employees adequate individual breaks. On the other hand, companies can adopt diversified ways to compensate for the resource consumption of employees working during non-working hours, such as creating a good scope of online communication, paying proper attention to individual employees' living conditions, to motivate employees to put into work with a more full state of mind.

What's more, positive affect helps individuals to carry out work resource recovery. Companies can enhance employees' sense of corporate culture, set up work groups to help employees better complete their work tasks, and enrich online learning content to improve employees' cognitive levels. Employees should set up personal long-term development goals, adjust themselves promptly, adapt to the working environment of electronic communication during non-working hours, and take appropriate breaks to supplement individual motivation.

Additionally, research results show that regulatory focus causes individuals to engage in more cognitive input. In reality, most employees experience work as "for living" and do not feel the pleasure and self-satisfaction of work. Therefore, companies need to first meet the material needs of individual survival, such as guaranteeing the salary level of employees and improving their welfare benefits. Individual employees also need to learn to shift their focus to the "gain" rather than the "loss" of their work. In this case, the employees have the psychological security of safety, so that they can be more confidently engaged in work recovery activities.

5.4 *Limitations and future prospects*

There are still some shortcomings and limitations in this paper, and the subsequent study can be further advanced and improved in the following aspects.

First, this paper mainly uses cross-sectional data to confirm the relationship between relevant variables, while work recovery changes with time, and cross-sectional data cannot effectively reveal the relationship between variable changes and dynamic work recovery. Therefore, in the future, the diary survey method or other qualitative and quantitative methods can be used to obtain data in regular segments to explore the mechanism of action between electronic communication and work recovery during non-working hours.

Second, future research could focus on the content and frequency of W_ICTs. The number and time of tasks for W_ICTs are diverse and may be influenced by different industries, types of companies, and work levels. In this paper, the above variables are studied as control variables, which can be varied in future studies to find the best arrangement of task quantity and work duration to provide suggestions for corporate practices.

Finally, the study in this paper only considers the role of individual prevention focus in mediating the mechanism between electronic communication and work recovery during non-working hours. In the future, boundary factors such as team or organizational level (leadership type, organizational support, etc.) can be further introduced to explore whether a cross-level moderating effect on the studied mechanism of action will be formed to find new ways out for corporate people management in a normalized epidemic.

REFERENCES

Bennett A. A., Bakker A. B., Field J. G. 2018. Recovery from Work-Related Effort: A Meta-Analysis[J]. *Journal of Organizational Behavior.*

Butts, Marcus M.; Boswell, Wendy R.; Becker. 2015. Hot Buttons and Time Sinks: The Effects of Electronic Communication During Nonwork Time on Emotions and Work- Nonwork CoYFlict (Article)[J]. *Academy of Management Journal* (3): 763–788.

Cao, Yuankun, Xu, Hongdan. 2017. A review of the Application of Regulatory Focus Theory in Organizational Management[J]. *Journal of Management* 14(08): 1254–1262.

Cavazotte F., Heloisa Lemos A., Villadsen K. 2014. Corporate Smart Phones: Professionals' Conscious Engagement in Escalating Work Connectivity[J]. *New Technology, Work and Employment* 29(1): 72–87.

Demerouti E., Bakker A. B., Sonnentag S., *et al.* 2012. Work-Related Flow and Energy at Work and at Home: A Study on the Role of Daily Recovery [J]. *Journal of Organizational Behavior* 33(2): 276–295.

Derks D., Bakker A. B. 2014. Smartphone Use, Work-Home Interference, and Burnout: a Diary Study on the Role of Recovery[J]. *Applied Psychology* 63(3): 411–440.

Derks D., Bakker A. B. Peters P., *et al.* 2016. Work-Related Smartphone Use, Work-Family Conflict and Family Role Performance: The Role of Segmentation Preference[J]. *Human Relations* 1045–1068.

Despoina Xanthopoulou. 2010. The Life of A Happy Worker: Examining Short-Term Fluctuations in Employee Happiness and Well-Being[J]. *Human Relations* 63(2): 301–303.

Higgins E. T., Spiegel S. 2004. Promotion and Prevention Strategies for Self-Regulation: A Motivated Cognition Perspective [D]. *In* R. F. Baumeister & K. D. Vohs *(Eds.)* 171–187.

Johnson Russell E. *et al.* 2015. Regulatory Focus Trickle-Down: How Leader Regulatory Focus And Behavior Shape Follower Regulatory Focus[J]. *Organizational Behavior and Human Decision Processes* 140: 29–45.

Kinnunen, U., Feldt, T., Siltaloppi, M., & Sonnentag, S. 2011. Work Demands-Resources Model in the Context of Recovery: Testing Recovery Experiences as Mediators. *European Journal of Work and Organizational Psychology* 20: 805–832.

Li Xingxing, Zou, Yan, Wang, Sihui. 2021. Are Inter-Work Micro-Breaks Beneficial for Work Performance Improvement? –A Moderated Dual Mediation Model[J]. *Journal of Lanzhou University of Finance and Economics* 37(02): 34–45.

Liao, H. H., Huang, L. and Hu, B. 2022. Application Of Resource Conservation Theory in Organizational Behavior: Evolution and Challenges[J]. *Advances in Psychological Science* 30(02): 449–463.

Ma, Li, Tang, Qiuqiu. 2022. How "Continuous Online" Connectivity Stimulates Individual Creativity – A Two-Path Model[J]. *East China Economic Management* 36(02): 109–118.

Matusik, S. F. & Mickel, A. E. 2011. Embracing or Embattled by Converged Mobile Devices? Users' Experiences With A Contemporary Connectivity Technology. *Human Relations* 64: 1001–1030.

Meijman T. F., Mulder G. 1998. Psychological Aspects of Workload[J]. *New handbook of work & organizational psychology.*

Mischel W., Shoda Y. 1995. A Cognitive-Affective System Theory of Personality: Reconceptualizing Situations, Dispositions, Dynamics, and Invariance in Personality Structure[J]. *Psychological Review* 102(2): 246.

Park, Y., Fritz, C. & Jex, S. M. 2011. Relationships Between Work-Home Segmentation and Psychological Detachment from Work: The Role of Communication Technology Use at Home. *Journal of Occupational Health Psychology* 16(4): 457e467.

Qin, Chia-Liang. 2021. A Review of the Application of Regulatory Focus in Organizational Management Research[J]. *Western Economic Management Forum* 32(03): 80-91+99.

Quick J. C., Tetrick L. E. 2011. *Handbook of Occupational Health Psychology [M]. American Psychological Association.*

Schieman, S. & Young, M. C. 2013. Are Communications About Work Outside Regular Working Hours Associated With Work-To-Family Coyflict, Psychological Distress And Sleep Problems? *Work & Stress* 27(3): 244–261.

Sonnentag S, Fritz C. 2007. The Recovery Experience Questionnaire[J]. *Journal of Occupational Health Psychology* 12(3): 204–221.

Sonnentag, S. 2001. Work, Recovery Activities, and Individual Well-Being: A Diary Study. *Journal of Occupational Health Psychology* 6: 196–210.

Tang H.-Y., Yue S.-S., Shi Y.-W., Ma H.-Y. 2019. To Work Better: The Connotation and Realization Machine Of Work Recovery[J]. *Psychological Science* 42(05): 1186–1193.

Tian Xizhou, Guo Xiaodong, Xu Hao. 2020. New Trends in Work Remodeling Research – Based on The Perspective of Regulatory Orientation[J]. *Advances in Psychological Science* 28(08): 1367–1378.

Wallace J. C., Johnson P. D., and Frazier M. L. 2009. An Examination of The Factorial, Construct, and Predictive Validity and Utility of The Regulatory Focus At Work Scale[J]. *Journal of Organizational Behavior* 30(6): 805–831.

Watson D., Clark L. A. and Tellegen A. 1988. Development and Validation of Brief Measures of Positive and Negative Affect: The PANAS Scales[J]. *Journal of Personality and Social Psychology* 54(6): 1063–70.

William A. Kahn. 1990. Psychological Conditions of Personal Engagement and Disengagement at Work[J]. *The Academy of Management Journal* 33(4): 692–724.

Xie J., Ma H., Zhou Z. E., *et al.* 2017. Work-Related Use of IYFormation and Communication Technologies after Hours (W_ICTs) and Emotional Exhaustion: A Mediated Moderation Model[J]. *Computers in Human Behavior* 79(feb.): 94–104.

Ye M., Tang H.-Y., Xie J.-L., Ma H.-Y., and Yue S.-S. 2018. The "Double-Edged Sword" Effect and Psychological Mechanism of Using Communication Technology To Process Work During Non-Working Hours[J]. *Psychological Science* 41(01): 160–166.

Yu, Songmei, Yang, Lizhu. 2003. A Review of Mitchell's Personality System Theory of Cognitive *Emotion [J]. Advances in Psychological Science* 11(2): 5.

Zhu B., Zhang Jialiang, Liu Jun. 2021. The Effect of Prevention Focus on Individual Creativity: A Mediated Model of Being Moderated[J]. *Journal of Management* 34(01): 43–55.

Zijlstra F., Sonnentag S. 2006. After Work is Done: Psychological Perspectives on Recovery From Work[J]. *European Journal of Work & Organizational Psychology* 15(2): 129–138.

Economic and Business Management – Lent & Zhang (Eds)
© 2023 the Author(s), ISBN 978-1-032-24482-2

Shandong iron & steel group company limited cost sticky and its influencing factors research

Na Xiao*
Yantai Shandong Technology and Business University, Yantai, China

ABSTRACT: The output of Chinese crude steel in 2021 has declined. This phenomenon has been very rare in the past 40 years. This signal tells us that China's steel industry has entered a "double carbon" period. In response to the call of the state, iron and steel enterprises take the initiative to undertake the task of reducing production and emission, At the same time, iron and steel companies will face greater competitive pressure and higher production costs. In this context, cost management is essential for enterprises. This paper selects Shandong Iron and steel, an important iron and steel enterprise in China, as a case. This paper uses Weiss model to measure its cost stickiness, studies the influencing factors of its cost stickiness, and puts forward corresponding suggestions. It is found that there are cost stickiness and anti-cost stickiness. Industry factors, agency problems, human capital and asset intensity will all affect its cost stickiness.

1 INTRODUCTION

1.1 *Research background and significance*

The iron and steel industry is an important industry for China's economic development. However, the development of China's iron and steel enterprises is restricted by various problems, such as excess iron and steel production capacity, increasing environmental pressure and the "double carbon" new policy. Under this background, how should iron and steel enterprises break through the "cold winter of development" and usher in new vitality of development. Cost management is an important work of business activities. Scientific cost management can help enterprises enhance market competitiveness. Cost stickiness is an important part of cost management. The traditional behavior model considers that the relationship between cost and business is linear. Scholars such as Banker and Johnson (1993) found that, there is a nonlinear relationship between sales revenue and cost, that is, the problem of cost stickiness. In the past, most of the scholars' studies on Cost Stickiness were empirical studies based on big data, and few of them studied a case. In this paper, Shandong Iron and steel, a representative enterprise of China's iron and steel enterprises, is selected as a case to study its cost stickiness. On the one hand, it can supplement the empirical study of Cost Stickiness and enrich the research framework of cost stickiness. On the other hand, it can provide corresponding reference for cost management of other iron and steel enterprises.

1.2 *Literature review*

American scholar Banker and Johnson (1993) found that there is a nonlinear relationship between sales revenue and cost. Anderson, Banker and Janakiraman (2003) found that the sales revenue increased by 1% and the expenses increased by 0.55%, while the sales revenue

---
*Corresponding Author: 957045701@qq.com

 DOI: 10.1201/9781003278788-36

decreased by 1% and the expenses decreased by only 0.35%, suggesting that the enterprise has the problem of cost stickiness. Subramaniam et al. (2003) changed the definition method of cost on the basis of Anderson's research and obtained the same conclusion, which confirmed the existence of cost stickiness. Subsequent scholars have done a lot of research on the causes of cost stickiness. Banker and Chen (2006) found that enterprises with a high proportion of fixed assets will also have higher adjustment costs, which is prone to cost stickiness. Calleja et al. (2006) found that the higher the capital intensity and human capital intensity of enterprises, the higher the Cost Stickiness of enterprises. Banker, byzalov and plehn-dujowich (2011) summarized the causes of Cost Stickiness as three factors: adjustment cost, manager expectation and agency problem. Kama and Weiss (2013) found that the operating conditions of enterprises also affect the Cost Stickiness of enterprises. The above studies on the existence and causes of cost stickiness are empirical studies based on big data. Few scholars take a single enterprise as a case study.

1.3 *Framework*

The first chapter is the introduction, which introduces the research background, research significance, research content and research methods; The second chapter is the case analysis. Firstly, the measurement method is introduced, and then the data acquisition and processing are explained. According to the measurement model and the obtained data, the measurement results of Shandong Iron and steel cost stickiness are calculated; The third chapter is the analysis of influencing factors, which studies the influencing factors of Shandong Iron and steel cost stickiness; The fourth chapter is the countermeasure suggestions and summary. According to the influencing factors of cost stickiness, it puts forward relevant adjustment suggestions, and summarizes the research of the full text.

1.4 *Working methodology*

(1) Literature research method: Before the research, I read a lot of literature related to cost stickiness, sorted out the existence, causes and research methods of cost stickiness, and found the innovation of the article by referring to previous research.
(2) Case study method: This paper adopts the method of case study, selects Shandong Iron and steel as the research object, which is a representative enterprise in China's iron and steel industry, calculates the Cost Stickiness of enterprises, and studies its influencing factors according to the characteristics of the industry.

2 CASE ANALYSIS

2.1 *Measuring method*

In this paper, Dan Weiss (2010) model is selected to measure the Cost Stickiness of Shandong Iron and steel. The reasons for choosing Weiss model are as follows: At present, the research on Cost Stickiness mainly adopts the "ABJ" model and Weiss model. Weiss model can measure the Cost Stickiness of a single enterprise, while "ABJ" model uses regression model to study big data and multiple samples, "ABJ" model is not suitable for this study, so this paper chooses Weiss model to study the Cost Stickiness of Shandong Iron and steel. Weiss research model is as follows:

$$sticky = \log\left(\frac{\Delta Cost}{\Delta Sale}\right)up - \log\left(\frac{\Delta Cost}{\Delta Sale}\right)down \tag{1}$$

Sticky = Cost Stickiness; Cost = Total operating costs; Sale = Total operating income; $\Delta Cost$ = Difference between operating costs of the next quarter and the previous quarter;

ΔSale = Difference in operating income between the next quarter and the previous quarter; Up = The quarter in which the operating income increase closest to the end of the year in the accounting period; Down = The quarter in which the operating income decreases close to the end of the year in the accounting period.

Sticky greater than zero indicates that the enterprise has the problem of cost stickiness. The larger the sticky value, the greater the Cost Stickiness; Sticky less than zero indicates that the enterprise has the problem of anti- cost stickiness.

2.2 Data source and processing

The relevant cost data required in this article comes from the financial report of Shandong Iron and steel and NetEase for financial. In order to use Weiss model for calculation, the data are processed as follows:

(1) Eliminate data whose cost change is inconsistent with the direction of business volume change; Weiss model requires that the change direction of cost should be consistent with the change direction of business volume.
(2) Eliminate the data of continuous increase and decrease of business volume in an accounting period; In Weiss model, up refers to the quarter in which the operating income increase closest to the end of the year in the accounting period, and down refers to the quarter in which the operating income decreases close to the end of the year in the accounting peri-od. If the business volume continues to increase or decrease, it cannot be calculated.

2.3 Calculation results

In this paper, the Cost Stickiness of 2007, 2008, 2009, 2010, 2011, 2013, 2019, 2020 and 2021 meeting the sample conditions are measured, and the measurement results are −0.16, 2.48, −1.19, −0.12, −0.04, 0.03, 0.14, 1.68 and 0.32 respectively (see Table 1). The average value is 0.24, indicating that the enterprise has cost stickiness, moreover, in 2007, 2009, 2010 and 2013, it showed the phenomenon of anti-cost stickiness. To sum up, Shandong Iron and steel has not only cost stickiness but also anti cost stickiness.

Table 1. Cost -sticky calculation table.

Accounting period	2007	2008	2009	2010	2011	2013	2019	2020	2021
Sticky	−0.16	2.48	−1.19	−0.12	−0.04	0.03	0.14	1.68	0.32

3 INFLUENCE FACTORS

3.1 Industry factors

The Cost Stickiness of Shandong Iron and steel decreased from 1.68 to 0.32 from 2020 to 2021. In 2020, President Xi Jinping clearly announced that the goal of "carbon-to-peak" and "carbon neutrality", steel companies were listed as high-emission enterprises. In response to the call of the national "double carbon" strategy, China's iron and steel industry has taken the initiative to undertake the task of reducing production and emission. The development of the iron and steel industry has changed from a period of high-speed development to a period of high-quality development. Due to the reduction of output, Shandong Iron and steel may reduce enterprise investment and control costs. Therefore, compared with 2020, the Cost Stickiness in 2021 has decreased.

3.2 Capital intensity factors

Iron and steel enterprises are capital intensive enterprises. Generally speaking, enterprises with high capital intensity will also have high cost stickiness. Capital intensive enterprises have a high proportion of fixed assets, and fixed costs do not change with the change of business volume. When the business volume of an enterprise suddenly drops, such costs cannot be adjusted in time, and the costs allocated to unit products will also increase, resulting in production stickiness, see Table 2.

Table 2. Capital intensity table.

100 million yuan	2007	2008	2009	2010	2011	2012	2013
Capital intensity	0.51	0.64	1.14	1.06	0.93	0.73	0.73

The capital intensity of Shandong Iron and steel showed an upward trend from 2007 to 2009, increasing from 0.51 to 1.14; From 2010 to 2013, the overall trend was downward, from 0.98 to 0.65. Shandong Iron and steel is a capital-intensive enterprise. From 2007 to 2009, the iron and steel industry is developing rapidly, and the enterprises are expanding rapidly. The financial crisis broke out in 2019. In order to alleviate the impact of the financial crisis in 2009, the management began to reduce capital expansion, slow down the company's development speed and adjust the capital structure. Therefore, the capital intensity of Shandong Iron and steel showed a downward trend in the next few years. The average cost stickiness from 2007 to 2009 was 0.38, and the average cost stickiness in 2010, 2011 and 2013 was −0.04. The Cost Stickiness in the rising capital intensity stage was much higher than that in the declining capital intensity stage.

3.3 Human capital factors

According to the adjustment cost theory, the higher the human capital of an enterprise, the higher the adjustment cost will be Calleja (2006). When the enterprise is in good development, in order to improve the professional and technical level of employees the enterprise usually increases the investment in education and training fees. When the sales revenue declines, the management will not lay off staff and retain human capital, which will eventually increase the Cost Stickiness of the enterprise. Because the management will consider the costs already paid, see Table 3.

Table 3. Human capital statue table.

	2020	2019	2018	2017	2016	2015
Number of employees	21398	19103	18881	18249	31307	31592
Per capita salary (10,000 yuan)	20.54	16.77	14.01	11.08	7.24	8.88

Shandong Iron and steel laid off many employees in 2017, which reduced the expenditure on human capital and alleviated the problem of cost stickiness to a certain extent. In addition, the per capita salary of employees is increasing year by year, which shows that enterprises pay more attention to recruiting and cultivating high-quality talents. On the one hand, it is conducive to the long-term development of the enterprise and can help the enterprise reduce the operating cost. On the other hand, the training of high-quality employees will increase the adjustment cost of the enterprise. When special circumstances require adjustment, it will produce greater cost stickiness.

3.4 *Agency problem factors*

Under the modern company system, the objectives pursued by the management and shareholders are different. In order to maximize personal interests, the management has the motivation to expand the scale of the enterprise and build a personal business empire. This behavior of the management often deviates from the best resource allocation of the enterprise, which is not conducive to the development of the enterprise and increases the Cost Stickiness of the enterprise. Shandong Iron and steel is a state-owned enterprise. Its strategic layout and expansion plan will be restricted by the government. If the management's decisions affect the development of the enterprise, they will not be approved. It limits the motivation of the management to meet private benefits through "building imperialism", which can effectively reduce the Cost Stickiness of the enterprise.

4 CONCLUSIONS AND RECOMMENDATIONS

4.1 *Cost Stickiness adjustment proposal*

4.1.1 *Pay attention to the adjustment cost of enterprises and reasonably allocate enterprise resources*

Iron and steel enterprises are capital intensive enterprises, which have the problem of high fixed assets and are prone to cost stickiness. When making decisions, the management should also consider the Cost Stickiness of the enterprise, reasonably allocate the enterprise assets, and prevent excessive purchase of fixed assets. In addition, the management should also pay attention to the issue of human capital. Hiring too many employees will also lead to higher adjustment costs. Short term employees can be considered in the period of business growth.

4.1.2 *Improve the supervision and reward mechanism of the management*

Based on the agency theory, the management's pursuit of private interests may lead to unreasonable resource allocation and high cost. On the one hand, it is necessary to strengthen the supervision of the management to reduce the opportunities for them to seek private interests and damage the interests of the company. On the other hand, it is necessary to strengthen the incentive mechanism for the management to coordinate the interests of shareholders and management.

4.2 *Conclusions*

This paper studies the existence of Cost Stickiness of Shandong Iron and steel and its influencing factors by calculating the cost data of Shandong Iron and steel from 2007 to 2021. Through the research, this paper draws the following conclusions: Shandong Iron and steel has the phenomenon of cost stickiness, and its cost stickiness is closely related to its industry attributes. The high capital intensity and high human capital of the iron and steel industry lead to its high adjustment cost, which leads to the existence of cost stickiness. In addition, its cost stickiness is also affected by industry factors and agency problems, which is universal. Therefore, the management of iron and steel enterprises should pay attention to cost management in their daily business activities to minimize the impact of Cost Stickiness on the enterprise.

REFERENCES

Banker R D, Chen L. 2006. Predicting Earnings Using a Model Based on Cost Variability and Cost Stickiness. *The Accounting Review* 81(2): 285–307.

Calleja K, Steliaros M, Thomas D C. 2006. A Note on Cost Stickiness: Some International Comparisons. *Management Accounting Research* 17(2): 127.

Dan, Weiss. 2010. Cost Behavior and Analysts' Earnings Forecasts. *The Accounting Review* 85(4): 1441–1471.

Kama ltay, Weiss Dan. 2013. Do Earnings Targets and Managerial Incentives Affect Sticky Costs?. *Journal of Ae counting Research* 51(1): 201–224.

Kenneth Calleja, Michael Steliaros, Dylan C. Thomas. 2006. A note on cost stickiness: Some International Comparisons. *Management Accounting Research* 17(2): 127–140.

Mark C. Anderson, Rajiv D. Banker, Surya N. Janakiraman. 2003. Are Selling, General, and Administrative Costs "Sticky"?. *Journal of Accounting Research* 41(1): 47–63.

Rajiv D. Banker, Holly H. Johnston. 1993. An Empirical Study of Cost Drivers in the U.S. Airline Industry. *The Accounting Review* 68(3): 576–601.

Weidenmier, Marcia Lynne, C. Subramaniam. 2003. "Additional Evidence on the Sticky Behavior of Costs." *SSRN Electronic Journal* 9.

Economic and Business Management – Lent & Zhang (Eds)
© 2023 the Author(s), ISBN 978-1-032-24482-2

A brief research on the development trend of transformation of scientific and technological achievements of universities in Shanghai

M.A. Weier Situ & Jingwei Xu*
University of Shanghai for Science and Technology, Shanghai, P.R. China

ABSTRACT: In recent years, the transformation of scientific and technological achievements has become the focus of attention of scientific research institutions, universities and research and development departments of enterprises. One of Shanghai's urban construction planning goals is to build a region-wide science and technology innovation center, and Shanghai universities have naturally become an important part of supporting this goal. By analyzing the exploration, experience and cases of the transformation of scientific and technological achievements in many universities in Shanghai, this paper lists the opportunities and challenges faced by the transformation of scientific and technological achievements in Shanghai universities, and puts forward suggestions for resource integration, multi-party cooperation and professional personnel training. This paper explores the development trend of the transformation of scientific and technological achievements in Shanghai universities.

1 GENERAL INSTRUCTIONS

With the intensification of the subdivision of economic activities, the economic competition has gradually evolved into the competition of science and technology. The transformation efficiency of scientific and technological achievements, especially the commercialization process of high-tech achievements, has gradually become a wind vane for the degree of industrialization and market share. The development of the economy depends on scientific and technological progress, and only by successfully transforming scientific and technological achievements into real productive forces and improving quality and efficiency can the economic mode be transformed from extensive to intensive. Under the guidance of the government, universities, enterprises, scientific research institutes and other relevant institutions have divided labor and cooperated, organized and operated through expert consultation, technology transfer, joint research and development, and co-located high-tech entities, and gradually formed complementary advantages and risks. These parties have gradually formed a diversified technology transfer community with complementary advantages, shared risks, shared interests and common development. This mode of combining economic and social benefits has effectively promoted the reform and development of the economy, science and technology and education systems, played an important role in promoting the close integration of science and technology and the economy, and achieved good results of win-win cooperation. As an important part of this kind of community, colleges and universities pay more and more attention to the transformation of scientific and technological achievements and technology transfer. How to directly and quickly transform the advantages of colleges and universities' scientific research technology and talent spillover efficiency into real productivity has become an important carrier for promoting technological innovation and progress in the industry and realizing the benign interaction between colleges and economic development.

---

*Corresponding Author:

DOI: 10.1201/9781003278788-37

The transformation of scientific and technological achievements is an important part of implementing the strategy of independent innovation, a key link for enterprises to achieve technological innovation and enhance their core competitiveness, and an important way to transform innovative achievements into productive forces. In September 2007, the Ministry of Science and Technology of China, the Ministry of Education and the Chinese Academy of Sciences jointly issued the "Notice on Printing and Distributing the Implementation Plan for National Technology Transfer Promotion Actions"[1], which aims to establish a good technology transfer mechanism, promote knowledge flow and technology flow, and establish a technological innovation system with enterprises as the main body, market-oriented, and the combination of production, education and research. In August 2008, the Ministry of Science and Technology designated 76 institutions including the National Technology Transfer Center of Tsinghua University as the first batch of national technology transfer demonstration institutions, hoping to promote the national technology transfer work through the exploration of different technology transfer models. In August 2015, the Standing Committee of the National People's Congress passed the "Decision on Amending the Law of the People's Republic of China on Promoting the Transformation of Scientific and Technological Achievements"[2], establishing and improving the results transformation law to meet the needs of economic and social development. On August 3, 2016, the Ministry of Education and the Ministry of Science and Technology of China promulgated "Several Opinions on Strengthening the Transfer and Transformation of Scientific and Technological Achievements in Colleges and Universities", etc.; in November 2019, Beijing issued the "Beijing Regulations on Promoting the Transformation of Scientific and Technological Achievements", etc. local management regulations. According to Annual Report on the Transformation of China's Scientific and Technological Achievements 2020, with the advancement of the country's deepening of the reform of the scientific and technological system, and also laying the foundation for the full implementation of the innovation-driven development strategy, China has successively adopted a series of major measures in resource allocation, plan management, and transformation of scientific and technological achievements, all of which have contributed to the transformation achievements. It provides an important policy basis for the transformation of results.

For the research on technology transfer theory and technology transfer system, the focus of domestic and foreign scholars is different. From the research content, foreign scholars focus on the research on the transformation of scientific and technological achievements, including Abrams I. (2009) and others' research on the division of scientific and technological achievements in Europe and the United States, Kenney M. (2009), Ilahiane H. (2016), Dragan I. F. (2018) and others lay particular emphasis on the analysis of the necessity of university achievements transformation, and William B (2016) and Leten B. (2016) mainly focus on the commercialization of scientific research achievements in colleges and universities. In general, Chinese experts and scholars started relatively late in the research on the transformation of scientific and technological achievements. Gao Feng (2005) mentioned in the article "On the Theory of Technology Transfer and the Transformation of my country's Scientific and Technological Achievements": Technology transfer is the diffusion process of the technical level knowledge group generated around a certain type of technology, that is, various forms of technology are received from the supplier to receiver. This movement can be carried out in geographic space or between different fields and departments. It is a dynamic process. When technology transfer activities cross national borders, it is called

---

[1]https://www.most.gov.cn/xxgk/xinxifenlei/fdzdgknr/fgzc/gfxwj/gfxwj2010before/201712/t20171222_137076.html, citation time: August 2022.
[2]https://www.most.gov.cn/xxgk/xinxifenlei/fdzdgknr/fgzc/flfg/201512/t20151204_122621.html, c. t: August 2022.

international technology transfer. For example, Zhang Yuchen (2009) mentioned in the book "Research on the Mechanism of Technology Transfer": Technology transfer refers to the process in which knowledge is transferred from technology owners to users in some form. At present, domestic and foreign academic circles have a relatively unified understanding of technology transfer: that is, technology transfer is a form of technology dissemination or technology diffusion, and mainly refers to the outward flow of technology or scientific and technological achievements, or between organizations and fields. During the last five years, Studies on technology transfer by Chinese scholars such as Zhong W. (2019), Zhang M. (2020), Zhu Y. (2021), Zong Q. (2022), Guan Y. (2022), Zheng J. (2022) mainly focus on foreign technology transfer systems, foreign multinational companies' technology transfer and university technology transfer modes. The research on university technology transfer mode is lacking in how to establish a technology transfer system that adapts to my country's basic national conditions and improve the technology transfer mechanism.

Through the study of some domestic and foreign related literature, as well as some policy settings for the transformation of scientific and technological achievements in China, the author has a preliminary understanding of the scientific and technological transformation achievements of 19 universities in Shanghai; Obtained some specific data on the transformation of scientific and technological achievements, analyzed these data and cases, analyzed the opportunities and challenges faced by Shanghai universities in this regard, and put forward relevant suggestions for promoting the transformation of scientific and technological achievements in universities.

3 ACHIEVEMENTS AND CHARACTERISTIC CASES

As the core area of national economic development and scientific and technological development, Shanghai has always attached great importance to the transformation of scientific and technological achievements. As the source of the transformation of scientific and technological achievements and achievements, the major scientific research institutions and institutions of higher learning in Shanghai have always been the main output carriers. In the second half of 2021, 19 universities in Shanghai will have exchanges on the transformation of scientific and technological achievements, including Fudan University, Shanghai Jiao Tong University, Tongji University, East China Normal University, East China University of Science and Technology, Donghua University, and Shanghai University, Shanghai Jiaotong University School of Medicine, Shanghai University of Traditional Chinese Medicine, Shanghai Normal University, University of Shanghai for Science and Technology, Shanghai Maritime University, Shanghai Ocean University, Shanghai University of Sport, Shanghai University Of Electric Power, Shanghai University Of Engineering Science, Shanghai Institute of Technology, Shanghai Second Polytechnic University and Shanghai Dianji University. Among these colleges and universities, although they belong to different types such as those directly under the Ministry of Education, co-constructed by ministries and provinces, and local high-level universities, various colleges and universities will carry out appropriate transformation of scientific and technological achievements according to their different characteristics and scientific research priorities.

Compared with the two main aspects of technology and patent transfer and achievement transformation, there is still a certain gap in the development status of these universities. For example, both Fudan University and Shanghai Jiao Tong University have contracts worth more than 100 million yuan for the transformation of achievements, and Fudan University and Shanghai University have more than 100 million yuan in patented technology transfer, all of which have opened a big gap with other universities. The following data tables and graphs show the disparities between universities very clearly.

It can be seen from the below tables and figures that the universities directly under the Ministry of Education of China or the universities that are deployed and co-constructed are significantly higher than the local universities in Shanghai or some specialized universities in terms of technology transformation, which is also related to the overall strength and ranking of the universities.

Table 1. Contract amounts of achievement transformation in Shanghai universities.

university name	achievement conversion contract (Mio.)
East China Normal University	7.0
East China University of Science and Technology	15.0
Shanghai Jiaotong University School of Medicine	45.0
Shanghai University	120.0
Fudan University	350.0
Shanghai Electric Machinery Institute	2.4
Shanghai Maritime University	0.9

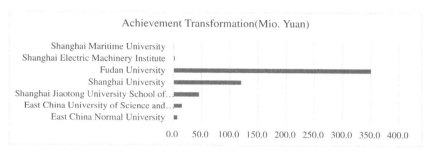

Figure 1. Contract amounts of achievement transformation in Shanghai universities.

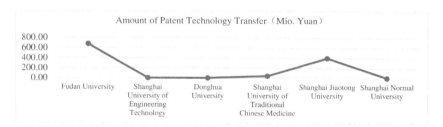

Figure 2. Contract amounts of achievement transformation in Shanghai universities.

3.1 *Case 1: Cooperation between DHU and COMAC*

As an institution directly under the Ministry of Education, Donghua University (DHU) started early in the transformation of achievements. Through the establishment of the Civil Aviation Composite Materials Collaboration Center, the school has participated in the support of scientific research projects for China's domestically produced large aircraft. Aiming at the problems of weak interface of aerospace-grade thermoplastic composites and poor wetting of fabrics by high-viscosity melts, researchers have developed a new technology system suitable for induction welding of aerospace-specific components, opening up the whole process of large-scale application of thermoplastic composites in the aerospace field, its materials can increase the structural strength of the aircraft, while greatly reducing weight, energy consumption and pollution. DHU has promoted the project in many large-scale international and domestic exhibitions such as the Industry Fair and the Express Train of Scientific and Technological Achievements, and actively exchanged and exchanged visits with COMAC (Commercial

267

Table 2. Amounts of patent technology transfer in Shanghai universities.

university name	patent technology transfer (Mio.)
Fudan University	680.00
Shanghai University of Engineering Technology	5.40
Donghua University	5.12
Shanghai University of Traditional Chinese Medicine	45.00
Shanghai Jiao Tong University	400.00
Shanghai Normal University	2.90

Aircraft Corporation of China Ltd.). In September 2021, the project completed a patent "CF/ PEEK composite material with full transverse crystal structure and its preparation method", and invested more than 5 million yuan in investment conversion.

3.2 Case 2: The "medical-industrial intersection" layout of USST

University of Shanghai for Science and Technology (USST) is a key applied research university in Shanghai that focuses on engineering and develops in coordination with multiple disciplines. The joint innovation research institutes, including the USST, the Department of Ophthalmology of Shanghai First People's Hospital, and the Shanghai High-end Medical Equipment Innovation Center, have opened up a new process of medical-engineering crossover and hospital-enterprise integration.

Through activities such as the "6th China Innovation Challenge (Shanghai) and the 4th Yangtze River Delta International Innovation Challenge High-end Medical Device Innovation Session", the school released 156 projects from clinicians, universities, enterprises, and professional service institutions. Innovation needs, 44 solutions and innovation achievements, and more than 10 innovation achievements were carried out on-site roadshows. At the same time, through the industrial docking and enterprise cooperation in the Yangtze River Delta region, breakthroughs have been made in basic research and key technologies, which has promoted the transformation and industrialization of scientific and technological achievements in colleges and universities.

3.3 Case 3: Attempt at the "pilot test base" of SIT

The school-enterprise cooperation features of Shanghai Institute of Technology (SIT) are remarkable. In June 2021, the technology transfer center of the school cooperated with Nantong Zhongxin Foundry Company to establish a "pilot test base", which made one of the scientific and technological achievements from the laboratory to the industrialization. Due to the conditions for the realization of the achievements, the difference is very large, and the probability of success is low. Therefore, the pilot base is very important in the process of technology transfer. However, the investment and occupation of the pilot base are large, and it is generally difficult for universities to independently undertake the construction of the pilot base. Therefore, it is convenient for the school to solve the problem through the cooperation of government, industry, academia and research. The establishment of the Nantong pilot test base will strengthen the pilot test services in the aspects of pilot scale amplification, achievement transformation, and verification testing, and enhance the carrying function of scientific and technological achievements transformation. This attempt not only enhanced Nantong's scientific research strength, but also helped to promote the introduction of talents and investment in the Tongzhou Bay Demonstration Zone, and injected fresh blood into its economic development; at the same time, this attempt also provided a pilot test for teachers and students The industrialization experimental base, to a great extent, embodies the mutually beneficial school-enterprise win-win model.

3.4 Case 4: Incubation and transformation of scientific and technological achievements in the Affiliated Hospital of SHSMU

Shanghai Jiaotong University School of Medicine (SHSMU) is a university that trains professional medical professionals. In order to accelerate the incubation and transformation and application of scientific and technological achievements, the affiliated mental health center of the school held a series of academic activities of the Oriental Psychiatry Forum on Sept. 16, 2021 – "Science and Technology Escort Lean Reality and Wisdom" The 2nd Mental Health Department The theme of the innovation forum is to "discuss the transformation of achievements in an all-round way, empower mental health with technological innovation, continuously explore the path of mental health and wisdom, and expand new channels for the transformation of scientific and technological achievements". In recent years, as a specialized hospital with obvious characteristics and advantages, the Mental Health Center has made outstanding achievements in accelerating the transformation of scientific and technological achievements into real productivity. As of the eve of the opening of the forum, the cumulative amount of transformation contracts has reached millions of yuan. At the forum, two achievements transformation technologies were signed. Through this operation, not only can the innovative ideas of medical staff continue to burst out, but these new achievements and new products in the field of psychiatry can truly go out of the laboratory and truly benefit patients.

4 THE CHARACTERISTICS, OPPORTUNITIES AND CHALLEGES

4.1 Characteristics of the transformation of scientific and technological achievements

The whole city of Shanghai has always adhered to the temperament of "accommodating all rivers and pursuing excellence", and has always been at the forefront of the country in the transformation of scientific and technological achievements. In general, in this work, relevant institutions and departments have unified the layout, removed the rough and extracted the essence, and gradually formed their own characteristics, which are mainly reflected in policy support, system layout and informatization, empowerment pilots, professional institution construction and personnel training, etc. several aspects.

4.1.1 Policy support for technology transfer and achievement transformation

On April 20, 2017, Shanghai passed the "Shanghai Regulations on Promoting the Transformation of Scientific and Technological Achievements", which came into effect on June 1 of the same year; On the basis of the 22 Opinions, the "Opinions on Further Deepening the Reform of the Science and Technology System and Mechanism and Enhancing the Sci-tech Innovation Center's Sourcing Capability" (also known as the "25 Articles of Shanghai Science and Technology Innovation") was revised and promulgated. These 25 reform measures cover six aspects: talent vitality, achievement transformation, optimization of scientific research management, cultural construction and integration into the global innovation network. In order to encourage the interest of scientific research workers in the transformation of scientific research achievements, the Ministry of Human Resources and Social Security also issued the "Notice on Issues Concerning the Incorporation of Cash Rewards for the Transformation of Scientific and Technological Achievements into Performance-based Salary Management for Scientific Research Staff in Public Institutions" in 2021. These policies have given scientific researchers and achievement transformation specialists a large degree of support, allowing them to have rules to follow, and also enhance the enthusiasm of scientific researchers; colleges and universities "tailor-made" according to these guiding opinions, deepening the system reform, Specific management rules in line with the actual situation of the school have been successively formulated, such as the "Administrative Measures for Incentives and Incentives

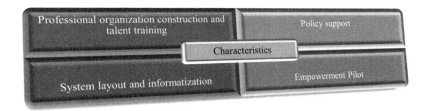

Figure 3. The characteristics of the transformation of scientific and technological achievements.

for the Transformation of Scientific and Technological Achievements of Shanghai Jiaotong University (Trial)", "Administrative Measures for Patents of Tongji University", "Administrative Measures for Technology Transfer Workstations of Shanghai University of Science and Technology", etc.

4.1.2 *Systematic layout and network information management*

With the increasing demand for scientific and technological achievements transformation and achievement transformation, various colleges and universities have successively launched a systematic layout. The key task is to set up their own technology transfer center or achievement transformation department, which generally includes two departments: first, technology transfer The Research Institute (Office of Technology Transfer, OTT) mainly focuses on national strategic needs and international academic frontier issues, and gathers resources to promote major technological innovation; through the combination of market-driven and technology-driven, it strengthens the interaction between schools and industry and forms collaborative innovation. Through the combination of standardized management and incentive services, management risks are avoided and an innovative and entrepreneurial culture is formed. Second, the Office of Technology Licensing (OTL), which is the daily office of the school's intellectual property management leading group, covers patent management, technology transfer, technology awards, policy and legal affairs, etc. Management shifts from "managing for results and focusing on quantity" to "focusing on quality and delivering value". Shanghai universities also have their own characteristics. For example, in 2021, Shanghai Jiaotong University established a coordinated division of labor and cooperation mechanism including reward distribution, state-owned assets filing, legal affairs, and human resources. The implementation is carried out in the mode assisted by the State-owned Assets Supervision and Administration Office, the Legal Affairs Office, the Human Resources Office and the Financial Planning Office. Tongji University has established an AI patent novelty search pre-assessment module through the development of a patent management information system. After obtaining the authorization of the State Intellectual Property Office in 2021, it will learn from the interdisciplinary work model, cultivate a single high-value patent achievement as a node, and use intellectual property rights as a node. Intelligence work is the starting point, tracking the entire process of patent application, protection, layout, and operation, and providing professional and accurate services.

4.1.3 *Promoting the pilot work of empowering scientific and technological achievements*

The empowerment of scientific and technological achievements is one of the highlights of the transformation of scientific and technological achievements. In May 2020, 9 departments including the Ministry of Science and Technology of China issued the "2021 Compilation of Typical Pilot Measures for Granting Scientific and Technological Achievements Ownership or Long-term Use Right to Scientific Research Staff", and selected 40 higher education institutions and scientific research institutions to carry out pilot projects in different fields. The ownership of scientific and technological achievements and the long-term use rights of scientific research personnel, implement the distribution policy oriented to increase the value of knowledge, optimize the management method of state-owned assets for the transformation of scientific and technological achievements, strengthen the management and service of the whole process of transformation of scientific and technological achievements, and strengthen the scientific and technological security of the transformation of scientific and technological achievements and scientific and technological ethics management, establish a due diligence exemption mechanism, and give full play to the role of professional technology transfer institutions. Shanghai University is one of the empowerment pilot units. The school allows teachers to apply for pre-transformation empowerment. The school gives teachers 70% of the ownership share of scientific and technological achievements. If teachers do not implement the transformation within three years, they should return the results to the school for free. 30% of the share, teachers have the right to give priority to transfer and representative transformation; no asset evaluation will be carried out for the scientific and technological achievements that grant teachers long-term use rights, and it is agreed that teachers will carry out continuous research and development activities on the basis of the results of long-term use rights. Schools or entrepreneurial enterprises can independently decide to apply for a patent for the derivative achievements of teachers; combine the empowerment policy with teachers' entrepreneurial activities in combination with teachers' entrepreneurial practice.

4.1.4 *Institutional construction and professional personnel training for the transformation of scientific and technological achievements*

University scientific research workers are the direct participants and upstream parts of the transformation of scientific and technological achievements, and the specific transformation of achievements needs the scientific research organization department, especially the downstream part such as the technology transfer center to implement and implement. Such professional talents have always been relatively scarce. The staff responsible for the transformation of university achievements are different from ordinary daily management personnel in universities. In addition to being experts in the industry, they also need to be paralleled with off-campus enterprises and competent departments at all levels. Units and so on. This puts forward higher requirements for such professional personnel: professional ability, ability to communicate with others, ability to respond on the spot, and certain economic professional ability and literacy. Due to the solidification of job promotion and professional title evaluation methods in colleges and universities, professionals who are engaged in technology transfer and achievement transformation are often in an embarrassing and free state within colleges and universities. In order to improve the enthusiasm of such personnel, many colleges and universities in Shanghai have begun to pilot the reform of professional title promotion for talents who transform scientific and technological achievements, and gradually open up some special channels for them to make them feel at ease in the work of technology transfer and achievement transformation. At the same time, through cooperation with Shanghai Zhangjiang University Collaborative Innovation Research Institute, Shanghai National Technology Transfer Alliance and other institutions, Shanghai universities have entrusted them to provide professional training for employees and continuously reserve high-quality talents for themselves.

4.2 *Opportunities for the transformation of scientific and technological achievements*

The transformation of scientific and technological achievements in Shanghai universities has certain advantages in terms of policies and locations.

4.2.1 *Shanghai's "five centers" construction orientation*

In 2017, the State Council of China approved the "Shanghai Urban Master Plan (2017-2035)", which proposes to build "five centers" of international economic, financial, trade, shipping, and technological innovation centers, an excellent global city and A socialist modern international metropolis with world influence, a desirable city of innovation, humanity and ecology[3]. Among them, the positioning of Shanghai's "science and technology innovation center" has risen to the national strategy. Shanghai has regional advantages such as Zhangjiang Comprehensive National Science Center and Lingang New Area. In November 2019, Shanghai was inaugurated in Lingang to establish the Shanghai Center of the "World Laureates Association (WLA)", becoming Asia's largest and the highest scientific institution in the region. Under the radiation effect of the universities in Shanghai, the achievements of scientific research and scientific and technological progress are further manifested. The positioning of the other "four centers" of international economy, finance, trade and shipping has just brought new opportunities for the transformation of achievements.

4.2.2 *Promotion of regional integration in the Yangtze River Delta*

In June 2016, China's National Development and Reform Commission and the Ministry of Housing and Urban-Rural Development jointly issued the "Yangtze River Delta Urban Agglomeration Development Plan", requiring Shanghai, Jiangsu, Zhejiang and Anhui to establish a sound collaborative working mechanism and strive to integrate the Yangtze River Delta. The urban agglomeration will be built into a world-class urban agglomeration with global influence. After that, in June 2018, Shanghai, Zhejiang, Jiangsu and Anhui provinces and one city jointly formulated the programmatic document of the "Three-Year Action Plan for the Integrated Development of the Yangtze River Delta Region (2018-2020)". The plan includes 12 cooperation topics, covering the scope includes 41 cities in Shanghai, Jiangsu, Zhejiang and Anhui. In October 2018, the "Yangtze River Delta Region Accelerates the Construction of a Regional Innovation Community Strategic Cooperation Agreement" to jointly build an ecosystem for innovation and entrepreneurship in the Yangtze River Delta region and build the G60 technology corridor. In the entire Yangtze River Delta region, the resources of universities in Shanghai are still concentrated, and the demand for the transformation of scientific and technological achievements is even greater.

4.3 *Challenges faced by the transformation of scientific and technological achievements*

There are still some problems in the transformation of scientific and technological achievements in Shanghai universities.

4.3.1 *Negative impact of the new crown epidemic*

Since 2020, due to the impact of the new crown epidemic, the activity of offline technology transfer work in colleges and universities has decreased. Although it is possible to communicate through online meetings and emails, the transformation of scientific and technological achievements and the transfer of technology are still constrained to a certain extent. Some scientific experiments and achievements transformation experiments require a longer period, and some economies themselves have also been greatly impacted, reducing the efficiency of scientific and technological achievements transformation.

4.3.2 *The scale of industry-university-research cooperation is small, and the number of scientific and technological achievements transformed is small*

Shanghai colleges and universities have different requirements for teachers' teaching and scientific research tasks, and teachers' energy investment in the output of scientific and technological achievements is limited. In such an environment, the scale of industry-university-research cooperation cannot truly meet market demand. Many colleges and universities have insufficient cultivation and mining of high-value patents in the stock patents,

---

[3]https://www.shanghai.gov.cn/nw42806/, citation time: August 2022.

lack of long-term planning and layout capabilities, and lack of understanding of the market. Due to different international and domestic standards, the transformation of scientific and technological achievements in colleges and universities can only be carried out domestically, and there is a certain gap from the goal of "dual circulation at home and abroad".

4.3.3 *Professional personnel training has a long way to go*
In the technology transfer center team, the number of full-time personnel with complex capabilities such as business, law, and technology is insufficient, and there is especially a shortage of experienced legal and business negotiating personnel. With the gradual development of the pre-examination of patent application proposals, the cultivation of high-value patent achievements and the cultivation and incubation of achievements, the problems of insufficient professional teams and insufficient effective standards and means for evaluating the value of achievements in transformation have become increasingly apparent. Especially for comprehensive universities, the dominant disciplines belong to many industry fields, and the professional and technical background of personnel engaged in achievement management and achievement transformation operations are relatively high. At this stage, the current situation of the professional talent team in colleges and universities and the implementation of plans by third-party professional institutions to promote the transformation of scientific and technological achievements on a large scale and in multi-disciplinary fields are relatively difficult.

5 CONCLUSIONS

As Engels said: "Technology depends to a large extent on the state of science, and science and technology depend to a greater extent on the state and needs of technology"[4]. As the financial center of China, Shanghai has great expectations for the transformation of scientific and technological achievements. Universities in Shanghai can think about the above opportunities and challenges from the following aspects:

First, through system revision and professional construction, the guarantee system for the transformation of scientific and technological achievements in colleges and universities will be more perfect. Explore the establishment of a patent application pre-examination system, comprehensively improve the quality of scientific and technological achievements, and carry out high-quality patent cultivation.

Second, strengthen cooperation with Shanghai Technology Exchange, Shanghai National Technology Alliance and other institutions to improve and simplify the implementation process of scientific and technological achievements transformation. We can establish a unified technology transfer output platform library to integrate the needs of enterprises and the future planning and development of the transformation of scientific and technological achievements in shanghai universities.

Third, strengthen the sorting of internal resources, encourage interdisciplinary collaboration to expand the scale of projects, expand external connection channels, strengthen school-local cooperation, school-enterprise cooperation, and expand achievement transformation platforms and channels. Give full play to the school's spillover advantages in technology and talents, and promote the high-quality development of university science and technology parks.

Fourth, regularly organize technology transfer center personnel to conduct relevant business training, organize and carry out various activities such as policy presentations, case analysis, and special discussions, and promote the professional quality of technology transfer center personnel. We could increase the communication between the personnel of the

---

[4]Selected works of Marx and Engels (Volume IV), Beijing, people's publishing house, 1995: pp.731–732.

technology transfer center in various forms, and improve their comprehensive ability through some methods, such as regular meetings and commissioned training.

Fifth, introduce third-party professional services, strengthen transaction risk prevention and control, build an intellectual property operation platform, strengthen intellectual property operation and implementation capabilities, improve patent quality, and increase the value of results.

FUNDINGS

The research is supported by the Foundation of 2021 Planning Research Project of Shanghai Higher Education Association with No. Y2-24.

REFERENCES

Abrams I., Leung G., Steffens A J. 2009. How are US Technology Transfer Offices Tasked and Motivated-Is It All About The Money. *Research Management Review* 1–34.

China Science and Technology Evaluation and Achievement Management Research Association 2021. *Annual Report on the Transformation of China's Scientific and Technological Achievements 2020*. Beijing: Science and Technology Literature Publishing House.

Dragan I. F., Dalessandri D., Johnson L. A., Tucker A., Walmsley A. D. 2018. Impact of Scientific and Technological Advances. *European Journal of Dental Education* 22(S1).

Gao F. 2005. On the Theory of Technology Transfer and the Transformation of my Country's Scientific and Technological Achievements. *Technical Economics and Management Research* 20–22.

Guan Y. 2022. The Present Situation and Countermeasures of the Transformation of Scientific and Technological Achievements in Universities in the Yangtze River Delta under Regional Integration. *Technology Entrepreneurship Monthly* 63–67.

Ilahiane H., Venter M. 2016. Introduction: Technologies and the Transformation of Economies. *Economic Anthropology* 3(2).

Kenney M., Patton D. 2009. Reconsidering the Bayh-Dole Act and the Current University Invention Ownership Model. *Research Policy* 1407–1422.

Leten B., Belderbos R., Looy B. V. Entry and Technological Performance in New Technology Domains. 2016. Technological Opportunities, Technology Competition and Technological Relatedness. *Journal of Management Studies* 53(8).

William B. Rouse. 2016. *Universities as Complex Enterprises: How Academia Works, Why It Works These Ways, and Where the University Enterprise Is Headed*. New Jersey: John Wiley & Sons.

Zhang M. 2020. Discussion on the Supply and Transformation Characteristics of Scientific and Technological Achievements in Colleges and Universities: Based on the Comparative Analysis of Technology Transaction Data from 2017 to 2019. *China University Science and Technology* 91–93.

Zhang Yuchen. 2009. *Research on the Mechanism of Technology Transfer: The Way to Find a Solution in Confusion*. Beijing: China Economic Press.

Zheng J. 2022. Current Situation Analysis on Transformation of Scientific and Technological Achievements of Universities. *Jiangsu Science &Technology Information* 7–10.

Zhong W., Chen Y. 2019. How Does the Government Promote the Transformation of Scientific and Technological Achievements in Universities: Based on the Experience of Developed Countries. *China Science and Technology Forum* 172.

Zhu Y. 2021. Research on the Influencing Factors and Countermeasures of the Transformation of Scientific and Technological Achievements: Taking the Local Universities in the Yangtze River Delta Region as an Example. *Science and Technology in Chinese Universities* 2021(4): 92–96.

Zong Q. 2022. Re-discussion on the Realistic Obstacles of the Transformation of Scientific and Technological Achievements in Universities and Its Cracking Mechanism. *Technological Progress and Countermeasures* 1–8.

Economic and Business Management – Lent & Zhang (Eds)

The new government-business relationship and firm value

He Zhang & Jiamin Chen*

School of Business, Macau University of Science and Technology, Macau, China

ABSTRACT: The government-business relationship is a significant factor that affects the firm value. General Secretary Xi Jinping proposed a new government-business relationship in the report of the 19th CPC National Congress. Can a new government-business relationship improve the regional business environment and exert a positive resource effect to promote firm value? This question has not been fully discussed in the existing literature. We selected the data of A-share listed companies in Shanghai and Shenzhen from 2017 to 2020 and constructed a structural equation model (SEM) to study the impact of the new government-business relationship on firm value. The results show that the new government-business relationship promotes the growth of firm value, especially in the "unsullied" government-business relationship. This study enriched the academic theories on the government-business relationship in China, while providing micro-level empirical evidence for the organic combination of efficient markets and responsive government.

1 INTRODUCTION

The government is able to exert a strong interventionist influence on resource allocation [16]. Since China's reform and opening up in 1978, the relationship between local governments and enterprises, as well as the relationship between government personnel, entrepreneurs and management has been affected by market regulation and government macro-control in an intricate manner. Under the development and promotion of the capital economy market, the closeness of the government-business relationship will determine to a certain extent the resources that the firm can obtain in the market as well as its competitive ability.

On the topic of government-business relationship, a part of scholars' general view is that the interaction between government and enterprises can bring certain economic benefits to enterprises [1,2,11,12,14], such as property rights protection, breaking regulatory barriers, alleviating financial inhibitions, government subsidies, tax preferences, bank credit [3], thus providing enterprises with greater resource support for their daily operation of production factor inputs and innovation activities and competitive space. Another group of scholars challenged the above view, arguing that the economic performance brought by government-business relationships is short-lived. Excessive reliance on government relations for resources not only breeds corruption between firms and officials, but also leads to the "curse" of political resources for firms [6]. Such enterprises are often accompanied by reduced market competitiveness, severe transfer of benefits, lack of innovation, and imbalanced investment landscape. In short, scholars with opposing views believe that the excessive closeness of government-business relationships can lead to the "curse" of political resources for enterprise development, especially for long-term sustainable development. On the issue of government-business relationships, in 2016, General Secretary Xi Jinping explicitly proposed the concept and guiding framework of a "new government-business relationship" in his report to the 19th Party Congress. The concept of the "new government-business relationship "refers to the "close" and "unsullied" government-business relationship proposed by

---

*Corresponding Author:511296163@qq.com

DOI: 10.1201/9781003278788-38

General Secretary Xi Jinping. So far, in the context of the new economy, can the new government-business relationship break the resource curse and positively affect the firm value? And what is the mechanism of its intrinsic effect? There is a lack of relevant literature, and no clear explanation has been given.

Therefore, our research focuses on improving the business environment and building a new type of "close" and "unsullied" government-business relationship. We try to solve two questions through theoretical analysis, modeling and empirical evidence: First, can the new government-business relationship improve the firm value? Second, what is the inner mechanism of the new government-business relationship to activate the firm value? The answers to two questions will not only enrich the academic theory of business-government relationship, but also provide empirical evidence for the organic combination of effective market and effective government.

The main contribution of our study is divided into two aspects. On the one hand, no scholars at home and abroad have explored the impact of new government-business relationships on firm value. This paper is the first to conduct a study on this topic, enriching the literature on the impact of institutional environment on the behavior of microeconomics. On the other hand, most scholars have used the institutional environment as a research context and failed to directly quantify the institutional environment and analyze its impact on firm behavior and performance in past studies [10]. This study quantifies the extent to which macro-level policies affect the market value of firms, which has implications for business managers, market participants, policy makers and market monitors to understand the boundaries between government and enterprises and for government to promote firm value more effectively.

2 THEORETICAL ANALYSIS AND RESEARCH HYPOTHESIS

2.1 *The new government-business relationship and firm value*

At present, China's market resource allocation mechanism is still not fully effective, and the legal system is not regulated, which leads to frequent rent-seeking behavior of government personnel. In an environment of market uncertainty and policy uncertainty, the more resources government personnel hold for the development of enterprises, the more discretionary power they have, which leads to a serious imbalance in the relationship between government and business. It is not conducive to the formation of a healthy business environment and the sustainable development of enterprises [4,15]. In other words, a healthy business environment is needed for enterprise value growth, and can help reduce market uncertainty and policy uncertainty, thus reducing the government's incentive and space for rent-seeking and achieving positive resource effects. The main purpose of the new concept of government-business relationship is to promote the formation of a healthy business environment. The "close" and "unsullied" government-business relationship are the important manifestations of a healthy business environment. The new government-business relationship reduces the probability of market failure and government failure, and achieves the optimal allocation of resources. So, what are the specific mechanisms by which the new government-business relationship affects the firm value? The new government-business relationship helps to form a good relationship government and enterprises, and makes it easier for the market mechanism to play its role. By playing the role of price and competition mechanism, the market makes it easier for enterprises to raise financing, enhances the efficiency of resource allocation, and enables enterprises to pursue the value of innovation, thus giving rise to a stronger positive resource effect. Business managers direct the production and operation of the enterprise under the influence of resource effects. Enterprises obtain various factors of production in the market and participate in competition and cooperation to achieve their expected goals and enhance their enterprise value [7]. In short, the new government-business relationship mainly affects the value of enterprises by giving play to the resource effect. The new government-business relationship solves the problems of financing constraints, resource allocation efficiency and enterprise innovation. In this way, the transaction cost of enterprises is reduced. The competitive advantage of enterprises will be improved. The sustainable development of enterprises will be realized, and the firm value will be realized. Therefore, we propose research hypothesis 1:

H1: The new government-business relationship promotes the enhancement of firm value.

2.2 The "unsullied" government-business relationship and firm value

An "unsullied" government-business relationship means that government officials should govern according to the law, while enterprises should comply with the law and provide quality products and services to society. The "unsullied" government-business relationship advocates unsullied and efficient government and transparent administration, which helps prevent the interference of rent-seeking behavior in business support policies and reduces policy uncertainty. The "unsullied" government-business relationship promotes firm value in several aspects: first, the government and enterprise personnel are strictly investigated for irregularities and violations, which will cause their rent-seeking costs to rise and cut off their rent-seeking behavior at the source [17]. With less rent-seeking behavior of government and business personnel, the probability of the government's rational allocation of resources and the exercise of free adjudication is greatly increased, which helps to give full play to the positive resource effect and ensure that enterprises focus on improving competitiveness and enterprise value. Second, the "unsullied" government-business relationship makes the interest chain between political and enterprise personnel gradually transparent, which makes it much more difficult and costly to maintain the original improper government-business relationship [5,18]. Therefore, the investment of enterprises in maintaining political relations will be greatly reduced, and enterprises will instead invest their resources in enterprise value growth points to win market recognition and enhance enterprise value; third, the "unsullied" government-business relations facilitate the construction of a healthy business environment. In a free market competition, market vitality will be stimulated. Enterprises will be more easily financed. The efficiency of resource allocation will be improved. Market vitality will be stimulated. Enterprises will pay more attention to the improvement of their sustainable development capability; fourthly, with a healthy political and business environment, enterprises will have more resources to redundantly invest in innovation activities and bring into play the value of enterprise innovation [8,19]. Therefore, we propose research hypothesis 2:

H2: The "unsullied" government-business relationship promotes the enhancement of firm value.

2.3 The "close" government-business relationship and firm value

The "close" business relationship requires the government to respect the rights of enterprises, provide fair competition environment and efficient service for enterprises, and at the same time, require enterprises to actively fulfill their social responsibility and participate in the obligation of political affairs. In a healthy "close" government-business relationship, the government will strengthen government services and reduce its intervention in the business, financing and investment activities of micro-economies. In a "close" government-business relationship, the government is inclined to take measures to improve the market system, provide public resources, and develop third-party support institutions to perform government service functions[1,2,3]. These measures help reduce information asymmetry between the

---

[1]http://www.niehuihua.com/uploads/soft/180514/1-1P5140J106.pdf

[2]http://nads.ruc.edu.cn/upfile/file/20191231162604_414000_57466.pdf

[3]http://nads.ruc.edu.cn/docs/2021-01/4ee6baa7834140a29a58b96032bd056a.pdf

government and enterprises, provide effective information for the government to regulate the economy, and thus reduce the impact of market uncertainty on enterprises. The improvement of the market system promotes the reform of the factor market, which allows enterprises to obtain production factors at low cost and relatively low financing costs [9], and enhances the efficiency of resource allocation, providing an important guarantee for the virtuous cycle of enterprise resources to boost the firm value. The improvement of the public resource system will attract a region's talents, capital, technology and other mobile factors to gather in the region, providing sufficient labor, finance, materials, policies and other resources to guarantee the subsequent development of enterprises. The government encourages the development of third-party intermediaries, such as analyst agencies, consulting agencies, accounting firms, law firms, and financing institutions, which have professional knowledge and practical experience to overcome information asymmetry in the process of business operation, financing, and decision-making, and facilitate the ability to bring into play the positive effect of enterprise resources under the condition of obtaining sufficient information to enhance firm value. Therefore, we propose research hypothesis 3:

H3: The "close" government-business relationship promotes the enhancement of firm value.

3 SAMPLE SELECTION AND VARIABLE DEFINITION

3.1 Sample selection

We select data from 2017 to 2020 for A-share listed companies in Shanghai and Shenzhen, and construct a structural equation model (SEM) to study the impact of the new government-business relationship on firm value. The SEM is a general linear statistical modeling technique, which makes up for the deficiency of traditional regression analysis and factor analysis. It is used to deal with the exploration and analysis of complex multivariate research data. It can not only reflect the separate relationship between elements in the model, but also reflect the mutual influence between elements [11]. The data are selected because the concept and framework of the new government-business relationship was proposed in 2016, and the new government-business relationship health index has been released year by year since 2017. The data are now updated to 2020. The final sample size obtained in this paper after excluding newly established enterprises in 2017, ST enterprises and missing values of variables is 6622. The new government-business relationship health index is measured from the Ranking of government -Business relationship in Chinese Cities published by the Institute for National Development and Strategic Studies of Renmin University of China. The rest of the financial data were mainly obtained from the CSMAR database.

3.2 Variable definition

3.2.1 Explained variable: firm value (EV)
In this paper, we measure firm value at two levels: short-term value and enterprise sustainability. For short-term value, we use three proxies, namely return on equity (NET), cost margin (CM) and return on assets (ROA). For enterprise sustainability, we use the market-to-book ratio (MB) and equity multiple (EM) as proxies, as shown in Table 1.

3.2.2 Explanatory variable: new government-business relationship (ZSGX)
The data on the new government-business relationship were obtained from the 2017, 2018 and 2020 editions of the report "Ranking of Government-Business Relations in Chinese Cities" published by Nie Huihua et al. of the Institute for National Development and Strategic Studies, Renmin University of China. The report was not released in 2019, resulting in the lack of data for 2019. We handled this by finding the average of the health indexes published in 2018 & 2020 to represent the new government-business relationship

Table 1. Definition of firm value.

Level	Index	Sign	Variable definitions
short-term value	return on equity	NET	Net profit divided by net assets
	cost margin	CM	Total profit/(Operating cost + selling expense + administrative expense + Finance expense)
	return on assets	ROA	Net income divided by average net assets
enterprise sustainability	market-to-book ratio	MB	Market value of outstanding stock divided by book value
	Equity multiple	EM	Total assets/Total shareholders' equity

health index in 2019. The new government-business relationship (ZSGX) is measured by the overall index of the health of government-business relationship in Chinese cities, which indicates the overall health of the city's government-business relationship. The "close" government-business relationship (QJ) is measured by the "close index" in the overall index of healthy government-business relationship in Chinese cities, which indicates the degree of closeness of government-business relationship in the city. The "unsullied" government-business relationship (QB) is measured by the "unsullied index" in the overall index of the health of government-business relationship in Chinese cities. The higher the index, the healthier the government-business relationship.

4   EMPIRICAL ANALYSIS

4.1   *Reliability and validity test*

The statistical results in Table 2 show that the combined reliability coefficient (CR) of firm value is 0.880, indicating that the measurement variable of firm value selected in this study has high reliability. The combined reliability coefficient (CR) of the new government-business relationship is 0.956, indicating that the measurement variables of the new government-business relationship selected in this study have high reliability. To sum up, there is a high internal structure consistency among the measurement variables, which means that the selection of measurement variables can well represent the latent variables.

Table 2. Confirmatory factor analysis.

Latent variable	Measurement variable	Standardized Coefficients	S.E.	CR	AVE
Firm value	CPS	0.805	0.004	0.880	0.710
	ROA	0.8	0.004		
	NET	0.917	0.003		
	MB	0.362	0.009		
	EM	0.803	0.009		
New government-business relationship	ZSGX	0.809	0.002	0.956	0.814
	QJ	0.867	0.002		
	QB	0.88	0.002		

The statistical results in Table 3 show that the Cronbach's α coefficient between firm value and measurement variables is 0.603, which is within the acceptable reliability range of the model. The Cronbach's α coefficient between the new government-business relationship and the measurement variables is 0.896, indicating that the measurement variables selected in this study have strong internal consistency and high correlation.

Table 3. Cronbach's α coefficients.

Latent variable	Measurement variable	Cronbach's α	N of Items
Firm value	CPS ROA NET MB EM	0.603	5
New government-business relationship	ZSGX QJ QB	0.896	3

4.2 *Overall model fitting test*

As shown in Table 4, the Chi-square degree of freedom ratio (X^2/df) is 2.885. When it is less than 3, it indicates that the overall fitting degree of the model is good, and the causal path of the overall model is relatively matched with the sample data. The root mean square error of approximation (RMSEA) is 0.078, which is in the range of 0 to 1, and the fitting index CFI = 0.98 and TLI = 0.95 are both greater than 0.9, indicating that the model structure is reasonable. On the whole, the overall model fitness of the theoretical model in this paper is acceptable based on the judgment of various indicators.

Table 4. Overall model fitting degree.

X^2	df	X^2/df	RMSEA	CFI	TLI	SRMR
11.54	4	2.885	0.078	0.98	0.95	0.026

4.3 *Research hypothesis testing*

As shown in Table 5, in H1 fitting test, the Chi-square degree of freedom ratio (X^2/df) is 2.66. RMSEA value is 0.06, and the X^2/d is 2.67 in H2 and H3 fitting test. The RMSEA value is 0.07. From the above absolute fitting index and relative fitting index, both show good overall model fitting degree.

Figure 1 is the statistical result of testing the relationship between the new government-business relationship and firm value. The results show that the standardized path coefficient of the new government-business relationship on firm value is 0.09, which is significant at the level of 1%, indicating that there is a significant positive correlation between the new government-business relationship and firm value, which means that the new government-business relationship helps improve firm value. H1 is established!

The results in Figure 2 show that the standardized path coefficient of the "unsullied" government-business relationship on firm value is 0.044, which is significant at the level of 5%, indicating that there is a significant positive correlation between the "unsullied" government-business relationship and firm value, H2 is established!

Figure 2 shows that the standardized path coefficient of the "close" government-business relationship on firm value is 0.042, which is significant at the 10% level, indicating that there is a significant positive correlation between the "close" government-business relationship and firm value. H3 is established!

Table 5. Fitting degree test of H1, H2 and H3.

Hypothesis	X^2	df	X^2/df	RMSEA	CFI	TLI
H1	45.31	17	2.66	0.06	0.98	0.98
H2/H3	29.38	11	2.67	0.07	0.98	0.96

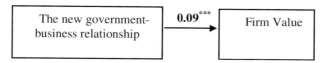

Figure 1. The causal relationship between the new government-business relationship and firm value.

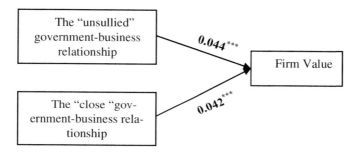

Figure 2. The causal relationship between the "unsullied" and "close" government-business relationship and firm value.

5 CONCLUSIONS

We empirically examine the relationship and mechanism between new government-business relationship and firm value by selecting data from 2017 to 2020 from Chinese A-share listed companies in Shanghai and Shenzhen and the "China City Government-Business Relationship Ranking". The results show that the new government-business relationship has a significant positive impact on firm value, especially in the "unsullied" government-business relationship. In addition, the answer to the question about the transmission mechanism of the new government-business relationship to promote the firm value is given in this paper. The new government-business relationship helps to form a good government-business relationship, and the market mechanism is more likely to play a positive resource effect, especially in terms of enterprise financing constraints, resource allocation efficiency and enterprise innovation capability, to guide enterprise production and operation. Enterprises obtain various factors of production in the market and compete and cooperate to achieve their expected goals and enhance their enterprise value.

This study deepens stakeholders' understanding of the boundary between government and business, as well as a new understanding of the role of the relationship between government and business in the process of enterprise development. Whether scholars' views advocate government intervention in the economy or free markets, they are not conducive to promoting government and business to achieve complementary resource advantages. The ideal government-enterprise boundary is one in which the market plays a leading role in resource allocation and the main position of enterprises in the capital market is affirmed. At the same time, the government should ensure that the market system can be effectively implemented and can play an effective regulatory role in case of market failure. The implementation of new government-business relationship can help to form the ideal boundary between government and enterprises [10].

We explored the influence mechanism of new government-business relationships on firm value and provided empirical evidence. Future research directions can be carried out in two aspects. On the one hand, we can explore the differences in the impact caused by the new government-business relationship among state-owned enterprises, state-controlled enterprises and other enterprises. On the other hand, this paper quantifies the relationship between new government-business relationship and firm value, and discusses the mechanism of the two in the hypothesis section. However, the mechanism between the new government-business relationship and firm value is not demonstrated by empirical test. In the future, scholars can conduct empirical studies on the mechanism of the relationship between new government-business relationship and firm.

REFERENCES

[1]   Amore M. D., Schneider C., aldokas A. 2013. Credit Supply and Enterprise Innovation [J]. *Journal of Enterprise Finance* 835–855.

[2]   Faccio M. 2006. Politically Connected Firms[J]. *American Economic Review* 96(1): 369–386.

[3]   Fisman, Raymond. 2001. Estimating the Value of Political Connections [J]. *American Economic Review* 91(4): 1095–1102.

[4]   He Xuan, Ma Jun, Zhu Lina, Li Xinchun. 2016. *China Industrial Economics* (12): 106–122.

[5]   Huang Shaoqing, Pan Siyi, Shi Hao. 2018. Anti-corruption, Transformation of Government-business Relationship and Corporate Performance [J]. *Academic Monthly* 50(12): 25–40.

[6]   Jiang changliu, Jiang Chengtao, & Zheng Dechang. 2021. Can a New type of Government-Business Relationship Break the Political Resource Curse of Enterprise innovation? *Soft Science* 35(6): 6.

[7]   Jiang Yanjun. (2021). Can pro-Qing Political and Business Relations Affect Enterprise Performance? – An Empirical Study Based on Data From the National Private Enterprise Survey. *Journal of Southwest Jiaotong University: Social Science Edition* 22(2), 10.

[8]   Jianli Li. 2009. Research on the relationship between exploratory innovation, exploitative innovation and firm performance: An empirical analysis based on the moderating effect of redundant resources [J]. *Studies in Science of Science*, (9): 1418–1427.

[9]   Jiang Ya-wen, Huang Yan, Xu Wen. 2011. Political connections, institutional factors and firms' innovation activities [J]. *Southern Economics*, (11): 3–15.

[10] Peng M. W., Wang D. Y. L., Jiang Y. 2008. An institution-based view of international business strategy: A focus on emerging economies[J]. *Journal of International Business Studies*, 39(5): 920–936.

[11] Qiu H. Z., Lin B. F. 2009. *Principle and application of structural equation model[M]*. Beijing: China Light Industry Press.

[12] Yang Sheng, Yu Feng. 2014. The Influence of Political Affiliation on Firm Innovation [J]. *Nankai Economic Research Journal* (6): 32–43.

[13] Yang Qijing. 2011. Enterprise Growth: Political Relevance or Capacity Building? [J]. *Economic Research Journal* 46(10): 54–66 +94.

[14] Yu Wei, Wang Miaojun, Jin Xiangrong. 2012. *Economic Research Journal* 47(9): 125–139.

[15] Yuan Jianguo, Hou Qingsong, Cheng Chen. 2015. The Cursing Effect of Firm Political Resources: A Study on Political Association and Firm Technological Innovation [J]. *Management World* (01): 139–155.

[16] Zhang Guoqing, Ma Li, Huang Fang. 2016. Xi Jinping's "Pro-Qing Theory" and the Construction of pro-Qing Political and Business Relations [J]. *Journal of Party School of the CPC Central Committee* (10): 5–12.

[17] Zhong Qinlin, Lu Zhengfei, Yuan Chun. 2016. Anti-corruption, Enterprise Performance and Channel Effect – Based on the Anti-corruption Construction of the 18th CPC National Congress [J]. *Financial Research* (9): 161–176.

[18] Zhou Xiaoyu, Fu Guoqun, Wang Rui. 2016. Whether relationship-oriented Strategy and Innovation-oriented Strategy replace or Complement each other – Evidence from Chinese Private Enterprises [J]. *Nankai Management Review* 19(4): 13–26.

[19] Zhou Jun, Zhang Yanting, & Jia Liangding. 2020. Based on empirical data of Chinese listed companies. *Journal of Foreign Economics and Management*, 42(5), 17.

Economic and Business Management – Lent & Zhang (Eds)
© 2023 the Editor(s), ISBN 978-1-032-24482-2

Author index